The Garden of Delights

THE MIDDLE AGES SERIES

Ruth Mazo Karras, Series Editor

Edward Peters, Founding Editor

A complete list of books in the series
is available from the publisher.

The Garden of Delights

Reform and Renaissance for Women in the Twelfth Century

Fiona J. Griffiths

PENN

UNIVERSITY OF PENNSYLVANIA PRESS

Philadelphia

Winner of the American Society of Church
History's Frank S. and Elizabeth D. Brewer Prize

Publication of this book has been aided by a grant from the Medieval Academy of America

10 9 8 7 6 5 4 3 2 1

Published by
University of Pennsylvania Press
Philadelphia, Pennsylvania 19104-4112

Library of Congress Cataloging-in-Publication Data

Griffiths, Fiona J.
    The garden of delights : reform and renaissance for women in the twelfth
century / Fiona J. Griffiths.
        p.   cm.—(The Middle Ages series)
    ISBN-13: 978-0-8122-3960-7 (cloth : alk. paper)
    ISBN-10: 0-8122-3960-1 (cloth : alk. paper)
    Includes bibliographical references (p.) and index.
    1. Herrad, of Landsberg, Abbess of Hohenburg, ca. 1130–1195. 2. Hortus
deliciarum. 3. Monastic and religious life of women—Germany—History—Middle
Ages, 600–1500. 4. Women in Christianity—Germany—History—Middle Ages,
600–1500. 5. Christian women—Religious life—Germany—History—12th century.
6. Germany—Church history—843–1517. I. Title. II. Series.
BX4210 .G75   2007
271′.90094309021—dc22

2006045670

To Ronald

Contents

Introduction

DURING THE LAST QUARTER of the twelfth century, Herrad (d. after 1196), abbess of the Augustinian monastery at Hohenbourg in Alsace, oversaw the production of what was to become one of the most famous of illuminated manuscripts: the *Hortus deliciarum* or *Garden of Delights*. A work of compilation, the *Hortus* comprised a rich selection of texts and images, skillfully woven together into a coherent and carefully structured presentation of salvation history. More than eleven hundred textual extracts, drawn from Christian authors from the early Fathers through the late twelfth century, appeared within an organizational framework defined by the manuscript's ambitious visual cycle. The result, a grand synthesis of word and image, is an extraordinary monument to the spiritual and intellectual culture of a female monastic community at the close of the twelfth century.

This magnificent manuscript, along with all the treasures of the Strasbourg library, was destroyed in the Prussian siege of August 1870. "One of the most ambitious and splendid manuscripts of the middle ages is irretrievably destroyed," lamented Rosalie Green of the Princeton Index of Christian Art.[1] Despite this loss, knowledge of the manuscript was preserved by some of the many scholars and antiquarians who had studied it before 1870.[2] Their notes conjure up parchment resplendent with images, texts written in a neat and regular hand yet crowded with marginal and interlinear notations, and folios of every shape and size, their irregularity a reflection of the many long years and cycles of revision that work on the manuscript involved. While the dramatic circumstances of the *Hortus* destruction have ensured that it continues to be widely remembered, these notes and the tracings that survived the manuscript permit its continued, although obviously imperfect examination; gathered together by a team of scholars under the direction of Rosalie Green, they form the basis for a reconstruction of the *Hortus*, published by the Warburg Institute in 1979.[3] This reconstruction has succeeded in presenting the essential structure and contents of the *Hortus* in such a way as to enable an integrated examination of the whole—for the first time since the manuscript was destroyed over a century ago.

The reconstructed *Hortus* provides a valuable witness to the culture of an otherwise little-known and little-celebrated monastic community during the last decades of the twelfth century. That this community was a women's community and the *Hortus* uniquely a women's book only adds to its intrigue: the *Hortus* was the product of a female mastermind and likely also the work of female scribes and artists. The purpose of the manuscript enhances its significance. Since it was never copied during the medieval period and seems not to have been known beyond Hohenbourg until the Renaissance, the *Hortus* was most likely intended primarily or even exclusively for domestic use: the education of the women of the community. Herrad herself confirms her authorship of the manuscript and intentions for it in her prologue. Describing herself as "a bee inspired by God" as she gathered the texts of the *Hortus* from "the various flowers of sacred Scripture and philosophic writings," Herrad dedicated the work to the women of her community with the hope that they would find "pleasing food" and spiritual refreshment in its "honeyed dewdrops" (*HD* no. 2). "May this book be useful and delightful to you," she wrote to them, "May you never cease to study it in your thoughts and memory" (*HD* no. 1).[4]

The particular circumstances of the production and reception of the *Hortus* at Hohenbourg make it especially useful as a witness to the religious life for women in a period of tremendous spiritual enthusiasm. During the eleventh and twelfth centuries, growing numbers of men and women converted to the religious life, abandoning the world and all its temptations for the rigors of the monastery. Inspired by the rhetoric of church reform, as well as the teaching of itinerant preachers, these women and men sought a life of greater faithfulness to the apostolic example than was thought possible within the secular sphere. Their conversions prompted a surge in monastic foundations: throughout the period new communities were established and old ones revived in order to house the crowds of new converts. The spiritual enthusiasm that inspired them is further reflected in the proliferation of new orders as the traditional Benedictine way of life gave way to include Cistercians, Carthusians, Augustinians, Premonstratensians, Gilbertines, Grandmontines, and others. The period was characterized by lively debates on such issues as the "true" nature of the apostolic life, the ordination of monks and their pastoral ministry, and the forms of worship permissible within the cloister. Among these many debates, a further question came to the fore, prompted by the increasing and enthusiastic conversions of women: what role did women have in the project of monastic reform? Did the *vita apostolica*, the apostolic life, include women, and if so how?

The *Hortus* provides one answer to these questions. When work on the manuscript began, sometime before 1175, Hohenbourg was a recently reformed community of Augustinian canonesses, facing many of the challenges typical of a new refoundation. Although the community's most pressing material needs seem to have been met by this time—its crumbling buildings had been refurbished and new chapels built—the women still required spiritual instruction and the consistent presence and pastoral care of a local priest. The provision of pastoral care, the *cura monialium* or care of nuns, was evidently the source of some concern at Hohenbourg: documents from the period reflect the women's dissatisfaction with the chaplains who served their community. In response, early in her abbacy Herrad established two new foundations for regular canons, both of which were to be dependent on the women's community and to provide spiritual service in its chapels. The *Hortus*, which was certainly well underway by this time, was a product of a similar impulse: it was designed to meet the community's need for instruction within the spiritual context of reform, providing its female audience with a wide-ranging theological education while at the same time equipping them with the ability to distinguish between "good" and "bad" pastors. In its breadth and theological complexity, the *Hortus* could supplement, and perhaps even displace, the teaching of Hohenbourg's male priests.

In keeping with these goals, the *Hortus* presents its audience with a challenging theological curriculum comparable to that which a monk-priest or student in the emerging schools of Paris might have expected. Its texts, which were drawn from a combination of monastic and scholastic works, favor contemporary authors. Herrad's major sources included the German Benedictines Honorius Augustodunensis (d. c. 1140) and Rupert of Deutz (d. 1129), authors who composed guidebooks for priests outlining their pastoral and liturgical duties, as well as the Parisian scholar Peter Lombard (d. 1160), whose work became standard reading for male university students. The intellectual currency of the *Hortus* is underscored by its inclusion of selections from Peter Comestor's (d. 1178) *Historia scholastica*, a text that was completed in Paris sometime between 1169 and 1173, not long before work on the manuscript began. The presence of these works in the *Hortus* testifies to the rich spiritual and intellectual context within

which it was produced and offers further proof of Herrad's didactic purpose. By incorporating texts written for priests and students of theology
into a work designed for women, Herrad claimed a body of knowledge
from which scholars have argued that women, since they could not study
within the university, were excluded.

Herrad was not alone in her attention to the religious lives of women.
At some point in the 1130s, the philosopher and monk Abelard (d. 1142)
received a letter from his once-wife, now sister-in-Christ, Heloise (d. 1164)
asking him to compose a monastic rule specifically for women—a thing,
as she writes, that "was never done by the holy fathers." Observing that
the Benedictine Rule was inappropriate for women, not least because it
neglected to account for their "monthly purging," Heloise urged Abelard
to consider the particular needs of women within the monastic life and to
draw up a rule for them to obey.[5] Abelard's response was twofold. First he
questioned the very basis of Heloise's petition, arguing against the need
for a gender-specific rule for women and invoking the inclusivity of the
religious life; "for as in name and profession of continence you are one
with us, so nearly all our institutions are suitable for you," he declared.[6]
Then, despite his initial misgivings, he proceeded to provide her with a
rule for women, albeit one riddled with contradictions and heavily reliant
on the sorts of male models that she had originally rejected.[7]

A different response to the sorts of concerns that had prompted Heloise's request can be found in the *Speculum virginum*, or *Mirror for Virgins*, a work of spiritual formation written by a monk at the south-German
reform house of Hirsau sometime around 1140.[8] Composed as a dialogue
concerning the spiritual life between a monk, Peregrinus, and a nun, Theodora, the *Speculum* was intended to serve as a sort of mirror reflecting
the path of the individual female soul in her journey to God. As its author
explains, it was to "provide Christ's studious virgins with a great incentive
for the preservation of chastity, an example of disdain for the present life,
and a model of desire for heavenly things."[9] Like Abelard's *Rule*, the *Speculum* was written at a time when questions about women's involvement
in the religious life had become critical. The enormous number of women
who had entered the religious life during the previous half century required not only buildings to house them, but also, as at Hohenbourg,
pastoral care: priests to hear their confession, celebrate the divine office,
and administer the sacraments within their communities. These priests, in
turn, required training in the guidance of their new female disciples. It was
to them that the *Speculum* was most immediately directed, even though

its ultimate audience was, obviously, the virgins invoked in its title. The manuscript history reflects this fact: Latin manuscripts of the work survive almost without exception from male, rather than female, houses.[10]

Like the *Hortus*, the *Speculum* combined word, image, and song in a presentation designed for a female audience. Although the structure and purpose of the two works differ—the *Hortus* embraced theology broadly speaking and was designed for an immediate female audience, while the *Speculum* pursued a more limited spiritual goal and was to be mediated for women by their male teachers—the two works share certain similarities. Both were designed in response to women's enthusiasm for the religious life during the twelfth century and both catered to their perceived spiritual needs. Moreover, both the *Hortus* and the *Speculum* emerged from the shared spiritual and political context of reform monasticism within the German-speaking Empire, although the *Speculum* reflects its Benedictine roots, while the *Hortus* was produced within an Augustinian framework. The shared context of the two works is further underscored by similarities in style and iconography and by the influence on both works of *On the Fruits of the Flesh and of the Spirit*, a treatise on the virtues and vices that may have been composed by the *Speculum* author and that Herrad evidently knew well.

Nevertheless, the *Hortus* and the *Speculum* represent very different responses to the spiritual needs of religious women. In keeping with his stated goal of providing spiritual guidance for women, the *Speculum* author avoided discussion of theological issues that might be distracting to his female audience. Contemporary Christological or sacramental debates find no place in his work, which is focused instead on the ultimate aims of the Benedictine life: simplicity, virtue, and knowledge of God. The contents and intellectual influences of the *Speculum* reflect this goal; while the text drew heavily on Scripture (especially the Psalms and the Song of Songs) and the writings of the Fathers, contemporary influences are rare. Herrad's *Hortus*, by contrast, demonstrates the broadening of the theological enterprise in the years after the *Speculum* was composed and reveals the greater receptiveness of Augustinian communities to new intellectual trends. As abbess of Hohenbourg, Herrad's primary concern was for the salvation of the women in her care, but she did not hesitate to address difficult theological issues, balancing care of the spirit with an awareness of the intellectual curiosity of her audience. Her texts, which fused monastic with scholastic sources, showcase her openness to new modes of thought and her effort to equip her audience with a first-rate theological education.

As such, the *Hortus* offers an important vantage point from which to examine the experiences of religious women in this period. Since the manuscript was written *by* women and designed *for* women, it provides unique access to the concerns and interests of religious women within the context of reform. Whereas Abelard and the *Speculum* author had written in response to women's spiritual enthusiasm and its results, they did so as observers rather than participants. Both men sought to develop a body of material—whether regulatory or devotional—that they deemed appropriate to the perceived spiritual needs of women; both grappled with the question of women's distinctiveness within the religious life; and both struggled to develop a model for men's involvement with them, whether as priests or as spiritual guides. However, both men assumed that women's religious life was qualitatively different from that of men (despite Abelard's initial hesitations). While their texts are useful as witnesses to men's engagement with religious women at this time, they provide little in the way of real insight into women's own understanding of their spiritual and intellectual experiences.

The *Hortus*, by contrast, provides an immediate witness to the spiritual and intellectual climate of a female community, revealing how religious women, following the Rule of Augustine, participated in the spiritual and intellectual vitality of the age. Not only was the manuscript produced by and for women, but it was written in a context that was largely free from male scribal influence or control, a fact that sets the *Hortus* apart from much medieval women's writing. As many scholars have observed, few women seem to have written during the medieval period; those who did often worked in collaboration with a male scribe, who was not infrequently also their priest or confessor. Such relationships influenced the sorts of texts that women produced, since, as John Coakley has argued, medieval men were drawn to religious women on the basis of their perceived difference: they assumed that women, whose liminality to the male ecclesiastical hierarchy was assured, had a unique channel to the divine.[11] These assumptions shaped men's interactions with women and their expectations of them. Studies of male-authored saints' lives have already shown the extent to which men's expectations of female sanctity affected their presentation of holy women;[12] in the same way, the expectations of male scribes and confessors influenced both the sorts of texts that women under their care wrote (or dictated) and the authority that they claimed.[13] Amy Hollywood cautioned some years ago that in reading medieval texts written for and about women, it is "crucial to ask who is speaking, from what position, and with what relationship to institutions and power."[14] These questions are equally important when considering women's own writings, in which they often downplay their learning and invoke divine rather than human authority.[15] The *Hortus*, which was written in an environment that was largely free from male authority and which assumes women's intellectual curiosity and competence, suggests that the spiritual and intellectual differences between medieval men and women that appear in many male- and female-authored sources of the period may be a function of men's expectations about women rather than a reflection of women's interests and abilities.

As we have seen, Herrad's primary audience—and likely also her only audience—was comprised of the women of her community at Hohenbourg. It is possible that she received assistance composing and executing the work, but this assistance came from Relinde (d. c. 1176), her predecessor as abbess of Hohenbourg, and not from a canon or priest from a nearby male monastery. Independence from male oversight seems to have provided Herrad with the freedom to produce a work that confounds modern expectations of medieval women's writing. Apart from its introductory texts (*HD* nos. 1–2), with their address to the women of Hohenbourg, and its penultimate folios (fols. 322v–23r; plates 1–2), in which the community as a whole is depicted in facing-page miniatures, there is little that marks the *Hortus* as a particularly "women's book." Herrad assumed that the key intellectual and theological issues of the day were appropriate topics for women's spiritual education.

It is this fact, more than any other, that may account for the remarkable absence of the *Hortus* from the recent spate of studies concerning medieval religious women. Although the loss of the *Hortus* manuscript poses certain undeniable obstacles to its study, this alone does not explain why it has failed to be the focus of research, especially since the reconstructed manuscript was published in 1979. The more likely reason is that it simply does not fit with established ideas concerning medieval female monasticism and particularly with prevailing scholarly paradigms of so-called female spirituality. Herrad's *Hortus* is neither affective nor visionary, characteristics that medieval and modern biographers have taught us to expect of women's piety. Instead it is rational and theological, characteristics most associated with male writers. Herrad's example argues against an automatic association—current in much contemporary scholarship—between immediacy, affect, and the feminine.

The *Hortus* and the Historiography of Medieval Women

Feminist scholarship is at an important crossroads. In the past, it was common for women to be excluded from studies of medieval writing (as they were from studies of medieval society more generally). Since the 1970s attempts have been made to remedy this exclusion. However, since they have focused primarily on the addition of women as ancillaries to a traditionally male canon, often through anthologies and university courses devoted to "women writers," these attempts have tended simply to perpetuate women's exclusion—both by defining women in opposition to the mainstream and by arguing for their involvement in a separate and even subversive discourse. Acknowledging this situation, Sara Poor draws attention to what she calls a "persisting and troubling dilemma" facing feminist literary scholars: "How," she asks, "does one advance the place and legitimacy of women authors in academic canons while also avoiding the pitfalls of essentializing and thus marginalizing them as women?"[16] Her solution is to avoid the category of "women," which she argues "continues to result in a stigmatization of women as deviant and therefore secondary to the (male) universal."[17]

Herrad's example further illustrates the wisdom of abandoning categories of analysis that define women exclusively according to their sex, with related assumptions of gendered behavior.[18] Unlike many of the female visionaries who have dominated recent discussions of medieval women's writing, Herrad invokes the inspiration of the Holy Spirit only perfunctorily in her prologue, highlighting instead her own learning and her reading of scriptural and philosophic texts. While female visionaries from the twelfth century on vigorously denied human learning and often emphasized their marginalization from the male-dominated spiritual and intellectual hierarchies of the medieval world, Herrad never downplays her learning and does not dwell on her sex. Obviously, this distinction is tied at least in part to the genre of her work, which was theological rather than visionary and therefore did not depend upon direct divine inspiration, and to her audience, which was exclusively female. However, the prologue and the work as a whole suggest that Herrad saw herself and the female community at Hohenbourg as full participants in the elite, Latin, and "masculine" intellectual culture of which the *Hortus deliciarum* is so rich a reflection.

Since Herrad did not present herself first and foremost as a woman, it would be a disservice to force an examination of her within the context of an artificially created tradition of "women writers." Barbara Newman warned some years ago against the tendency to impose a group identification on medieval women (she refers specifically to female saints), for whom such an identification would have been anachronistic, or to divorce them from their broader cultural context. She writes, "it can be misleading to study female saints as if they formed a subculture unto themselves, isolated from the overwhelmingly male culture that surrounded them."[19] Her caution is equally valid—if not more so—for women writers, who tend to be grouped together whether or not they saw themselves as a group or laid claim to a "feminine" self-perception. Herrad was well aware of the particular difficulties faced by women within the context of medieval monasticism; her activities beyond the *Hortus*, as abbess and administrator at Hohenbourg, are proof enough of her astute negotiation of gendered categories of male and female religious propriety, as is the *Hortus* itself, which may well have been created in response to some of the difficulties that she faced as abbess. Nevertheless, she clearly placed herself within an elite Latin culture—usually presumed to be "male"—and a tradition of scholarship that extended from the Church Fathers to the intellectual centers of northern France. If she recognized the irony of her participation in that culture—after all, she is the only known female author whose work appears in the *Hortus*—she did not comment on it or draw attention to her exceptionalism. Indeed, one of the most striking aspects of the *Hortus*, in comparison to such contemporary male-authored works for women as the *Speculum virginum* and Abelard's *Rule*, is that it does not depict Latin learning or theological discourse as unusual or inappropriate for a female audience.

Herrad's *Hortus deliciarum* urges a reconsideration of the ways in which medieval women's spheres of activity and their spiritual and literary authority have been defined. My purpose in this book is therefore to place the manuscript (and the women who made and read it) within the spiritual and intellectual context of the twelfth century and in so doing to offer (1) a new reading of renaissance and reform, the two developments most central to our understanding of the twelfth century, and (2) a new framework within which to understand female monasticism during the period. Much recent work on medieval religious women has been premised on the as-

sumption of their exclusion from the literate domain and their nonpartici-
pation in the intellectual and spiritual currents that comprise what we have
termed renaissance and reform. Indeed, the twelfth century is typically
seen by historians as an era of declining female influence, when the twin
movements of renaissance and reform ushered in a profound increase in
overt clerical misogyny.[20] For female religious communities, once vibrant
centers for women's education and independence, renaissance and reform
are seen as having dealt a swift but certain blow—at once displacing the
monastery as a center of learning and reinforcing the traditional association of women with sexuality, sin, and temptation.[21] However, the *Hortus*,
with its sophisticated and self-confident engagement with the major spiritual issues and intellectual currents of the twelfth century, poses a strong
challenge to this long-accepted model of decline.

The association between decline for women and reform begins with
the institutional reform movement of the eleventh century, or so scholars
have argued. The eleventh-century drive to reshape the church led to increased attention to the moral standing of priests and, above all, to the
enforcement of clerical celibacy. Whereas previously many priests had
maintained wives and families, a heightened concern with the purity of the
church resulted in the abolition of priestly marriage and a marked increase
in clerical misogyny. Within the monastic sphere, however, reform
seemed—at least initially—to breathe new life into the Pauline model of
equality. As Paul had written in his letter to the Galatians (Galatians 3:28),
sexual difference was no longer relevant for the Christian community,
since—like differences between class and race—differences between the
sexes had been swept away with the coming of Christ. Now, as Paul informed his audience, "you are all one in Christ Jesus." Records from the
late eleventh and early twelfth century reflect a similar emphasis on inclusivity as an ideal: they abound with descriptions of preachers marching bare-
foot through the countryside accompanied by hordes of followers from all
groups in society—including every class, all ages, and "both sexes." In
Germany and parts of France, reform meant the establishment of what are
known as "double" monastic houses, which included both male and female communities.[22] Yet, the growing numbers of women in the religious
life and the pastoral care that they required created a new problem for
ordained monks: how to provide care for women (the *cura monialium*)
while still resisting what many saw as the polluting influence of contact
with the opposite sex. For many, the answer was total segregation.[23]

As many scholars have recently observed, "reform" is a vague and imprecise term.[24] But in almost whatever way it is used—whether to refer to a papacy embroiled in conflict over investiture, a church occupied with the reorganization of the canons and moral reform of the priesthood, or a popular spiritual movement—"reform" has been constituted as having either excluded or opposed women.[25] Whereas the focus by earlier generations of scholars on the institutional aspect of reform meant that it was rarely discussed in relation to women or the laity, reform, recently redefined as a contest between purity and pollution, is now identified with heightened anxiety concerning the interaction of religious men with women and the increasing opposition, even revulsion, to women that is associated with male monasticism in this period.[26] The result is a general sense that women had no place either in the papal reform movement, which was essentially the concern of priests and powerful laymen, or in the popular reform movement, which manifested itself in a profusion of new monastic orders. The tendency to focus on the reform congregation of Cîteaux—which ultimately rejected women—has reinforced this picture of women's exclusion from new spiritual trends and confirmed their passive position as "objects" of reform.[27] This tendency is exacerbated by reliance on the prescriptive documents of male monastic orders rather than the saints' lives, letters, and documents of practice that record both friendships between men and women and women's involvement in reform.[28]

Herrad's *Hortus* offers an important vantage point from which to reevaluate the decline model as it relates to twelfth-century reform. Not only was the *Hortus* produced within this context, but it reflects Herrad's own interest in the broader concerns of church reform, notably the need for pastoral care and for the adequate training of the pastorate, the concern with incipient materialism, the desire to embrace a life of apostolic poverty according to the example of the early church, and, most important, the effort to improve the moral standing of the clergy. These concerns were not unique to women's communities, but infused the reform movement as a whole. Significantly, Herrad does not acknowledge the pollution fears suggested by the decline model, nor did she include misogynist warnings against clerical involvement with women. Instead, corrupt clerics are the subjects of Herrad's most biting criticism, suggesting that, from her perspective at least, they were the true source of danger and contamination.

As a manuscript produced within the Empire, the *Hortus* broadens our geographic understanding of monastic reform, which has been informed—at least within English-speaking scholarship—primarily by studies of Benedictine houses in France and Italy. In the Empire, reform communities—notably those connected with the Benedictine reform center of Hirsau—were famed for their early openness to women. As the *Speculum virginum* attests, there were men who were interested in the spiritual needs of religious women and committed to providing them with pastoral care, despite concerns regarding the interaction of men and women. Hohenbourg, which was situated within the Hohenstaufen domain, offers further evidence of the distinctiveness of women's experience within the Empire; Herrad almost certainly enjoyed support from nearby Augustinian canons in her work on the *Hortus*. The tendency to ignore Augustinian communities like Hohenbourg has contributed to an overly negative view of reform. Whereas the Benedictine Rule made no provision for women, as Heloise pointed out, the Augustinian Rule included both a male and a female version and seems to have been particularly favored by male monastic communities in which involvement with women and provision of the *cura monialium* formed a central part of their religious observance. Significantly, the Augustinian Rule was adopted at both Sempringham and Fontevrault by the male members of the community, who, as canons and priests, provided pastoral care for the women. Attention to Augustinian communities like Hohenbourg, and not simply Benedictine houses—chief among them Cîteaux—may yield a more positive picture of men's engagement with religious women in the reform period.

A second development associated with decline for twelfth-century religious women is intellectual: the emergence of the first universities in northern France. From the early decades of the twelfth century, wandering scholars gathered in the great cathedral cities of northern France, debating publicly and offering instruction to the many students who flocked around them. Although the rise of the university as we might recognize it did not occur for another century, this early period of intellectual enthusiasm provides a basis for the claim that the twelfth century witnessed its own "renaissance."[29] However, since women could not study within the schools, which were intended only for the training of clerics, scholars have identified the beginnings of the university with the exclusion of women from the elite culture of Latin scholasticism and their marginalization from the key intellectual developments of the period. The shift from the monastery to the cathedral school—and ultimately the university—is associated with a deterioration in women's education and Latinity, and with a general decline in the intellectual vitality of the female monastery. Whereas prior to the twelfth century, nuns, like monks, were able to study within the monastery and attain a high level of education, by the twelfth century monastic schools had largely been eclipsed by universities. Of course, this development had a significant effect on monks as well as nuns, but they could choose to attend the university if they wished, an option that would not be open to women until the nineteenth century.

Yet as the example of the *Hortus* makes clear, Herrad was an active participant in the very textual culture that is often deemed responsible for relegating women to positions of marginality and inferiority during this time. The *Hortus* includes texts drawn from both monastic and scholastic authors, demonstrating Herrad's interest in the theological debates of the Parisian schools and confirming that women did have access to university knowledge. Moreover, Herrad's work on the *Hortus* and her involvement in theological study were not thwarted but rather were actively encouraged by male communities and clerics. These men provided strong support for Herrad, even as she produced a text that is marked by a profound engagement with the supposedly "masculine" realms of philosophy, allegory, biblical learning, Latin, and the liberal arts. Not only did a certain "Conrad" and "Hugo the priest" contribute poems to the *Hortus*, but canons at the nearby Augustinian monastery of Marbach may have provided Herrad with access to their well-stocked library. Marbach's willingness to enter into collaborative projects with women is confirmed in the *Guta-Sintram Codex*, a manuscript that was produced in 1154 by Guta, a female scribe and canoness from Schwartzenthann, in cooperation with Sintram, a male artist and canon from Marbach.[30] Like Guta, Herrad may have looked to Marbach for support in her work on the *Hortus*. In addition to its witness to women's involvement in renaissance and reform, then, the *Hortus* also suggests that historiographical commonplaces regarding male-female relations during the twelfth-century need to be rethought. Herrad's cooperation with men offers a striking, but by no means unique, testament to the many positive and productive relations between men and women that existed at this time.

Here again the Empire offers a distinctive example that cuts against the grain of much recent scholarship concerning medieval female monasticism. Marbach's example suggests that within certain monastic circles, the care of women—their minds as well as their souls—was seen as an integral part of men's spiritual lives. There were women like Herrad and Guta attached to reform communities elsewhere in the Empire; these women were actively involved in scribal work and book production, providing ample evidence of their education and engagement with the written word. While many scholars—especially those focusing on France, England, and

the Low Countries—have pointed to women's decreasing Latinity from
the twelfth century on, within the Empire religious women had a long and
illustrious tradition of learning that continued even into the later Middle
Ages.[31] Herrad's contribution provides one example of a trend that was
certainly broader than current scholarship might suggest. Indeed, religious
women within certain Germanic communities continued to read and write
in Latin even into the fourteenth century.[32] At Helfta in the late thirteenth
century, both Mechthild of Hackeborn (d. 1298) and Gertrud of Helfta
(d. 1301/02) wrote in Latin, while nuns at the Alsatian convent of Unterlinden in the early fourteenth century produced their Sister-Book in Latin,
eschewing the by-then common practice of writing in the vernacular.[33]
Similarly, nuns at Maria Medingen in the fourteenth century were not only
literate in Latin, but according to the letters of Heinrich of Nördlingen (d.
after 1356) read Latin works by both Heinrich Seuse and Thomas Aqui-
nas.[34] In those cases where women did write in the vernacular, it may be
that their vernacularity was a choice and not simply a function of their
failed Latinity.[35]

These examples suggest a richer intellectual culture for medieval monastic women than scholars have tended to allow. Though Herrad's
achievement in the *Hortus* is unique, both in its scope and ambition and
especially among extant works by women,[36] there is at least one important
parallel: the *Scivias* of Hildegard of Bingen (d. 1179). The *Scivias*, like the
Hortus (and the *Speculum virginum*), included lavish imagery alongside
texts and music in a presentation that was intended for a female audience.
Indeed the *Scivias* may have been designed first for the women of Hildegard's own community, although, unlike the *Hortus*, it ultimately commanded a wide audience and was promoted by no less a champion than
the abbot Bernard of Clairvaux (d. 1153). The similarities between the *Hortus* and the *Scivias* are telling. Like the *Hortus* (and also the *Speculum
virginum*), the *Scivias* was a product of Germanic reform monasticism;
Disibodenberg, the Benedictine monastery to which Hildegard was
attached as a child, was related to the Hirsau reform and reform concerns
pervade the *Scivias*. Like the *Hortus*, the *Scivias* was sharply critical of
contemporary churchmen. Furthermore, both works provide an overview
of salvation history, both emphasize the Church, the sacraments, and the
personified Virtues, and both were heavily influenced by the writings of
Rupert of Deutz and Honorius Augustodunensis. However, the *Scivias*
was a visionary work, while the *Hortus* was essentially a textbook of theology. So while Herrad generally acknowledged her sources, Hildegard pro-

fessed her freedom from human learning and disdained the scholastic knowledge that Herrad so readily embraced.

The comparison between Hildegard and Herrad serves as a useful a case in point. Despite similarities between the two women and their spiritual and, at least to some extent, intellectual frameworks, Hildegard and Herrad nonetheless present different traditions of female spirituality and achievement. While Hildegard depicted herself as a prophetess and sought a public, male audience for her visions, Herrad wrote only for the education and edification of the women of her own community. This difference in purpose and audience informed each woman's self-presentation: Hildegard stressed her role as a visionary reliant on divine inspiration and emphasized her lack of learning and notional inferiority as a woman, while Herrad's work is largely free of references either to feminine weakness or to divine inspiration. Although scholars have begun to recognize that Hildegard's claims to be unlearned must not be taken at face value,[37] the very fact that she chose to downplay her learning points to one of the reasons why Herrad continues to appear so unusual among monastic women: scholars in the past were too willing to accept as genuine women's rhetorical self-deprecation, mistaking their claims concerning the primacy of their visionary experience for an actual lack of education. Hildegard's learning was deeper than either she or many of her medieval and modern admirers have been prepared to admit.

The last twenty years have witnessed a dramatic upsurge in studies of medieval European women and of feminine imagery and symbolism within medieval religion and society. Despite this interest, the extent and richness of women's intellectual accomplishments remain largely unexamined. The result is the mistaken perception that the medieval intellectual tradition was a product exclusively of male efforts and the assumption that women's interests and achievements lay more in the realm of the flesh than of the spirit. In 1984, Peter Dronke called for an intellectual history of medieval women, observing, "while the history of medieval women in its social, legal and economic aspects has made real progress of late, most of their intellectual and imaginative achievements are still neglected . . . Whereas the number of books and articles *on* medieval women increases yearly, the greater part of what survives *by* medieval women has remained virtually unknown."[38] My study of the *Hortus deliciarum* takes up this challenge, fuelled by the realization that more than twenty years later, there is still very little sense of medieval women's intellectual achievements.

Research in this field is still in its infancy. In the past, attempts to sketch out the intellectual landscape of medieval religious women were hampered by skepticism concerning women's authorship and involvement in book production. Indeed, one of the most significant barriers to a study of Herrad's intellectual accomplishment is the enduring skepticism with which her claim to authorship has traditionally been met. Writing in 1910, Albert Marignan expressed his doubts that the *Hortus* could have been the work of a woman, given its intellectual currency and complexity. He proposed instead that Herrad's prologue and her claim to authorship be recognized as a "pious fraud."[39] Subsequent scholars, although willing to accept that Herrad did produce the *Hortus*, have tended to characterize it as an elaborate cut-and-paste job that required little in the way of creativity, originality, or inspiration. The tendency to categorize the *Hortus* as an encyclopedia or a florilegium—terms that suggest anthologizing but not necessarily reflection or careful organization—continue to minimize Herrad's achievement. A central purpose of this book, then, is to rethink the *Hortus* in light of the medieval conception of authorship and so to offer a stronger understanding of Herrad's own claims to have "authored" this work.

My study of the *Hortus* is only a first step toward an intellectual history of medieval women. There is certainly more to discover concerning women's intellectual interests and activities, both from the archives and from unexamined primary sources, many of which are only now beginning to attract the attention of scholars. Inspired by the work of Bernhard Bischoff and Rosamond McKitterick, Alison Beach's recent study of women's scribal activity in Bavaria during the twelfth century offers one example of the ways in which new sources are being plumbed for evidence of women's engagement in the spiritual and intellectual culture of twelfth century.[40] Julie Hotchin's study of the community of Lippoldsberg, a Hirsau-reform house that owned some of the texts that Herrad cites, demonstrates that twelfth-century women were reading monastic and scholastic authors, even if they did not produce a work on the scale of the *Hortus*.[41] In Germany, Susann El Kholi and Katrinette Bodarwé have demonstrated the breadth and richness of book ownership and scribal activity at women's communities.[42] These examples, and the many more that await scholarly analysis, suggest that Herrad was not alone as a monastic woman whose piety was firmly grounded in theological study and reflection.

Chapter Outline

The *Hortus deliciarum* provides rich evidence for women's direct participation in both reform and renaissance and, by implication, in spiritual and
intellectual concerns that continue to be associated with a literate and elite
male priesthood. In the first chapter, I present the *Hortus* within the political and spiritual climate of the twelfth century and specifically within the
context of the reform movement, which provided the catalyst for intellectual renewal from the eleventh century. My purpose in this chapter is to
outline the conditions that both inspired the *Hortus* project and enabled
Herrad, and the women of Hohenbourg, to bring it to completion. The
Hortus was the product of a newly reformed community and, as such, the
history of reform at Hohenbourg is crucial to our understanding of the
manuscript. Hohenbourg's position as an independent community of canonesses, its adoption of the Augustinian Rule at the middle of the twelfth
century, and the benefits it received through the patronage of the emperor, Frederick Barbarossa (d. 1190), provided the spiritual, intellectual,
and material context for the creation of the manuscript. However, as I
argue in this chapter, difficulties in securing pastoral care for the women
of the community supplied the immediate impetus for the project. The
cura monialium had traditionally been a source of conflict for Hohenbourg and was a marked concern for its two reforming abbesses, Relinde
and Herrad. Both women consciously sought sympathetic male communities for support and cooperation. Their resourcefulness in arranging
for the provision of pastoral care at Hohenbourg offers a robust challenge
to the model of female passivity that has held sway in discussions of the
cura.

The production of the *Hortus deliciarum* marks the culmination of
reform at Hohenbourg. In the second chapter, I present the *Hortus* within
the context of the particular concerns of the women at Hohenbourg in
the first generation of reform. Chief among these was the desire to secure
reliable pastoral care by what later documents insisted must be a "suitable" priest—one who was appropriately trained and willing to provide
care for women. The *Hortus* reflects this concern and was designed at
least in part to reduce the community's reliance on priests for theological
training. Herrad designed the *Hortus* to replicate priestly reading patterns,
affording the women of her community direct access to the theological
education that their priests would have had. Her decision to feature works

by Honorius Augustodunensis and Rupert of Deutz provided her female audience with essential texts that had been written for ordained monks within the context of reform. The *Hortus* was therefore one solution to the problem of the *cura monialium* at Hohenbourg—an alternative to uncooperative and intransigent priests. At the same time, the manuscript is evidence of women's interest in the ideas emerging from the Parisian schools. Indeed, one of the most remarkable aspects of the *Hortus* is its integration of contemporary scholastic and monastic texts. Herrad's interest in both monastic and scholastic books—and her access to them—offers persuasive evidence of women's engagement in the twelfth-century renaissance and suggests that the school and the cloister were less distinct than modern scholarship has assumed.

In the third and fourth chapters, I explore Herrad's role as the author of the *Hortus deliciarum*, first through her symbolic presentation of herself as a "bee," and then through the evidence of the manuscript itself: its organization, visual program, and physical construction. Although Herrad wrote only a few of the texts that appear in the manuscript, she nonetheless asserts her claim as its author in her prologue to the work, describing herself famously as "a little bee inspired by God" (*quasi apicula Deo inspirante*) (*HD* no. 2). Herrad's presentation of herself as a bee offers important clues as to her sense of herself and her work, since bees were associated in medieval thought with wisdom, the cognitive processes of memory, and, most important, authorship. To her audience, these associations would have been clear, announcing Herrad as a learned woman and her project as a work of intellectual sophistication. In Chapter 3, I argue that Herrad's description of herself as a bee was deliberate, a metaphor coded with precise messages particular both to the learned culture of classical antiquity and that of the medieval world. By describing herself as a bee, Herrad invoked at once the classical understanding of the bee as author within a tradition of literary *imitatio*, the spiritual associations of the bee in Christian thought, and the identification of the bee with the Old Testament prophet Deborah, a model of wisdom for women.

Chapter 4 continues to investigate Herrad's "authorship" of the *Hortus*, turning to the logistics of her work on the manuscript: exactly how her textual "flowers" were transformed into the "honeycomb" of sources that comprised her final product. Although Herrad provides no details concerning the practicalities of her work on the *Hortus*, it is clear from the manuscript's structure and organization that it was a carefully planned project, and not merely an anthology of texts and images. Herrad edited her textual sources, cutting them, adding to them, and often combining sections from different texts and authors in order to achieve her intended presentation. Rarely does she duplicate a textual section, suggesting that she took careful notes as she worked, perhaps even on the original manuscripts she consulted. The coherence of the *Hortus*, which was the result of continuous attention to revisions over the many long years that work on it required, provides further evidence of Herrad's editorial skill; additions and interpolations throughout the original manuscript reflect her efforts to maintain a clear organizational plan. The sophisticated interplay of text and image within the *Hortus* suggests that, in addition to her role as editor of the manuscript, Herrad should also be recognized as the architect of its visual cycle. Given the length of time that work on the manuscript required and the continuous revisions to which it was subjected, it is likely that she was supported in her work by female scribes and artists from her own community at Hohenbourg.

In the fifth chapter, I explore the spiritual significance of the title Herrad chose for her work—the *Garden of Delights*—as an indication of her attitude toward learning and the education of women. For a work that was devoted to the presentation of salvation history, Herrad's title was especially appropriate, suggesting at once the Fall and expulsion from the earthly garden, which marked the beginning of humanity's exile from God, while at the same time offering the promise of salvation in an eventual and eternal reunion with the Creator. Most important to Herrad, the garden image was not to be detached from its moral significance; the first biblical garden, the Garden of Eden, necessarily evoked the tree of knowledge at its center. Having eaten from the fruit of this tree, in disobedience to God, Adam and Eve were expelled from Eden and separated from him. Herrad's garden title stands as a reminder to her female audience that knowledge, when used inappropriately, was the source of humanity's exile from God; however, when used properly, as Herrad teaches it can be, knowledge could become the means for reconciliation. The chapter concludes with a detailed examination of Herrad's famous depiction of *Philosophia* and the liberal arts (fol. 32r; plate 9), set against attitudes toward philosophy within monastic thought and toward women's education within the religious life.

Having situated Herrad as author in earlier chapters and discussed both the extent of her learning and her epistemology, I turn my attention in Chapter 6 to the *Hortus* as a pedagogical tool, suggesting some of the ways in which the book may have been received by its female readers.

Although we have no records of how the manuscript was read at Hohen-bourg and few explicit directions from Herrad, it is possible to draw certain conclusions regarding the probable reception of the manuscript from its design—the size of the book, its page layout, the type and density of its glosses, and last, but not least, its illuminations. The *Hortus* clearly assumed an audience that had already mastered the trivium; its purpose was not to provide training in the introductory subjects of grammar, rhetoric, and logic, but to furnish the women of Hohenbourg with a rigorous theological education. However, Herrad does more than simply transmit knowledge: she moves beyond her sources, achieving a presentation of salvation history that was at once a product of her sources and an interpretation of them. Her most notable innovation is pedagogical. In the *Hortus*, Herrad presents a grand synthesis of text and image, a visual *summa* in which word and image functioned together to convey its teachings. In the final section of the chapter, I discuss the place of images in the *Speculum virginum* and the author's justification for them as concessions to unreading women, and suggest, by contrast, how the richly symbolic and theological images in the *Hortus* might have been understood by its female audience.

In the seventh and final chapter, I return to the spiritual context of the *Hortus*, examining the manuscript for evidence of its reform message and concerns. Designed by Herrad in the wake of Hohenbourg's restoration at the mid-twelfth century, the *Hortus* was profoundly engaged with the project of religious renewal: its goal was to provide an orthodox theological education for the newly converted Augustinian canonesses and to direct them in their religious life. Reformist concerns are prominent in the manuscript, not simply in Herrad's choice of Honorius Augustodunensis and Rupert of Deutz as two of her major sources, but even more strikingly in the manuscript's miniatures. Of the "triple abuse" tackled by reformers—lay investiture, clerical marriage, and simony—Herrad was most concerned with simony, as her repeated warnings concerning the evils of avarice and of private property and her praise of *contemptus mundi* demonstrate. Criticism of greedy monks, immoral priests, and wayward churchmen are rife in the manuscript's images and served as a warning to future generations of Hohenbourg women against unscrupulous and degenerate pastors. Significantly, Herrad avoided the typical equation of women with moral failure, directing her most biting criticism at churchmen; men, and not women, appear in the *Hortus* as agents of corruption within the church. In its reformist inspiration and message, the *Hortus* offers proof of women's concern for the issues of ecclesiastical reform and, most important, for the integrity of the clergy on whom they were forced to rely for the *cura monialium*.

The conclusion revisits the question whether or not the *Hortus* differs from contemporary works for men—that is, if it is gendered female. Did Herrad see a particular role for women within reform, as both Abelard and the *Speculum* author ultimately did? Or did she subscribe to a vision of the religious life that presupposed women's intellectual and rational capacity on a level similar to men? Although the *Hortus* was intended for a female audience and explicitly dedicated to women, it contains few pointed references to a female readership. There is no sense in which Herrad made concessions to her female readership and no indication that she saw their spiritual needs as differing in any fundamental way from the potential needs of religious men. However, the context in which the *Hortus* was written and the factors that motivated and enabled Herrad's project were specific to women. The need for well-trained and reform-minded priests to provide the *cura monialium* at Hohenbourg provided the catalyst for a project that sought to replicate priestly training, thereby reducing the women's reliance on sometimes-unreliable male support. Herrad's freedom to embark upon such a project, and to avoid the usual declarations of female deficiency, was a function of the particular circumstances at Hohenbourg. Unlike many other religious women at the time, Herrad was the abbess of an independent female community; as such, she enjoyed greater autonomy than did either Hildegard of Bingen or Elisabeth of Schönau (d. 1164/5), both of whom were active during her lifetime. These women lived in double communities in which the women were practically and theoretically subordinate to male authority. Hildegard's and Elisabeth's self-presentations as unlettered prophetesses were mediated through male scribes and may well have been calculated to satisfy a male audience. By contrast, if Herrad had male scribal support, that scribe is not named and remained, in any case, subordinate to her own overarching authority.

The fragmentary state of knowledge of the *Hortus* means that there are significant limitations to what can be known about the manuscript. Indeed, even if we had an exhaustive knowledge of its contents and structure, it would still be impossible to discuss either its codicology or paleography, or specific aspects of its artistic program—topics that might shed more light on the development of the *Hortus* project, the chronology of its revisions, and the immediate circumstances under which it was produced: the scriptorium at Hohenbourg. Losses to the manuscript exacerbate these problems. Losses—particularly in the central portion of the manuscript, which included the cycle of images detailing the life of Christ—leave a gaping hole in our understanding of the iconographic program of the manuscript; the absence of some thirty folios of texts from Peter Lombard remove what might have been a key to Herrad's editorial practice; and the notice of suggestive texts on church reform included in a small booklet (which was not copied) leave as a tantalizing possibility the deeper involvement of the Hohenbourg women in church reform.

Despite these limitations, it is possible to consider the significance of the *Hortus* in broad terms and to employ it as a basis for a new history of religious women in the second half of the twelfth century. Hohenbourg's charters and other documents reveal how women negotiated reform; the *Hortus* provides evidence of their interest and involvement in the reform movement more broadly. The *Hortus* demonstrates that women *were* in fact reformers. At the same time, it provides a unique witness to the history of women's education: a working curriculum that incorporated not only texts traditionally found within male monastic libraries, but also those from the emerging schools of Paris.

As an intellectual rather than an overtly spiritual, visionary, or devotional work, Herrad's *Hortus deliciarum* is singular among extant women's writings. However, the fact of Herrad's distinctiveness need not undercut the case for the *Hortus* as proof of a wider cultural phenomenon. The *Hortus*, and the situation at Hohenbourg in which it was produced, points to the potential for women's engagement in the major spiritual and intellectual trends of the twelfth century, despite current models that stress women's decline at this time. It was certainly possible for religious women to attain a high level of education and for them to involve themselves in both monastic and scholastic theological debates, as they did at Hohenbourg. The fact that we have few other examples similar in scope and sophistication to the *Hortus* may indicate the processes by which certain texts have survived and the limitations on women's public activity more than it does their actual interests or abilities. The privileging of certain types of spiritual behaviors and their association with women by both medieval and modern audiences have contributed to a one-dimensional image of so-called female spirituality, one that the *Hortus* undercuts.

In seeking to outline both the education available to religious women and the richness of scholarship within a female community during the early scholastic period, this book challenges the construction of Latin literacy as masculine and misogynistic, while at the same time contributing to discussions about women writers, women readers, and the visual culture of female communities. But it also forces a reconsideration of the two most important developments of the twelfth century, intellectual renaissance and spiritual renewal, arguing that the picture that has been painted of these movements is incomplete. While women have traditionally been excluded from histories of medieval culture, recent attempts to include them have all too often emphasized the spiritual rather than the intellectual, presenting their participation as marginal rather than mainstream. As the *Hortus* makes abundantly clear, some women were thoroughly interested and implicated in the "elite" and "masculinist" cultures of the twelfth century; like Herrad, they ought to be understood as intellectuals and reformers in their own right.

Reform and the *Cura monialium* at Hohenbourg

IN 1153, FREDERICK BARBAROSSA, the newly elected king and soon-to-be emperor of Germany, paid a single visit to the ancient monastery at Hohenbourg, high in the Vosges mountains of Alsace not far from Strasbourg. As with so much of medieval history, Barbarossa's visit is recorded only by chance in a diploma that he issued during his stay; no light is shed on the reason for his visit, its length, or the nature of his relationship to the monastery.[1] Yet despite this silence Barbarossa's purpose at Hohenbourg can be understood in light of the secondary evidence: the developments that were associated with his visit and that are recorded in a bull issued some thirty years later by Pope Lucius III (1181–1185). Reflecting what was most likely the sequence of events as they were enshrined in the community's collective memory, Lucius recalls first how Hohenbourg had been invaded and left "almost destroyed" by Barbarossa's father, Duke Frederick II of Swabia (d. 1147), and then how Barbarossa, wanting to "regain the grace of the eternal king," had undertaken to make amends for his father's transgressions, through the restoration of the community.[2] As Hohenbourg's self-designated reformer, Barbarossa's first known action was to summon a woman named Relinde to assume the abbacy of the monastery and to execute his plan for its physical and spiritual renewal.

Although the details are scarce, Barbarossa's visit to Hohenbourg must have played some role in his plan for the monastery's reform. It may be that he had already turned his attention to the community before 1153, in which case his visit allowed him the opportunity to meet with Relinde and to inspect the progress of the reform that he had chosen her to implement. It is equally possible that his visit preceded reform, in which case it must have sparked his interest in the community and marked the beginnings of his active involvement there. In either case, Barbarossa's reform of Hohenbourg and Relinde's arrival there sometime around the middle of the twelfth century ushered in a period that must be reckoned the most vibrant in the monastery's history. Under Relinde's care, Hohenbourg's buildings were restored, its scattered properties reclaimed, and the spiritual life on the mountain, long jeopardized by inconstant and quarrelsome clerics, at last renewed. As a central part of her reform agenda, Relinde orchestrated Hohenbourg's adoption of the Augustinian Rule, bringing the monastery into the mainstream of religious reform in Alsace and inaugurating the beginning of its "golden age," an age that is identified above all with Relinde's successor, Herrad, and with the *Hortus deliciarum*.

Little is known of Hohenbourg in the centuries before Barbarossa's attention thrust it into the spiritual and political spotlight. Legend has it that Duke Adalric of Alsace had founded the monastery in the late seventh or early eighth century and later given it to his saintly daughter Odile.[3] But Hohenbourg's early history and association with Odile are uncertain; the two are linked only by the late ninth-century or early tenth-century *Vita Odiliae*.[4] Even the nature of Hohenbourg's first rule, which had allegedly been established by St. Odile herself, is unknown, although by the time that her *vita* was written, the community most likely followed the *Institutio sanctimonialium*.[5] The obscurity of Hohenbourg's early history is exacerbated by a series of twelfth-century forgeries that intentionally confused the community's past. One of these, a false diploma of Louis the Pious (d. 840), was produced at Hohenbourg; the others, a pretended *Testament of St. Odile* and a falsified *Chronicon Ebersheimense*, came from Hohenbourg's rival monasteries at Niedermünster and Ebersheim.[6] Each of these sought to recast Hohenbourg's special relationship to St. Odile in order to gain advantage in the monastic rivalries of the twelfth century.

Despite the obscurity of Hohenbourg's early history, the monastery to which Relinde was called at the middle of the twelfth century was one of real significance, not only within Alsace, but also across southern Germany. Hohenbourg's connection to St. Odile was central to its importance. Since the monastery housed Odile's shrine, it was (and, indeed, continues to be) the most popular pilgrimage destination in Alsace. It is even possible that Barbarossa's visit in 1153 was a pious one, inspired by his desire to seek intercession at the shrine of St. Odile, as so many other pilgrims had before him. Hohenbourg's ties to St. Odile may also have provided the basis of its appeal to the counts of Eguisheim, whose most prominent son, the reforming pope Leo IX (1049–1054), paid two separate visits to Hohenbourg in the mid-eleventh century. In the immediate wake of a fire in 1045, which had ravaged the monastery, Leo, then Bishop

Bruno of Toul, visited Hohenbourg and consecrated the church that was about to be constructed there. He dedicated the church to the Virgin and to St. Nicholas, as the ceremony took place on his saint's day, December 6.[7] During a second trip through Alsace after he had become pope, Leo visited the monastery again and issued a papal bull in its favor.[8] Leo's interest in Hohenbourg may have been deepened by his relationship to one of the community's eleventh-century abbesses, but it was founded on his devotion to St. Odile, about whom he composed a series of responses.[9]

In addition to Hohenbourg's historical and spiritual significance, the monastery occupied a position of real political and military consequence within Alsace—a region that formed the western border of the Empire. Perched at the top of Mont Sainte Odile and surrounded by a pre-Christian wall evocative of earlier battles, the monastic compound at Hohenbourg comprised a natural fortress above the Alsatian plain.[10] Its strategic importance had been confirmed earlier in the twelfth century by Duke Frederick II, whose "invasion" continued to be remembered at Hohenbourg until at least the thirteenth century.[11] The nature of Duke Frederick's assault on Hohenbourg has been a source of disagreement among scholars, some of whom have seen it as evidence of Hohenbourg's entanglement in the battles of the investiture controversy, and specifically Frederick's campaign in Alsace in about 1115, while others interpret his actions simply as those of an overzealous advocate claiming the assets of his monastery.[12] However, it is clear in either case that the Hohenstaufen viewed Hohenbourg as an important prize.

Duke Frederick II's possible advocacy of Hohenbourg may explain Barbarossa's royal and, later, imperial patronage of the monastery. Certainly by the time of Barbarossa's son, Duke Frederick V (d. 1191), the Hohenstaufen had officially assumed advocacy of Hohenbourg, confirming their, by then long-standing, relationship with the monastery.[13] Hohenbourg's continued importance within the empire, even after Frederick Barbarossa's death in 1190, is demonstrated by Henry VI's (d. 1197) decision to imprison Queen Sibylle of Sicily there following her exile from Sicily in 1194. Sibylle's presence at Hohenbourg is recorded in Otto of St. Blasien's *Chronicle*, where she is mentioned together with one daughter, and possibly also on folio 323r of the *Hortus*, where a woman identified simply as "Sibilia" appears among the *conversae* (*HD* Cat. No. 346; plate 2). While this "Sibilia" may have been the imprisoned queen, if she was, then she was represented without her daughter, or daughters, whose names—reportedly Albinia, Medania, and Constantia—do not appear in the list of Hohenbourg women.[14]

Relinde of Hohenbourg (d. c. 1176)

As with the early history of Hohenbourg and the immediate context of its reform, little is known of Relinde, the woman who launched the community into its most celebrated and intellectually significant period. She appears only once in the *Hortus*, on the penultimate folios of the manuscript. Here the legendary foundation of the monastery by Duke Adalric in the seventh or eighth century is shown facing a group portrait of the women who lived at Hohenbourg when the *Hortus* was produced: forty-six canonesses and twelve novices (fols. 322v–23r; plates 1–2).[15] Although this is Relinde's only appearance in the manuscript, her centrality to the history and renewal of the community is clear. Shown to the left of the assembled women, Relinde is depicted both as a second Odile, a second founder of the community, and as co-abbess and mentor to her successor, Herrad. Above all, however, it is Relinde's reforming activity that is emphasized. An inscription identifying her records that: "In her time, Relinde, venerable abbess of the church of Hohenbourg carefully restored the things that had been demolished and wisely reformed the divine service, which had been almost destroyed."[16] No further information is given, even though Relinde must have provided the spiritual and material context of the *Hortus* project. The details of her life and, in particular, the chronology of her abbacy are unknown. Only the day of her death, August 22, is sure, since it is noted in the necrologies of both Zwiefalten and St. Arbogast in Strasbourg.[17] Neither source mentions the year of her death. Beyond these witnesses, only one charter has survived from Relinde's abbacy, which, since it is undated, sheds no further light on the chronology of her abbacy. In the absence of other evidence, the date of her arrival at Hohenbourg can only be proposed based on Frederick Barbarossa's visit in 1153 and his reform of the monastery.[18]

Even more curious than the chronology of Relinde's abbacy is the question of her origins and early career: where was she when Frederick Barbarossa called her to come to Hohenbourg? Until fairly recently, it was thought that Relinde had come to Hohenbourg from the abbey of Bergen on the Danube, which she had purportedly been sent to reform from her home community, the Benedictine reform house at Admont.[19] This con-

nection—tantalizing for a number of reasons—has its origins in the work
of the sixteenth-century scholar, Gaspard Bruchius. Working from a catalogue of abbesses for Bergen that has since disappeared, Bruchius remarked on the existence of two abbesses of Bergen, both by the name of
Relinde. The first and elder Relinde he identified as Relinde of Hohenbourg, suggesting that she had been called from Bergen to Hohenbourg
by Frederick Barbarossa. Although he admitted that he could find no details concerning her origins or abbacy, Bruchius nonetheless specified that
she had died on August 22, the date assigned to Relinde of Hohenbourg
in the necrologies of St. Arbogast and Zwiefalten. Bruchius's second Relinde was a less mysterious figure: a nun from Admont, she had been sent
by the Abbot Geoffrey, along with seven of her sisters, to reform Bergen
in 1156. The activities of this Relinde are confirmed in the *Annales Admontenses*; she died on April 4, 1169.[20] These two figures were subsequently
conflated, and their achievements attributed to a single woman, who was
supposed to have been first a Benedictine nun at Admont, then the abbess
of Bergen, and finally the Augustinian reformer of Hohenbourg.[21] Adding
to her fame, Peltre, author of a seventeenth-century *Vie de Ste Odile
Vièrge*, suggested that Relinde had also been a princess of the Empire, the
niece of none other than the emperor himself. He proposed 1167 as the
date of her death.[22]

Nineteenth-century scholars expressed reservations concerning this
account of Relinde's origins, yet the idea that she had come to Hohenbourg from Admont, by way of Bergen, proved too tempting for it to be
dismissed entirely. Few twelfth-century female communities are so well
known for their learning and scribal activity as Hohenbourg and Admont;
a connection between them, although almost certainly illusory, is seduc-
tive in its simplicity. Moreover, such a connection would explain many of
the artistic and intellectual influences that the *Hortus* shares with certain
Bavarian manuscripts. The manuscript's emphasis on the works of Honorius Augustodunensis and many of its images, which reflect compositions
popular in Bavarian monasteries, strengthen the Bavarian connection, as
do its German glosses, which indicate that Bavarian was most likely the
mother tongue at Hohenbourg.[23] Moreover, the names of the women of
Hohenbourg, which are listed alongside their portraits on the penultimate
folios of the *Hortus*, confirm that many of them had come from Bavarian
families.[24]

In a reconsideration of Relinde's origins, Will argued against the Ber-
gen-Hohenbourg connection on chronological grounds. Since Lucius III

records that Relinde had been appointed by Frederick Barbarossa and had worked alongside Bishop Burchard of Strasbourg in her reform of the monastery, Will concluded that she must have arrived at Hohenbourg between 1147, the death of Duke Frederick II, and 1162, that of Burchard. This dating would exclude her removal from Bergen, which a sixteenth-century history of Bergen dates to 1163.[25] Will then compared what is known of Relinde of Hohenbourg with what is known of Relinde of Bergen. Obviously both women were reformers who reinvigorated the spiritual lives of their monasteries. However, Relinde of Bergen introduced the rule of St. Benedict, while Relinde of Hohenbourg placed her monastery under the rule of St. Augustine, making it unlikely, although not impossible, that they were the same person. The case for a distinction between the two Relindes is supported by Lucius III's reference to Relinde of Hohenbourg as simply *idonea persona*, a description that would rule out a prior career as abbess at another monastery, or a relationship to the emperor.[26] On this basis, Will concluded that Relinde, abbess of Hohenbourg, had not come from Admont, had not ruled Bergen, and was not related to Frederick Barbarossa. Finally, he showed that Peltre's suggestion of 1167 as Relinde's date of death was founded on a simple mistake: rather than printing 1176, as internal references suggest that he had intended, Peltre inadvertently switched the numbers, writing 1167 instead. Relinde's death should be placed closer to 1176.[27] This date is consistent with what is known of Relinde's successor, Herrad: her name first appears as abbess in charters for Hohenbourg in 1178.[28]

Relinde and Augustinian Reform at Hohenbourg

Relinde's contribution to the physical and spiritual renewal of Hohenbourg was substantial. Not only did she see to the repair of the monastery—"for love of God diligently rebuilding the things that had been destroyed" (*pro Dei amore destructa diligenter reedificans*) as Lucius III records—but she also brought about the religious renewal that provided the spiritual foundation for the *Hortus*. Her most important achievement in this regard was to place the women of Hohenbourg under the Augustinian Rule, which she did with the help and counsel of Bishop Burchard of Strasbourg.[29] Hohenbourg's adoption of the Augustinian Rule reflects the monastery's involvement in the movement for spiritual renewal that was sweeping across Alsace and, indeed, all of Europe at the mid-century.

At the same time, it brought Hohenbourg into direct contact with other reformed Augustinian communities in Alsace, the most important of which was the reform center of Marbach.

Hohenbourg's adoption of the Augustinian Rule sometime during the middle of the twelfth century is consistent with trends in female monasticism more generally. Prior to Relinde's abbacy, the community had most likely been a house of secular canonesses, following the *Institutio sanctimonialium* of Aix.[30] According to this rule, canonesses were not required to make a vow and could therefore leave the community either to marry if necessary or to travel if they wished. They were also free to hold private property. Given these freedoms and the traditional association of canonesses with the high nobility, houses of canonesses tended to attract women from the ruling classes, who were able to maintain many of the comforts of their secular lives while still giving themselves over to lives of prayer and devotion to God.[31] Most important, since canonesses were not required to make a vow, young girls could be sent to their communities to be educated, with no expectation that they would remain once they had completed their studies.[32]

By the twelfth century, however, few houses of secular canonesses remained. Many had already been reformed during the tenth century, when efforts had been made to regularize observance of the religious life and to restore monasticism to its supposedly original ideal. It is likely that attempts were made at that time to introduce the Benedictine Rule at Hohenbourg and to convert the canonesses there into nuns, as happened elsewhere. However, the women of Hohenbourg, no doubt anxious to defend their ancient rights and way of life, resisted the reformers' efforts. The *Vita Odiliae*, which purported to chronicle the community's foundation in the late seventh or early eighth century, provides evidence for opposition to reform at Hohenbourg, casting the canonical life of the community as a part of St. Odile's legacy. The *vita* records that, soon after Hohenbourg's foundation, Odile gathered the women of the community together and offered them a choice, "whether they wished to live the canonical or the regular life." Although such a choice could not yet have existed at the time of Hohenbourg's foundation, the *vita* reports that:

All responded unanimously that they preferred to follow the regular life. But she said to them with humility and gentleness: "Indeed I know, most dear sisters and mothers, that you are most eager to bear every difficulty and hardship for the name of Christ. But I fear that if we should choose the regular life, a curse shall be on our successors, since this place, as you know, is truly ill-suited and awkward for the religious life. Truly it is not even possible to secure water without great effort. Therefore it seems to me, if it pleases your kindness, that it is better that you remain in the canonical life." Then, according to her advice, they all chose the canonical life, in which those still in the aforementioned monasteries [Hohenbourg and its sister-foundation at Niedermünster] continue, following the pattern of those who have gone before.[33]

By presenting justifications for the community's original adoption of the canonical life and depicting the ultimate decision as Odile's, the author of the *vita* (who may have been one of the Hohenbourg canonesses)[34] may have intended to resist or forestall the imposition of the Benedictine Rule.[35] If this was the case, then the *vita* is an eloquent testimony not only to the women's opposition to reform at this time, but also to their deliberate manipulation of the historical record in order to maintain and defend their way of life.

By the time that Relinde became abbess, resistance to reform was evidently no longer either practical or desirable at Hohenbourg. The drive to reform houses of canonesses had been given increased urgency in the first half of the twelfth century by the legislation of the Second Lateran Council (1139), which condemned canonesses for their supposed lack of discipline and implicitly called for their regularization according to an accepted rule.[36] Less than ten years later, the condemnation of canonesses was repeated at the Council of Rheims (1148), in conjunction with a now-explicit call for their adoption of a recognized rule.[37] In these increasingly hostile circumstances it is little wonder that implementation of the Augustinian Rule accompanied reform at Hohenbourg, or that both events took place within only a few years of Rheims.

Relinde's program of reform at Hohenbourg and her introduction of the Augustinian Rule set the stage for the spiritual and intellectual vitality that is demonstrated in the *Hortus deliciarum*. Reform of the secular canonesses was part of the broader movement for church reform that had first taken hold in Italy during the second half of the eleventh century. At that time, the men who served in the cathedral chapters of Europe—known as "canons" (*canonici*) by virtue of their appearance on the bishop's list (his *canon*)—became the focus of a more general impulse to reform the church and to restore it to the original apostolic ideal of the New Testament.[38] Since cathedral canons were at the forefront of the church's pastoral ministry, their reform was central to the purpose and mission of the ecclesiastical reform movement as a whole. Efforts to reform these canons centered on

such issues as their ownership of private property, purchase of church office, and luxurious manner of living. The remedy to these perceived evils
was to subordinate communities of canons to the communal life under
the authority of a rule, which was most often the Rule of Augustine. It
was among reformed canons, then, who gradually came to be known as
"regular" canons to distinguish them from the unreformed or "secular"
canons, that the earliest references to the Augustinian Rule appear.[39] The
Rule gained prominence quickly. By the second quarter of the twelfth
century, it was an established option both for communities of reformed
cathedral canons and for the communities of canons and canonesses that
had been founded in the wake of reform, as well as those, like Hohenbourg, that had been recently reformed.[40]

Although many of these new communities had no ties to the bishop's
cathedral, the original connection between canons and the care of souls
(*cura animarum*) continued. Canons maintained their right to preach, to
be ordained, and to receive tithes, topics that were the focus of heated
debates between them and monks.[41] In many ways, there were few real
differences between the two groups. However, the dedication of canons
to teaching, both within their communities and beyond them, provides
one point of clear contrast. As Caroline Bynum argues, the concern to
educate and to edify, which stemmed from the association of Augustinian
canons with the priesthood, sets them apart from Benedictine monks.[42]
The Parisian community of St. Victor is a prime example of what she identifies as the Augustinian devotion to teaching and of the canons' ability to
combine scholarship with contemplation.[43] The *Hortus deliciarum* demonstrates that the Augustinian dedication to teaching was not limited to
male communities. As the product of Herrad's (and Relinde's) desire to
provide the newly reformed community of women at Hohenbourg with a
complete moral and intellectual education, the *Hortus* showcases women's
involvement in an Augustinian tradition of teaching *verbo et exemplo*.

The Reform Center at Marbach

In addition to its intellectual implications, Hohenbourg's adoption of the
Augustinian Rule placed the monastery in the mainstream of the reform
movement in Alsace, which centered on the male community of Marbach.[44] Marbach's early history is bound up with the quarrels of the investiture controversy and its support for the papacy. Founded in 1089 by

Burchard of Gerberschweier, a vassal or ministerial of the Strasbourg church, Marbach had already emerged as a significant reform center within a decade of its foundation, largely due to the influence of Manegold of Lautenbach (d. c. 1103). A scholar, Gregorian polemicist, and imperial adversary, Manegold had come to the new community as provost in 1094.[45] His life had been devoted to the cause of church reform. Following a career of teaching and scholarship, which, if Richard of Poitiers is to be believed, involved both his wife and daughters,[46] he adopted the religious life as a canon at the Alsatian reform center of Lautenbach. There, sometime around 1085, he composed two polemical tracts in support of the reformed papacy. In the first, the *Liber ad Gebehardum*, which he addressed to the reforming Archbishop Gebhard of Salzburg, Manegold defended the reforms initiated by Pope Gregory VII (d. 1085) and criticized the position held by the emperor, Henry IV (d. 1106).[47] In his second work, the *Liber contra Wolfhelmum*, he linked reliance on philosophy with the obstinacy of the imperial party, which he termed the "madness of the German kingdom."[48] Not surprisingly, Manegold's outspokenness earned him the enmity of the imperial party. At some point, presumably while he was still at work on the *Liber ad Gebehardum* but after he had completed the *Liber contra Wolfhelmum*, imperial supporters destroyed the community at Lautenbach and forced its inhabitants into exile. Manegold fled to the Bavarian monastery of Rottenbuch, which was widely known as a refuge for Gregorian supporters; he remained there as dean until he was called to be provost of Marbach in 1094.[49]

The earliest contemporary record of Manegold's career at Marbach is provided by Bernold of Constance, the scholar turned Benedictine monk whose writings detail in glowing language the vicissitudes of Gregorian and monastic reform in Germany.[50] Bernold records that Manegold reignited the fire of religious enthusiasm throughout Alsace. The scene that he describes at Marbach is reminiscent of the religious enthusiasm that he records elsewhere in his *Chronicle* and that emptied entire villages as men and women from every age and station flocked to the religious life.[51] Crowds flocked to Manegold, too, seeking from him reconciliation with Rome and absolution from excommunication, papal prerogatives that Urban II had authorized him to grant.[52] As Bernold notes, Manegold's ability to free men from excommunication attracted crowds of erstwhile imperial supporters, including "almost all the greater nobility and knights of that province."[53] However, it also "aroused great envy" among the "perfidious," an outcome to which Bernold remarks that Manegold gave little thought, "because he did not doubt that it was actually a most glorious thing to be despised, for the name of God." Henry IV's reaction to the challenge that Manegold posed was swift: four years after he had arrived in Alsace, Manegold was thrown into prison. Bernold writes:

Manegold, the venerable prior of the canons dwelling at Marbach, was held in captivity for a long time by Henry the King because he refused to obey the schismatics who rejected the authority of the Church. For this reason the whole Church far and wide grieved for him.[54]

Although Manegold probably died soon after his release in 1103, his legacy of spiritual vitality and commitment to church reform lived on in the Marbach customs, a set of guidelines designed to supplement the short text of the Augustinian Rule and to provide for the practical details of the community's religious life.[55] By the mid-twelfth century, some twenty-five houses had begun to observe Marbach's customs, while other monasteries shared with Marbach in an extensive web of prayer confraternities evident in its surviving necrologies.[56] These necrologies, which in many places read like a roll call of Gregorian reformers, reveal Marbach's ties to Benedictine reform monasteries of the Hirsau circle—proof that the community continued in its dedication to church reform even after Manegold's death. At its height in the mid-twelfth century, Marbach formed the nucleus of a large reform network that spread beyond Alsace to include monasteries in Bavaria as well as Switzerland.[57] Hohenbourg may well have been a part of this network, although there is no proof that the women themselves adopted Marbach's customs. They did, however, seek connections with Marbach, establishing a confraternity of prayers with the community and even selecting the Marbach customs to govern the religious life of Hohenbourg's (male) daughter house.

Hohenbourg's adoption of the Augustinian Rule, which placed it within the Alsatian reform circle defined by Marbach, also brought it into contact with communities marked by openness to women. Alongside its reforming zeal, Marbach maintained a particular concern for the spiritual lives of women—a characteristic feature of many late eleventh-century reform communities, and particularly those associated with Hirsau.[58] In many cases, the reform or foundation of a male house was accompanied by the establishment of a female community, a model that may have been followed at Marbach in 1089. A fifteenth-century tradition claims that Burchard had founded Marbach with the help of his wife and daughter, Judenta and Margaretha. Their names were added in a fifteenth-century hand to the community's 1241 necrology.[59] Although this account cannot be corroborated by contemporary evidence, a female community was attached to the male foundation at Marbach, if not at its inception, then soon thereafter. These women formed part of the Marbach community until a gift of land in about 1117 made it possible for them to establish their own house at Schwartzenthann, some six kilometers away. In recording this gift, the Marbach annalist simply notes that land at Schwartzenthann had been received "by the congregation of the women of Marbach," indicating that in its early years Marbach had indeed been a double community.[60]

Marbach's attention to women may have been a function of its Augustinian affiliation. Indeed, the attraction of women to the Augustinian Rule and the shared involvement of both men and women in many Augustinian communities are factors that distinguish Augustinians from Benedictines, despite the fact that certain Benedictine reform communities, like Hirsau, were also committed to the care of women. The difference between the two stems from the relative attention paid to women in the Augustinian as opposed to the Benedictine Rule. In the 1130s, when Heloise wrote to Abelard, one of her chief complaints was that the Benedictine Rule, which was observed at the Paraclete, was inappropriate for women. Requesting that Abelard furnish her community with a rule "suitable for women" (*quae feminarum sit propria*), Heloise goes on to explain that since the Benedictine Rule had been written for men alone "it can only be fully obeyed by men."[61] Unbeknownst to Heloise, the Augustinian Rule had always included a feminine version. Augustine's letter 211—one of the three texts that may be seen to comprise his monastic writings—was addressed to a female community and included both a "reprimand to quarreling nuns" and a "rule for nuns."[62] Since the "rule for nuns" was identical to the rule for monks in everything but the gender of the text, it has never been clear which community—male or female—Augustine had first addressed. While scholarly opinion has recently declared in favor of the masculine version as the original form of Augustine's Rule,[63] medieval commentators were not always so sure. Indeed, some thought that the derivation was the other way around—that is to say, that Augustine's Rule had been written in the first instance for women and only later adapted for men.[64]

The question of Augustine's original intention and audience in writing the Rule is in many ways irrelevant to its appeal during the twelfth century and to its perceived association with women. What matters is that

Augustine was widely believed to have concerned himself equally with the
spiritual lives of both sexes. The strongest confirmation of this point appears in the *Guta-Sintram Codex*, a manuscript that was produced in 1154
through the cooperation of Guta, a female scribe and canoness from
Schwartzenthann, and Sintram, a male artist and canon from Marbach. In
this manuscript, Augustine's attention to both men and women is made
explicit in a full-page miniature, where he is shown with two canons on
his right and two canonesses on his left (*CGS*, p. 11; plate 3). The symmetry
of the image reflects the spiritual parity of men and women within the
Augustinian order, and especially amongst those houses associated with
Marbach.

Marbach and the *Cura monialium*

The presence of the Augustine image in the *Guta-Sintram Codex* provides
a crucial link to the history of Hohenbourg and its adoption of the Augustinian Rule at the mid-century. As a manuscript produced by a female
scribe within an Augustinian community, the codex offers an obvious parallel to the *Hortus deliciarum* and has much to reveal concerning the female scribal culture in Alsace at the mid-twelfth century. Most striking is
the example of male-female collaboration in book production that it provides. Guta and Sintram worked together—possibly even side by side—as
they brought the manuscript to completion. The collaborative nature of
their relationship is highlighted on the manuscript's dedication page
(*CGS*, p. 9; plate 4).[65] Here both Guta and Sintram are shown paying
homage to the Virgin Mary, with Sintram on the Virgin's right and Guta
on her left. The visual symmetry of the image, which anticipates the Augustine image some pages later, underscores Guta's partnership with Sintram and their shared responsibility for the codex. Inscriptions within the
image's central panel complete the message of cooperation, presenting
Guta and Sintram as co-supplicants in a prayer to Mary.[66] Mary's response
confirms their unusual partnership: "Together, you have adorned this
work, which you have dedicated to me, with letters and figures achieved
with skill. Together I will make you to share in the same repose."[67]

The intimacy of Guta's working relationship with Sintram was mir-
rored in the close ties that bound their two communities. As we have
already seen, it is likely that Marbach had initially been founded as a double community; the women only moved when a gift of land allowed them

to establish their own house at Schwartzenthann. Importantly, the women's move did not alter their ties to Marbach. The two communities continued in their special relationship, as the *Guta-Sintram Codex* makes clear. Not only does the manuscript signal tangible cooperation between the two houses, but its contents reflect the ties—past, present, and future—that bound them together. The most obvious connection was commemorative: the bulk of the manuscript comprised the shared necrology of Marbach and Schwartzenthann, which, despite the loss of its last three months, lists in excess of 4,000 names.[68] These include members of both communities as well as donors, patrons, and others who were connected to them in some way. In addition to the necrology, the codex contains a homilary, a copy of the Rule of St. Augustine, a commentary on the rule entitled the *Expositio in Regulam beati Augustini*, and the famous customs of Marbach, which were evidently observed at Schwartzenthann as they were elsewhere in Alsace and across Germany and Switzerland.[69]

The ties that brought Guta and Sintram together and that bound their two communities were characteristic of a general policy of support for the lives of religious women among the canons at Marbach. This policy finds its most eloquent expression in a text, excerpted from one of Abelard's sermons (sermon 30) for the Paraclete, which appears in the *Guta-Sintram Codex* on the page facing the Guta-Sintram dedication image (*CGS*, p. 8).[70] Beginning with the words of Matthew 5:3—"blessed are the poor in spirit" (*Beati pauperes spiritu*)—the text argues that the true poor, those who had committed themselves to the religious life, comprised not only men but also women. Although it includes no salutation and is presented anonymously, this text is clearly addressed to a male audience with the exhortation that they pay special attention to the spiritual care of religious women. Its message is one of obligation and privilege. While arguing that men should care for women, the text also presents the opportunity to serve women as a tremendous privilege; as brides of Christ, religious women enjoy access to him unavailable to men. Quite apart from the bridal relationship, the text goes on to argue that women have greater spiritual potential than men, since their natural weakness has made their virtue more acceptable to God than men's. The result is that the pastoral care of religious women—the *cura monialium*—is presented as an obligation for priests: by becoming brides of Christ, religious women gain authority over all of Christ's servants.

Abelard's arguments were powerful, and evidently had real impact at Marbach, where they were used to justify the sorts of relationships with women that the canons there maintained. Such justification was necessary: Marbach was increasingly out of step with trends in the religious life during the second half of the twelfth century. By the time that the *Guta-Sintram Codex* was written, few male communities maintained the close contact between the sexes that had been characteristic of the initial spirit of reform. The decline in shared communities in the second half of the twelfth century was at least in part a result of legislation against the co-celebration of the liturgy enacted by Lateran II. Henceforth men and women were not to sing in the same choir, a stipulation that dramatically increased the difficulties for shared communities with a single church.[71] In response, many male communities that had initially included a female component chose either to move the women away to a more distant spot or to cut ties with them altogether.[72] This is evidently what happened to the community of women at Steinbach. Although they had originally been placed under the authority of the nearby Cistercian monastery at Lucelle, soon after the Cistercian General Chapter in 1152–1153 they were abandoned by Lucelle and left without pastoral care.[73] Marbach's response to Steinbach's situation is emblematic of its approach to pastoral care and to women generally. In 1157, the bishop of Basel decreed the incorporation of Steinbach to Marbach, which immediately dispatched a canon to serve as priest for the women of the community, just as Marbach canons provided care for the women of Schwartzenthann.[74]

Marbach's attention to the spiritual lives of women is in keeping both with its historical orientation toward reform and the *vita apostolica*, and with its Augustinian affiliation. Reformed communities, especially in Germany, had often included both men and women in imitation of the model of the early church that was provided in Acts. In the immediate aftermath of Jesus' ascension into heaven, Acts describes how the community of Christians gathered together in Jerusalem to pray "with the women and Mary the mother of Jesus" (Acts 1:14). There was no denying that the early church, which the reformers claimed as their exemplar, had comprised both men and women or that men were expected to care for women, a fact that is emphasized in accounts of the crucifixion. While Jesus had provided a model of care for women during his life, even from the cross his concern was to ensure that his mother was adequately provided for. Exhorting John to adopt Mary's care, he presented her to his disciple, saying, "Here is your mother" (John 19:27). Jesus' commendation to John was cited by both men and women during the twelfth century as a model for men's obligation to provide pastoral care for women.[75]

In addition to the biblical example, Augustinian communities were inspired by the perceived association of Augustine with women. Not only was the Augustinian Rule particularly attractive to communities that sought to institutionalize the shared involvement of men and women in the religious life, but it was also adopted by male communities that had been established explicitly to provide spiritual care for women. At Sempringham and Fontevrault, for instance, the women followed the Benedictine Rule, while the men, who as canons and priests were to provide the women with pastoral care, were placed under the Rule of Augustine.[76]

Marbach's dedication to the care of women is crucial to the history of Hohenbourg and its reform in the twelfth century. As we have seen, in adopting the Augustinian Rule at Hohenbourg Relinde placed Hohenbourg within a network of vibrant Augustinian communities of which the monastery of Marbach had been the center since its foundation in the late eleventh century. It may be that Marbach's fame had even inspired Relinde in her reforming activities. In addition to the many achievements that Lucius imputes to her in his 1185 bull—the rationalization of Hohenbourg's properties, the restoration of its buildings, and the reorganization of its religious life under the Rule of Augustine—she also sought to establish bonds with Augustinian communities in Alsace, chief among them the reform center at Marbach. At some point, probably after she had introduced the Augustinian Rule at Hohenbourg, Relinde paid a visit to Marbach. Marbach's 1241 necrology states: "The venerable abbess Relinde, who restored the order of canonical rule in Hohenbourg, coming to us, faithfully asked us the following: that in prayers and in other observances we make such prayers for the deceased nuns of Hohenbourg, as we are accustomed to do for our sisters. But since they have fewer priests than we do, they promised to give thirty prebends to the poor at the death of any of our canons so that they might pay for the prayers with alms."[77] Relinde's concern to establish a link with Marbach is confirmed through the sole charter that has survived from her abbacy.[78] Listed first among the witnesses is Dipold, the provost of Ittenwiller, a community that had been founded in 1115 as a daughter house of Marbach, possibly even its first.[79] Dipold's presence among the witnesses to Relinde's charter suggests that her ties to Marbach extended beyond the confraternity of prayers that the Marbach necrology records; it is likely that Relinde also solicited help in the practical matters of monastic administration either from Marbach or from its dependencies. Since many of the houses that adopted Marbach's customs also adopted its concern for women, Ittenwiller too may have absorbed some of the spirit of *Beati pauperes* during the course of its early years.[80]

The probable chronology of Relinde's visit to Marbach and the connection between the two communities that it initiated raise questions concerning the factors that prompted Relinde's attraction to the Marbach canons. Even if Relinde had become abbess as early as 1147, she might not have approached Marbach concerning the possibility of confraternity with Hohenbourg before the 1150s—the decade during which there is the most evidence for Marbach's involvement with women. In fact, it might be that Relinde was drawn by Marbach's reputation for dedication to the religious lives of women. Although there is no indication that she knew of the *Guta-Sintram Codex* or that Guta knew of her—neither Relinde nor Herrad appears in the necrology of the codex—the relationship that Relinde sought with Marbach suggests that she was aware of its care for women. Relinde's attraction to Marbach must be judged more than coincidental: during her abbacy, Marbach took on the care of Steinbach, engaged with Schwartzenthann in the production of at least two, if not three manuscripts in addition to the *Guta-Sintram Codex*,[81] and possibly even formulated in *Beati pauperes* a theory for the reciprocity of men and women in the religious life.[82]

The *Cura monialium* at Hohenbourg

Relinde's appeal to Marbach may have taken on increased urgency given the fate of women within other reform communities in the second half of the twelfth century. Like the Cistercian monks of Lucelle, many male communities appear to have been increasingly unwilling—or unable—to take on female members or dependent houses for women by the mid-twelfth century. This reluctance may have been the result of Lateran II's ruling against the co-celebration of the liturgy, or it may simply have been a function of increased bureaucratization as a community matured and the spontaneous early associations of men and women were subjected to mounting oversight. By the mid-twelfth century it was evidently increasingly difficult for women to find suitable care, even such women as Hildegard of Bingen and Heloise. Hildegard had to apply to Pope Alexander III (1159–1181) to resolve a conflict between her community at the Rupertsberg and the men's community at Disibodenberg, which had failed to fulfill its obligation to provide the women with a provost after the death of her secretary Volmar in 1173.[83] The pope referred the matter to Hildegard's nephew, who arranged for a priest named Gottfried to serve at the Rupertsberg until his own death in 1176. While there is no record of a similar conflict at the Paraclete, Heloise too worried about the community's future ability to appoint a suitable priest. She revealed her concerns in a letter to Abelard: "After you we may perhaps have another to guide us, one who will build something upon another's foundation, and so, we fear, he may be less likely to feel concern for us, or be less readily heard by us; or indeed, he may be no less willing, but less able."[84] Given that attention to women at Marbach evidently extended beyond the early reform period and into the more cautious climate of the later twelfth century, the community would have been especially attractive to religious women in Alsace, a fact that Relinde evidently recognized. Like Heloise and Hildegard, both of whom aggressively asserted their claim to pastoral care and took great pains to ensure that it was properly provided, Relinde's actions offer a persuasive challenge to the model of female passivity that is so often associated with the *cura monialium*. Her decision to ally herself with the canons at Marbach suggests that the Hohenbourg women recognized Marbach's reputation for the care of women and were strategic in securing the attention of the canons there.

Relinde's heightened concern for the *cura monialium* was unquestionably a product of Hohenbourg's tumultuous history in the early part of the twelfth century and even into her own abbacy. One of the most important aspects of her role as a reforming abbess was to normalize relations with the priests who celebrated the divine service at the community's chapels.[85] Like most female communities, Hohenbourg had contractual arrangements with chaplains (*hebdomadarii*) who lived in close proximity to the monastery—although not within the monastery itself—and who provided spiritual service at its altar while also representing the community in its secular dealings. Relationships with these chaplains could be difficult. Hints that all was not well in Hohenbourg's relationship with its priests in the early years of the twelfth century can be found in a partially falsified papal bull of Leo IX.[86] Although this bull was issued at the mid-eleventh century, portions of text that were added in the early decades of the twelfth century shed light on Hohenbourg's situation at that time.[87] These additions reveal the monastery's particular concern with encroachment on its properties at the summit of Mont Sainte Odile, within the area enclosed by the pre-Christian wall.[88] Although encroachment on this land was a problem that continued to trouble Hohenbourg, as a charter issued by

Bishop Conrad of Strasbourg in the 1190s reveals,[89] in the immediate context of the early twelfth century, it appears that Hohenbourg's own chaplains were the culprits. An addition to the end of the bull offers a stern warning to these chaplains that they should stop disturbing the monastery and content themselves with the properties that they had already been given by the abbess. The twelfth-century forger (who may have been one of the women) reminded the community's priests of their obedience to the abbess: "Let him be struck by the same anathema, if any of the weekly priests (*hebdomadarii*) should dare to oppress the Hohenbourg church either by strife or by rebellion. Moreover, the weekly priests themselves shall possess nothing more on the mountain than the houses they require, which are granted to them by the abbess as a benefice. Amen."[90]

Conflict with its own chaplains did not mark the end of Hohenbourg's troubles. The provision of pastoral care at the monastery was further complicated in the twelfth century by quarrels with the Benedictine monks of Ebersheim, who had traditionally supplemented the spiritual care of the chaplains at Hohenbourg. Ebersheim traced this relationship back to the time of Hohenbourg's foundation, alleging that, at that time, Odile had made an agreement with its abbot that governed the men's provision of spiritual care. This agreement, which appears only in a forged document included in Ebersheim's *Chronicle*, required that a delegation of monks should minister at Hohenbourg at Christmas, Easter, and Pentecost, while the abbot himself should celebrate the mass for the Nativity of the Virgin. In return for these services, Odile was purported to have given Ebersheim certain lands and revenues.[91] Ebersheim's *Chronicle*, which dates to 1163 at the earliest, adds to our admittedly scant knowledge concerning Hohenbourg's relationships with its priests during Relinde's abbacy. In this case, the point of contention appears to have been the lands that Ebersheim claimed it had been given by Odile in return for spiritual service. These same lands were among those to which Hohenbourg laid claim in its own forgery, a false diploma of Louis the Pious.[92] Although it is possible that both communities could legitimately own land in the same places, the overlapping land claims and the curious fact of a double forgery could well be evidence of conflict between the two communities; such conflict would certainly have jeopardized pastoral care at the women's community.

When Herrad succeeded Relinde as abbess, probably in 1176, her most immediate task was to find a workable solution to the problem of pastoral care at Hohenbourg. Her remedy was at once ambitious and direct: between 1178 and 1180 she established two new foundations for regular canons near Hohenbourg, both of which were to be dependent on the female community and to provide spiritual service in its chapels. The first, St. Gorgon, was founded in 1178 at the base of Mont Sainte Odile and given to the Premonstratensian canons of Étival; it was to house two canons.[93] The canons of St. Gorgon were obliged to provide one priest to say the daily mass in the chapel of St. Odile and another to perform the weekly office. The abbot of Étival was to come in person to celebrate the office on particular feast days. In return, Hohenbourg provided St. Gorgon with lands, revenues, and material goods: wheat and wine.[94] Two years later, Herrad established a second community at Truttenhausen on the other side of the mountain, slightly farther away than St. Gorgon. Truttenhausen was a larger community than St. Gorgon with resources to support twelve canons, who were to come to the new foundation from Marbach.[95] Although Truttenhausen did not provide priests to celebrate a daily service at Hohenbourg, as St. Gorgon did, the community's provost was required to visit the community and to say mass at a number of feasts: the Purification of Mary, Palm Sunday, Holy Thursday, the Nativity, the Beheading of John the Baptist, the Assumption of Mary, and the Feasts of St. Michael, All Saints, and St. Odile. In addition, he was to celebrate the first mass of the day for the Nativity, the Feast of Odile, and the feast commemorating the dedication of her chapel.[96] Sometimes representatives from both houses were required at Hohenbourg so that, for instance, for the Feasts of Odile and of the dedication of her chapel, both the provost of Truttenhausen and the abbot of Étival would be present; for the Nativity of Mary, the abbot of Étival and possibly also the abbot of Ebersheim; and for Christmas, the provost of Truttenhausen and the abbot of Ebersheim, together with his retinue. This solution effectively freed Hohenbourg from its previous dependence on its chaplains and the monks of Ebersheim. It also made Hohenbourg the focal point of a small circle of reform houses and added to Herrad's prestige, since, as the abbess of Hohenbourg, she maintained ultimate authority over the provost of each new house. While the canons of St. Gorgon and Truttenhausen were given the freedom to elect their own provost, he was to receive his authority at the hands of the abbess of Hohenbourg, underlining his subordination and the subordination of his house to Hohenbourg.[97]

Herrad's foundations represent a natural continuation of Relinde's reforms and an extension of her policy regarding the *cura monialium*. Like Relinde, Herrad sought connections with male communities that

were already known for their care of women. This is most clearly illustrated
in her foundation at Truttenhausen in 1180. With the help of Günther of
Vienhege, a ministerial of Hohenbourg,[98] she bought the land on which
the monastery was to be built and proceeded to oversee the construction
of a chapel dedicated to the Virgin, a church dedicated to St. Nicholas,
and a monastic enclosure that included both a guest house and a hospice
to receive pilgrims.[99] In the community's necrology, Herrad was remembered for her role in its foundation.[100] She may also have worked in
cooperation with her brother, whose name is also recorded in the Truttenhausen necrology, although no mention is made of his role, if indeed he
played one.[101]

From the first, Herrad intended that her new foundation at Truttenhausen would be inhabited by regular canons who followed the Augustinian Rule and the Customs of Marbach, "in honor of God and of the
monastery of Hohenbourg," as Lucius records.[102] Her decision to establish the Customs of Marbach at Truttenhausen, from the very moment of
its inception, raises questions concerning her familiarity with them. Although there is no record that they were observed at Hohenbourg, adoption of the Marbach customs tended to coincide with the moment of
reform and conversion to the Augustinian Rule in the case of other Mar-
bach-affiliated communities. Reform at St. Arbogast in 1143 had followed
this pattern when it was reformed under the guidance of Bishop Burchard
of Strasbourg. It is possible that Burchard's role in advising Relinde in
her adoption of the Augustinian Rule also extended to recommending
Hohenbourg's adoption of the Marbach customs. In any case, Herrad
was certainly familiar with Marbach: her decision to affiliate herself with
Marbach in her foundation at Truttenhausen demonstrates her continuation of Relinde's policy. For their part, the canons who came to Truttenhausen from Marbach in all probability brought with them both their
famous customs and their tradition of service and cooperation with
women.

Herrad's foundation at St. Gorgon two years before had followed a
slightly different course. Instead of buying the land herself and seeing to
the establishment of the community, Herrad had donated the property at
St. Gorgon to the abbot of Étival with the intention that he should build
a chapel and a priory and provide the two canons who would inhabit
them.[103] Her donation must have been at least partly motivated by the
desire to provide a solution to the spiritual needs of the women of her
community; however, in her charter she also expressed the hope that it

would form the basis for a "bond of affection" between Hohenbourg and Étival.[104]

As with Relinde's attraction to Marbach, Étival's appeal to Herrad may have lain in its tradition of service to women, in this case Étival's long-standing relationship with the female community at Andlau, to which the canons had been subordinated since the late ninth century.[105] When Étival adopted the Augustinian Rule in the middle of the twelfth century, it had first to secure permission from the abbess of Andlau, who continued to maintain her authority over the male community.[106] Only in 1172 did the abbess of Andlau finally cede control over Étival, retaining only the right of investiture over the abbot and allowing the male community what Parisse calls "quasi-independence."[107] In return, the abbot of Étival owed spiritual service at Andlau: each year he was to celebrate the feast of Saints Peter and Paul at the female community and to accompany the abbess in the event that she was summoned to the imperial court. The unusual subordination of Étival to Andlau meant that, like Marbach, Étival too had a history of cooperation and collaboration with women.[108] It may be that this is what appealed to Herrad when she chose to make the community a partner in her first foundation at St. Gorgon. Since her plan was to subordinate this new community to Hohenbourg, it made sense for her to identify a community in which subordination to women was already accepted. Wernher, the abbot of Étival who helped in the foundation of St. Gorgon, would not have balked at Herrad's condition that she maintain the right to invest its provost, since he had already received his investiture at the hands of a woman—the abbess of Andlau.

The *cura monialium* was not Herrad's only concern, although it was certainly a major one. Herrad also continued Relinde's efforts at rebuilding the monastery, turning her attention to its properties and proving herself an able business manager. In addition to founding St. Gorgon and Truttenhausen, Herrad sought to consolidate Hohenbourg's lands, encouraging donations to the monastery, reconstituting domains that had been unjustly usurped by local landholders, and reasserting her authority in the surrounding area. Several charters record her efforts. One charter from the early years of her abbacy notes the donation of a house at Rodesheim to the monastery by Willebirc, a noble woman of Andlau.[109] The importance of this donation is reflected in the fact that it was confirmed by Frederick Barbarossa on October 12, 1178, when he also confirmed Herrad's donation of St. Gorgon to Étival.[110] It is possible that Willebirc entered the monastery after the death of her husband, Bernhier, who is mentioned in her donation to Hohenbourg; a woman by the same name is shown among the women of Hohenbourg on folio 323r of the *Hortus* (plate 2). Additional charters record that Berthold of Ingmarsheim gave nine fields in Ingmarsheim and that Burckhard of Strasbourg gave a mill at Ottrott in 1189.[111] Three further charters record donations of land at Rodesheim that were made to Hohenbourg in lieu of unpaid debts. Two of these, both undated, compensate for debts that had been owing *de oblatione Bennonis*.[112] A third charter records that Conrad of Lutzelbourg gave lands at Rodesheim to Hohenbourg to compensate for debts that were owed to the monastery.[113] In addition to calling on Hohenbourg's creditors, Herrad also reasserted the monastery's rights over lands that belonged to it. She restored the offices of chairman and forest guard of the village of Ingmarsheim, which Leo IX had listed among Hohenbourg's assets in 1051, stipulating that the villeins there should propose candidates for these positions.[114] Finally, she reclaimed lands at Rodesheim that had been unjustly usurped.[115]

Once Herrad had completed this work of foundation and restitution, she was careful to ensure that her achievements were recognized by papal and episcopal authority. Both Lucius III and Bishop Conrad of Strasbourg make explicit reference to her "petition" in their confirmations, Lucius in 1185 and Conrad in the 1190s. Herrad used these instances of official endorsement as occasions to reinforce her authority and that of her house. In the cases of Truttenhausen and St. Gorgon, that meant getting papal endorsement for Hohenbourg's authority over the canons of both communities as well as papal warnings against any sort of disruption. Lucius's bull offered a particularly stern caution against the men's disobedience, warning that canons who disrupted the peace at Hohenbourg would be stripped of their benefices and replaced by new priests, to be chosen by the women of the community.[116] He further advised the canons that the "divine will" would be done to any miscreants. Not fully content with this confirmation, Herrad sought an additional charter from Bishop Conrad of Strasbourg some years later, repeating the prohibition against colonization within the confines of the pre-Christian wall and enforcing once more the abbess's right to select the priests who would serve at Hohenbourg's altar.[117] Evidently her efforts were successful: the peaceful presence of regular canons at Hohenbourg during Herrad's abbacy is confirmed through the record of several canons in the witness lists to Herrad's charters. Berthold, a cleric (*Bertholdus clericus*), and Gerhard, a canon (*Gerhardus canonicus*), witnessed one charter, while another charter again lists Berthold among the witnesses, this time describing him as "the canon Berthold, a brother at Hohenbourg and *magister* of the hospital in that place" (*Bertholdus canonicus, frater in Hohenburc et magister hospitalis ibidem*).[118] The fifteenth-century necrology of Truttenhausen confirms this picture, listing several priests among the sisters of Hohenbourg and Niedermünster, and several women among the "brothers of this house."[119]

Conclusion

The self-confidence that both Herrad and Relinde demonstrated in their negotiation of reform, in their management of Hohenbourg's properties, and, above all, in their reorganization of Hohenbourg's arrangements with its priests offers a robust challenge to the depiction of women as objects of reform and also to the model of female passivity in the face of difficulties related to the *cura monialium*. Herrad and Relinde saw to it that Hohenbourg had able and willing priests, seeking out relationships with reform-minded male communities like Marbach and even founding new houses in order to achieve this goal.

The *Hortus deliciarum* was a product of reform and of the specific circumstances at Hohenbourg in the latter half of the twelfth century. As a newly reformed community, Hohenbourg needed books to support the spiritual lives of the canonesses. As with monasteries elsewhere, notably those connected with Hirsau, book production emerged as a natural corollary of reform. Hohenbourg's history as a community of canonesses, its relationship to the emperor, and its probable wealth provided Herrad with the means to produce a luxury manuscript. As we have seen, canonesses in the Empire had traditionally been engaged in education and the transmission of knowledge. The community's Augustinian conversion and ties to Marbach anchored the *Hortus* within the reform movement and provided the spiritual and practical context in which the production of the manuscript was possible. Marbach's support for Schwartzenthann and collaboration in the production of such books as the *Guta-Sintram Codex* provides one possible model for the *Hortus*. Finally, Hohenbourg's continued autonomy throughout the twelfth century, which must be attributed at least in part to its imperial connection, allowed Herrad the independence to produce a book that was largely free from male influences and expectations. In other reformed communities, the tendency to separate what had initially been "double" houses and to relocate the female component was accompanied by the juridical subordination of the women's community. Reformed houses for women, especially those associated with Hirsau, were inevitably subordinated to the headship of a male provost.[120] Hohenbourg's independence is reflected in the fact that, while Relinde and Herrad maintained the title of abbess, the heads of female communities within Hirsau circles were simply termed *magistrae*. This explains why Hildegard of Bingen was never abbess of the Rupertsberg, despite her fame and spiritual authority.[121] In contrast, Herrad was not only "venerable" but also the "faithful and prudent abbess of Hohenbourg"—a title that reflected Hohenbourg's distinctiveness as a reformed yet autonomous community for women.

The *Hortus deliciarum*:
A Book for Reform and Renaissance

THE *HORTUS DELICIARUM* MARKED a critical stage in the progress of reform at Hohenbourg. Some twenty years had elapsed since the first flush of reform enthusiasm had begun to transform the community from a neglected outpost—locked in struggles both with its own chaplains and most likely also with the neighboring monasteries of Niedermünster and Ebersheim—to a vibrant spiritual center for the female religious life. As we saw in the last chapter, that transformation had been effected over the course of several years, beginning with the attentions of the emperor, Frederick Barbarossa, and spanning the careers of both Relinde and Herrad. By the time work began on the *Hortus*, sometime before 1175, Hohenbourg was already entering its second generation of reform. Many of the difficulties that must have marked the early years of Relinde's abbacy were no longer as pressing as they had been. The monastic buildings—once in disrepair—had been restored and some new ones had been built. More important, the spiritual life of the community had been renewed and the women placed under the Augustinian Rule in accordance with the dictates of several church councils and in probable obedience to the bishop of Strasbourg. Although we have few details concerning the spiritual life at the community during this early reform period, it is clear that Relinde sought relationships with other reform-minded communities, chief among them the male reform center at Marbach. Her arrangement with the canons there reinforced Hohenbourg's reform stance and set the stage for Herrad's foundation at Truttenhausen. The relationship with Marbach may also, as I discuss in this chapter, have provided Herrad with the library access that her work on the *Hortus* presupposed.

Despite the many successes of Relinde's abbacy, one major task remained unfinished in the early 1170s: the establishment of reliable pastoral care for the women of the community by what later documents insist must be a "suitable" (*idoneus*) priest. Given the defensive context in which this term usually appears in Hohenbourg's records—alongside strict warnings against attacks on either the women or their property—"suitable" seems at the very least to have meant that these priests should harbor no ill-will toward the community. However, the term obviously meant more than this bare minimum, given Hohenbourg's recent refoundation and evident commitment to reform. Like other reformers, Herrad and Relinde were deeply concerned with the proper instruction of priests, their preparation for the care of souls, and, above all, their moral standing, a topic that appears repeatedly throughout the *Hortus*. Against this background it is likely that a suitable priest meant not simply one who would do no damage to the community, but who was well equipped and eager to guide the women in their spiritual lives.

In their concern for the quality of the pastoral care that they would receive, Relinde and Herrad were very much in tune with the most pressing issues of the contemporary reform movement: the instruction and preparation of priests had been a preoccupation of church reformers since the late eleventh century. During the twelfth century, these concerns gained new force with the ever-increasing ordination of monks and the extension and solidification of the church's administrative reach. Although the contexts of monastic and secular ordination were certainly different, the issues of education and preparation were shared; both were viewed as central to the ultimate success of reform. In 1179, the year following Herrad's foundation at St. Gorgon, the Third Lateran Council laid down guidelines for the provision of education within each diocese to ensure that proper training for the priesthood would be universally available. Some forty years later, the Fourth Lateran Council (1215) extended these requirements, noting that "to guide souls is a supreme art" and calling for the careful preparation and selective ordination of candidates to the priesthood. Reminding church leaders that "it is preferable, especially in the ordination of priests, to have a few good ministers than many bad ones," the council invoked the warnings of Matthew 15:14 and Luke 6:39—if "a blind man leads another blind man, both will fall into the pit."[1] Properly trained and spiritually minded priests formed the front line of the church's reforming efforts. It was to them, then, that reformers increasingly turned in order to secure the viability of the reform movement as a whole and to ensure the orthodox instruction of laypeople.

Concern to establish relationships with reform-minded male communities and to secure appropriate pastoral care was sustained throughout the abbacies of Relinde and Herrad and animated many of their known activities. Hohenbourg's connections to male communities at Marbach, Ittenwiller, and Étival were predicated on their potential provision of pastoral care. In the cases of Marbach and Étival, that potential was strengthened by the men's reputation for attention to the spiritual lives of women, as we saw in the last chapter. Both houses were implicated in Herrad's foundations at St. Gorgon and Truttenhausen. By establishing these two communities, Herrad ensured the provision of suitable pastoral care at Hohenbourg, effectively by-passing the monastery's previous dependence on secular chaplains and the monks of Ebersheim, while at the same time establishing a new context for the *cura monialium* in which the superiority of the abbess of Hohenbourg was assured and the spiritual vitality of the male communities guaranteed—at least in the immediate period of the foundation.

The *Hortus* is a product of the same reforming impulse as these two foundations, both of which date to the very decade during which work on the *Hortus* was at its most intense. Indeed, the establishment of St. Gorgon and Truttenhausen and the initiation of work on the *Hortus* should be seen as twin prongs of a single reforming initiative: to ensure that the women of Hohenbourg had access to an orthodox and reform-minded theological education. Assuming that the canons at St. Gorgon and Truttenhausen fulfilled their responsibilities to Hohenbourg, it might have been possible for the women to rely on them entirely for spiritual instruction, as, for instance, the male-authored *Speculum virginum* assumed that women should. However, Relinde and Herrad were not naïve; they knew that relationships between communities could sour and obligations fall by the wayside. It was crucial, therefore, that Hohenbourg not be totally dependent on priests for spiritual instruction—even those priests who were most closely tied to the community and most dedicated to it. In the same way that Herrad had tried to avoid dependence on a single male house for pastoral care (it is likely that she founded two houses for this very reason), it was important that the women should have a source of theological knowledge that was exclusive of their priests, a source that would not be subject to the vagaries of human interaction and the possible waning of human piety and enthusiasm. That source was—obviously—the *Hortus*.[2]

Dating of the *Hortus*

The dating, textual sources, and organization of the *Hortus* reflect its roots in Hohenbourg's reform period and its purpose to furnish the women with a comprehensive theological training. Like many other twelfth-century works, including those on which Herrad relied, the *Hortus* was a work of compilation that drew on texts from a wide variety of different sources, but that nonetheless presented them within a new conceptual framework. Herrad wrote very few of these texts. Instead, in her prologue to the manuscript, she drew attention to its collective composition, describing its diverse sources as textual "flowers." Dedicating the work to the women of Hohenbourg, Herrad writes: "like a little bee inspired by God, I collected from the diverse flowers of sacred Scripture and philosophic writings this book, which is called the *Hortus deliciarum*, and I brought it together to the praise and honor of Christ and the church and for the sake of your love as if into a single sweet honeycomb" (*HD* no. 2).[3] Although she does not discuss her sources in the prologue, the texts to which she turned in the subsequent work were overwhelmingly contemporary and marked by a clear orientation toward reform. Works by Honorius Augustodunensis and Rupert of Deutz, Benedictine reformers committed to the training of monastic priests; Ivo of Chartres (d. 1115/6), a canonist and patron of the Augustinian order; and Walter of Châtillon (d. 1202/3), a pro-papal poet of the mid-twelfth century, are just a few of the reformist sources that Herrad used.

The contemporary emphasis of these authors points to one of the most striking aspects of the *Hortus*: the bulk of the manuscript is comprised of twelfth-century works of theology, biblical history, and canon law. Although the *Hortus* showcases Herrad's knowledge of the Scriptures and of both patristic and early medieval texts, direct excerpts from these sources were not emphasized. Scattered selections from the sermons of St. Gregory and Bede, as well as excerpts (falsely attributed to Jerome) from Eusebius's *Ecclesiastical History* do appear in the manuscript. However, the stock figures of monastic composition—Ambrose, Augustine, Jerome, Cassiodorus, John Chrysostom, and Boethius—are mentioned primarily in passing, either in glosses to other texts, in texts excerpted from other authors, or in false attributions. Only two early sources were featured: Freculph of Lisieux's (fl. 825–852) *Chronicle* and the fourth-century pseudo-Clementine *Recognitiones*. Instead, most of the works that Herrad cites are quite late—some nearly contemporary with the *Hortus* itself. Herrad's inclusion of Peter Comestor's *Historia scholastica*, several of Walter of Châtillon's poems, and a sermon ascribed to Geoffrey of St. Thierry (c. 1200) place the *Hortus* firmly within the intellectual milieu of northern France in the late twelfth century.

Since Herrad provided no firm dates for the *Hortus*, either in a colophon or in her prologue, the sources that she used provide the only clues that we have as to the chronology of her project. Her extensive use of Peter Comestor's *Historia scholastica*—which appears first on folio 41r—helps to establish the earliest date for the beginning of the project. Since Peter completed the *Historia* in Paris sometime between 1169 and 1173,[4] and work on the construction of the *Hortus* could not long have predated the dissemination of this text from Paris to the Vosges region, the *Hortus* cannot be dated much earlier than the mid-1170s. However, evidence within the *Hortus* indicates that the *Historia* was known at Hohenbourg soon after it was completed—a fact that hints at the close ties that must have linked Paris with the monasteries of Herrad's circle. A note introducing the computus on folio 319v states: "this page was completed in the year 1175" (*HD* no. 1160).[5] It is clear that work on the manuscript was underway by this point and we can assume that Herrad had secured a fairly early manuscript of the *Historia*.[6] This dating of the *Hortus* suggests that work on the manuscript began before Herrad's foundations at St. Gorgon and Truttenhausen and may even have been intended to fill the need for theological training at a time when there were few priests at Hohenbourg.

A second clue for the dating of the *Hortus* is provided by the catalogue of popes that appears between folios 316r and 317v (*HD* no. 1156) and that, beginning with Christ, details each of his vicars from St. Peter until Clement III (1187–1191). Paleographic evidence from the original list, recorded by de Bastard, reveals the various stages in which work on the *Hortus* was conducted. Evidently the list was written in the same hand until the papacy of Lucius III (1181–1185), suggesting that the first stage of work on the *Hortus* was completed before 1185, at which point the first scribe stopped writing.[7] Moreover, it appeared to de Bastard that the names of three popes had been scratched from the vellum and replaced by three others who now appear in the list: Alexander III (1159–1181), Lucius III, and Urban III (1185–1187).[8] In its original format, the manuscript had presumably recorded the names of the three anti-popes who were recognized within the Empire before Frederick Barbarossa's submission to Alexander III had put an end to the eighteen-year-long schism (1159–1177).[9] With its close ties to the emperor, the monastery of Hohenbourg evidently reflected Barbarossa's politics in its catalogue of popes, naming anti-popes Victor IV, Pascal III, and Calixtus III (1168–1178) in place of Alexander III. Following Barbarossa's reconciliation with Alexander, the scribe at Hohenbourg dutifully erased the names of the three intervening anti-popes and put Alexander III in place of the first. Since the last of the three expunged anti-popes must have been Calixtus III, this folio must have been prepared in the first instance during his reign, yet before Frederick Barbarossa's submission to Alexander III in 1177. This places it sometime between 1168 and 1177, dates that are consistent both with the composition and assumed dissemination of the *Historia scholastica* and with the testimony of *HD* no. 1160.

In addition to providing evidence for the inception of the *Hortus* project, the list of popes points to the date of its likely completion. Once the first scribe had corrected the list of popes to reflect Frederick Barbarossa's reconciliation with Rome, she continued writing until the reign of Lucius III, when a second hand took over, continuing until the papacy of Clement III. At this point, work on the manuscript seems to have stopped. No further additions were made, despite the fact that the following folio (fol. 318r) had been left blank, presumably for the purpose of maintaining the catalogue. Since Clement became pope in 1187 and died in 1191, work on the manuscript must have been substantially completed during this period. Given that the last charter issued during Herrad's abbacy was dated 1196, the *Hortus deliciarum* must have been completed during her lifetime.[10]

Relinde and Herrad

This dating of the *Hortus* raises important questions concerning the authorship of the manuscript and the specific circumstances under which the project was begun. Although Herrad claims sole responsibility for the work in her dedication to the women of Hohenbourg—describing herself as "like a little bee inspired by God"—work on the manuscript clearly began before she became abbess in around 1176. This fact prompts a reevaluation of Relinde's role in the genesis, if not the realization, of the *Hortus*. From the chronology of the project, it seems that Herrad must have collaborated with Relinde, at least in the project's planning stages.[11] The impetus for the work may even have come from Relinde, who, as abbess of Hohenbourg, would have had final say concerning the substantial material resources that the project would have required, as well as access to men beyond the monastery who might have been able to furnish the community with manuscripts of such recent works as the *Historia scholastica*. Relinde's probable involvement in the planning stages of the *Hortus* strengthens the argument that the manuscript project formed part of the larger reform context at Hohenbourg and was not an individual achievement to be identified with Herrad alone.

Herrad's silence in her prologue concerning Relinde's probable involvement in the *Hortus* project is surprising, particularly since the two women appear as partners elsewhere in the manuscript. In the penultimate folios of the *Hortus* (fols. 322v–23r; plates 1–2), where the community and history at Hohenbourg are featured, Herrad and Relinde are presented together as joint leaders of the community. A gloss to the image explains that it depicts all those who had been resident in the community, "in the times of the abbesses Relinde and Herrad."[12] In a striking visual manifestation of their shared leadership of the community, the two women are represented symmetrically, standing on either side of the assembled canonesses and novices and each presenting a poem to them.[13] Of course, by the time that the *Hortus* project was brought to completion, Relinde had been dead for many years and so her presence is more symbolic than actual.[14] However, the image confirms Herrad's intention that she and Relinde would be remembered together as coleaders of the community.

The Hohenbourg folios link Relinde and Herrad in another, less egalitarian way: as teacher and disciple. In addition to featuring Relinde as a coleader of the community, Herrad paid tribute to her predecessor, making clear the enormous intellectual and creative debt that she owed her. The text above Herrad's head identifies her as "Herrad abbess of Hohenbourg, appointed and instructed according to the admonitions and examples of Relinde."[15] Although this short tribute provides the only information that we have as to Herrad's intellectual formation, it suggests that she may have been educated at Hohenbourg and that Relinde may have been her teacher. Herrad's acknowledgment of Relinde's influence on her strengthens the case for Relinde's involvement in the early years of the *Hortus* project.

More concrete evidence for Relinde's role in the planning, if not the execution, of the *Hortus* and for her partnership with Herrad is provided in a twelfth-century stone sculpture, which can still be seen at Hohenbourg. In addition to St. Leodegarius (St. Léger), the seventh-century bishop of Autun, who had been linked by the author of the *Vita Odiliae* to St. Odile,[16] and St. Odile, the stone depicts Relinde and Herrad at the feet of the Virgin and Christ child, holding between them an open book.[17] There has been much debate over the content of this book. Haupt cited it as evidence for his erroneous association of a German paraphrase of the Song of Songs with the monastery of Hohenbourg,[18] while Bischoff posited that it could represent either the foundation charter of the monastery, or, more interestingly, the manuscript of the *Hortus*.[19] If the book was meant to represent Hohenbourg's foundation charter, then Herrad and Relinde are shown together as the monastery's second founders, as, indeed, the Hohenbourg folios of the *Hortus* would seem to suggest. However, if it was intended to signify the *Hortus deliciarum*, then Relinde was evidently remembered as an author of the project, alongside her now more famous student. In either case, Relinde is depicted as Herrad's teacher, collaborator, and partner, providing an exception to the model of male guidance and scribal support more common among medieval women writers.

Reform Context of the *Hortus*

The dating of the manuscript and the probable collaboration of Relinde and Herrad in its early stages reinforce the reform context and purpose of the *Hortus*. It was a project that emerged in the decades following Hohenbourg's reform, was actively supported by the community's first reforming abbess, Relinde, and was executed by Herrad in the very years during which her attentions were most focused on the question of pastoral care. The manuscript's textual sources reflect its reform context and confirm the reforming zeal that motivated the project as a whole. Many of Herrad's sources were drawn from authors who were explicit in their support for the papacy and for the reform movement: Honorius Augustodunensis, her most significant source, and Rupert of Deutz had both been staunch supporters of reform, as had Ivo of Chartres, whose solution to the disputed election at Beauvais in 1100 had been reflected in the settlement at Worms in 1122. Most striking is Herrad's inclusion of the poet Walter of Châtillon, who composed several poems in support of Alexander III. Not only was Walter one of the main authors of the polemical literature that was produced during the schism of 1159–1177, but his poetry revived the Gregorian language of papal supremacy. In a poem entitled "That the pope is supreme and the emperor is beneath him," Walter wrote that

"Caesar therefore receives the temporal power from him who possesses the pastoral care."[20] Although his work appears in only a few places in the *Hortus*, his presence is a sign of Herrad's willingness to include the writing of an imperial opponent, despite Hohenbourg's close ties to the Hohenstaufen.

A second source goes even further than Walter in its assertion of papal prerogatives and its challenge to the policy of the Empire. The text, which appears in the *Hortus* under the unremarkable title "Item de romana Ecclesia," claims for the papacy the right to excommunicate anyone, anywhere (*quoslibet per totum mundum*), freedom from deposition, and "all power in the world" (*pape omnis potestas mundi subdi debet*) (*HD* no. 799). Also known as *Proprie auctoritas apostolice sedis*, this text was probably drafted in the period between the papacies of Victor III (1086–1087) and Calixtus II (1119–1124), before the settlement at Worms but after the tumultuous period of Gregory's reign.[21] Although it retreats from the more radical claims of *Dictatus papae*, notably its deposition claim, *Proprie auctoritas apostolice sedis* is nonetheless an unusually powerful statement of papal authority.

Like *Dictatus papae*, *Proprie auctoritas apostolice sedis* had a narrow circulation, which makes its presence in the *Hortus* all the more curious: apart from the *Hortus*, it is known from only four manuscripts.[22] How Herrad came across this text and why she included it in the *Hortus* are questions to which there are no clear answers. It is possible that Hohenbourg's connections to other reformed houses in Alsace (like Marbach) gave her access to the polemical literature of reform, although, if they did, she rarely chose to include it in the *Hortus*. The relative absence of polemical texts makes Herrad's decision to include *Proprie auctoritas apostolice sedis* all the more striking. Moreover, its radically pro-papal stance calls into question her acknowledgement of Barbarossa's popes. Herrad's fidelity to the imperial candidate was evidently tempered by a deeply felt sympathy for the reformed papacy and its prerogatives; indeed, at several points in the manuscript, she directs criticism at "false popes" and "corrupt prelates," suggesting her lack of support for Frederick Barbarossa, since most of the German bishops were the emperor's men. It is possible that Herrad included *Proprie auctoritas apostolice sedis* in the *Hortus*, buried within its folio pages and away from the more prominent papal catalogue that appeared toward its end, as a challenge to Barbarossa's papal policies, which she otherwise appeared to follow. Together with the poems of Walter of Châtillon, the presence of *Proprie auctoritas apostolice sedis* in the *Hortus* argues against a simplistic "pro-papal" or "pro-imperial" interpretation of Herrad's reform stance.

Herrad's apparent support for Barbarossa's popes may well have been a function of Hohenbourg's position as a beneficiary of imperial patronage. However, it must also be seen in the context of the later twelfth century, and of the general support of the German church for Barbarossa, at least in the early stages of his conflict with Alexander. Unlike the struggle between Henry IV and Gregory VII, in which many of the German bishops and most reformed monastic and canonical communities had supported the papacy, in the 1159–1177 schism the German church sided almost unanimously with the emperor. Not even the German bishops, with the exception of the bishops of Salzburg, supported the papacy of Alexander III.[23] Among reformed monastic communities—notably those associated with Hirsau and Marbach, which had been ardent supporters of Gregory VII—few remained that were not now closely connected to Frederick Barbarossa, a testimony to the success of his early ecclesiastical policy. Even Marbach received a bull from the anti-pope Victor IV in 1159 and maintained the imperial protection that Barbarossa had granted it in 1152, before the beginning of the schism.[24]

In addition to the changed political climate, it is clear that the reforming spirit itself had undergone a marked shift after about 1130, away from the divisive political issues that had characterized the early reform movement and that had focused on the church's external foes, and toward a more internal and individual program of renewal.[25] No longer concerned primarily with the political and spiritual issues that had occupied reformers in the late eleventh century, the reform movement by this time had turned toward an increasingly sharp criticism of the weakness and inefficacy of the contemporary church. As Bernard of Clairvaux wrote, reflecting contemporary anxiety surrounding the potential failings of the church:

Today a foul corruption permeates the whole body of the Church, all the more incurable the more widespread it becomes, all the more dangerous the more it penetrates inwardly. . . . Called to be ministers of Christ, they are servants of Antichrist. Promoted to honors over the possessions of the Lord, they pay the Lord no honor. Hence that bogus splendor that you see every day, that theatrical apparel, that regal pomp. . . . Such is the goal they aim at when they seek a prelacy in the Church, to be deans or archdeacons, bishops or archbishops.[26]

These two factors—the general support for Frederick Barbarossa within the German church and the shift within reform—help to explain the response of German prelates and reformers to Barbarossa, the papacy, and the schism. Most useful for the purposes of comparison with Relinde and Herrad are the examples of Hildegard of Bingen and her younger contemporary, Elisabeth of Schönau. Both women are recognized as visionaries, if not always explicitly as reformers, and both were contemporaries of Relinde and to some extent of Herrad too, although Elisabeth died before Herrad became abbess and Hildegard very shortly thereafter. The connection of these two women to Hirsau houses farther down the Rhine valley—Hildegard to the male community at Disibodenberg and Elisabeth to the double house at Schönau—completes their shared spiritual context, since Marbach, with which Hohenbourg had forged links, also maintained close ties to Hirsau.

Hildegard's relationship with Frederick Barbarossa is most instructive.[27] The abbess and seer wrote to the emperor soon after his election as king in 1152 and she accepted his invitation to visit him at his palace at Ingelheim at some point in the mid-1150s.[28] Their relationship survived Barbarossa's split with the papacy in 1159 and continued despite his excommunication the following year. Although it grew increasingly difficult as the schism wore on, Hildegard maintained close contact with the emperor; her community at the Rupertsberg received a charter from him in 1163.[29] Around the same time, however, she cited distress at the schism as the reason for her inability to continue preaching: in a letter to the clerics of Cologne (c. 1163), she explained that "because the church was divided, I have kept quiet."[30] After 1164, when Victor IV died and Frederick Barbarossa prolonged the schism by naming Paschal III to replace him, Hildegard's writings were increasingly colored by distress concerning the state of the church and preoccupation with the schism.[31] Her disillusionment intensified in 1168, when Barbarossa appointed a further anti-pope at the death of Pascal. In 1173, she wrote to Alexander III, in lieu of Barbarossa's papal candidate, to petition for the restoration of pastoral care at the Rupertsberg. But she added her own advice concerning the state of the church: "Be the Morning Star," she writes, "which precedes the sun, a guide to the Church, which, for far too long, has been lacking in the light of God's justice because of the dense cloud of schism."[32] The schism continued until just shortly before Hildegard's death in 1179.

Despite her disapproval of the emperor and her distress over the schism, Hildegard did not focus her criticism on either the emperor or the papacy; instead, she condemned both equally. Already in *Scivias*, which she wrote between 1141 and 1151, Hildegard had presented the grotesque image of *Ecclesia* apparently giving birth to antichrist, suggesting that the church itself would harbor its own greatest enemy.[33] In her later sermons and prophecies, she was similarly harsh on the contemporary clergy, whom she saw as having polluted the church with their avarice, lechery, and evil living.[34] Ultimately, Kerby-Fulton observes that "Hildegard castigated popes and emperors alike, prophesying the end of *both* seats of power well before the Last Judgment."[35]

Elisabeth of Schönau's response to the schism was more markedly imperialist than Hildegard's, perhaps because she did not live to see either its deepening in 1167, when Alexander renewed his excommunication of Frederick Barbarossa, or Barbarossa's prolongation of it in 1168. Elisabeth's only pronouncement on the schism appears in a letter that she wrote to Hillin, archbishop of Trier, shortly after the disputed election in 1159. Presenting her message as "a certain small spark sent from the seat of great majesty," she writes that "you should know that the one who has been chosen by Caesar is more acceptable to me."[36] Instead of focusing on the details of the schism, Elisabeth directed her attention to the failings of the church, launching pointed attacks on both church and clergy in the *Liber viarum Dei*, the very text that she had ordered the bishops to preach. Her indictment is damning. She writes: "The head of the Church has languished and its members are dead, for the apostolic seat is filled with pride, avarice is cultivated, and it is full of iniquity and impiety. They scandalise My sheep and make them go astray when they should have been protecting and guiding them."[37] Although there is little reason to assume that Elisabeth was influenced in her response to the schism by her brother Ekbert, Ekbert's close friendship with Rainald of Dassel, the man who was both archbishop of Cologne and chancellor to Frederick Barbarossa, signifies the openness to the imperial party that characterized even reformed communities by this time.[38] Like Hildegard, who was virulent in her contempt for the effeminate age (*muliebre tempus*), which had forced women into positions left vacant through the inaction of men, Elisabeth's visions left more room for criticism of the church than of the secular powers, against whom the earlier generation of reformers had set themselves.

Clearly, the issues in the latter half of the twelfth century were complex.[39] Fidelity to the church coexisted with a nagging disillusionment with the church hierarchy, and with criticisms of priests, bishops, and even the papacy itself. By this time, the confidence of the early reform period, when the enemies of the church had seemed clearly identifiable, had been replaced by a sense of confusion and concern for adversaries that appeared to assail the church from within. There was a pervasive sense—evident in the writings of Hildegard, Elisabeth, Bernard, and others—that the church was failing in its spiritual mandate, and that its failure was the result of such internal evils as avarice, pride, and sexual sin. Given the clear link between the education and preparation of priests and the moral health of the church as a whole, this sense of failure was matched by an urgency to recall priests to their duties and to ensure that they were prepared to fulfill them. Both Hildegard and Elisabeth focused criticism on the failure of the contemporary clergy to teach and to lead their flock. Hildegard's criticisms were public, many of them delivered during the four preaching tours that she undertook beginning in 1158. In her Trier sermon, she berated the clergy for their inaction and neglect of their pastoral duties: "The teachers and superiors refuse to blow the trumpet of God's justice. Therefore, the East of good works, which illumines the entire world and is, as it were, the mirror of light, has been extinguished in them."[40] Between 1161 and 1163, Hildegard traveled down the Rhine to Bopard, Andernach, Siegburg, and Werden, preaching at the cathedral at Cologne and criticizing the clergy there for their indolence in the face of Catharism.[41] In her Kirchheim sermon, Hildegard's criticisms took the form of a vision of *Ecclesia*, who appears battered and abandoned by the very priests who had been charged to protect her:

Those who nurtured me—the priests, that is to say—were supposed to make my face glow like the dawn, my clothes flash like lightning, my cloak gleam like precious stones, and my shoes to shine brightly. Instead, they have smeared my face with dirt, they have torn my garment, they have blackened my cloak, and they have soiled my shoes. The very ones who were supposed to beautify me with adornments have all failed miserably. This is the way they soil my face: They take up and handle the body and blood of my Bridegroom while defiled by the uncleanliness of their lustful morals, poisoned by the deadly venom of fornication and adultery, and corrupted by the avaricious rapine of buying and selling improper things.[42]

Elisabeth too exhorted the clergy to bestir themselves from their spiritual lethargy, chastising them especially for their failure to use their learning in the service and edification of the church. She wrote, "You, however, who are learned, study the books of the New Testament and remember their words and you will find great fruit. Be renewed in the Holy Spirit and revive your souls in the structure of the church."[43]

It is in this later twelfth-century context that the *Hortus* must be understood. By this time, the focus on institutional reform had been joined by a growing concern for the individual's path of salvation and a strong sense of the need for individual reform. The *Hortus* reflects these concerns. In her introductory poem, *Salve cohors virginum*, which appears on the opening folios of the *Hortus*, Herrad outlines the main themes of the manuscript, balancing joyful expectation of union with Christ in heaven with the reality of spiritual battle on earth and the urgency of contempt for the world (*HD* no. 1). While Herrad promises that Christ awaits each woman in heaven, she nonetheless warns her audience that they must strive to please him through their freedom from sin, especially sexual sin. Her message is at once celebratory and joyful, yet cautionary:

Christ prepares a wedding
Wonderful in delights,
May you await this prince
By keeping yourself a virgin. (*HD* no. 1)[44]

The *contemptus mundi* (contempt for the world), a reform theme that is sustained throughout the texts of the *Hortus*, appears in Herrad's emphatic advice to her community. "Scorn, scorn the world," she encourages the women of Hohenbourg, warning them that Christ "hates the blemishes of sins."

For he hates the blemishes of sin
And scorns the aged wrinkles of a guilty soul,
His desire is for beautiful little maidens
Ugly women he drives away. (*HD* no. 1)[45]

Although Herrad does not mention creation, the fall, the incarnation, the person of Christ, or the work of the cross in her prologue, there is no mistaking her focus on salvation: both her own and her audience's. This focus is amplified in her poetic dedication of the manuscript to the women. She writes:

Suffer bitterness now
Despising the fortunes of the world
Be now a partner in Christ's cross,
And thereafter sharer in his kingdom. (*HD* no. 1)[46]

Meanwhile for herself she begs:

And may you never cease to pull me with you
By your prayers
To Christ, the sweetest Bridegroom
The Son of the virgin.

So that I may be found a sharer
In your victory and great glory,
Let me be rescued
From earthly peril. (*HD* no. 1)[47]

The image of the soul's journey to God—made visually explicit later in
the manuscript, most dramatically in the full-page depiction of the Ladder
of Virtues (fol. 215v; plate 5)—is reinforced in Herrad's prologue where
she depicts herself, like Peter, walking on the water, supported by the
prayers of the women of Hohenbourg as she is again "pulled" by them to
heaven. Echoing the prayer of her *Salve cohors virginum*, Herrad writes:
"And now as I pass dangerously through the various pathways of the sea,
I ask that you may redeem me with your fruitful prayers from earthly passions and draw me upwards, together with you, into the affection of your
beloved" (*HD* no. 2).[48] A gloss (or unidentified text) that appears later in
the manuscript explains that the "sea" is to be understood as the world:
"through the sea this world is to be understood, which is constantly battered by the innumerable storms of adversity" (*per mare hoc seculum intel-
ligitur, quod innumeris adversitatum procellis jugiter colliditur*) (*HD* no.
403).[49] Reiterating the image of the soul as a traveler through the sea of
the world, Herrad encourages the women to view themselves as travelers
through the world en route to their eternal homeland, the *patria* to which
Christ invites the women in a poem on folio 322v (plate 1; *HD* Cat. No.
345). She writes:

Navigate through this sea
Pregnant with holiness
When you leave this mortal vessel
May you attain holy Syon. (*HD* no. 1)[50]

Finally, she promised that the virgin mother Mary, who is described elsewhere in the manuscript as the *contemptrix mundi* (fol. 176v; *HD* Cat. No.

235; plate 7), would guide the women on their journey, joining them to Christ in the heavenly Zion.

Then may Mary, the sea's shining star,
The only virgin mother,
Join you to her son
With a perpetual pledge of love. (*HD* no. 1)[51]

These themes of struggle and reward are revisited in the final folios of the *Hortus*. On folio 322v (plate 1), Christ appears at the center of the image, presiding over the legendary seventh-century or early eighth-century foundation of the monastery by Duke Adalric for his daughter Odile. In his left hand, he holds a scroll containing a poetic address to the women: *Vos quas includit*. The poem promises eternal rest for those who suffer trials and torment on earth (*HD* Cat. No. 345). In response, the women pray:

O Christ, be the gracious reward of our labors.
Count us in the number of your elect. (*HD* Cat. No. 346)[52]

Reform Sources

Like Hildegard and Elisabeth, Herrad was deeply concerned with the training and moral standing of the clergy, topics that were particularly pressing in the period during which work on the *Hortus* likely began. Herrad's major textual sources—Honorius Augustodunensis and Rupert of Deutz—reflect her reforming interests and concern to provide orthodox theological training, in this case for women. Both Honorius and Rupert were ardent supporters of the papal cause and had dedicated their lives to the goal of church reform. Both were, ultimately, Benedictine monks whose reforming efforts took the form of education; both wrote guidebooks for the use of priests in their pastoral duties and personal devotions. Like Herrad, they believed that proper theological training was essential to the work of reform.

Of the two, Honorius was Herrad's most significant textual source and the inspiration behind countless images in the *Hortus*. Little is known of Honorius's origins and, indeed, it appears that he intentionally concealed his identity, publishing many of his works anonymously and naming himself only in a late work, *De luminaribus ecclesiae*. There he described himself as "Honorius, priest and 'scholasticus' of the church of 'Augustodunensis' "—a descriptor that has given scholars no end of trouble. He also listed twenty-two of his major works and declared that he had "flourished" during the reign of Henry V (1106–1125).[53] Evidence from Honorius's writings furnishes some further clues as to his biography. Although he had originally been a canon, it is clear from the progression of his writings, which are listed chronologically in *De luminaribus ecclesiae*, that his sympathies shifted toward the end of his life from canons to monks, with whom he probably spent his last days. While his early work, *Liber duodecim quaestionum*, reflected his support for the canons in their disputes with the monks, in his later tract, *Quod monachis liceat predicare*, he argued against the canons in favor of monastic involvement in the *cura animarum*.[54] Given this shift, it is likely that Honorius converted to monasticism later in life, in accordance with the vocational progression that he outlined in *Quod monachis liceat predicare*.

Based on the evidence, Flint has proposed a biography for Honorius that places him firmly within the ecclesiastical reform movement of the early twelfth century. She suggests that the designation "Augustodunensis" referred to the *Alte Kapelle* of the city of Regensburg and that Honorius was there between 1109/1110 and 1133/1134. Before moving to Regensburg, he had been in England, probably in Canterbury, to which he had been drawn sometime after Anselm had become archbishop in 1093. Following Anselm's death in 1109, Honorius moved to Regensburg, possibly with the marriage retinue of the soon-to-be empress Matilda. There, he converted to the monastic life, probably adopting the unusual name Honorius as he did so. He spent the last years of his life as an enclosed monk at the Benedictine monastery of Lambach.

Honorius's first work, the *Elucidarium*, may have been composed while he was still in Canterbury and reflects the influence of his mentor, Anselm. Subtitled the *summa* of all theology (*summa totius theologiae*), it contained all the knowledge that Honorius thought was necessary for the understanding of salvation.[55] It was written to educate priests and to provide them with an orthodox theological program so that they could revitalize the church from the inside—a purpose that was central to early twelfth-century reform.[56] The text was divided into three parts: the first detailed creation, the incarnation, and redemption; the second addressed the role of the church in a fallen world; and the third dealt with Last Things. In keeping with Honorius's perennial concern for his audience, it was composed as a dialogue between a master and his disciple: the figure of the disciple allowed him to pose probable questions, underscore potential opposition, and provide an orthodox response in every instance.[57] The range of subjects treated in the *Elucidarium* together with Honorius's pastoral approach ensured that it was the most widely read of all his works. These characteristics may also explain its appeal to Herrad: she imported almost the entire text into her *Hortus*.

Honorius's later projects, the *Speculum ecclesiae* and *Gemma animae*, both works that also appear in the *Hortus*, were planned as complementary guides to the liturgy of the church. In the *Gemma animae* he explained the liturgy and outlined the liturgical year, while in the *Speculum ecclesiae* he provided relevant sermons. Although these sermons were written for practicing priests, they were directed ultimately at a lay audience. Given this fact, Honorius strove to make them interesting and accessible. They were to be clear and concise, seasoned with anecdotes and illustrations, and not too long or too boring. In the Siren sermon, his suggested text begins with a strikingly modern promise—to be brief. "For some of you have come from afar, and will have a long journey home. Some may have guests at home, or wailing infants," Honorius suggests as an appropriate introduction.[58] The clarity and simplicity of the *Speculum*, combined with Honorius's use of narrative illustrations, or word pictures, ensured its enormous popularity. Not surprisingly, the *Speculum ecclesiae*—a work that was much longer than the *Elucidarium*—was the most widely used of any of Herrad's sources. Although she did not include the entire text, as she had with the shorter *Elucidarium*, Herrad imported some three hundred sections from it into the *Hortus*. The *Gemma animae* provided her with some thirty further extracts. These selections from Honorius are largely responsible for the simple, pastoral tone that infuses the *Hortus* and that made its lessons so readily accessible.

The heavy reliance on Honorius in a manuscript designed for the use of women is striking, since he wrote originally for the guidance of priests in the service of reform.[59] In his prologue to the *Speculum ecclesiae*, Honorius explicitly addressed an ordained audience, presenting the text as a mirror in which priests could compare themselves with the ideals toward which they should strive, and then work to improve themselves.[60] In many cases, the guidance that Honorius offered his priestly audience extended beyond the provision of crib notes to which they might refer as they preached. In the *Speculum ecclesiae*, he gave meticulous instructions concerning the actual delivery of the sermon, remarking that the priest should take care to modulate his voice so that, "your hearers will think they actually see the events instead of hearing you."[61] The visual agenda of the *Hortus* may well have been inspired by Honorius's emphasis on seeing rather than just hearing.[62] Herrad mined the *Speculum ecclesiae* for images that formed the basis for several of the miniatures in the *Hortus*.[63] The Leviathan (fol. 84r; plate 8), the Ladder of Virtues (fol. 215v; plate 5), and the depictions of Ulysses and the Sirens (fols. 221r–v) are directly related to texts from the *Speculum*; the Microcosm image (fol. 16v) is linked to a section of dialogue from Honorius's *Elucidarium*.[64]

Herrad's reliance on Honorius, who described himself as both *presbyter* and *scholasticus*, reflected her interest in blending the theological with the pedagogical and ensured the pastoral aspect of the *Hortus*. However, Honorius was obviously more concerned with pastoral issues, particularly the concerns of his intended audience, than he was with contemporary theological debates.[65] Possibly in recognition of this fact, Herrad balanced her reliance on Honorius with the writings of Rupert of Deutz, which appear in some seventy excerpts in the *Hortus*. Like Honorius, Rupert was a staunch supporter of the papal reform movement.[66] Born sometime around 1075, he had been given as a child to the Benedictine abbey of St. Lawrence outside Liège. His formative years were shaped by the abbey's vicissitudes in the investiture controversy. In 1092, conflict with the bishop of Liège forced a group of monks into a three-and-a-half-year exile from the monastery. Rupert was a part of this group. His experience of exile solidified his opposition to simony and strengthened his commitment to papal reform. In 1119, he fled the hostility of the clerics at St. Lawrence for Deutz, where he was soon appointed abbot and where he remained until his death in 1129.

In his writing, Rupert devoted himself single-mindedly to reform. His *De divinis officiis*, completed in 1112, was designed as a guide for fellow monk-priests, especially those who would say the mass privately each day without understanding it. "But to celebrate these sacraments without understanding their causes," Rupert charged, "is like speaking in a language without knowing its meaning."[67] Unlike Honorius, whose ultimate audience was the laity, Rupert was concerned in this work only to provide guidance for the private use of priests within a monastic context. As such, he allowed digressions in his text in order to treat major theological issues of the day. He began with the daily service performed by ordained monks, rather than with a more general discussion of the mass or of the church year, and then proceeded to discuss the various theological controversies that occupied contemporary monks and schoolmen, evidence of what John van Engen has called Rupert's "theologizing" tendency.⁶⁸ Herrad included some seventy excerpts from Rupert's *De divinis officiis* in the *Hortus*. Less important for her was Rupert's commentary on the Song of Songs, the *Commentaria in Canticum canticorum*: she included only four excerpts from this text, despite the fact that it was Rupert's most widely read work and the first wholly Marian interpretation of the Song.⁶⁹

Herrad's reliance on Honorius and Rupert is testimony to her reforming purposes in the *Hortus*. The texts that she selected from these authors had been composed in the first half of the twelfth century and were explicitly directed to an audience of priests, many of them the monk-priests who comprised Honorius's and Rupert's communities. They were intended to meet the need of these men for proper theological, liturgical, and pastoral training. Although, as in the case of the *Speculum ecclesiae*, Herrad removed all indications that her extracts had originally been sermons designed to be spoken, she nonetheless ensured that they conveyed the essential information. So although the *Hortus* does not allow for the recreation of Honorius's scripted sermons by the women at Hohenbourg, it would have enabled them to penetrate to the core of his message, deriving from it the instruction that he had intended. Significantly, these texts were the very same as those to which Hohenbourg's priests may have turned for instruction. By providing Honorius and Rupert directly to the women of her community, Herrad ensured that they would have a theological foundation and understanding similar, if not identical, to that of their chaplains.

The dissemination of Honorius's and Rupert's works confirms the monastic and sacerdotal reading patterns that Herrad was trying to duplicate at Hohenbourg. Flint counts more than 265 twelfth-century manuscripts of Honorius's works, primarily from libraries in Austria and southern Germany, where he was especially popular, and from England, where he had been resident for some time.⁷⁰ The libraries of Benedictine monasteries, and particularly those associated with the Hirsau movement, top this list, a fact that is not surprising given that Honorius was, with Rupert and Idung of Prüfening, most vocal among Benedictines in his defense of monastic preaching, a central concern of Hirsau communities.⁷¹ However, Honorius's popularity was not limited to Benedictine readers. Observing that Augustinian houses, as well as Cistercian ones, also possessed manuscripts of Honorius, Flint notes, "Honorius did his job so well that he was copied not merely by the Benedictines but by their rivals and their critics."[72] The *Elucidarium*, the only work that Herrad included in its entirety, was also the most widely copied of Honorius's works, surviving in some 329 medieval manuscripts and fragments. Notably, its readership and purpose were almost exclusively pastoral.[73]

A similar picture emerges from the manuscript dissemination of Rupert's works, which survive in 266 manuscripts, more than half of which date from the twelfth century.[74] In terms of their provenance, these manuscripts are split between the lowlands, where Rupert lived and wrote, and the monasteries of southern Germany and Austria, where Honorius's works were also popular. The connection between Honorius and Rupert, whose works were similar in many respects and obviously attracted a shared readership, may have been provided by Cuno of Raitenbuch (d. 1132), abbot of St. Michael's in Siegburg (1105–1126) and later bishop of Regensburg (1126–1132).[75] As abbot of St. Michael's, Cuno had given Rupert much-needed encouragement to write and, in response, Rupert dedicated his *De divinis officiis* to him. When he was named bishop of Regensburg in 1126, Cuno may have taken with him copies of Rupert's works, which he circulated as he traveled. Upon his arrival in Regensburg, Cuno became patron to another reformer: Honorius. Like Rupert before him, Honorius also dedicated certain of his works to Cuno, and presumably received from him manuscripts of Rupert's writings. These had an enormous influence on Honorius's later work and particularly on his advocacy of monastic ordination. Both men wrote texts in defense of monastic preaching, Rupert the *Altercatio monachi et clerici, quod liceat monacho praedicare* and Honorius *Quod monachis liceat predicare*.[76]

Similar conclusions concerning the reforming context of the *Hortus* can be drawn from the manuscript dissemination of one of Herrad's other sources, Ivo of Chartres. In addition to works of pastoral theology and biblical history, Herrad included in the *Hortus* twenty-nine texts—primarily concerned with magic, spells, incantations, and sorcery (largely fols. 183–185)—from Ivo's *Panormia*. A canonist, priest, and, from 1090, bishop of Chartres, Ivo was active during the late eleventh-century revival of Roman law and is considered one of the most significant French reformers as well as an important patron of the Augustinian canons. He gained his intellectual and spiritual formation first as a student in Paris and then at the Benedictine monastery at Bec where, with Anselm, he was a pupil of Lanfranc. Later, as abbot of the new Augustinian foundation at St. Quentin, Beauvais, Ivo saw the community develop into a center for Augustinian reform. His *Panormia* was in wide use as a handbook of canon law soon after its appearance. It continued to be popular throughout the twelfth century, particularly among monastic houses associated with re-form, despite the growing prominence of Gratian's *Decretum* within the urban schools. As Bruce Brasington writes, "The extant manuscripts of Ivo's *Panormia* undercut assumptions that the monastery was quickly eclipsed by the urban school during the twelfth century."[77] The presence of Ivo's *Panormia* among the texts of the *Hortus* demonstrates Herrad's interest in legal scholarship and confirms her place amid late twelfth-century monastic reformers.

As ordinary as Herrad's reading of Honorius, Rupert, and Ivo would have been within the context of Benedictine monasticism, it is important to remember that Herrad was neither Benedictine nor, more importantly, a monk. Of the extant manuscripts of works by these three, few can be traced to an independent female community, a fact that may reflect the fate and ephemeral nature of women's libraries and houses more than it does their reading patterns.[78] Several have been identified with communi-ties that housed both men and women—notably Admont, a community in the archdiocese of Salzburg that was associated with the Hirsau reform and that is famous for its community of nun-scribes.[79] However, books in so-called double communities may have been produced for, and possibly also read primarily by, the community's male inhabitants. Beach argues that female scribes at the Premonstratensian community of Schäftlarn did not have permission to read even those books that they had produced.[80] Although the nun Irimgart copied Rupert's *De divinis officiis*, her colo-phon indicates that she did so only with the permission of the prior.[81] The copy then passed into the men's library, where it was used to train or-dained members of the community. At Admont, the women's library was separate from the men's, and the volumes that it contained—according to Beach's reconstruction—included few works that were not directly con-nected to the women in some way. Of the twelve manuscripts that may have formed part of the nuns' library, only a volume of homilies and a collection including the *Hexameron* and *Sigillum Beatae Mariae* were not immediately connected to the women's community.[82] Of course, it is pos-sible that the women at Admont had some access to books in the men's library and could borrow volumes, just as it is clear that they lent their own volumes to the men;[83] however, they did not own the range of texts that appears in the *Hortus*.

Recent studies of libraries from female communities present a limited picture of women's reading and book ownership, suggesting that, in general, books owned by female houses—or copied or commissioned by them—were of a liturgical or devotional rather than theological nature.[84] Few women's communities seem to have owned the sorts of contemporary theological texts that Herrad included in the *Hortus*.[85] A notable exception is the northern German monastery of Lippoldsberg, which had been established sometime around 1090 and reformed according to the Hirsau observance some ten years later.[86] According to the community's twelfth-century library catalogue, which was inserted into the 1151 chronicle of the prioress Margaret, Lippoldsberg owned copies of Honorius Augustodunensis, Hugh of St. Victor (d. 1141), and Anselm of Canterbury, as well a number of reform texts, among them a tract against heretics and married priests, the *Adversus Simoniacos* of Bruno of Segni, and a tract concerning the sacraments of heretics by a certain Godfried.[87] A series of letters between Gunther, provost of Lippoldsberg, and Sindold, librarian at the abbey of Rheinhardsbrunn, indicates a lively exchange of books between the two houses and records that the women at Lippoldsberg were actively involved in the copying of texts. Their work was commissioned by Sindold, who wrote detailed instructions concerning the texts that they were to copy and apparently also sent parchment and ink.[88] In one letter, Sindold requests a copy of Hugh of St. Victor's *De sacramentis*, complaining of a faulty version of the text, which had evidently caused difficulties. At the same time, he requested Rupert's *De divinis officiis*, a text that is not listed in the catalogue but that Lippoldsberg evidently owned: "If you should have also Hugo, send it to me through the present messenger, in order that ours might be corrected from it. Also, allow one or other of my sisters to copy Rupert's *De divinis officiis* from your exemplar on the parchment that I send."[89]

Despite the paucity of the physical evidence, women did read works by Honorius and Rupert, and probably also those by Ivo, as the *Hortus* demonstrates. In addition to the witness from Lippoldsberg, it is clear that Hildegard was familiar with Rupert, whose influence on her own visionary experience has been widely accepted.[90] However, Herrad's reliance on both Honorius and Rupert was calculated to provide the basics of a theological education for the women of her community, an education, as we have seen, that had been designed in the first instance to meet the needs of priests. As such, Honorius and Rupert demonstrate an important aspect of Herrad's purpose in the manuscript, one that goes beyond the broad category of reform monasticism that their presence (and that of Ivo) would suggest. The training that Herrad provided in the *Hortus* was designed to equip the women of Hohenbourg with the knowledge necessary to select the "suitable" priests who are featured in Hohenbourg's charters and whom Herrad ensured the women the legal freedom to choose. The *Hortus* could also substitute for the presence of priests; it represented one important way in which Herrad responded to the problem of the *cura monialium*.

Renaissance Sources

Both Honorius and Rupert were authors who were fairly unexceptional within the context of male monasticism in southern Germany during the twelfth century, although their presence in a book designed for women is, of course, unusual. More striking in terms of the intellectual context of the *Hortus* is the manuscript's clear orientation toward the emerging Parisian schools. The most remarkable aspect of the *Hortus* is the presence of Peter Lombard's *Sentences*, which was composed in Paris between 1155 and 1157, and Peter Comestor's *Historia scholastica*, which, as we have seen, provides a start date for the manuscript and suggests the immediacy of Herrad's access to contemporary scholastic texts. Herrad's incorporation of these two authors demonstrates her interest in the intellectual climate of the schools, with their ways of questioning and learning, and their new approach to biblical studies and theology.[91] The sentence collections that began to emerge from the beginning of the twelfth century sought to systematize theological knowledge, introducing topics as questions or disputes, which were then subjected to dialectic. Herrad's interest in these new ways of thinking is demonstrated in her emphasis on Peter Lombard, whose *Sentences* offered a systematic exposition of the Christian faith and, according to Colish, a "reconsideration of the nature of the theological enterprise."[92] Herrad selected approximately 250 excerpts from the *Sentences* for inclusion in the *Hortus*. These were drawn mostly from the fourth book, which outlined the sacraments and Last Things, and are largely grouped toward the end of the *Hortus*. Despite the unusual way in which the *Sentences* appear in the *Hortus*, as a block of texts that Herrad does not integrate into the main body of her manuscript, there is no sign that Peter Lombard's inclusion was an afterthought. Herrad must have known that the *Sentences* was the last word in sacramental theology; although she copied almost all of the *Elucidarium*, she pointedly omitted

Honorius's discussion of the Eucharist, baptism, and marriage, choosing rather to deal with these subjects with excerpts from the more recent *Sentences*. The Lombard's presence in the *Hortus*, together with Peter Comestor, showcases Herrad's ability to identify important texts, especially since tradition had not yet attached great importance to the writings of these men. Particularly in the case of Peter Comestor, whose *Historia* was "hot off the press" when Herrad first saw it, Herrad's incorporation is testimony to her discrimination and discernment.

By the early thirteenth century, the centrality of both the *Sentences* and the *Historia* to the education of the schools was assured. In 1215, Innocent III approved both works, and shortly thereafter the Dominican General Chapter in Paris named them, together with the glossed Bible, as essential to the study of theology and required reading for all theological students.[93] The timing of this acknowledgment is further proof of Herrad's prescience. By 1223/7, the Lombard's *Sentences* had become the principal textbook of theology at Paris,[94] the "door," as Southern describes it, "through which every aspiring theologian in the scholastic tradition had to enter."[95] However, some fifty years before it was established in the theological faculty at Paris—where women could not study—the *Sentences* had been taught to the nuns of Hohenbourg by Herrad in the *Hortus*.[96]

The presence of Peter Lombard and Peter Comestor in the *Hortus* adds another dimension to the reforming focus that is revealed in Herrad's reliance on Honorius and Rupert. Where these men had symbolized the Augustinian tradition of theological enquiry and had written in the service of reform for a largely monastic audience,[97] Peter Lombard and Peter Comestor wrote for scholars and university students. They were representatives of a new generation and type of scholarship that was met with skepticism and outright hostility among some of the older monastics.[98] Both men combined ecclesiastical administration with scholarship: Peter Lombard as bishop of Paris from 1159 and Peter Comestor as chancellor of the school at Notre Dame from about 1164 (or 1168). The two certainly knew each other. Peter Comestor was responsible for glossing Peter Lombard's *Sentences*, and possibly also his commentary on the Psalter;[99] moreover both men retired to the Augustinian reform center of St. Victor toward the end of their careers. Peter Lombard's relationship with St. Victor may even have dated to his early years in Paris. Indeed, he is first mentioned in the 1130s in a letter from Bernard of Clairvaux to the prior of St. Victor. It is even possible that he lived at St. Victor before becoming a canon at Notre Dame.[100] Certainly Victorine ideas had an enormous influence on

him, as they did on Peter Comestor. In fact, Peter Comestor finished work
on the *Historia scholastica* at St. Victor, following his retirement from
teaching. The influence of Hugh of St. Victor on this work is also
marked.[101] In his *Didascalicon*, Hugh had expressed the need for a Christian history.[102] Peter's *Historia scholastica*, a text that he claims to have
written at the request of his friends, was designed to fill precisely this need:
to provide a foundation in Christian history as a background for further
allegorical and tropological readings of the Bible.[103] For his efforts, Peter
Comestor became known as "Master of Histories," just as the Lombard
had earned the title "Master of Sentences."[104]

The St. Victor connection may help to explain how manuscripts of
Peter Comestor and Peter Lombard found their way so quickly to Alsace
and to Hohenbourg. As Bynum has shown, the culture of the Augustinian
canons was one in which teaching was held in high regard and the contemplative life existed alongside the scholarly. The distinct intellectual and
spiritual culture of St. Victor has been characterized by Zinn as one that
was "open to the currents of intellectual life stirring in the Parisian schools
yet maintaining steadfast fidelity to the ancient traditions of *lectio divina*
and monastic spirituality."[105] That the community produced a significant
number of theologians and exegetes during the twelfth century—among
them Hugh, Andrew, and Richard—is testimony to the success of its commitment to education and openness to new scholarship.

Until recently, St. Victor has appeared anomalous, alone in a world
in which the contemplative life is thought to have been separate from, if
not also inimical to, the scholastic. Leclercq's model of a monastic way
of "doing" theology that was distinct from that of the schools has long
held sway, creating the impression of unremitting hostility between
the two, the sort of hostility that characterized Bernard's relationship
with both Abelard and Gilbert of Poitiers (d. 1154).[106] However, the existence of sometimes-significant intellectual cross-fertilization between the
cloister and the school is gradually being recognized.[107] Some monks
and canons studied at universities, just as some scholastic texts are to be
found in monastic libraries. Manuscript evidence demonstrates this cross-
fertilization. Indeed, the fact that the first extant manuscript of Peter Lombard's *Sentences* (1158) is from Clairvaux is proof, according to Colish, that
"it was read in circles that went well beyond those of the scholastic class-
rooms of Paris and environs where one would expect to find it."[108] Mews
draws a similar conclusion from his examination of extant twelfth-century
manuscripts from Zwiefalten, a Hirsau reform monastery that included

both a female community and at least one female scribe. Among the manuscripts in Zwiefalten's extensive library were copies of Peter Comestor's *Historia scholastica* and Honorius's *Gemma animae*, as well as manuscripts containing texts by Ivo of Chartres, Hildegard of Bingen, Bernard of Clairvaux, and Hildebert of Lavardin.[109] From his examination of this wide-ranging collection, Mews concludes that "the concept of 'monastic theology' imposes a degree of cultural uniformity on twelfth-century monasticism which is difficult to sustain."[110] Herrad's incorporation of all of these authors indicates that cross-fertilization between the monastic and the scholastic worlds could extend to include communities of women as well.

Herrad's Library Resources

How did monastic and canonical communities obtain works from the schools? And how, in particular, might such texts have found their way into the *Hortus*? It was not uncommon for male houses to receive news of intellectual developments within the schools from canons or monks who had traveled to them in order to study. On their return, they might contribute school notes or manuscripts to the community's library, as was the case at Frankenthal. Iohannes, a scribe and member of the Frankenthal community, spent ten years in Paris, most likely as a student at St. Victor. On his return to the community, Cohen-Mushlin suggests that he brought with him a copy of Peter Lombard's commentary on the Pauline epistles.[111] Although the women of Hohenbourg could not travel to Paris to get copies of Peter Comestor's *Historia* or other contemporary texts, they might have had access to such texts through the library of a neighboring male community. Unfortunately, as with so many other details concerning the construction of the *Hortus*, Herrad does not discuss the library (or libraries) that she consulted during the course of her project. We cannot assume, as El Kholi does, that the sources that appear in the *Hortus* formed part of the library collection at Hohenbourg.[112] There is no evidence to support such a hypothesis and, indeed, the inspiration of the *Hortus* project would seem to argue against this idea. If Herrad had had ready access to the works that she cites in her own library at Hohenbourg, there would have been little need for her to compile them as she did.

Given the recent refoundation of the monastery at Hohenbourg, it is unlikely that the community's library was adequate to meet Herrad's needs. Although it is possible that Relinde had brought some books with her when she came to Hohenbourg, her probable arrival around the mid-century predates certain of Herrad's most important sources, such as the *Sentences* and the *Historia scholastica*. Certainly, some books may have been given to the women at Hohenbourg in the years following the community's refoundation, as they were at Schwartzenthann. Gifts of books were recorded in the necrology of the *Guta-Sintram Codex*, alongside other donations to the community.[113] Even so, it is unlikely that the collection of books at Hohenbourg—for which there is no extant evidence—was large. Indeed, Herrad's motivation in the creation of the *Hortus* may have been to provide a proxy for the sort of library that Hohenbourg lacked. If this was the case, then her activities were consistent with what is known of other recently reformed houses, especially those connected with Hirsau, in which book production followed fast on the heels of reform.[114]

Assuming that Hohenbourg did not have a substantial book collection, Herrad's work on the *Hortus* suggests that she had access to a well-stocked library elsewhere and that she was involved in a network of book lending and borrowing, such as that which existed between Rheinhardsbrunn and Lippoldsberg.[115] The most obvious candidates for this sort of a relationship are the two established male communities with which Hohenbourg was closest: Marbach and Étival. The library at Marbach may have been particularly useful to her.[116] Although the library itself was destroyed in 1632, several of its manuscripts survive and are now housed in libraries in Colmar, Sélestat, Paris, Laon, Nuremberg, Freiburg, Strasbourg, and Basel.

The following twelfth-century manuscripts form part of the extant Marbach collection. At the Bibliothèque municipale, Colmar: Augustine, *Enarrationes in psalmos* 1–50 (MS 24); a composite manuscript including Didymus of Alexandria's *De Spiritu Sancto*, letters to Hugh Etherien from Hugo of Honau and Peter of Vienna, both men who had ties to Gilbert of Poitiers, and Boethius's commentary on Aristotle's *Categoriae* (MS 58); a composite manuscript containing the polemical pro-monastic treatise *De vita vere apostolica, De officio et ordine ecclesiastico*, a selection of Abelard's sermons, including *Adtendite a falsis prophetis*, and texts by Hugh of St. Victor, including his *De verbo incarnato* (MS 128);[117] a collection of sermons and theological treatises by Hugh of St. Victor, Hildebert of Lavardin,[118] and Peter Comestor, which included two sequences for the dedication of the church, sometimes attributed to Adam of St. Victor (MS 187);[119] and a manuscript of Geoffrey of Monmouth's *Historia Regum Britanniae* (MS 448). At Sélestat: the *Historia Trevirorum* of Justin (MS 93/

2). At the Bibliothèque municipale in Laon: the *Evangeliary of Marbach-Schwartzenthann* (MS 550).[120] At the Germanisches Nationalmuseum in Nuremberg: a schoolbook containing a collection of texts related to the teaching of the trivium, including, among other things, an *ars metrica* together with excerpts from the *Isagoge* of Porphyry and the *Rhetorica ad Herennium* (MS 27 773).[121] Finally, at the Universitätsbibliothek, Freiburg: a manuscript containing Boethius's *Opuscula sacra* together with Gilbert of Poitiers's highly controversial commentary (MS 367).[122] To this list, Reinhardt adds a late twelfth-century manuscript now in the university library at Basel (O.II.24), which contains Gilbert of Poitiers's commentary on Boethius and which he argues is closely connected to both Freiburg MS 367 and Laon MS 550. In addition to these surviving manuscripts, Marbach may have owned copies of the historical works used by the author of the *Marbach Annals*,[123] as well as the texts that appear in the *Guta-Sintram Codex*, most of which, like the section from Abelard's sermon 30 in Colmar MS 128, were presumably copied from Marbach exemplars.[124] Of the texts that influenced the *Annals*, only Freculph's *Chronicle* also appears in the *Hortus*; apart from these two witnesses, no other Alsatian manuscript of his work is known.[125]

It is difficult to draw firm conclusions regarding Herrad's library access from this evidence, since few of the authors or texts that survive from Marbach's library appear in the *Hortus*. Of her three major sources, Honorius, Rupert, and Peter Lombard, not one appears in this listing, although Marbach did own texts by Hildebert of Lavardin (d. 1134), Peter Comestor, and Hugh of St. Victor, all of whom appear in the *Hortus*, as well as certain sequences associated with St. Victor. However, the intellectual and spiritual profile of Marbach that emerges from its surviving manuscripts suggests the sort of monastic-scholastic crossover that Colish and Mews note elsewhere and that is manifested in the *Hortus* as well. At a time when monastic and canonical opinion was increasingly turning against Peter Abelard and Gilbert of Poitiers, Marbach's library collection included texts by both men. The Augustinian polemicist Gerhoch of Reichersberg (d. 1169) issued strict warnings against reading Gilbert's work, as did Bernard of Clairvaux, whose attacks on Gilbert and Abelard have been seen to epitomize monastic opposition to the schools.[126] Yet despite these warnings, Gilbert continued to be read and studied at Marbach, as he was in Austria, where Häring has identified readers whose marginal manuscript notations indicate that they were often sympathetic to him.[127] Manuscripts of Gilbert's work are not numerous; however, they are to be found in many monastic libraries, among them several in southern Germany and Austria.[128] Most striking, as far as the intellectual history of Marbach is concerned, is the fact that in the Basel manuscript of Gilbert's work, which Reinhardt associates with Marbach, Gilbert is depicted twice in author portraits with a nimbus, suggesting that rather than being studied cautiously, he may even have been revered at Marbach.[129] Similarly, although Abelard's sermons appear anonymously in Colmar MS 128, they were read by the canons, who even copied selections from his sermon 30 into the *Guta-Sintram Codex.*[130]

Bernard's opposition to both Gilbert and Abelard does not appear to have influenced opinion at Marbach. In fact, opinion at the community may have been turned against the Cistercians instead. The presence in Colmar MS 128 of Abelard's sermon, *Adtendite a falsis prophetis,* which was critical of the Cistercians, suggests that canons at Marbach were sympathetic to Abelard's objections and possibly also resistant to the spread of Cistercian monasteries.[131] It may be no small coincidence, then, that Bernard of Clairvaux is not featured in the *Hortus.* Although Herrad cites his work six times, she does so generally under the title *in sermone cujusdam doctoris,* an indication that she did not know his name, despite his fame and his relatively recent visit to Alsace, when he had preached the second crusade at Strasbourg in 1145.[132] Notably, the earliest Marbach manuscript containing works by Bernard dates to the thirteenth century.[133]

Strikingly absent from Marbach's surviving twelfth-century manuscripts are works by the Augustinian polemicists, Gerhoch and Arno of Reichersberg (d. 1175), Anselm of Havelberg (d. 1158), and Philip of Harvengt (d. 1183). This absence is paralleled in the *Hortus,* which makes little reference to the Augustinian life and which bypasses the most important Augustinian writers, with the exception of Ivo. Nor is there any special reference to Augustine as the patron of the Augustinian order to which Hohenbourg had recently converted, beyond a short text on folio 224v: "Augustine, the light of the world and the salt of the earth, the honest vessel of Catholic teaching, the greatest of pearls, distinguished with the gems of the apostolic life, which he, having followed, restored, and he usefully preserved his writings for posterity."[134] Despite these lacunae, clues to Hohenbourg's Augustinian context do appear in the manuscript. *Beata illa patria,* a poem that appears in a miniature of the celestial court on folio 244r (*HD* Cat. No. 317), is one such clue. Although both Autenrieth and Bischoff attribute this poem to Herrad, *Beata illa patria* is in fact the fourth stanza of *Interni festi gaudia*, a sequence that appears in the twelfth-century graduals of St. Victor and Ste. Geneviève and that was attributed to Adam of St. Victor during the late fifteenth century.[135] Margot Fassler identifies this sequence as "an early-twelfth-century piece for St. Augustine" that "appears almost exclusively in Augustinian books during the twelfth and early thirteenth centuries."[136] Its presence in the *Hortus* is a rare marker of the monastery's Augustinian connections.

There is no proof that Herrad used Marbach's library in her work on the *Hortus*. Nonetheless, from what remains of Marbach's collection it is clear that the community owned a wide-ranging selection of texts, many of which came from Paris and which as a whole reflect the same intellectual openness as marks the *Hortus*. The closeness of Marbach's ties to Paris, and in particular to the Augustinian community at St. Victor, is suggested by its possession of twelfth-century copies of Peter Comestor, Peter Abelard, Gilbert of Poitiers, Hildebert of Lavardin, Hugh of St. Victor, and Adam of St. Victor. Of these, three are securely identified with St. Victor: Peter Comestor, Hugh, and Adam. To these, we might add Peter Abelard, whose old teacher William of Champeaux has long been held as the founder of St. Victor. Works by Abelard and Hugh of St. Victor often appear in the same manuscripts, as they do in Colmar MS 128, an indication that they were read and disseminated together.[137] As we have seen, one possible explanation for the scholastic emphasis at Marbach is that a canon (or canons) from the community had studied in Paris, possibly at St. Victor, and brought manuscripts with him for the Marbach library on his return. These manuscripts may have included works by Walter of Châtillon and Hildebert of Lavardin, both of whom appear in the *Hortus*. If this hypothesis is correct, then the almost complete absence of Victorine texts in the *Hortus* is all the more mystifying. Although Herrad shares much in common with Hugh of St. Victor and, indeed, her *Hortus* is structured according to the historical framework that Hugh advocated, only one extract from Hugh appears in the *Hortus*, and even then it appears anonymously. Like Bernard, Hugh's text is identified simply as *in sermone cujusdam doctoris* (*HD* no. 114). Significantly, it was drawn from the *De verbo incarnato*, a work that Marbach did own.

The evidence from Étival is less complete, since most of the community's manuscripts were lost in the upheavals of the Revolutionary period.[138] Despite these losses, an idea of Étival's manuscript holdings can be gleaned from two eighteenth-century catalogues: first, the catalogue of père Blampain (1737–1739) and second, that which was produced at the

behest of the revolutionary government in February 1792.[139] Based on
these catalogues, links between Étival and Hohenbourg appear unlikely.
The single connection is an excerpt from the martyrology of Florus of
Lyon (*HD* no. 695), a text that Bischoff suggests derives from the diocese
of Toul, the diocese in which Étival, but not Hohenbourg, lay.[140] In any
case, Étival was not the most important medieval monastic library in Lorraine; the library at Moyenmoutier, a community with which Hohenbourg
had no ties, was much more significant.[141]

Whether or not Herrad borrowed books from Marbach or even Étival
must, at the moment, remain a subject for conjecture. However, her collaboration with male religious is certain. Poems on the penultimate folios
of the manuscript address the monastery of Hohenbourg directly and contain in acrostics the names of their authors: Conrad (*Hohenburgensibus
Conradus*) and Hugo the Priest (*Hugo Sacerdos*) (*HD* nos. 1162 and 1163).
In addition to Conrad and Hugo, Herrad incorporated poems by a third
poet, who might also have been known to her from the circle at Hohenbourg: *Godescallcus*.[142] Otherwise unknown, Godescallcus was most likely
the author of four poems (*HD* nos. 298, 300, 302, 722) in the *Hortus*; he
provides his name in acrostics in *HD* no. 300. Who these men were and
what their involvement in the *Hortus* project may have been is, again, a
question that, for the moment at least, cannot be answered definitively.
Probably they were canons at Truttenhausen charged with the provision
of spiritual service to Hohenbourg. Whoever they were, the inclusion of
their poems in the *Hortus* indicates that the possibility for interaction between religious men and women, a promise held out by the early reformers
and predicated on the *vita apostolica*, still existed in the Rhineland at the
close of the twelfth century.

Conclusion

The model of decline for women in the latter half of the twelfth century
is predicated on women's exclusion from the exciting intellectual and spiritual movements by which the period is now largely defined: renaissance
and reform. As this chapter has demonstrated, the *Hortus deliciarum* offers evidence of women's participation in both movements and of their
concern to provide themselves with a first-rate theological education. Herrad's major sources—Honorius Augustodunensis, Rupert of Deutz, and
Peter Lombard—include typically monastic as well as typically scholastic

texts, demonstrating her access to both traditions. The currency of her sources makes clear her engagement in contemporary debates; through the *Hortus*, women at Hohenbourg had access to the very texts that both their priests and male students at Paris were reading.

The *Hortus* was the product of reform at Hohenbourg. It represents Herrad's response to the particular concerns of a women's monastic community and, especially, to the need for priests to provide pastoral care, which Hohenbourg's charters reveal was a source of ongoing anxiety. In the *Hortus*, Herrad provided the tools with which the women of Hohenbourg could evaluate their priests; she also provided them with an education to rival and even surpass that of clerics, reducing their dependence on men for theological instruction. At the same time, however, the *Hortus* suggests that Hohenbourg enjoyed productive and positive relations with male monastics. The manuscript's contents hint at Herrad's library access and probable cooperation with neighboring monasteries in networks of book lending and borrowing. Together these attest to a community of women at Hohenbourg who were actively involved in reform concerns both locally and generally and who participated in the intellectual vitality of the age.

3

A Bee in the Garden of the Lord

As we saw in the last chapter, Herrad wrote only a handful of the texts that are included in the *Hortus*. Indeed, her authorship can be declared with certainty for no more than two, both of which she explicitly claims to have written: the first, *Salve cohors virginum* (*HD* no. 1), the poem with which the manuscript opens and which she addressed to the women of Hohenbourg, and the second, the prose prologue (*HD* no. 2), in which she dedicated the manuscript as a whole to her community. In addition to these two, it is likely that Herrad also wrote the four short poems that appear on the manuscript's penultimate folios: *Vos quas includit, O pie grex, Esto nostrorum,* and *O nivei flores*. If these poems were Herrad's, then she was clearly practiced in different forms of versification. *Vos quas includit*, an example of *versus raportati*, requires the reader to read vertically, matching the verb in line one with the subject of the action in line two, so that, for instance, prison (*carcer*) confines (*includit*) the audience of the poem (*vos*).

> o
> Vos quas includit,   frangit, gravat, atterit, urit,
> in terris
> Hic carcer, mestus,   labor, exilium, dolor, estus;
> in celis
> Me lucem, requiem, patriam,   medicamen et umbram,
> Querite, sperate,   scitote, tenete, vocate. (*HD* Cat. No. 345)

> O
> You whom prison confines,
> Sorrow breaks,
> Labor burdens,
> Exile and grief wear down,
> And passion burns here on earth;
> Seek me as light,

Hope for me as rest,
Know me as your homeland,
Hold me as balm,
Call me as cooling shade
In heaven.

The poem on Relinde's cross, *O pie grex*, can be read either horizontally or vertically and is governed by a triple internal rhyme scheme (e.g., *grex / lex / fex*).

O pie grex,   cui celica lex   est, nulla doli fex;
Ipse Syon mons   ad patriam pons,   atque boni fons;
           est
Qui via, qui lux,   hic tibi sit dux,   alma tegat crux.
           castitatis   eternitatis   Christus
Qui placidus ros,   qui stabilis dos,   virgineus flos
           grex
Ille regat te   commiserans me,   semper ubique;   amen.
   (*HD* Cat. No. 345)

O pious flock to whom the heavenly law is given, in whom there is no residue of
   deceit;
He is the mount of Syon, the bridge to paradise, and the fount of good;
May he who is the way of chastity, the light of eternity, Christ, be your leader;
May the gracious cross protect you.
O flock, may he who is the peaceful dew, the stable dowry, the virginal flower,
   guide you,
Having mercy on me, always and everywhere. Amen.

The last two poems, *Esto nostrorum* and *O nivei flores*, are examples of leonine verse, where the syllable just before the caesura rhymes with the last syllable on each line:

O nivei flores   dantes virtutis odores (*HD* Cat. No. 346)

Beyond these poems, which were certainly associated with Hohenbourg in form and content, a further group of poems may be attributed to Herrad on stylistic grounds: *De primo homine* on folio 109v (*HD* no. 374) and *Rithmus de Domino* on folio 166v (*HD* no. 595).[1]

The other texts in the *Hortus* were selected from what Herrad simply calls the "diverse flowers of sacred Scripture and philosophic writings"—the works of such men as Honorius, Rupert, Peter Lombard, and others. Although Herrad chose each of these texts, and excerpted, edited, and rearranged them in their new context in the *Hortus*, she did not write them. Instead, as she acknowledged both in her prologue, where she described the textual "flowers" she had gathered, and in the title—*Garden of Delights*—that she chose to give her work, the *Hortus* was explicitly a work of compilation.

This fact has important ramifications for the study of the *Hortus*, for its value as a witness to the educational culture at Hohenbourg and, most important, for estimations of Herrad's role in the planning and construction of the manuscript. On the one hand, the composite nature of the *Hortus* enhances its value as a witness to the reading patterns and intellectual interests of the women at Hohenbourg. While library catalogues for female communities in the twelfth century are rare, the contents of the *Hortus* indicate the full range of study at Hohenbourg, a range that rivaled even the most intellectually engaged of contemporary male communities. From the *Hortus*, we know not only that women read scholastic and pre-scholastic texts, but also how they read them, what subjects they found most important, and how they chose between conflicting authorities or, more simply, two writers who both treated a single subject. At the same time, the contents and currency of the manuscript hint at the broader networks of book borrowing and lending in which Hohenbourg must have been involved. While the women at Hohenbourg were clearly educated within their community, the *Hortus* suggests that they were also engaged in relationships beyond their monastery, which provided them at the very least with recent works such as the *Historia scholastica* and possibly also with friendship and more intimate intellectual exchange as well. The picture that emerges from the compiled texts of the *Hortus* is one of remarkable intellectual vitality and collaboration—both within the monastery and beyond it.

However, the fact that the *Hortus* was a work of compilation has been seen to confirm women's failure as authors even while it offers firm evidence of their reading and education.[2] Since the *Hortus* is characterized primarily as an encyclopedia—a characterization that is, importantly, less appropriate for the manuscript's visual program than it is for its textual content[3]—Herrad tends to be seen as the compiler of the manuscript and not as its author. This distinction may seem a fine one, perhaps even an irrelevant one in light of the "death of the author" hailed by poststructur-alist theorists some decades ago.[4] Nevertheless, it is important in two re-spects: first, since modern concepts of authorship have negatively affected appraisals of Herrad's work and recognition of her as an intellectual figure; and second, since authorship and authority—in the medieval sense—were central to Herrad's understanding of her project, its purpose, and her own role in bringing it to completion.[5] As I argue in this chapter, Herrad did see herself as the author—both in the modern sense of the "inventor," with its connotations of individuality and self-expression, and in the medieval sense of the "authority" behind the *Hortus* as a whole, if not each individual text.[6]

The clearest indication of Herrad's authorial self-perception appears in her prose prologue to the *Hortus*, where she claims responsibility for the entire manuscript, even while she acknowledges its composite nature as a garden of textual flowers.[7] Describing herself famously as "a bee in-spired by God," she writes:

Herrad, by the grace of God, abbess, although unworthy, of the church of Hohen-bourg, to the sweetest virgins of Christ faithfully working at Hohenbourg as though in the vineyard of the Lord Christ, grace and glory, that the Lord will give. I make it known to your holiness, that, like a little bee inspired by God (*quasi apicula Deo inspirante*), I collected (*comportavi*) from the various (*ex diversis*)[8] flowers of sacred Scripture and philosophic writings this book, which is called the *Hortus deliciarum*, and I brought it together (*compaginavi*) to the praise and honor of Christ and the church and for the sake of your love as if into a single sweet honeycomb (*unum mellifluum favum*). (*HD* no. 2)[9]

At first glance, the most striking aspect of Herrad's prologue is her identi-fication of herself and implicit claim to authorship of the manuscript as a whole.[10] In the poem that preceded this text, *Salve cohors virginum* (*HD* no. 1), she had already asserted her claim to authorship twice—first in her introduction of the piece as "The poem of the abbess Herrad by which she lovingly salutes the Hohenbourg virgins and with good wishes invites them to faith and love of the true bridegroom,"[11] and then again in its second stanza:

Herrad,
Your most devoted and faithful
Mother and little handmaid
Sings songs for you. (*HD* no. 1)[12]

However, her claim to authorship of this piece, while unambiguous, is limited ("I wrote this poem"). By contrast, in her prologue, Herrad extended her identification of herself as author beyond the immediate context of the piece ("I wrote this prologue") to encompass the entire *Hortus*, which she tells us that she put together "like a little bee inspired by God."

The fact that Herrad named herself in these opening pieces is an important indication of the way in which she understood and wished to communicate her role in the *Hortus*, especially since not all medieval writers chose to name themselves in prologues to their work. Honorius Augustodunensis preferred to remain anonymous, declining to name himself out of fear that his detractors would cause his work to be discounted.[13] Other writers had more prosaic reasons for their decision to remain unknown: their anonymity reflects their sense of their own unimportance in comparison to the work that they had created. Compilers of florilegia—a modern term comprised of *flos* (flower) and *legere* (to read) that has been used to describe medieval collections of excerpts[14]—tended not to name themselves out of modesty and deference to the authors from whose works they cited.[15] The compiler of the *Liber florum*, an early twelfth-century compilation from either Normandy or England, explains the reasons for his anonymity in this way: "I do not wish to affix my name to the title in the usual way, lest I seem insolently to apply to myself authority which rightly belongs to others."[16] Herrad's decision to name herself in the prologue is therefore the first and most direct indication that she saw herself as the author of the *Hortus* and that, importantly, her authorship extended beyond what modern readers might think of as mere compilation. By naming herself, she explicitly claimed responsibility for the entire work that followed, establishing herself as its *auctor*, literally the person who guaranteed its authority. In keeping with her assumed responsibility for the texts of the *Hortus*, Herrad alerted her readers to reservations concerning the orthodoxy of the pseudo-Clementine *Recognitiones*, warning of their mixed reception by the ecclesiastical authority.[17]

Herrad's sense of herself as an author may explain a second aspect of her prologue, her failure to cite her textual sources in the prologue as many compilers of florilegia and encyclopedists did. By listing their sources, these compilers tried to enhance the credibility of their work. The compiler of the seventh-century *Liber scintillarum* remarked on this very phenomenon, explaining his desire to give his work "authority" through the identification of his sources: "Lest this work, more or less authorless (*quasi sine auctore*), be regarded as of doubtful authenticity (*apocrifum*), I have written the name of the author for each excerpt."[18] Herrad's decision not to name her sources in her prologue is telling, particularly since she generally did identify works that she used in titles that accompanied each excerpt. Such headings as *Ex Sententiis Petri Lombardi*, *In Speculo Ecclesiae*, and *Rupertus* are common in the *Hortus*, and they appear in much the same way as Herrad's own name does in the titles to her poem (*HD* no. 1) and prologue (*HD* no. 2)—a further sign that she saw herself as an authority akin to the other authors whose work she cites. Given that she generally did name her sources elsewhere in the *Hortus*, Herrad's silence on the subject in her prologue suggests that she thought her own name sufficient to guarantee the credibility of the *Hortus* as a whole. Evidently she saw no need to rely on borrowed authority, as other compilers did, a fact that may reflect the limited audience to which the manuscript was dedicated, but which is nevertheless a sure sign of her intellectual self-confidence.

Finally, the boldness of Herrad's claim to authorship of the *Hortus* is consistent with the lack of a rhetorical apologia in her opening pieces. Although she is humble enough in describing herself as the "abbess of the church of Hohenbourg, although unworthy" (*Herrat . . . Hohenburgensis ecclesie abbatissa licet indigna*), her admission that she was "unworthy" was a moral rather than an intellectual judgment and was, moreover, in such wide usage by the twelfth century as to be virtually part of the abbatial title. Herrad never depicts herself as unlearned or *indocta*, an epithet that was common as a modesty topos among male authors who were demonstrably not *indoctus*,[19] but that was ubiquitous in the works of female writers, where the disqualification of their supposed lack of learning was compounded by that of gender.[20] Peter Lombard describes his *Sentences* as a *tractatus* and echoes Augustine in his pious hope for readers who will be able to remedy his mistakes[21]—posturings that are entirely absent from Herrad's prologue. Moreover, where Peter Lombard, like Honorius, Peter Comestor, and countless others, invokes the insistent pleas of his brethren as the catalyst for his writing, Herrad resists the familiar trope of external pressure—whether from her sisters, her superior, or an external patron. Even more strikingly, she does not appeal to divine authority as the basis for her work. Unlike visionaries who often disclaim learning, presenting themselves merely as conduits for the divine message, "inspiration" marks the extent of the credit that Herrad is willing to give to God for the work that she produced ("like a little bee inspired by God"). For the rest, she relies on no other authority than that of her own wide reading and erudition.

Yet despite these signs that Herrad saw herself as more than a compiler, she has rarely been taken seriously as an author, with the result that her achievement in the *Hortus* has repeatedly been minimized or denied. Writing in 1910, Marignan expressed his doubts that the manuscript could have been the work of a woman, proposing that Herrad's prologue and its claim to authorship be recognized as a "pious fraud"—a suggestion that few, if any, ever took up, but which has nonetheless haunted studies of the *Hortus* and assessments of Herrad's role in its creation.[22]

Herrad's claim to responsibility for the manuscript is no longer questioned, yet Marignan's doubts as to her authorship linger on. In part, these doubts stem from flawed perceptions of the *Hortus* as a whole. The tendency to characterize the work as an encyclopedia—with its connotations of comprehensiveness, universality, and inclusiveness but not originality—merely confirms the assumption that, beyond the selection and arrangement of texts, Herrad's influence on it was minimal. In fact, there are several drawbacks to the now widely accepted categorization of the *Hortus* as an encyclopedia, the most obvious of which is the fundamental ambiguity of the term.[23] Even specialists disagree about what, exactly, constitutes an encyclopedia.[24] The problem is acute for the medieval period since "encyclopedia" is not a medieval term and was not used by medieval authors to describe their works.[25]

One way to resolve the question of genre is to start with how Herrad presented her work. Did she intend the *Hortus* as an encyclopedia in the way that we might accept Isidore's *Etymologies* to define the medieval genre?[26] She was certainly aware of the encyclopedia and used at least one—the *Summarium Heinrici*—in her work on the *Hortus*.[27] This text, a late eleventh-century or early twelfth-century reworking of the *Etymologies*, provided material information that appears in thirty-three of Herrad's textual extracts—some of which, for instance the long section on the parts of a ship (*HD* no. 755), are fairly arcane—as well as some seventy marginal notes to other texts. Herrad turned to the *Summarium Heinrici* consistently throughout the *Hortus*: the first intact chapter appears on folio 4r of the *Hortus*, the last on folio 220v. However, she used this text as she did not want the *Hortus* to be used: as a reference tool. Like all of her sources, she took from the *Summarium* what was germane to her project and left the rest. By contrast, in her organization of the *Hortus*, Herrad intentionally omitted book or chapter divisions, which suggests that she wanted to prevent the use of the *Hortus* as a reference book.

A further explanation for the denial of Herrad's authorship by modern scholars has to do with the competing definitions of authorship—medieval versus modern. While ancient and medieval writers reflect assumptions about authorship that emphasize participation in a literary tradition founded on the authority of past authors, post-Enlightenment society disdains the old and privileges the new: "originality" has become the exclusive test for modern authorship, so that medieval works—often deemed unoriginal—are simply ignored. This is particularly the case with works of compilation, which are seen to transgress all of the rules of modern authorship, appearing to be both "derivative" and "unoriginal."

Of course, even medieval authors saw that there was a difference between compiling the words of others and being an *auctor* oneself. Like the compiler of the *Liber florum*, who refused to name himself, the encyclopedist Vincent of Beauvais (d. 1264) explained the limits that were placed on him as a compiler in the prologue to his *Speculum maius*. Distinguishing carefully between his own role and the *auctoritas* of his textual sources, Vincent admitted that the *Speculum* contained, "few or almost none of my own words; I say the *auctoritate* is theirs, the *ordinatione* alone is ours."[28]

Vincent's denial of "authority" reflects what was, by the thirteenth century, an accepted hierarchy of authorship in which compilation fell below the more highly regarded work of authorial creation. According to Bonaventure (d. 1274), there was a clear progression of ways in which a book could be made, with each displaying an increase in authorial intervention:

The method of making a book is fourfold. For someone writes the materials of others, adding or changing nothing, and this person is said to be merely the scribe. Someone else writes the materials of others, adding, but nothing of his own, and this person is said to be the compiler. Someone else writes both the materials of other men, and of his own, but the materials of others as the principal materials and his own annexed for the purposes of clarifying them, and this person is said to be the commentator, not the author. Someone else writes both his own materials and those of others, but his own as the principal materials, and the materials of others annexed for the purpose of confirming his own, and such must be called the author (*auctor*).[29]

Bonaventure's distinctions are clear enough and have been repeated often; however, it is little known that his enquiry into the varieties of textual creation was prompted by a simple dilemma: whether or not Peter Lombard could rightly be considered to be the author of the *Sentences*. Bonaventure concludes that he can, since his compiling of authoritative *sententiae* served only to support his own conclusions on various topics. The Lombard's work, then, was undergirded by a thesis that was the basis both of his compilation and his authorship.

To a modern audience, the very question that Bonaventure poses seems odd. Far from questioning Peter Lombard's status as an "author," we have celebrated his *Sentences* as one of the most significant achievements of the twelfth-century schools. And yet, the Lombard described his work in words that refer explicitly to compilation, and not authorship. "Volumen, Deo praestante, compegimus," he writes, choosing "compingere," a common word that means "to unite parts into a whole," to represent his authorial activity.[30] At the same time, he explicitly notes that the *Sentences* brings together the sayings of the Fathers and that he has only placed them side-by-side in his own work.[31] Even so, Bonaventure was content in the final analysis to recognize the Lombard as an "author."

The disparity with which "authorship" is granted by modern commentators reflects a general and subjective valuation of intellectual work—one that has had the effect of privileging the work of men over that of women. Abelard is seen as an author, even though, apart from his correspondence with Heloise, his best-known work, *Sic et non*, contains almost none of his own prose; yet few would claim that Abelard was not its "author." Meanwhile, the authenticity of Heloise's letters has been the subject of fierce debate and her *Problemata* is most often gathered together with Abelard's works rather than her own. Similarly, Hildegard's "authorship" of her visionary and other works has repeatedly been questioned, although she names herself as a visionary and writer, while Chaucer is celebrated as the most significant medieval English "author," even though he preferred to name himself only as a "maker" or "compiler," and not an "author" (*auctor*), a term that he uses only to identify his sources.[32] Few would now call Chaucer a compiler, recognizing him instead as one of the foremost authors of the English language. Yet Herrad, who scorns to call herself a compiler or to differentiate herself from the textual authority of her sources, is most often denied the "authorship" that she claims in her prologue.

Summit comments on the apparent absence of women authors from the canon, answering the question: "Were there women authors in the Middle Ages?" by problematizing the terms of the debate: "The answer depends on which term we consider to be in question, 'women' or 'author'."[33] According to the modern sense of the author as a "self-expressive individual and original creator,"[34] there are generally reckoned to have been few, if any, medieval women authors. As such, Summit argues for the need to extend definitions of "author" beyond the modern sense in order to include not only the creation of texts we might consider "new" or "original," but also the re-presentation of texts already in existence, whether by translation, compilation, or even the superficially conservative act of textual copying.[35] It is, of course, now common to see in the trope of translation the insertion of new ideas, or the presentation of old ideas within a new framework. However, the latitude for a figure such as Ælfric to be considered as the "author" of his translations has not yet been extended to such women as Clemence of Barking, whose "translation" of the *Vie de sainte Catherine* has yet to be considered a work of genuine creativity.[36]

Summit's point is well taken; however, it should be joined by another: if originality is to be the litmus test for medieval authorship, then few men would earn the title either, since most medieval texts were skillful (and sometimes not so skillful) tapestries of ideas and excerpts drawn from past authorities. A more interesting question has to do with authorial self-presentation: how did medieval writers see themselves: as authors, or as compilers? In order to solve the dilemma of Herrad's authorship, it may be that we must simply pay more serious attention to how she presents herself in her prose prologue, which is, after all, the logical starting point for any examination of the manuscript as a whole.

Quasi apicula

The most remarkable manifestation of Herrad's own authorial claim is her description of herself as a "little bee" inspired by God. Often cited, but little understood, Herrad's bee metaphor has been interpreted both as an expression of her humility and as further evidence that her role did not extend beyond the gathering of texts. According to this view, her reading—capricious, whimsical, and even somewhat aimless—might be likened to the erratic path of a bee buzzing from flower to flower in pursuit of nectar. Guided by winds and weather rather than plan or purpose, her path was unpredictable, unplanned, and spontaneous and the resulting *Hortus* a jumble of loosely organized texts. The image is, at least superficially, a touching one. However, it is an image that obscures the very serious intent of Herrad's prologue and the audacity and intellectual sophistication that her metaphor rightly implied. Like so much else in the *Hortus deliciarum*, Herrad's description of herself as a bee was deliberate—but not in the simple and engaging way that it has typically been read. Instead, it was a metaphor coded with precise messages particular both to the learned culture of classical antiquity and that of the medieval schools. To the educated medieval reader, these messages would have been clear, announcing Herrad as a learned woman, and her project as a carefully crafted work of erudition and of invention.

As an animal rich with symbolic potential, the bee had a long history of figurative representation in ancient cultures.[37] Bees were prized not only for the honey that they produced, but for the example that they were thought to set of communal living, particularly in their peaceful, hierarchical organization. Their symbolic importance was further enhanced by the model of hard work, diligence, and selflessness that they provided, as well as by their putative connection to the supernatural. For medieval Christian authors, the moral and communal characteristics of the bee were its most important aspects. Bestiaries report on the harmonious spirit of bees, who were considered as model citizens and exemplars for the monastic life, while in the liturgy the bee was celebrated as a symbol of the Virgin Mary since, like her, bees were thought to reproduce without sexual intercourse.

However, the symbolic significance of the bee within the classical world lay not in its moral significance—its evocation of purity and idealized community—but in its association with wisdom and with the cognitive processes of memory.[38] The activities of the bee in gathering nectar from various flowers and storing it in the cells of the hive provided a popular analogue to the workings of human memory—the gathering of nectar recalled the compilation of memory materials, while the cells of the hive, like the memory houses of antiquity, suggested the logic and organization that was implicit in memory making.[39] As far as the *Hortus* is concerned, the process of honey-making was significant for its potential to represent not only memory making, but also, more importantly, the making of thoughts. Seen in this light, the bee could also serve as a metaphor for composition—which constitutes Herrad's primary use of the image.

The bee as a symbol for composition is most associated with the writings of Seneca and, in particular, with his *Epistulae morales*. Although Seneca was not the first to make the connection between bees and memory, he did link memory to composition in a passage so popular that it continued to be cited, often anonymously, until the Renaissance.[40] Describing the processes of composition, Seneca emphasized the value of combining reading with writing, taking as his model the activities of the honey-bee. He writes:

We should imitate bees and we should keep in separate compartments whatever we have collected from our diverse reading, for things conserved separately keep better. Then, diligently applying all the resources of our native talent, we should mingle all the various nectars we have tasted, and turn them into a single sweet substance (*unum saporem*), in such a way that, even if it is apparent where it originated, it appears quite different from what it was in its original state.[41]

Seneca's extension of the bee's traditional symbolic role in the gathering and organization of memory to the making of ideas marked a significant shift in conceptions of literary *imitatio* and composition. Although the apian metaphor had been common in the ancient world as a way to characterize the work of gathering that preceded composition,[42] Seneca transcended this traditional portrayal of the bee's work. However, in order for him to adopt the bee as a symbol of composition, it was important for him to ask what, exactly, the bee *did* in order to make honey. The key question, obviously, was whether or not the bee "adds" a new element to her gathered nectar in the process of mellification, that is, whether honey is something more, or even something different, than the sum of its constituent parts. This question was an important one for authors, whose writings inevitably drew on a wide variety of sources, but could nonetheless constitute something original or "new"—the "single sweet substance" that Seneca described.

Immediately following his initial presentation of the bee metaphor, Seneca subjected it to a detailed interrogation, explicitly asking whether the bee functions only as an aggregator of materials, or if her role extends beyond the mere collection of pollen. In short, he asked if the process of making honey is more than assemblage or compilation—if, in fact, it is a process of creation. "It is not certain," he wrote, "whether the juice which they [the bees] obtain from the flowers forms at once into honey, or whether they change that which they have gathered into this delicious object by blending something therewith and by a certain property of their breath."[43] After noting differing opinions on the subject—including the possibility that honey is produced through natural fermentation and the belief that, in India, honey is gathered from the leaves of certain plants as though it were dew—Seneca concluded that honey, that "single sweet substance" that is the end result of the bee's labors, does indeed constitute a new material, something that can be the sum of its parts and yet transcend them, both at the same time.

Seneca's model of authorship as a sort of creative compilation of existing ideas transformed into something new has important implications, particularly for medieval compilation. As Hathaway has observed, the borrowing of texts, or what we would now call compilation, was sharply distinguished from the work of original composition by medieval writers and each type of work described by its own vocabulary.[44] Before the twelfth century, *compilo* and related terms were rarely used by authors to describe their own works of compilation, since they retained the negative connotations of their classical origins—*compilo* meaning to plunder or rob. Notably, Herrad avoids the negative implications of compilation, describing her work not as *compilatio*, but by the verbs *compaginare* and *comportare*.[45] Although borrowing could be defended under certain circumstances, medieval authors recognized that there was an important difference between borrowing texts from other authors and actually being an author oneself. As we have seen, some medieval compilers make this distinction explicit, even going so far as to deny "authorship" of the works that they produced. Like Vincent of Beauvais, the compiler of the *Liber florum* denied authorship, protesting: "I am not the author of these *sententiae*, but rather like a collector of flowers from the meadows."[46] However, for other writers, Seneca's bee metaphor offered a way to bridge the divide between mere gathering and real authorship by analogy to the mysterious process of mellification—Seneca's model of authorial transformation.

Seneca's confidence in the novelty of the bee's honeyed produce is an important reminder of the profound differences between medieval and modern attitudes toward composition and an important clue to the correct interpretation of Herrad's prologue. Herrad, like Seneca, was functioning within a cultural and intellectual context very different from our own, one in which "newness" (or originality) was not so much the aim of education as were such factors as careful reading, interpretation, and application of canonical texts. Within that context, Herrad claimed that the *Hortus* was a "new" creation and that she was its author. Her use of the apian metaphor to evoke the transformative nature of her work on the *Hortus* is all the more striking given that Seneca's letter and its encouragement to imitate bees was not always adopted as he had intended. Although Seneca had stressed transformation in the making of honey, the apian metaphor could equally be used in its traditional sense: to emphasize simply the gathering of materials.[47]

The transformative potential of the bee is absent from Macrobius's (c. 400) use of the metaphor. Although he took the image of the bee as a guiding principle in the composition of his *Saturnalia,* a work that he dedicated to the education of his son Eustachius, and even followed Seneca verbatim in places, there was an important difference between Macrobius's interpretation of the bee's role in the transmission of ideas and that which had been promoted by Seneca. As we have seen, Seneca argued that the creation of something new—honey—from existing materials was the bee's primary achievement. A less popular metaphor, designed to reinforce the idea that something new could be created from preexisting sources, was his further analogy between composition and the digestion of food. While not so palatable—and, in the sense that intestinal workings did not produce a carefully ordered product, also less appropriate to his purpose— the intestinal metaphor called attention to the active role that digestion required, even once the raw materials had been amassed. Tasting, chewing, swallowing, and ultimately incorporating food into her own body, the eater made food her own in the same way as the reader claimed knowledge. Seneca's point was that authorship involved collecting and literally digesting existing textual sources, processes by which an author could ultimately assimilate the objects of her reading into her own unique product. Yet for Macrobius the bee metaphor appears primarily as a justification for textual borrowing, and not as a claim for the originality of his own writing, even though he was obviously familiar with Seneca's argument for the digestive aspect of reading and writing, and the "single flavor" of the honeycomb that the bee's labors produced.[48] In his preface, Macrobius offered his son this apology for the collective nature of his finished work:

You should not count it a fault if I shall often set out the borrowings from a miscellaneous reading in the authors' own words (for the present work undertakes to be a collection of matter worth knowing, not a display of my command of language), but be content with information of things of ancient times, sometimes set out plainly in my own words and sometimes faithfully recorded in the actual words of the old writers, as each subject has seemed to call for an exposition or a transcript.[49]

In the same way, in his *vita* of Eigil (d. 822), the schoolmaster and later abbot of Fulda, the monk Candidus described Eigil's learning, commenting that his progress was such that he appeared to imitate bees in the gathering of flowers (*ut etiam apes esurientes in colligendis floribus imitari videretur*). There is no sense here of the crucially transformative function of the bee, nor of the honey produced through his efforts—although, of course, even the use of the metaphor was intended by Candidus to underscore the extent of Eigil's learning.[50]

Whether or not the bee image was always used as Seneca had intended, the positive view of textual borrowing that it allowed suggests that modern disregard for medieval works of compilation, or for those that weave together ideas from disparate sources, has been too hasty. To a large extent, this disregard reflects the sense that compilation or "borrowing" is merely a passive activity, just as memorization has been deemed a largely passive form of learning. However, as Carruthers has shown, within ancient and medieval cultures memorization was seen as an active way of literally "digesting" knowledge.[51] Rather than being inimical to real creative thought, memory held a place of particular importance within education and especially within the trivial arts—grammar, rhetoric, and logic. As such, it was memory, and not imagination, that was central to learning and to creativity. The model that Carruthers offers for the reinterpretation of memory, and of learning, is directly relevant to evaluations of medieval authorship, since literary *imitatio*, like memory, involved reading, contemplation of a text, assimilation of that text through memorization, and, ultimately, recreation. Indeed, memorization and composition were intricately connected since Seneca's bee metaphor was inspired by the existing association of bees with wisdom and memory.

In salvaging memory from modern censure, Carruthers contrasts the modern preoccupation with the imagination as the source of creativity with the medieval emphasis on memory—which she rightly notes has misled modern commentators to assume that the medieval world was one, less of creativity than of imitation. Since medieval learning was not concerned with novelties, but with the mastery of existing thought and with contribution to an existing edifice of learning, drawing on the work of another author was not shameful, but could become an act of scholarship and even creativity.[52] Indeed, quite apart from the Senecan idea of "creation" in imitation, there were those who valued the art of compilation as one that rivaled and even surpassed the initial process of writing. The early tenth-century Arabic encyclopedist Ibn 'Abdarabbih of Córdoba drew a clear distinction between his work of selection and the original work of authorship, yet he does not apologize for his work, but rather argues that it represents a more sophisticated achievement than had the original text.

He writes that: "The selection of texts is more difficult than composing it. People have said: A man's choice is a messenger of his mind. A poet has said: We recognized you by your choice, since the intelligent man is indicated by his choice."[53] According to this view, the ability to select appropriately from an original work is a manifestation of true understanding that surpasses even that of the original author. Ibn 'Abdrabbih's positive evaluation of compilation was anticipated—although less radically—by Jerome who had characterized compilation as a means of seizing the power of an *auctor*: "To wrench the club from the hand of Hercules is to have great power."[54] The implication is that reuse of texts, like the incorporation of spolia into works of art, was a rich and powerful way of engaging elite intellectual culture. Obviously the Enlightenment concept of authorship—which divorced originality from tradition—would not have occurred to medieval writers: their honey was considered sweet because it combined the fragrant knowledge of past masters. It could not have been created from nothing.

It is within the context of debates concerning the *Hortus* as a whole and Herrad's role as its author that her use of the bee metaphor is so important. Quite apart from the creative aspect of the bee's work and the potentially positive implications of compilation, the bee was also a common symbol within ancient and medieval culture for reading, study, and wisdom. Indeed, the image of the bee suggested itself to Seneca for a variety of reasons that strengthen his argument that honey was more than processed nectar, and the bee more than a compiler of its juices. The rhetorician Quintilian compared intellectual production to the manufacture of honey, likening the orator to a bee making honey, "whose taste is beyond the skill of man to imitate, from different kinds of flowers and juices."[55] Like Seneca, Quintilian assumed the relationship common within ancient cultures between bees and wisdom, and between honey and divine or secret knowledge—topics discussed by both Aristotle and Virgil, who devoted significant attention to bees in the fourth book of his *Georgics*, even arguing that bees had a share in the divine mind.[56] The connection between the bee and wisdom was most powerfully expressed in the topos of the infant fed by bees, a story that attached itself to mythological figures as well as poets and philosophers. Cicero relates how bees had settled on Plato's lips as he lay in his cradle, concluding, "thus his future eloquence was foreseen in his infancy."[57] The sweetness of knowledge, and possibly also its unusual origins, was stressed in epithets for both Plato, who was known as the "Athenian Bee," and Sophocles, the "Attic Bee," with whom miraculous bee-feeding was also associated. Ultimately, the bee became the symbol of an educated man, particularly in the writings of Plutarch, who saw the bee's ability to extract sweetness from thorny plants as a model for the wise man, who derives profit from difficult texts—a motif that was later taken up by Augustine and others.[58]

In addition to the intellectual connotations of the bee metaphor, the bee was an important spiritual symbol within medieval Christian thought. Despite its supernatural and even cultic associations in the ancient world, the bee was easily Christianized during the early Middle Ages and subsumed within a moral framework.[59] Since the bee had already been established in ancient texts as a model not only for intellectual endeavor but also for community (the hive) and diligence (the manufacture of honey), it could serve equally well as a model for the ideal Christian society. As an established metaphor for divine wisdom in biblical literature, the bee's produce—honey—equally had a spiritual connotation.[60] The Psalmist writes: "How sweet are thy words unto my taste! yea, sweeter than honey to my mouth!" and elsewhere, describing God's judgments, "More are they to be desired than gold, yea, than much fine gold; sweeter also than honey and the honey-comb" (Psalms 118:103 and 18:11). Accordingly, medieval authors consistently describe the Scriptures as a honeycomb, and spiritual knowledge as honey. Rhabanus Maurus, for instance, writes: "Divine Scripture is a honeycomb filled with the honey of spiritual wisdom."[61] Beyond these spiritualized attributes, the metaphor of the bee was appropriate for Herrad's purposes in that the allegorized bee was often depicted as finding nourishment in the word, or the love of God.[62]

Herrad's use of the bee metaphor suggested a range of interpretations, both Christian and classical. However, she used it primarily as Seneca had intended—to express the production from existing materials of a new creation, which is now clearly marked with the stamp of the new author. Indeed, she deviates from him only in one place: she Christianized the metaphor, describing herself not only as a bee, but more specifically as a bee *inspired* by God. In so doing she introduced a new element—divine inspiration—to Seneca's formulation of composition.

Had Herrad read Seneca? Certainly his letters were known within certain circles during the twelfth century and played a role in the medieval *ars dictaminis*. Reynolds lists more than twenty twelfth-century writers who cite sections from Seneca's letters, among them Rupert of Deutz, Abelard, Bernard of Clairvaux, William of St. Thierry, Otto of Freising, Hildebert of Lavardin, John of Salisbury, Peter Comestor, and Alan of

Lille—groupings that suggest knowledge of the letters particularly in the Parisian schools.[63] Déchanet's suggestion that the Premonstratensians were especially involved in the dissemination of Seneca's letters is interesting in light of Herrad's connections to the Premonstratensians at Étival, as is the obvious overlap between many of her sources and those who knew Seneca—in particular Rupert, Peter Comestor, and Hildebert.[64] However, neither Seneca nor Macrobius was mentioned in the *Hortus* although Macrobius was certainly known in Alsace and was evidently a subject of discussion at Lautenbach where Manegold had originally been a canon.[65] Yet this absence is in many ways irrelevant. Macrobius did not cite his source when he quoted Seneca, and it is likely that Herrad would have been familiar with the exhortation to "imitate bees" whether or not she knew the precise details of its origins. In any case, Herrad's interpretation of the apian metaphor is reminiscent of Seneca's "single sweet substance" (*unum saporem*)—she describes the *Hortus* as a "single sweet honeycomb" (*unum mellifluum favum*)—and evokes Seneca's belief in the bee's creation of a new intellectual product.

Herrad's use of the bee image as a marker of intellectual engagement and production is especially interesting in light of the tendency, by the twelfth century, to read the bee in a predominantly moral or spiritualized light or, like Macrobius, to obscure the transformative aspect altogether.[66] Within monastic circles by this time, the bee had become primarily a symbol of perfection in the religious life. The cooperation of bees, their hierarchy, division of labor, and even the cells of the beehive offered countless opportunities for moralizing and allegorizing in works of monastic direction. Already in the *vita* of Bishop Ulrich of Augsburg (d. 973), the work of the gathering bee had been divorced from its intellectual context and likened instead to the Bishop's increase in virtue; the result of his labor is *mella spiritualia*.[67] In the same way, although John of Salisbury (d. 1180) maintained the intellectual associations of the bee, he too emphasized the moral rather than the merely intellectual aspect of the apian metaphor, obscuring Seneca's interest in the metamorphosis through which nectar becomes honey. When John cited Seneca's injunction to imitate bees in his *Policraticus* (completed 1159), he did not emphasize the crucial intellectual aspect of the bee's transformative power, commenting instead: "Whatever we have acquired by our varied reading let us also turn to virtue's purpose, that all may combine into a category of things to be transacted by the directing force of reason."[68] By contrast, Herrad resisted the primarily moralistic use of the metaphor, focusing instead on the bee as a creator and a symbol of the generation and organization of thoughts. The intellectual implications of the bee, and not its moral significance, inspired her decision to describe herself as a "little bee."

The Christianized Bee

Beyond the authorial connotations of the bee metaphor, there were other reasons why Herrad might have chosen to describe herself as a bee, or rather why such a description would have resonated particularly with her intended audience—the women of her community. As I have already noted, bees were important exemplars for the monastic life and for the female monastic life especially. In its industry, communal living, and subordination of the individual to the community, the bee had traditionally been held up as a model citizen and its hive as a model state. The harmony of bee society was praised in classical texts, and above all in Book Four of Virgil's *Georgics*, a text that provided an exhaustive supply of bee lore to later authors.[69] However, the centrality of the bee to the store of Christian symbolism was assured by Ambrose (d. 397), who praised the bee for its hard work, cooperation, and peaceful hierarchy. He wrote:

All have the same abode and are confined within the limits of one native land. They engage in the same labor. They share the same food and partake of the same activities. . . . Scripture rightly commends the bee as a good worker: "Behold the bee, see how busy she is, how admirable in her industry, the results of whose labors are serviceable to kings and commoners and are sought after by all men." Do you hear what the Prophet says? He enjoins on you to follow the example of that tiny bee (*apicula*) and to imitate her work. You see how pleasing it is and what labor it entails. Her fruit is desired and sought after by all men. . . . It supplies without distinction the same sweetness to kings and to commoners.[70]

Although the bee gathering nectar was an obvious image of diligence and industry, for Ambrose the diligence of the bee as it might be observed in nature was supplemented by scriptural praise for the ant in Proverbs 6:8, a passage that had been appropriated by early Christian writers in praise of the bee—as Ambrose did too. Ambrose's enthusiasm for the bee was reflected in his biography, where Paulinus records that, in the tradition of Plato and others, he had received a visitation from bees while still an infant. Settling on his mouth, the bees ensured that the words of the proverb should be fulfilled: "Good words are a honeycomb."[71]

Within the monastic community, the qualities associated with bees were deemed desirable and necessary; the hive, a medieval commonplace for the model state, was adopted as a symbol of monastic perfection. The communal living of the bee lent itself to an interpretation of the bee as a symbol of service to others.[72] This image of the bee as a selfless worker was enforced in medieval bestiaries where bee society was depicted as one in which a natural hierarchy existed alongside division of labor and cooperation.[73] The physical structure and the natural geometry of the honeycomb confirmed for medieval observers the orderliness and tranquility of the hive. Finally, the hum of the bees in their community, known as their "murmur," was adopted as an analogy for the type of contemplative reading aloud that accompanied the *lectio divina*.[74]

The bee recommended itself as a model for the monastic life in another way: as an animal that was thought to procreate without coitus (through parthenogenesis), the bee was typically a symbol of chastity. Although this association almost certainly began in error—bees were thought by some to grow from the rotting carcasses of cows[75]—it seemed to confirm the apparent absence of coupling among bees and certainly added to the effectiveness of the bee as a model for the monastic life. Ambrose was most influential in popularizing the virginal reputation of the bee, presenting the bee as a symbol of purity in his *De virginibus*.[76] The bee was subsequently widely adopted as a symbol of virginity; among others it appears in the writings of pseudo-Augustine, who taught that bees reproduce without desire (*sine libidine*),[77] Venantius Fortunatus, for whom the bee was "fertile in its chaste bed,"[78] Ælfric, who wrote that bees give birth in purity,[79] and Aldhelm, who comments, "The bee, I say, by virtue of the special attribute of its peculiar chastity, is by the undoubted authority of the scriptures agreed to signify a type of virginity and the likeness of the Church."[80] The idea appears too in the writings of Hildebert of Lavardin, who stated simply: "The virgin is a little bee (*apicula*), who makes wax and procreates without coitus."[81]

Hildebert's identification of the virgin with the bee appeared in a sermon for the Feast of the Purification; the virgin to whom he referred was none other than the Virgin Mary—who, increasingly, became associated with the bee since, like her, it brought forth its young without sin. As Ælfric commented:

There is no woman like her, for neither before nor since was there a virgin who bore a child and afterwards remained a virgin, save her alone. Nevertheless, there are some creatures who propagate without intercourse and both mothers and daughters are virgins: these are bees. They bring forth their offspring in purity. From the honey they nourish their brood and the young are brought forth in virginity and the older ones remain virgins.[82]

The eleventh-century poem *Vestiunt silve* (*Carmina Cantabrigiensia* no. 23) conflates distinctions between the bee and the Virgin entirely:

None among the birds is like the bee,
who represents the ideal of chastity,
if not she who bore Christ in her womb
        inviolate.[83]

In a similar vein, pseudo-Augustine's assertion that the bee reproduced without desire appeared in his sermon on the wax of the Easter candle (*De cereo Paschali*).[84] The connection between the bee—who by its labors supplied wax for the liturgical candles—and the Virgin Mary was also underscored in the liturgy for Holy Saturday. The *Exultet* explicitly likens the bee's chastity to that of the Virgin; both bring light to a dark world, the bee literally through the wax of the candle, and the Virgin spiritually through her son, Christ.[85] Ultimately the bee was honored not only as a symbol of human perfection, but was also thought actually to *be* pious. In a popular exemplum, versions of which appear in both Caesarius of Heisterbach's *Dialogus miraculorum* and Thomas of Cantimpré's *Bonum universale de apibus*, a text that marks the culmination of medieval bee theory, the bee figures as a protector of the consecrated Host. According to the story, a Host, which had been stolen and hidden in a tree, was later discovered within a shrine of honeycomb that had been built by a swarm of bees to protect it.[86]

The bee image of Herrad's prologue drew on all of these associations at once. While it functioned primarily according to Seneca's model of learning and composition, it also served to confirm Herrad's monastic status and to encourage the perfection of the hive as a model for the community at Hohenbourg. Herrad's choice of the bee metaphor would have resonated particularly with her audience, some of whom may even have been involved in bee-keeping at Hohenbourg—an essential monastic occupation since bees were prized both for their honey and for the wax that they produced and that alone could be used in the manufacture of liturgical candles. Above all, the bee image was most directly appropriate to Herrad's audience in that the bee, *apis* or *apicula*, was almost always gendered

female, despite the widespread assumption that a king bee led the hive and
the prevalence of martial imagery in descriptions of bees from Virgil, Seneca, and Lactantius, as well as Isidore.[87]

Yet even within a Christian reading of the metaphor, Herrad's bee
image was not primarily moralistic, but instead allowed her to reinforce
the intellectual component already implicit in the classical bee metaphor—
with one important twist. Since the bee was almost always gendered female, she could function as a model not simply for the educated man, as
bees had in the world of classical antiquity and particularly in Plutarch's
writing, but more particularly for the learned woman. To the established
connection between bees and wisdom, medieval writers often added a
third factor—women. This is how Aldhelm uses the bee image in his writing for the nuns of Barking, whom he describes as bees, "roaming widely
through the flowering fields of scripture," as well as those of history,
grammar, and metrics. The sophisticated image that he offers captured the
broad ranging and almost insatiable intellectual curiosity of the nuns. He
writes:

For just as the swarm, having left in companies and throngs the restricted openings
of the windows and the narrow entrance-halls of the beehive, pillages the beautiful
meadows of the countryside, in the same way your remarkable mental disposi-
tion—unless I'm mistaken—roaming widely through the flowering fields of scripture, traverses (them) with thirsty curiosity, now energetically plumbing the divine
oracles of the ancient prophets foretelling long in advance the advent of the Saviour with certain affirmations; now, scrutinizing with careful application the hidden
mysteries of the ancient laws miraculously drawn up by the man [i.e. Moses] who
is said to have cruelly smitten the Memphitic realms [i.e. Egypt] with ten most
savage afflictions of plague . . . ; now exploring wisely the fourfold text of the
evangelical story [i.e. the four Gospels], expounded through the mystical commentaries of the catholic fathers and laid open spiritually to the very core and
divided up by the rules of the fourfold ecclesiastical tradition according to *historia*,
allegoria, *tropologia* and *anagoge*; now, duly rummaging through the old stories
of the historians and the entries of the chroniclers, who by their writing have
delivered to lasting memory the chance vicissitudes of times gone by; now, saga-
ciously inquiring into the rules of the grammarians and the teachings of experts on
spelling and the rule of metrics (as they are) measured out into accents (and) times,
fitted into poetic feet, broken up into cola and commata—that is, into pentimem-
eres and eptimemeres—and, indeed, divided individually into a hundred kinds of
meter.[88]

During the twelfth century, the most famous bee-woman was Heloise, Herrad's near contemporary and a woman famed for her learning.

Hugh Metel writes in rapturous terms of the "honey" of Heloise's wisdom: "Your discourses are sweet to my throat. And how sweet? Sweeter than honey and the honeycomb. They are sweeter than honey and the honeycomb, and are the mirror of your prudence."[89] More strikingly, Peter the Venerable used the image of Heloise as a bee to convey his respect for her and his esteem for her learning. After encouraging her to assume command in the "army of the Lord," since "it is not altogether exceptional amongst mortals for women to be in command of women," Peter encouraged Heloise to see herself equally as a teacher of women, extending the bee metaphor to encompass public instruction by and for women. Paying tribute to Heloise's wide learning and mastery not only of Latin and Greek, but also Hebrew, Peter writes:

And because the name of Deborah, as your learning knows, means "bee" in the Hebrew tongue, you will be a Deborah in this respect too, that is, a bee. For you will make honey, but not only for yourself; since all the goodness you have gathered here and there in different ways, by your example, word, and every possible means, you will pour out for the sisters in your house and for all other women. In this brief span of our mortal life you will satisfy yourself with the hidden sweetness of the Holy Scriptures, as also your fortunate sisters by your public instruction.[90]

The connection between wisdom, bees, and honey may have been a more natural one for medieval writers than even for their ancient counterparts since, as Peter the Venerable notes, the biblical judge Deborah, a venerable model for Christian women, had been associated with the bee by Origen and the connection transmitted to Latin audiences by Jerome.[91] The association of the bee with Deborah adds to the traditionally intellectual and gendered aspects of the bee figure the further connotation of counsel and wisdom. Indeed, the bee emerges in Peter the Venerable's hands as a kind of female counselor or wise woman. In addition to Peter's letter to Heloise, the connection between Deborah and the bee appears in the writings of such eleventh-century and twelfth-century figures as Peter Damian, Guibert of Nogent, and Rupert of Deutz, as well as in the *vita* of Hildegard of Bingen.[92] Clearly, Peter expected that Heloise would be as familiar with the many meanings of the bee metaphor as he was himself. However, it is significant in this context that Peter's use of the metaphor extended not only to the making of intellectual or textual honey, but also to the public instruction for which Heloise may also have been famed.[93]

We cannot know how Heloise responded to the admiration of Peter the Venerable, although it is likely that she did not react well to the flattery of Hugh Metel, as his second letter to her hints.[94] However, nowhere, at least in her extant writings, does Heloise apply the bee metaphor to herself. This is not unusual; in most cases, as we have seen here, wise women are described as bees by their male admirers. So, for instance, Baudry of Bourgeuil wrote to Emma (probably a nun at Notre-Dame du Ronceray, Angers), indicating that he wanted to be her student and referring to the "swarm of female students" (*examina discipularum*) who flocked to her in order to be revived by her honey—the honey of the "queen bee" (*melle parentis apis*).[95] Yet, the predominantly male use of the image makes Herrad's arrogation of it to herself that much more striking. In claiming the bee image for herself, Herrad drew on the association of the bee with learned women, monastic discipline, chastity, wisdom, and, of course, the production of honey—in this case signifying the theological knowledge that the *Hortus* contained.

Conclusion

The metaphor that Herrad provided of herself culling texts from the flowers of Scriptures was by no means original; as a standard image for compilation, it can be found not only in the writings of Jerome, Abelard, and Lambert of St-Omer, but also in the prefatory epistle to the *Speculum virginum*. However, Herrad is singular in that she moves beyond the merely poetic or moralistic use of the metaphor, in order to imbue it with the sort of transformative, creative implications that Seneca had intended, as well as the gendered implications of female wisdom and learning. So although Lambert of St. Omer likened his *Liber floridus* (c. 1120) to a bouquet of flowers and stated his intention that "the faithful bees may come to it and draw from it the sweetness of heavenly savour,"[96] his use of the bee metaphor deviated from that intended by Seneca. According to Seneca, Lambert himself, and not his readers, should properly represent the bee. Similarly, the *Speculum virginum* presents the books into which it is divided as "meadows" containing flowers which it presents as the mystical senses of the divine word. However, the virgin appears less as a student and more as a bride ornamenting herself to meet the bridegroom. In the text, Peregrinus exclaims: "Look! While browsing through the meadows of Scripture, we have at the same time gathered flowers to weave a crown for the virgin's head, until we are able to cover the rest of her body as well with mystical garments—so that, beautifully adorned, she may proclaim to her bridegroom, 'He has clothed me with the garment of salvation, he has covered me with the robe of justice'."[97] In other echoes of Seneca's injunction to imitate bees, medieval writers often describe themselves as gathering flowers, but do not add in the crucial process by which flowers, or more particularly their nectar, are transformed into honey. Abelard, for instance, uses the floral metaphor, among others, to describe his work in preparing his *Rule* for the women of the Paraclete, but does not describe the finished product as a whole in terms consistent with Seneca's transformative model.[98]

It is against this background of the bee as author and the bee as wise woman that Herrad's metaphor should be read—as a serious comment on the construction and integrity of the *Hortus* and on Herrad as its author. In her *Book of Memory*, Carruthers makes this point, warning that the bee metaphor "should be understood not as a mere decoration but a complex model of the process of composition and authorship."[99] Herrad's bee was not simply the decorative, or the touching image that it has so often been considered. Indeed, the bee image enabled her to communicate succinctly to her audience her claim to authorship of the text and her hopes for its use, both as spiritual refreshment ("honeyed dewdrops") and intellectual nourishment.

Herrad's bee image is reprised only once more in the *Hortus*, in Conrad's poem, *Rithmus de monte Hohenburc*, which Herrad may have commissioned and which she presented on the manuscript's final facing pages. Adopting Herrad's image of the *Hortus* as containing the nectar of Scripture and her invocation of the learned woman as a bee—particularly as the "little bee" (*apicula*) of her prologue—Conrad writes:

On this mountain of Hohenbourg, the little sheep
Drink from the living fountain of the Holy Spirit,
The little bees gather
The nourishing doctrine of life, without strife.

They drink freely
The clear nectar of the Scriptures,
May they drink now, may they drink in the future,
May they live now and always, may they all live eternally. (*HD* no. 1162)[100]

Although these were not Herrad's verses, they nevertheless echo her emphasis on the spiritual significance of the "honeyed dewdrops" that the

Hortus contained. Like the Vatican Bestiary, which depicts the gathering of nectar from flowers as the harvesting of God's love, Conrad's poem expresses the joyfulness of the women as they gather the nectar, which is the sweetness not only of learning, but also the true sweetness that is the love of God. Conrad's verses were neumed, although no trace of the neumes now survives.[101] However, the spirited tone of the poem, which as Saxl points out reads "like a drinking song" in places, provides a clear sense of how it was sung by the women in community.[102] The representation of the Hohenbourg women as bees drinking not the honey that Herrad had produced, but rather nectar from the flowers in her garden (the *Hortus*), hints at Herrad's hopes for the continuation of scholarship at Hohenbourg—independent of her teaching. In Conrad's poem, the bee-canonesses of the community are shown in a reiteration of Herrad's creative cycle, producing their own honey from the "various flowers of sacred Scripture and philosophic writings" that had been gathered together by Herrad in the *Hortus*.[103]

4

From Nectar to Honeycomb:
Constructing the *Hortus*

IN HIS DISCUSSION OF HONEY making as an analogy to composition, Seneca leaves unanswered the question of what the bee actually *did* to transform nectar into honey: the process of mellification remains, ultimately, a mystery. In the same way, although Herrad describes herself as a bee and the *Hortus* as a honeycomb in her prologue, she does not make explicit the details of her work on the manuscript—exactly *how* the textual flowers of her sources were transformed into the honeycomb that she describes. The silence in her prologue concerning the sources of the *Hortus* extends to the manuscript's visual program, its organization, and its physical structure, as well as the collaborators (including Relinde) who must certainly have helped her in her work. Yet despite Herrad's silence on these practical matters, it is possible to piece together a picture of what work on the *Hortus* may have entailed from what is still known of the manuscript—its contents, their order, and the overall structure of the book. These allow some idea of the processes by which the *Hortus* must have been constructed, the stages of planning and organization and the types of resources, both material and human, that it required, and even a sense of the immediate context of the workshop in which the manuscript was produced. Insofar as they can be determined, these details support the striking authorial claim that Herrad made in her prologue to the manuscript, confirming that she was the mastermind of the *Hortus* project.

Organization: A "Single Sweet Honeycomb"

The first clue to the composition of the *Hortus* comes from Herrad's description of the manuscript as a "single sweet honeycomb" (*HD* no. 2). Like her bee metaphor, the honeycomb image was coded with important information concerning the manuscript's structure and organization, topics that Herrad does not explicitly address, but that were nonetheless carefully planned. As Carruthers points out, the honeycomb was a common metaphor for the organization of knowledge and was especially important in connection with the cognitive processes of memory training and recall.[1] The natural structure provided by the constituent cells of the honeycomb symbolized the organization and storage of knowledge, and its sweetness the pleasures of learning and divine wisdom. As such, Herrad's use of the honeycomb metaphor for the *Hortus* conveyed her sense both of the book's order and coherence and of its ultimate purpose: the education and spiritual edification of the women of Hohenbourg. Moreover, it underscores the essential unity of the *Hortus*, suggesting that Herrad saw the book as a coherent theological system, which shared with the honeycomb a certain order, symmetry, and logic. Like individual cells in a honeycomb, the many texts of the *Hortus* had been brought together to form a single structure, whose unity was ensured through the overarching structure of salvation history. Each of the manuscript's folios, from the Creation to the Last Judgment, contributed to this narrative, which was centered on the person of Christ and the work of salvation brought about by his incarnation and crucifixion. Herrad's fidelity to the outline of salvation history places the *Hortus* among other contemporary works of theology, including Honorius Augustodunensis's *Elucidarium* and Peter Lombard's *Sentences*, sources on which she relied heavily, as well as Hugh of St. Victor's *De sacramentis* and Hildegard's *Scivias*. Salvation history was equally significant for Rupert of Deutz, who saw in its progression from creation through redemption a way to understand the Trinity.

As with other salvation histories, Herrad's presentation contains roughly four sections. It begins with a typological reading of the Old Testament, followed by a largely narrative account of the person and the work of Christ and an allegorical reading of the Church as the *sponsa Christi*, and culminates in a consideration of Last Things. This fourfold division does not take into account the unusually distinct series of texts taken from Peter Lombard's *Sentences* (fols. 264r–94r) and the pseudo-Clementine *Recognitiones* (fols. 295r–308v), which follow the eschatological section of the manuscript. Nor can it be taken to represent the proportional emphases of the *Hortus*. Obviously, the narrative presentation of Christ's life formed the focal point of the manuscript, as it does of salvation history in general. Indeed, based on her examination of the images, Green suggests that the *Hortus* is a "great triptych whose centre is a narrative life of

Christ."[2] At the heart of the manuscript, the life of Christ presented an almost unbroken sequence of narrative images, most of which are no longer extant. What might the effect of this sustained visual cycle, page after page "glowing with gold and colour," as Green imagines, have been on the reader?[3] It is little wonder that the narrative of Christ's life was one of the most heavily illustrated sections of the entire *Hortus*; in terms of its salvific message, it was also the most significant.

Herrad's organization of the *Hortus* according to the unfolding narrative of salvation history compensates to some extent for the manuscript's lack of book or chapter divisions, finding tools that would have appeared in several of her sources. Since the developments of Christian history would be well known to any Christian person, religious or lay, the structure of salvation history would have made the most basic finding tools largely unnecessary. No one would have thought, for instance, to look for Joshua and the Spies in Canaan (fol. 53r) before the Israelites in the Sinai desert (fol. 40), or for Dives and Lazarus (fol. 123r–v) before the rejection of Christ at the Synagogue in Nazareth (fol. 107v). The biblical narrative dictated its own order, which, with few exceptions, was maintained in the *Hortus*.[4] Herrad's genius was to make this order highly visible. The manuscript's images provided an obvious and practical structure to the book and could be used to navigate its pages.[5] The image of the Israelites dancing around the golden calf while Moses met with God at the summit of Mount Sinai (fol. 40v), for instance, provided an easy reference point for the account of the Exodus, details of which were then explored in texts from Honorius, the Bible, the *Glossa ordinaria*, and Peter Comestor's *Historia scholastica*. Similarly, the now-missing image of the spies in Canaan, most likely with their bountiful cluster of grapes, pomegranates, and figs, would have marked the arrival of the Israelites in Canaan. No less impressive is the presentation of Judith as the deliverer of her city, Bethulia: who could forget the images of Judith, with Holofernes's head cradled in her sleeve, and later on a pike displayed above the city walls (fol. 60r)?[6]

Other images, which did not perform a narrative function, but required interpretation, could also serve as "markers" in the text. Most notable were those that formed part of the striking psychomachia cycle, which extended across five consecutive openings (fols. 199v–204r). Equally useful were the full-page *Philosophia* (fol. 32r; plate 9) and Ladder of Virtues (fol. 215v; plate 5) images, which in their beauty and monumentality would not easily have been forgotten. Even though these images were not illustrations of biblical events, they could nonetheless serve as finding tools within the manuscript, since their proper interpretation was bounded by their place within the narrative of salvation history: the psychomachia cycle taught the reality of spiritual warfare at the outset of the *Ecclesia* section; the *Philosophia* image warned against the misuse of knowledge in the wake of the fall; and the Ladder of Virtues taught contempt for the world within the context of the contemporary church. Clear proof of Herrad's intent that the images should serve as finding tools is provided in an excerpt from the *Gemma animae*. A marginal note advises the reader: "Read also in the sentences of Peter Lombard, the rubrics at the end *after the Bosom of Abraham* [my italics], concerning ecclesiastical orders, from this place: *Nunc ad considerationem*, until: *Cum alia sacramenta*."[7] The reading in question is likely *HD* no. 1019, *De ordinibus ecclesiasticis* (*Sentences*, IV, d. 24, c. 1, 2), an excerpt that was included in the block of texts following the final *Hortus* image—the Bosom of Abraham (fol. 263v). Herrad's marginal note instructs her reader to turn to the Bosom of Abraham image—which was obviously toward the end of the manuscript since it depicted the rest of the just at the end of time—and from there to locate the appropriate section in the *Sentences*.

Elsewhere in the manuscript, Herrad used images to mark transitions from one section to another.[8] The transition from the Old Testament to the Life of Christ is marked through a section of almost twenty folios (fols. 67r–84r), beginning with a double-sided folio of paired *rotae*, each of which constitutes a typological commentary on the connection between Old and New Testament (fol. 67r–v; plates 11–12).[9] Following these *rotae* are excerpts from the *Speculum ecclesiae*, which provide a textual recapitulation of the Old Testament in keeping with the typological emphasis of the image, to which they are clearly linked. At the beginning of the text section, Herrad explains, "here begin the mysteries of the Old Testament which the previous pictures illustrate" (*Incipiunt mysteria quedam veteris Testamenti que elucidant antecedentem picturam . . .*) (*HD* no. 229). Similarly, the end of this first transition, which indicates the beginning of the Christological section, is marked by the Leviathan image, which provides a visual commentary on Christ's dual nature and leads into the narrative of his life (fol. 84r; plate 8). A second transition, between the Christological and the ecclesiological sections, is similarly visually delineated: the transitional section is bounded by parallel images of baptism—first of Synagogue being baptized by Peter (fol. 167v) and then of an Ethiopian woman (*Ecclesia*) being baptized by Paul (fol. 199r). As Curschmann points out, these two transitions were designed intentionally as parallel sections within the manuscript: both include historical recapitulations that Herrad selected from Freculph's *Chronicle* in such a way that the second section picks up almost exactly where the first had left off (*HD* nos. 268–95 and *HD* nos. 705–7).

Herrad also used images to mark a progression within the narrative of salvation history: turning the page moved the reader from one moment in the narrative to another. An example of this technique is provided in the first two images in the manuscript, which appear on opposite sides of a double-sided painted folio leaf (fol. 3). Coming after only one full folio of texts (fol. 2r–v), the first image confronts the reader with a depiction of the first day of creation. God the creator is shown in the top half of the folio, displaying an open book on his lap, in the act of creation. Directly below him a youthful and comely Lucifer is flanked by angels. Lucifer's proximity to the Father is palpable but, of course, impermanent. His rebellion is not yet inevitable. However, with a turn of the page, Lucifer plots rebellion, and is expelled from Heaven. Like an early animation shown in frames, Lucifer's downfall occurs in stages: he appears first as the guardian cherub of Ezekiel 28:14, then he plots rebellion, and finally he plunges to destruction. With the turn of the page, the reader sets into motion the cycle of sin and salvation with which the entire *Hortus* is concerned. Indeed, by turning the page and initiating Lucifer's transformation, the reader is made complicit in the ensuing narrative.

Constructing the *Hortus*

As the preceding discussion suggests, the *Hortus* was a carefully planned and executed project, which was the result of several decades of work. Much of this work must have preceded the actual physical construction of the manuscript. Before Herrad started writing, or even taking notes, she must have read widely and systematically among works of contemporary theology. She may even have drawn inspiration from the sorts of composite manuscripts being produced in Bavaria and to which the *Hortus* bears some resemblance.[10] This first phase of work already presupposes an elite intellectual culture at Hohenbourg with access to a wide range of books as well as parchment and ink for note taking. Obviously, the most important factor at this stage was Herrad's library access. The way in which she selected texts—often picking and choosing individual sentences rather than complete sections—demonstrates that she must have worked with full copies of many of her sources, and certainly all of her most important ones. With few exceptions, Herrad's use of her sources excludes the possibility that she worked from florilegia or similar collections of excerpts. Given the resources that the project required in these planning stages and the tremendous cost of the project, Herrad would have needed the support of Relinde and the other women of Hohenbourg. The cost of the project may explain why work on the manuscript took so long—money would have been needed to restore the provisions of parchment and ink that it required.[11]

The second phase of the project required that Herrad sift through the texts that she had read, selecting some for inclusion in the *Hortus* and rejecting others, all the while refining her plan for the manuscript. It is here that Herrad's editorial skill can best be seen. Since she wished to avoid duplication of topics, Herrad chose between her primary sources when they treated the same subjects. Her choices reflect her desire to include only the most relevant and recent discussions as well as her ability to determine which discussions those were. So, although two of her core sources, the *Elucidarium* and the *Sentences*, both included sections on the sacraments, Herrad omitted Honorius's treatment of the Eucharist, baptism, and marriage, in favor of Peter Lombard, whose discussion was more current. Her omission of aspects of Honorius's sacramental theology is made all the more striking since she imported almost the entire *Elucidarium* into the *Hortus*, excluding only those topics that she realized had been better addressed by Peter Lombard. Her handling of the *Gemma animae* and *De divinis officiis* demonstrates a similar judgment; although the contents of these texts often overlapped, Herrad was careful to avoid duplication. Among other things, she turned to Rupert for his discussion of baptism and Easter, which appears in the *Hortus* between the burial and resurrection of Christ (fols. 151v–58v),[12] and to the *Gemma animae* for Honorius's treatment of the church, its dedication, and the orders of clergy and laypeople, subjects which appear in several long blocks of text on folios 228r–33v.

Given that this process of selection occurred before work on the *Hortus* proper had begun, Herrad must have taken detailed notes as she read, documenting her selections either in a notebook, on wax tablets, or even on the source manuscript itself.[13] This stage differentiates her work from that of Lambert of St. Omer, who seems to have worked directly onto his fair copy of the *Liber floridus*, probably because he lacked adequate materials for a rough draft.[14] One indication that Herrad did work from notes is provided toward the end of the *Hortus* in the Peter Lombard and pseudo-Clementine *Recognitiones* section, which Curschmann argues may represent an unrevised insertion of Herrad's preliminary notes into the final manuscript.[15] The texts in this section appear in their original order and include neither interpolations nor images, omissions that are uncharacteristic of Herrad's editorial practice. The distinctiveness of the section suggests that it may represent a preliminary stage in the development of the *Hortus* project: these may be the notes that Herrad took as she read.

In tandem with her reading and selection of textual extracts, Herrad must have worked to determine the group of images that form the core of the manuscript. However, her silence on this subject is absolute; she offers no discussion of the purpose of the images or of the way in which they were chosen, a fact that is surprising given their centrality to the structure of the *Hortus* and the communication of its message. It is possible that Herrad was confined by her own symbolic presentation: the bee metaphor does not expand, nor does she expand it, to include the process by which she selected the manuscript's images. It is equally possible that her silence on the subject of the *Hortus* images signaled her refusal to apologize for them, a common practice in other works from this period. The *Hortus* avoids the traditional justification of images as "books for the illiterate."[16]

Despite Herrad's silence, it is clear that she selected, shaped, and in some cases created the *Hortus* images based on an extensive repertory. The visual sophistication of the manuscript's images is suggestive of Hohenbourg's deep involvement in the world beyond the cloister, whether through its connections to the emperor, the periodic admission of such noble women as Sibylle of Sicily, the implied connection with Marbach, or the network of book lending in which the monastery must have participated. Unlike the "repetitive, unskilled craftsmanship" of some later medieval illustrated prayer books for women, which Hamburger cites as evidence for "the paucity of models in an enclosed environment," the *Hortus* was a work of visual, as well as textual, complexity.[17] The influence of Byzantine models on the manuscript is marked; Green notes similarities to the Cotton Genesis (especially in the Adam and Eve cycle, fol. 17), the Byzantine Octateuchs (fols. 34–54), and the lost frescoes of Regensburg (c. 1166–1184) (fols. 112r, 241r, 261v), as well as others.[18] The master artist obviously had several manuscripts close at hand from which to draw visual inspiration.[19]

Phase three of the *Hortus* project involved delicate editorial work:

Herrad shaped the texts that she had selected in order to prepare them for the new context of the *Hortus*. On the most basic level, this meant removing them from their original textual framework and subordinating them to the thematic plan of the *Hortus*. Rather than copying texts sequentially, Herrad skipped back and forth in her sources so that even verses from the Bible are cited out of their original order. This sort of reorganization is most apparent in her use of Honorius's *Elucidarium*, which, like the *Hortus*, was organized according to the narrative of salvation history. Although she copied almost the entire text, she shuffled excerpts from it so that they do not appear sequentially in the *Hortus*. Similarly, Herrad subordinated the *Speculum ecclesiae* to the plan of salvific history that was outlined in the *Hortus*, rather than including its sermons as they originally appear, according to the liturgical calendar. Herrad's creative use of the *Speculum* is most clear in her recapitulation of the Old Testament (fols. 68r–72v; *HD* nos. 229–60), which is comprised of *Speculum* excerpts. Even though the *Speculum* provides the content for this section, Herrad did not simply lift excerpts sequentially, but chose them from sermons scattered throughout Honorius's text and then rearranged them according to her plan for the transition to the life of Christ. This "shuffling" is clear proof that Herrad did not simply copy from her sources, but rather that she read, sifted, and reorganized them—in literal obedience to Seneca's injunction to "imitate the bee."[20]

In addition to reordering her sources, Herrad edited them either to remove indications of their original context or to add introductory material that would aid in their understanding by the women of Hohenbourg. Sermons were transferred from direct address to a narrative voice, while pointed temporal references were muted—*hodie* (today) is generally removed and, in those cases in which identification of a feast or saint's day was necessary to the sense of the text, replaced by a generic reference. In many cases, Herrad prefaced her sermon excerpts with a short introduction that provided the sort of background information that would have been clear to its original audience from its position within the church calendar.[21] In certain cases, she also added material that was relevant to Hohenbourg, as, for instance, in the case of the list of female saints excerpted from Honorius's *Speculum ecclesiae* (*HD* no. 700). While the original list had included such virgin martyrs as Tecla, Cecilia, Agatha, and Agnes, Herrad added names that would have been more familiar to the women of Hohenbourg: Odile, the legendary founder of the monastery and patron saint of Alsace, Waltpurg, who had been associated with Boniface's circle and whose cult was especially strong in Bavaria, and Brigid, the famed Irish saint. These changes, like the German glosses that appear throughout the manuscript, were designed to make the work as a whole more familiar to its audience at Hohenbourg. Only in a few cases does Herrad's editorial practice break down; isolated excerpts from Honorius's sermons address readers of the *Hortus* as Honorius must have addressed his original audience—as *karissimi*, or even simply, "brothers."[22] These rare lapses were most likely the result of scribal error.

Herrad's use of textual excerpts is the final and most clear manifestation of her authorship: she extracted from her sources only the material that served her purpose and presentation of salvation history. The excerpts that she chose were included in the *Hortus* for particular pieces of information and not for the broader context or purpose that they had served in their original location. In the case of the *Speculum ecclesiae*, this meant that Herrad extracted the biblical narrative and allegorical interpretation from Honorius's sermons and left behind his larger message. For example, his sermon for the second Sunday in Lent provided information for a short section, *De transmigratione Babilonis* (*HD* no. 265), in which the Babylonian captivity was read allegorically as a battle between pride, represented by Nebuchadnezzar, and faith, hope, and charity, symbolized by the three walls surrounding Jerusalem. His sermon for the first Sunday after Pentecost offered a section that appears under the title *De David et Golia* (*HD* no. 258), and that presents David, who is glossed as Christ, the "true David," using a slingshot representing Christ's humanity and a rock representing his divinity in order to defeat the devil.[23] As with the *Speculum ecclesiae*, Herrad's use of the *Gemma animae* and Rupert's *De divinis officiis* extended beyond textual reorganization. In order to shape excerpts from these works for their new purpose, Herrad divorced them from their liturgical context. All three works were incorporated into the *Hortus* by subject, rather than according to the liturgical year, as they had been composed. Similarly she mined the *Historia scholastica* for information concerning the Old Testament, particularly the tabernacle and priestly vestments (*HD* nos. 157–70, 198–99), and the *Summarium Heinrici* for German and Latin glosses, which appear throughout the *Hortus*. The two *vitae* that she included were also selected for specific content. Rather than providing biographical information, the *Vita Leonardi* contributed a discussion of creation (*HD* no. 31) and the *Vita Silvestri* a section detailing the passion of Christ (*HD* no. 493).

To view the *Hortus* simply as a compilation is to miss the tremendous care with which Herrad selected and shaped her textual extracts. This care is most clear in her treatment of Honorius's *Speculum ecclesiae*, the work to which she turned most often. Comparison of *HD* no. 420 with the original *Speculum* text, to take one example, shows Herrad choosing certain sentences and passing over others, and even over entire paragraphs, reducing the text by about half as she excerpted it for inclusion in the *Hortus*.[24] In other cases, a single source text was divided between several different excerpts in the *Hortus*, as in the case of Honorius's sermon *De omnibus sanctis*. From the first part of the sermon, Herrad selected the texts that appear in the *Hortus* as *HD* no. 700. From the second, she chose the text of *HD* no. 241. The split between the two sections is sharp: *HD* no. 700 ends only the sentence before *HD* no. 241 begins.[25] Similarly, Honorius's sermon *De inventione sanctae crucis* provided textual material for *HD* nos. 519 (taken in three separate sections), 95, 230, 236, 244, 247, 250 (the text is missing), and 520 (taken in two separate sections). Again, there were no overlaps, an achievement that points to the care with which Herrad selected her excerpts, and the certainty that she kept a note, possibly on the manuscript of the *Speculum* itself, of the sections that she had already copied.[26] Of course, in a work of this size some duplication was unavoidable; still, duplication was fairly minimal proportional to the number and extent of the *Hortus* excerpts.[27]

Just as interesting as those instances in which Herrad took a single sermon from the *Speculum* and divided it among several *Hortus* texts are those cases in which a single excerpt reflects the careful blending of different sections from a single source text. One example, *HD* no. 11, *De sancta Trinitate*, blends texts from some seven places in Honorius's *Elucidarium*, a clear indication that Herrad did more than simply copy her sources directly. In other cases, a single excerpt in the *Hortus* blends texts from several disparate sources. *HD* no. 456, although entitled *In Speculo ecclesiae*, is just such a blend, which brought together selections from both Honorius and Rupert. Less than half of the text as we have it now is from the *Speculum ecclesiae*; the rest is drawn from two places in Rupert's *De divinis officiis*. This blending of source texts is most clear in Herrad's use of the *Summarium Heinrici*. In addition to her practice of combining source texts, Herrad's use of the *Summarium* as a source for both Latin and German glosses meant that most excerpts in the *Hortus* were composites in one way or another.

Herrad's deft handling of her sources is part of the process by which the nectar of her sources was transformed into honey. Obviously, she did not subscribe to the idea that altering her source texts was unethical or, worse, iniquitous. Although Alcuin had warned scribes against interfering with the sacred texts they copied and Hildegard had laid a curse on anyone who tried to change her inspired words, Herrad selected, cut, edited, and altered her sources with apparent impunity. Rarely do excerpts appear as blocks of text, as in the case of the Peter Lombard section toward the end of the manuscript. Instead, they were meticulously gathered, in many cases sentence by sentence, and then blended together seamlessly into the *Hortus*. Most of these so-called excerpts were in fact a skillful précis of the original. The result was that few of Herrad's textual "flowers" are immediately recognizable in their new context. In part this is because they have been selected and edited in such a way as to highlight only one aspect—for instance the Babylonian exile, or the allegorical meaning of the battle between David and Goliath. However, Herrad also directed her readers toward the particular interpretation she wished to emphasize through the titles that she used to introduce each excerpt. For works such as the *Speculum ecclesiae* and *Elucidarium*, which were without chapter divisions, Herrad supplied her own titles.[28] Nichols cautions against discounting the interpretive importance of titles, commenting that, "the rubric . . . does not simply 'explain' or describe what is to be found in the miniature or passage it introduces. Appropriating to itself the role of commentary or directed reading, the rubric focuses attention at specific moments, telling us what it is we are to see in the visual scene or laying out the narrative thrust of the verbal text."[29] According to this argument, even Herrad's titles were interpretative tools, designed to guide still further the reading of texts that she had already selected and edited according to her plan. Nichols's observation is particularly appropriate to the *Hortus*, which has tended to be examined as a compilation, with little recognition of the ways in which the whole manuscript—image, text, gloss, page layout, and rubric—functions together to convey Herrad's message.[30]

Herrad's attention to the structure and organization of the *Hortus* is most clear in the fact that the manuscript was not originally bound, a fact that allowed for ongoing additions and revisions in order to refine its message and enhance its internal coherence.[31] The high proportion of half leaves and interpolations, which Evans estimates at about twenty percent of the whole, together with an independent booklet (fols. 309–315), and what Green suggests was an intrusive quire (fols. 10–16), indicate that work on the manuscript continued, even once its basic structure was in place.[32] There was no "fixed" text. Instead, the manuscript was subject to

continuous revision, possibly even in response to the practical experience
of using it within the classroom at Hohenbourg—in which case the revisions may guide us toward a greater understanding of how the manuscript
was used. Since work on the *Hortus* appears to have drawn largely to a
close by 1191, some five years before Herrad died, these additions and interpolations must, with few exceptions, be attributed to her. This conclusion is strengthened by the fact that some obvious additions, for instance
the image on folio 176v, appeared in the same hand as original parts of the
manuscript.[33]

A final manifestation of the organizing spirit that marked Herrad's
selection and coordination of texts is the skillful way in which she integrated text and image throughout the manuscript. Few folios were devoted either to text or to image, but instead displayed some combination
of the two so that the message of the *Hortus* was presented at the intersec-
tion of the textual and the visual, with image glossing text, and vice versa.
Only in rare instances did either text or image predominate. The psychomachia cycle (fols. 199v–204r) is one example of an entirely visual presentation, in this case of the battle between the Vices and the Virtues that
introduces the *Ecclesia* section. The images here are presented devoid of
almost all text, except for the tituli that identify the personified Virtues
and Vices and certain explanatory sentences. Similarly, the section of the
manuscript that follows the image of the Bosom of Abraham (fol. 263v) is
devoted entirely to texts, selections from Peter Lombard's *Sentences* and
the pseudo-Clementine *Recognitiones.* In general, though, text and image
are mutually dependent. As Curschmann puts it, in the *Hortus* "picture
and text are made for each other and linked as equal partners in pursuit of
a common goal."[34]

Herrad's practice of interspersing text with image extended into the
images themselves, which were often heavily glossed, so that they needed
literally to be "read" to be understood.[35] Glosses on the *Hortus* images
fall into certain categories. Sometimes they were single words that identified aspects of the image. For the most part these are demonstrative rather
than interpretive, although in some cases the gloss provides the key to the
allegorical meaning of the image, as for instance in the Leviathan image,
where the "hook" that catches the Leviathan is clearly labeled as the
"hook of divinity" (*aculeus divinitatis*)—indicating that the reader should
interpret the image as an allegory for the triumph of the cross (*HD* Cat.
No. 101; fol. 84r; plate 8). In the *Hortus* image it is Christ's divinity, dis-
guised by the weakness of his human flesh, which is the hook that catches

the Leviathan.[36] Like the Leviathan, Satan had been deceived by Christ's humanity at Calvary and had therefore been unable to recognize his divinity. Short glosses might also provide liturgical indications for the feast day on which a particular biblical character or event was remembered. So, for instance, the image of the burial of Moses is glossed with the note: "II. Non. Sept. obitus Moysi prophete" (fol. 54r; *HD* Cat. No. 76).[37]

A second type of gloss comprises textual extracts, most often biblical verses but also paraphrases or excerpts from Herrad's sources, or short verses or sequences that are inscribed within or alongside the image.[38] Source texts were taken primarily from Honorius's *Speculum ecclesiae*, which inspired several of Herrad's images, although excerpts from his *Gemma animae* and *Elucidarium* also appear, as do texts from and references to the *Sentences* and Rupert's *De divinis officiis*. In general, these sections provide allegorical explanations for images that might otherwise be read as narrative. A section from Honorius's *Gemma animae* inscribed alongside an image of Abraham preparing to sacrifice Isaac (*HD* Cat. No. 45; fol. 36r), reminds the reader that, in his willingness to sacrifice Isaac, Abraham signifies God the Father. Although Isaac escaped death, the flesh of Christ was sacrificed, just like the ram that took Isaac's place. However, Christ's divinity—always Honorius's and Herrad's favorite point—escaped unscathed.

A third type of gloss provided cross-references to texts found elsewhere in the manuscript, often to Peter Lombard's *Sentences* but sometimes also to sections from Rupert's *De divinis officiis*. In two cases, an image contains the explicit instruction to "read here" (*hic lege*), with the text to be read provided (*HD* Cat. Nos. 4 and 6; fols. 3v and 8r).[39] In other cases, only the name of the author or work to be referenced was provided, in which case the gloss simply says *Rupertus* or *Ex sententiis Petri Lombardi*, with no further information provided. In these cases, it is not clear how the reader was to locate the text that Herrad intended.[40] This sort of cross-referencing is equally common between texts, so that a section from Honorius on baptism (*Gemma animae* III, 113–16) is linked through a gloss to a similar discussion excerpted from Peter Lombard (= *Sentences*, IV, d. 2–7).[41] In these cases, the gloss provided a suggestion for further reading: "read also" (*lege etiam*) with reference to the suggested text. Finally, glosses might echo or repeat nearby excerpts, furthering the textual embeddedness of the image. I mention here only a few of the many instances in the manuscript: *HD* no. 308 (fol. 83v) was evidently repeated on the facing-page image of the Leviathan image (fol. 84r; *HD*

PLATES

Plate 1. Monastery of Hohenbourg, 1: Foundation (*HD* fol. 322v). By permission, the Warburg Institute and the Bibliothèque nationale de France.

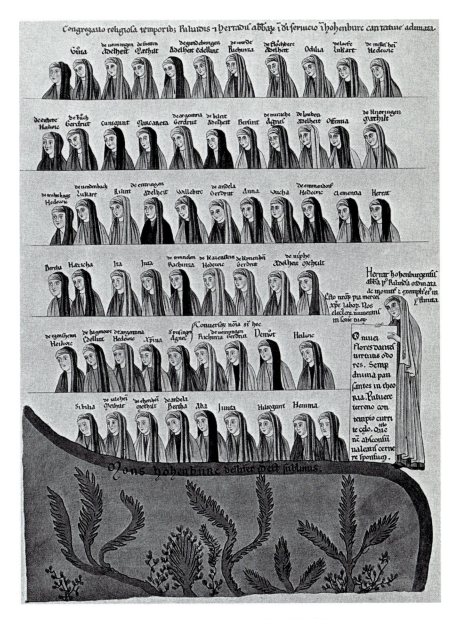

Plate 2. Monastery of Hohenbourg, 2: Congregation (*HD* fol. 323r). By permission, the Warburg Institute and the Bibliothèque nationale de France.

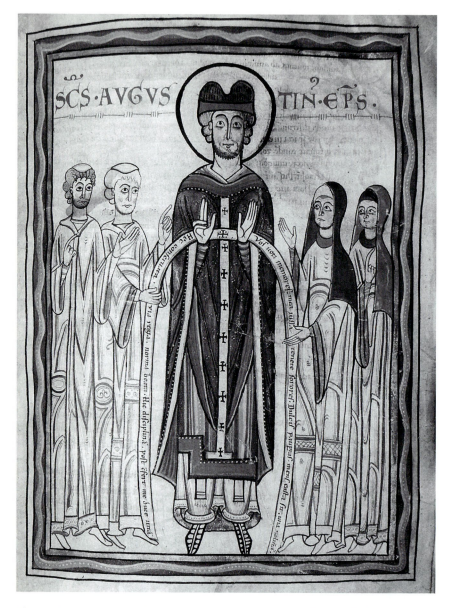

Plate 3. St. Augustine, with Canons and Canonesses (*Guta-Sintram Codex*, Bibliothèque du Grand Séminaire de Strasbourg, MS 37, p. 11). Artwork J.-Cl. Stamm. Copyright Inventaire général / ADAGP, 1974.

Plate 4. Guta and Sintram with the Virgin Mary (detail, *Guta-Sintram Codex*, Bibliothèque du Grand Séminaire de Strasbourg, MS 37, p. 9). Artwork J.-Cl. Stamm. Copyright Inventaire général / ADAGP, 1974.

Plate 5. Ladder of Virtues (*HD* fol. 215v). By permission, the Warburg Institute and the Bibliothèque nationale de France.

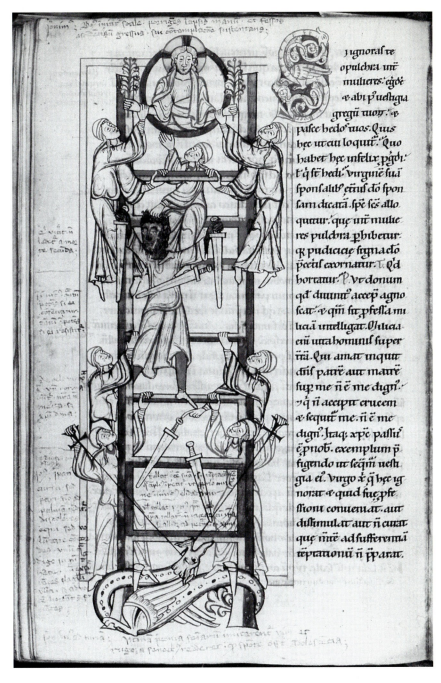

Plate 6. Ladder (*Speculum virginum*, Historisches Archiv der Stadt Köln, W 276a, fol. 78v). By permission, Historisches Archiv der Stadt Köln.

Plate 7. Virgin Mary and Evangelist John as Guardian of Virgins (*HD* fol. 176v). By permission, the Warburg Institute and the Bibliothèque nationale de France.

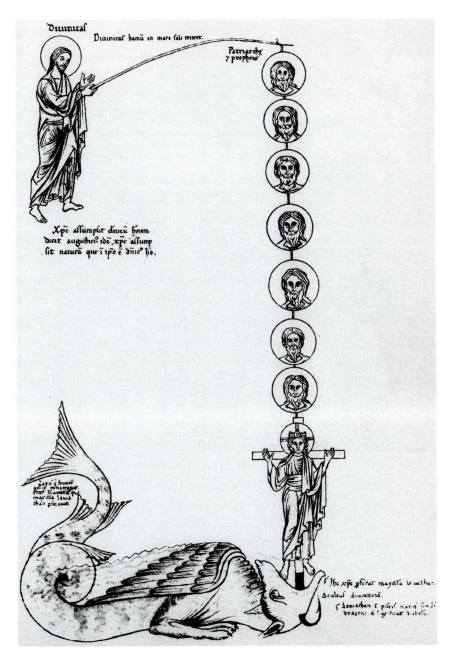

Plate 8. God Capturing Leviathan, Christ on the Cross as the Hook (*HD* fol. 84r).
By permission, the Warburg Institute and the Bibliothèque nationale de France.

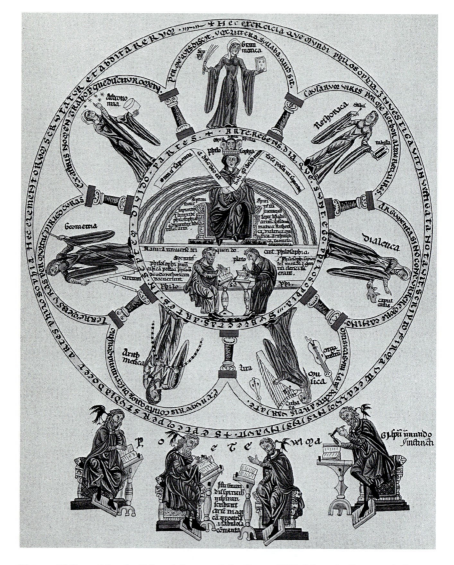

Plate 9. Philosophia, the Liberal Arts, and the Poets (*HD* fol. 32r). By permission, the Warburg Institute and the Bibliothèque nationale de France.

Plate 10. Bronze bowl depicting Philosophia with Representatives of the Liberal Arts (sketch by Joseph Aldenkirchen; Xanten, Domschatzkammer, inv. No. Hölker: B-4). By permission, Domschatzkammer, Xanten.

Plate 11. Old and New Testament Sacrifices United (*HD* fol. 67r). By permission, the Warburg Institute and the Fondation de l'Oeuvre Notre-Dame, Strasbourg.

Plate 12. Christ as King and High Priest Surrounded by Virtues (*HD* fol. 67v). By permission, the Warburg Institute and the Fondation de l'Oeuvre Notre-Dame, Strasbourg.

Plate 13. Structure of the Church (*HD* fol. 225v). By permission, the Warburg Institute and the Bibliothèque nationale de France.

Plate 14. House of Wisdom (*Speculum virginum*, British Library, Arundel 44, fol. 114v). By permission, the British Library.

Plate 15. Hell (*HD* fol. 255r). By permission, the Warburg Institute and the Bibliothèque nationale de France.

Plate 16. Avaritia Gathering the Spoils (detail, *HD* fol. 202v). By permission, the Warburg Institute and the Bibliothèque nationale de France.

Plate 17. Chariot of Avaritia (*HD* fol. 203v). By permission, the Warburg Institute and the Bibliothèque nationale de France.

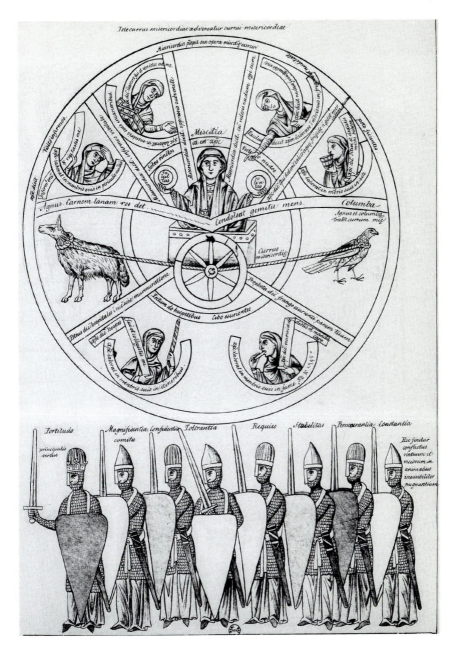

Plate 18. Chariot of Misericordia (*HD* fol. 204r). By permission, the Warburg Institute and the Bibliothèque nationale de France.

Cat. No. 101); part of *HD* no. 719 (fol. 211r) is repeated on the image of Solomon receiving the Queen of Sheba on folio 209v (*HD* Cat. No. 292); *HD* no. 836 (fol. 245v) is repeated on the image of the Celestial Court on folio 244r (*HD* Cat. No. 317); and *HD* no. 881 (fol. 257r–v) is repeated in the image of the Whore of Babylon on folio 258r (*HD* Cat. No. 340). In these cases, the repetition of a certain text or text fragment was intentional and served Herrad's pedagogical purpose: by connecting a particular excerpt to a nearby image through a linking text, Herrad underscored the point of contact between the two and strengthened the interpretation of each in light of the other. In the case of the typological image on folio 67r (plate 11), key inscriptions are repeated in *HD* nos. 224 and 226 on the facing page, possibly to ensure that they could be read more easily than they might in the image itself. Often, as with texts inscribed around the circumference of *rotae*, the repeated text functioned as the image's "motto."[42]

Herrad's integration of text and image meant that the textual and the visual could literally gloss each other, so that an image might promote a particular reading of the text, or a text encourage a certain interpretation of an image.[43] This is certainly the case with the Judith image (fol. 60r), which at first appears to serve a purely narrative function. However, a text on the facing page, loosely taken from the *Speculum ecclesiae*, reminds the viewer that Judith's victory over the tyrant Holofernes is to be understood as the victory of Christ's flesh over the devil (*HD* no. 208).[44] In the same way, Herrad explains the purpose of the sequence of images that follows the psychomachia cycle in a gloss on folio 221v: "Solomon and the wheel of fortune and the ladder and the sirens admonish us concerning contempt for the world" (*HD* Cat. No. 299).[45] Although these images were accompanied by texts, Herrad does not mention them, since in this case it was the images that functioned as the primary vehicle for her message of *contemptus mundi*. Similarly, her purpose in the psychomachia cycle was to make visible the invisible spiritual battle between virtue and vice, a goal that could largely be achieved through image alone.[46]

The most striking examples of visual exegesis—the use of images to summarize texts, or even to gloss or replace them[47]—are provided in the manuscript's diagrammatic illustrations and, most notably, in the typological *rotae* that mark the beginning of the transition from Old to New Testament (fol. 67r–v, plates 11–12). These images have been examined by Krüger and Runge, who note the intrinsic typological unity of both Testaments that they present. Other images allowed Herrad to move beyond her textual extracts, so that she could insert her own editorial comment into the manuscript. This is particularly true of the Cleansing of the Temple (fol. 238r), which presented reforming ideas that transcended those of her textual sources. These images communicated complex ideas economically, fulfilling the role envisioned by the author of the *Rhetorica ad Herennium*: "Often we encompass the record of an entire matter by one notation, a single image."[48]

The extent to which text and image are interconnected in the *Hortus* strengthens the argument that Herrad was the sole mastermind of the entire project, the *spiritus rector*, as Curschmann describes her.[49] As mastermind, Herrad was equally responsible for the visual and the textual elements of the manuscript. Since the visual and the textual function together throughout the *Hortus* as two aspects of a single, coherent spiritual message, we must consider the images as part of her work if we are to accept the responsibility that she claims for the selection, editing, and organization of the *Hortus* texts. It is unlikely that Herrad chose the texts of the *Hortus* without at the same time determining the images that form its core, especially since it was particularly through the images that she presented her editorial commentary, highlighting some sections of the manuscript and offering reinterpretations of others. Many of the themes that she stressed, both in her own poems and in her textual selections, are reinforced through the manuscript's images. The reality of the devil and of spiritual warfare that appears in Herrad's introductory poem, *Salve cohors virginum* (*HD* no. 1), is expressed visually in the psychomachia cycle (fols. 199v–204r), as well as in the Ladder of Virtues (fol. 215v; plate 5) and *Ecclesia* image (fol. 225v; plate 13), which shows demons and angels battling on the roof of the church while the souls of those within hang in the balance. The bitterness of life on earth, the temptations of the devil, and the need for rescue from worldly dangers, additional themes of Herrad's poetry, appear in other images. The consequences of failing to resist sin are laid out in an image on folio 123v, where demons are shown waiting at Dives's deathbed in order to seize his soul, while angels watch over Lazarus who lies poor and naked on his doorstep. The wages of sin are also emphasized in the Judgment cycle (fols. 247v, 251r–v, 253r–v) and vivid Hell image (fol. 255r; plate 15). Similarly, the potential of each soul to fall from grace— whether through pride, avarice, or disobedience—is emphasized in the motif of the falling figure, which recurs throughout the manuscript: Lucifer falling from heaven, Pride (*Superbia*) from her horse in the psychomachia cycle (fol. 199v), the figures on Fortune's wheel (fol. 215r), the lay couple, cleric, monk, recluse, and hermit who fall from the Ladder of Virtues (fol. 215v; plate 5), and finally the Whore of Babylon, who tumbles to her fiery punishment (fol. 258v).

There can be no question that the images and texts of the *Hortus* were chosen as part of a single process of selection, an observation that raises the question of Herrad's artistry: was she the artist as well as the intellectual architect of the *Hortus*? The combination of both roles in a single figure would not be unprecedented: the Augustinian canon Hugh of Fouilloy (d. 1172/4) might have designed the miniatures for his *Aviarum* and painted them as well.[50] Similarly, based on the interconnectedness of text and image within the *Liber floridus*, Derolez concludes that Lambert might have executed the manuscript's images in addition to writing its texts. He comments: "The pictures in the L.F. have such an eminent role in communicating the leading ideas of the book, they are so idiosyncratic and interwoven with the text, they so often replace the text as a medium, that they can hardly be the work of an artist other than the very man who conceived the book."[51] Lewis makes a similar argument in support of Matthew Paris's (d. 1259) role in designing the images that accompany his texts. She writes that "the whole corpus of marginal drawings appears to form a personal and highly inventive pictorial commentary on the text, too heavily larded with the distinctive eccentricities of the author to have been done by anyone else, even by an assistant working from preliminary sketches."[52] The same is true—even more true—of the *Hortus*.

Even so, the exact nature of Herrad's role in the visual component of the *Hortus* is difficult to determine. Many of the *Hortus* images draw from well-established traditions and were not, like the visual cycle of Hildegard's *Scivias*, new compositions. In some cases, images fused elements from several traditions, such that images were compiled just as texts were. Godwin notes that the Judith illustration was a fusion of three different cycles of Judith images, a fact that she attributes to "the evidently large library at Herrad's disposal."[53] The creative synthesis of these different visual traditions suggests both that the *Hortus* artists were well trained and conversant in various schools of representation and that the visual repertory to which they had access was extensive. As we have seen, the artists probably had several gospel books on hand. They may even have worked from a model book, as Cames has suggested. He proposes that three fragmentary leaves recovered from the flyleaves of Baroque manuscripts in the Freiburg Municipal Archives (now Freiburg Augustinermuseum Inv. No.

G 23/1a–c) may have formed part of a model book that inspired the *Hortus* images, a suggestion that has not been widely accepted.[54] Although many of the scenes that this book seems to have contained overlap those that appear in the *Hortus*, reliance on model books may not have been as widespread as some scholars have tended to think. Still, Herrad must have had access to a wide range of models, whether in other illuminated gospel books, wall paintings, or even through periodic contact with the itinerant artists who may have passed through Alsace.[55]

Whatever the situation, there can be little doubt that Herrad exerted control over the visual aspect of the manuscript, just as she determined its texts. Although we have no record of how she chose the *Hortus* images, the example of Ceraunia, wife of Bishop Namatius of Clermont, is instructive. In his *History of the Franks*, Gregory of Tours describes how Ceraunia commissioned a wall painting, chose the images it was to depict, and personally oversaw the work of the artists:

The wife of Namatius built the church of Saint Stephen in the suburb outside the walls of Clermont-Ferrand. She wanted it to be decorated with coloured frescoes. She used to hold in her lap a book from which she would read stories of events which happened long ago, and tell the workmen what she wanted painted on the walls.[56]

In the same way, Herrad must have suggested some of the *Hortus* images on the basis of texts that were significant to her. Indeed, while many of the *Hortus* images contain aspects that are reminiscent of earlier depictions, a significant minority may have been designed specifically for the manuscript, either in order to accompany an excerpt or to communicate an idea that is not made explicit in the text. For these images, no pictorial precedents are known. Examples include the depiction of the Journey of the Israelites on folio 51r (*HD* Cat. No. 67), the images of Ulysses and the Sirens on folio 221r–v (*HD* Cat. Nos. 297–99), and the image of Christ appearing to Peter and James on folio 160v (*HD* Cat. No. 220). Some images seem to have been directly inspired by Honorius Augustodunensis—Herrad's primary source. For others, Herrad must have drawn on visual models that were known to her—either directly, in the form of gospel books that were on hand, or indirectly, through her store of images and visual memories. The Microcosm image (fol. 16v) shares much in common, including many of its inscriptions, with a depiction in a *Glossarium* from Prüfening (c. 1158–65).[57] The *Philosophia* image (fol. 32r; plate 9) is paralleled in a twelfth-century bronze bowl from Horst (plate 10).[58]

Still other images were rare compositions or even entirely new creations: these include the lost Idolatry image (fol. 32v); the *rotae* that mark the transition between Old and New Testament (fol. 67r–v; plates 11–1 2); the baptisms of Synagoga and the Ethiopian woman (fols. 167v and 199r); the Virgin and John as guardian of virgins (fol. 176v; plate 7); the Solomon series (fols. 204v, 209r, 209v, 215r); the Cleansing of the Temple (fol. 238r); and the fall of the Whore of Babylon (fol. 258v), which Green calls a "superb new creation."[59]

Like all visual depictions, those in the *Hortus* were the result of a two-stage process, which involved first the design or selection of the images and then their execution. These two stages might have been distinct, as in the case of Ceraunia, who selected the subject matter of the images for the artists who then painted them. Or they might have been combined as in the case of Lambert of St. Omer, who most likely chose and painted the images of the *Liber floridus* himself. Obviously, Herrad played an important role in the first stage of this process—the selection of the images. On this basis, it is certainly appropriate to consider her as their designer, just as Hildegard of Bingen must be considered the designer of the images that accompany the *Scivias*. As Caviness concludes, "I believe that Hildegard can be credited with the quintessential part of creativity . . . , that is, *idea* or concept."[60] However, she notes that "a role as the designer of these pictures seems to be the last area of Hildegard's multimedia outpouring that has been denied to her by recent scholars, even though most posited her supervisory intervention in the process of 'illustration'."[61] Like Hildegard, Herrad supervised the entire construction of the *Hortus* and must be allowed the artistic as well as the intellectual credit to which she laid claim in her prologue.

More difficult to determine are Hildegard's and Herrad's roles in the second stage of the visual composition—execution. Again, Caviness comments, "a variety of unarticulated possibilities are hidden under the repeated formula that she [Hildegard] directed the production of this manuscript [*Scivias*]."[62] What might Herrad's role in the execution of the *Hortus* images have been? For Caviness, Hildegard was an artist in addition to a visionary and author.[63] Could it be that Herrad too was an artist as well as the conceptual designer of the *Hortus* images? In order to answer these questions, it is necessary to explore the evidence that we have for the *Hortus* scribes and artists, the nature of their working relationship, and the workshop in which the manuscript was produced.

The *Hortus* prologue is the logical starting point for questions concerning the construction of the manuscript. However, as we have already seen, Herrad does not name a collaborator in the project or give details concerning the identities of the scribes or artists who must have worked with her over the course of the project. With the exception of the role played by "divine inspiration"—which is never clearly defined—Herrad admits no assistance in her project. Nonetheless, it is plain that she had help: de Bastard notes the presence of three scribal hands in the manuscript, proof that Herrad was not responsible for the entire text. The presence of at least three hands in the miniatures suggests that the same is true of the manuscript's visual cycle.[64] Of course these six hands may have overlapped, so that a scribe also functioned as an artist, a situation that was not uncommon, as we have seen.[65]

Who were Herrad's collaborators? From the chronology of the project, we can assume that Herrad drew some support from Relinde in its planning stages, although she probably died around the point at which work on the construction of the manuscript began in earnest and so cannot be considered as one of the *Hortus* scribes or artists. However, Herrad must also have drawn on the talents of the other women at Hohenbourg, whether as scribes and artists, or as assistants and advisers in the intellectual work of the manuscript's planning stages. Some, perhaps all, of the *Hortus* scribes may have come from among the women of Hohenbourg, a proposal that is consistent with the activity of other nun-scribes in Alsace and elsewhere in southern Germany and Austria during the twelfth century.[66] Like Guta of Schwartzenthann, several female scribes can even be known by name; the most famous of these is Diemut of Wessobrunn, who copied more than forty books for Wessobrunn, the Hirsau reform community where she was a recluse, probably during the first half of the twelfth century.[67] As we saw in Chapter 1, it is likely that female scribes were active at Hohenbourg: members of the community most likely produced both the *Vita Odiliae* and the monastery's twelfth-century forgeries. Herrad also had support from Conrad and Hugo, and possibly also Godescallcus— men who, though unidentified, were probably canons at either St. Gorgon or Truttenhausen. Although there is no evidence to suggest that the involvement of these men extended beyond the composition of their poems, their participation in the project demonstrates that at least some of Herrad's collaborators came from beyond her own community.

The slightly earlier *Guta-Sintram Codex* showcases the sorts of collaboration that the *Hortus* may have involved. It is clear from the codex's dedication page, which shows Guta and Sintram together before the Vir-

gin, that Guta and Sintram worked together on the manuscript. The closeness of their working relationship is confirmed by the paleographical
evidence. Although Guta names herself as the scribe and Sintram as the
artist, she nonetheless records that Sintram had completed the texts of the
codex, "et ad finem usque perductum," indicating that in addition to his
artistic contribution, he had played a role in the scribal work of the manuscript.[68] In keeping with this scenario, two hands can be seen in the manuscript: hand A, which belonged to Guta, and hand B, which was most
likely that of Sintram.[69] The nature of their collaboration is suggested by
the alternation of their hands on a single page—a situation that occurs on
page 4, where the replacement of hand A by hand B occurred in the middle of a line. After switching, hand B continued to write until page 9, at
which point hand A reappeared. As Beach has argued, where paleographical evidence points to the presence of both men's and women's hands
within the same folio, and even within a single line, it is likely that collaboration occurred within a single scriptorium.[70]

In addition to Sintram, Guta acknowledges the help that she had received from two women in her community at Schwartzenthann: Trutwib
and Gisela.[71] The role played by these women in the manuscript's genesis
is unclear. Since only two primary hands are apparent in the manuscript—
those of Guta and Sintram—it is unlikely that Guta intended to acknowledge Trutwib and Gisela principally as scribes, although they may have
served a secondary scribal role. In addition to hands A and B, other hands
appear in the charters on page 2, the necrology, pages 96–110 of the martyrology, and possibly also the computus. These may well have been Trutwib's or Gisela's, or the hands of other anonymous Schwartzenthann
women.

The evidence of the *Guta-Sintram Codex* indicates that female scribes
were active in the circle of Augustinian houses to which Hohenbourg belonged and, moreover, that collaboration between men and women on
projects of book production was possible. It is certainly conceivable that
Herrad was herself one of the scribes whose hand is visible in the manuscript, just as it is possible that she was one of the manuscript's artists.
Although neither conjecture can be proven, all evidence points to a very
close working relationship between architect, scribe, and artist, suggestive
of Herrad's activity in each of these areas. Just as the integration of the
Hortus images suggests that the architect of the manuscript's images and
the architect of its texts must be one and the same, so too the physical
integration of text and image suggests that there must have been close

cooperation, if not actual overlap, between the manuscript's scribes and artists. Commenting particularly on folio 176v (plate 7), where the Virgin Mary, described as *contemptrix mundi*, appears together with John the Evangelist, depicted as the guardian of virgins (*custos virginum*), Green notes that the tasks of writing and illuminating were probably carried out in tandem. In her view, the outline of the miniature was first drawn onto the folio, after which the scribe copied the text, and then the artist painted the outlined miniature.[72] According to this scenario, the *Hortus* artists and scribes must have worked closely together, either in the same room, or in close enough proximity that the folios could easily be passed back and forth.[73] A similar integration of text and image is apparent in the text and images on folio 119r–v (*HD* Cat. Nos. 164–67). Here the text was written so that the words appeared directly beside the images to which they referred. The glossing of text on image and the direct references that link the two add further weight to the argument that the *Hortus* scribes and artists must have worked closely, and may even have overlapped, as does the ruling of folios designed to include both text and image. In these cases, the ruling would have had to accommodate the image—which was surely planned in advance of the text. If, as I have already argued, the composition of the *Hortus* required Herrad's direct oversight, then the manuscript must have been produced either near or at Hohenbourg and both the scribes and the artists must have been in close contact with her.

This observation has important implications for the *Hortus* workshop. The sort of cooperation between scribes and artists that the construction of the *Hortus* required continued for some fifteen years (ca. 1175–before 1191), suggesting that both groups would have had to be in residence either near, or even at, Hohenbourg for that entire time. Given the close working relationship that characterized the *Hortus* team, it is unlikely that the manuscript's artists could have been itinerant professionals, who contracted their work for specific projects. These sorts of artists could not have provided Herrad with the extended commitment and proximity that she required. Moreover, they would have moved on once the project had been completed. Evidence from the flabellum of Hohenbourg, a magnificent strip of illuminated parchment now in the British Library, demonstrates that the *Hortus* scribes and artists continued to work together on other projects.[74] On the basis of comparison between the flabellum and tracings from the *Hortus*, Green suggests that the flabellum artist was also responsible for certain scenes in the *Hortus*, including John the Baptist baptizing (fol. 98v) and the Queen of Sheba (fol. 209r–v).[75] Brown draws a similar conclusion from his examination of the paleographic evidence, suggesting that the flabellum scribe also worked on the *Hortus*. "Short though it is," he observes, "the inscription on the flabellum of Hohenbourg includes more than enough detailed points of likeness to the legends in HD to establish that the same scribe wrote both."[76] Finally, the subject of the flabellum—the life of John the Baptist—confirms the shared spiritual context of the two works. Devotion to John the Baptist was strong at Hohenbourg and is especially associated with Odile. Odile's devotion to John the Baptist is a feature of her *vita*, and is also recalled in the depiction of her in the *Hortus* (fol. 322v; plate 1). Not only does Odile appear immediately to John's left, but he is described as "St John the Baptist, whom St. Odile loved particularly, beyond all the other saints" (*S. Johannes baptista quem singulariter pre ceteris sanctis dilexit S. Odilia*) (*HD* Cat No. 345).

The overlap between the scribes and the artists of the flabellum and those of the *Hortus* makes it unlikely that Herrad could have relied on itinerant artists.[77] Although such artists may have had some role in the *Hortus*, possibly even sharing images from a model book as they traveled through Alsace, it is more likely that the *Hortus* artists were members either of the community at Hohenbourg, or that they were resident in the neighborhood—close enough to facilitate the sort of collaboration that the interdependence of text and image in the *Hortus* would have required. As we have seen, the *Guta-Sintram Codex* offers one model of collaboration between scribes and artists. Although Guta and Sintram had produced the codex some twenty years before work on the *Hortus* began, Sintram's community at Marbach continued to be known for its book illumination in the latter part of the twelfth century, at which time the Laon Evangeliary and the Freiburg Boethius were produced. Collaboration with Marbach, or with canons from Marbach now resident at Truttenhausen, is, therefore, a possible scenario in the illumination of the *Hortus*, although it must be treated cautiously since there are few stylistic similarities between the extant Marbach manuscripts and the *Hortus*.[78]

It is equally possible that Herrad contracted with lay artists in the vicinity of Hohenbourg to produce the images. At the female community of Obermünster in Regensburg between 1177 and 1183, the canonesses collaborated with professional artists in the production of a richly illuminated necrology.[79] Among the *familiares* associated with the female community, two painters are depicted.[80] These men may have been the two professional artists who had collaborated with the female scribes of the necrology, much as Sintram had collaborated with Guta.

Finally, it is possible that the *Hortus* images were produced at Hohenbourg by members of the community. Indeed, there are few other options that would have allowed for the degree of oversight that Herrad must have had in the selection and composition of images, the length of time that work on the manuscript required, and the sustained integration of text and image that the manuscript presents.[81] Alternative scenarios—which exclude the possibility that the Hohenbourg women were active as scribes and artists in the construction of the *Hortus*—create unnecessary complications. If the *Hortus* was not produced at Hohenbourg, then where was it produced? Would Herrad have been able to exert the sort of influence that the manuscript's texts and images demonstrate from a distance? And how would she have communicated with the artists?[82] There are no easy answers to these questions if the possibility of a Hohenbourg workshop is ruled out.[83]

Previous generations of scholars simply assumed that the *Hortus* scribes and artists were male. Resistance to accepting Herrad's artistry is still to a large extent based on the perceived incongruity of a female artist. And yet, female artists were certainly active at other Germanic monastic communities during the twelfth century. The otherwise unidentified Guda wrote and illuminated a collection of homilies, to which she attached both a self-portrait and a colophon naming herself as scribe and artist: "Guda peccatrix mulier scripsit quae pinxit hunc librum."[84] In addition to Guda, whose monastic affiliation is not known, female artists seem to have been active at Admont, where Seeberg argues that women painted the initials in the nuns' breviary.[85] Women may also have produced the Sélestat *liber precum* (ca. 1150), as Jeffrey Hamburger suggests.[86] In conjunction with the evidence for women's scribal activity, these examples suggest a context in which women were deeply involved in book production, and in particular in the production of illustrated books—for which it is possible, probable even, that they provided the images too.[87] The sustained and lengthy process required to produce the *Hortus*, together with Herrad's watchful involvement throughout the entire production effort, suggests that this was the case at Hohenbourg: women in Herrad's community would have been the most readily available source of scribes and artists for the work.

Regrettably, few ancillary sources exist that might shed greater light on the monastery of Hohenbourg in the period during which the *Hortus* was completed. There are no library catalogues, no letter collections, no narrative sources—no *vita*, for instance, of either Herrad or Relinde—and only the handful of charters discussed in Chapter 1. The *Hortus* is the only manuscript that can be securely identified with Hohenbourg, and the only known text from the monastery's twelfth-century library. However, we know from Herrad's testimony that she guided the composition and production of the *Hortus*, we know that female scribes were active in other female communities associated with Marbach in the twelfth century, and we know that female scribal activity was part of a more general increase in book production among reformed communities. It is true that we know nothing of scribal training at Hohenbourg and, lacking the paleographic evidence, cannot comment on the possibility of a school for scribes at the monastery. Nevertheless, comparative evidence from other female monastic communities with known scribes and scribal networks may assist us in developing a model of scribal activity at Hohenbourg.

One possible point of comparison is the monastery of Zwiefalten. Founded as a daughter house of Hirsau in 1089, Zwiefalten had already established a female community by 1100, in keeping with the Hirsau tradition of attention to the spiritual lives of women. Zwiefalten was also part of the circle of reformed houses to which Hohenbourg also belonged: the twelfth-century necrology of Zwiefalten is one of the few records of Relinde's death on 22 August.[88] The extent to which Relinde was known at Zwiefalten remains a mystery since there is no other indication of a direct connection between the two houses; it is possible that her death was reported simply through a *rotulus*, or circulating obituary scroll. However, by the time of Relinde's death, probably in 1176, Zwiefalten was already an important intellectual center, as the evidence of its extensive library indicates. Of the 285 manuscripts that have been identified with the community, some one hundred date from the twelfth century.[89] Many of these were illuminated, often with the sorts of diagrammatic images that appear in the *Hortus*. Indeed, for the Leviathan image (fol. 84r; plate 8), the only earlier depiction appears in a manuscript from Zwiefalten.[90]

The scribal activity that must have characterized Zwiefalten during its first century is reflected in the community's necrology. Although the names of just two scribes appear, one of these was a woman: in addition to "Albert, a monk of our congregation," the necrology makes special mention of "Mathilda of Nifen, *conversa* of our congregation, who wrote many books of St. Mary" (*Mahtilt de Niphin m^a n. c.; ista multos libros s. Marie conscripsit*).[91] Mathilda may provide a further connection with Hohenbourg. A woman with a similar name appears among the women of Hohenbourg, who are pictured on the penultimate folios of the *Hortus* (fol. 323r; plate 2). On the fourth line from the top, far right (almost level with Herrad) are two women noted as "de Níphe," one Adelheit and one Mehtilt (*HD* Cat. No. 346).[92] It is possible that the "Mehtilt de Níphe" shown here was the same woman who is listed in the Zwiefalten necrology as the *conversa* "Mahtilt de Niphin." Although such a connection cannot be proven, it is tempting: did female scribes (like some male scribes and artists) travel in order to complete projects? Were they sought for projects for which their skills would be commissioned? If Matilda did travel, is it possible that she brought with her sources for inclusion in the *Hortus*? Among the holdings in Zwiefalten's library were copies of Peter Comestor's *Historia scholastica* and Honorius's *Gemma animae*, texts that suggest spiritual and theological interests that were close to Herrad's. Although it is not clear which books with Zwiefalten provenances came from the women's library, or whether the women there had access to them, Zwiefalten provides a useful example of book production in the context of reform.

The Zwiefalten connection must—at present—remain more tantalizing than concrete. However, the *Hortus* does offer one further clue as to the female scribal culture at Hohenbourg. The famous depiction of *Philosophia* and the seven liberal arts that appears on folio 32r (plate 9) contains an unusual image of *Rethorica*, personified as a young woman holding a *stilus* and a *tabula*—one of the very few medieval pictorial indications of a woman writing.[93] Although the wax tablet represents schoolroom practice or note taking rather than scribal work proper, in conjunction with Herrad's claim of authorship, the physical proof of the *Hortus* itself, and the examples of Schwartzenthann and Zwiefalten, this image strengthens the suggestion that the *Hortus* was produced at Hohenbourg, by women within the community and perhaps also with the aid of canons from Truttenhausen, St. Gorgon, or Marbach.

Conclusion

By describing her work as a honeycomb, Herrad communicated to her audience the tremendous care with which she had selected and combined its texts and images, and the resulting coherence of the manuscript. The *Hortus deliciarum* was no random miscellany of excerpts, but a carefully planned presentation of salvation history. In this chapter, I have explored

Herrad's role as author of the *Hortus* through the evidence of the manuscript itself: its order and organization, the integration of text and image within its folio pages, and the remarkable precision with which Herrad determined its textual contents. This evidence strengthens Herrad's claim as author of the *Hortus*. That her authorship included not only the texts of the *Hortus*, but also its images, is suggested by the way in which text and image work together throughout the manuscript. The interconnectedness of text and image is the result of their selection—or composition—at the hands of a single creator, who can only have been Herrad.

The Tree of Knowledge

Blessed is the man who finds wisdom,
and is rich in prudence,
for she is more profitable than silver
and yields better returns than the purest gold.
She is more precious than all riches;
nothing that is desired can compare with her.
Long life is in her right hand;
in her left hand are riches and honor.
Her ways are beautiful ways,
and all her paths are peaceable.
She is a tree of life to those who embrace her;
he who lays hold of her will be blessed. (Proverbs 3:13–18)

IN THE PROSE PROLOGUE that introduced the texts of the *Hortus delici-arum* (*HD* no. 2), Herrad provided her readers with two distinct meta-phors for the manuscript. The first is the title that she had given the work and with which she explicitly commends it to the women of Hohen-bourg—the *Garden of Delights*. There is no question that Herrad chose this title, at least in part, to reflect the extensive work of compilation that the manuscript represented and its foundations in what she describes as the "diverse flowers of sacred Scripture and philosophic writings." As I argued in Chapter 3, however, Herrad's authorial self-presentation ex-tended beyond the role of the gatherer or editor that the garden image suggests. By describing herself as a bee, Herrad claimed the role of author and creator of the *Hortus deliciarum*. Her second metaphor is more in keeping with this role: she presents the *Hortus* to her readers as a "single sweet honeycomb." The image of the honeycomb, which was associated with the transformation of nectar and the creation of honey and also, ac-cording to Seneca, with the processes of authorial invention, memory, and the ordering of information, provided Herrad with a poetic yet precise way to assert once again her authority in the creation, and the *authoring* even, of the manuscript.

Given Herrad's insistence on her role as the author of the *Hortus*, her presentation of the work as a garden is somewhat curious: the garden image, which suggests beauty but not order, does not invoke the same sense of authorship and organization as the bee metaphor. As we have seen, Seneca argued that honey is a new creation, while the garden is simply a reorganization, however artful, of unchanged raw materials. This poses an interesting dilemma: why would Herrad offer two metaphors for her work, which, although complementary in the sense that each drew from the same general pastoral imagery, were at the same time contradictory? It is unlikely that she misunderstood her metaphors or failed to notice that they delivered mixed messages concerning her authorial role. Rather, it must be that the garden metaphor served a purpose that was central to Herrad's overall goal for the manuscript, a purpose that transcended the traditional floral and "gathering" imagery that it has so often been taken to represent. In this chapter I argue that Herrad's garden was not simply a delightful place, or one in which different textual flowers were gathered together; instead it was a place where the women of her community could meet God—and meet him expressly in study and in the pursuit of all forms of knowledge.

Biblical Gardens: Eden, the *Hortus conclusus*, and Paradise

The *hortus deliciarum*, the pleasure garden of Herrad's title, was a source of continuous medieval commentary. To Isidore of Seville, whose *Etymologies* was widely read throughout the medieval period, the *hortus deliciarum* represented the earthly paradise, the *paradisus voluptatis* of Genesis.[1] This was the most obvious reading of the garden of delights and one that appeared in the *Hortus* in an excerpt from Honorius Augustodunensis's *Elucidarium*. In answer to the disciple's question "What is paradise, or rather where is it?" Honorius responded:

It is a most delightful place (*locus amenissimus*) in the east, in which, by the grace of the Word, trees of different kinds were planted against diverse weaknesses, so that if a man should eat from one at the right time, he would never more be hungry, at the right time from another and he would never again thirst, from another and never again be tired; finally if he should eat from the tree of life he would not age further, never become infirm, and never die. (*HD* no. 76)[2]

Although Honorius here presents paradise in the historical sense as the Garden of Eden, where Adam and Eve had met regularly with God before the Fall, elsewhere he expanded his reading of paradise, which he called the *hortus deliciarum,* to include the church (which in the *Expositio in Cantica canticorum* he describes as the *paradisus religionis*), the paradise of the individual soul (*paradisus virtutis*), and the heavenly paradise (*paradisus exaltationis*), where God and man would once more be united.[3]

Herrad's decision to present her work as a "garden of delights," while drawing from these various interpretations, was not motivated by the association with just one garden. Instead, throughout the *Hortus* she consciously evoked three of the preeminent biblical gardens—the Garden of Eden, the enclosed garden of the Song of Songs, and the promised garden of Paradise (Revelation 22). Of these, the most immediately significant to the women of Hohenbourg was the enclosed garden of the Song of Songs, the *hortus conclusus,* which could be interpreted variously as the monastery, the soul, the virgin, or the church.[4] In terms of Herrad's presentation of salvation history, the *hortus conclusus* afforded a contemporary image that could always be read in the present tense. While the Garden of Eden signified humankind's past—the fall from grace, expulsion from the garden, and separation from God—and the garden of Paradise symbolized the potential for future reconciliation with God at the end of time, the *hortus conclusus* suggested the possibility for spiritual union with God in the present and on earth and not simply in humankind's sinful past or glorious future. Each of these gardens—past, present, and future—represented a place in which human beings could encounter God. In Eden, Adam and Eve had talked with God during his visits and, in Paradise, the just would be reunited with God and see him face to face. However, on earth men and women could encounter him in the metaphorical *hortus conclusus*—whether by that garden the soul, the church, the monastery, or the purity of virginity was intended.

The archetypal medieval garden—both literally and allegorically—was the monastery.[5] In a literal sense, gardens were an important part of the monastic compound since they were necessary to grow food for the community, and to keep the bees whose wax would provide for the liturgical candles and whose honey might sweeten the monastic cuisine. Given that monasteries were often situated in picturesque or remote locations, or depicted themselves as such, the cultivated garden within the monastery was matched by descriptions of the natural garden beyond the monastic enclosure—the boundless natural garden within which the entire monastery was located. Hohenbourg, perched at the summit of Mont Sainte Odile, gave views across the Vosges mountains and down into the surrounding valleys. Although it was not a garden in the strict sense, the mountain and community of Hohenbourg as Herrad envisioned them in the *Hortus* were unquestionably pastoral; in her depiction of the community on folios 322v–23r of the *Hortus* (plates 1–2), Herrad's mountain appears green and leafy and the women who populate it are described as "snow white flowers" (*nivei flores*) (*HD* Cat. No. 346).[6] The monastery in this image is shown as a verdant garden rather than a building; there is little sense of the monastery as an enclosure or of its surrounding walls, which twelfth-century monastic women were increasingly encouraged to safeguard.

Enclosure, Virginity, and the *Hortus conclusus*

The implied monastic enclosure of the *hortus conclusus* was equally appropriate for monks and nuns. However, it held particular significance for religious women, since the enclosed garden of the Song of Songs was most frequently used to denote virginity.[7] Indeed, the lover suggests as much when he describes the beloved as a garden enclosed in Song of Songs 4:12. Praising the beloved's beauty—her flawless teeth, scarlet lips, elegant neck, and the perfection of her breasts—the lover associates her attractions with her inaccessibility, and perhaps even locates them there:

A garden enclosed, sister my bride
a garden enclosed, a fountain sealed[8]

The hermetically sealed garden, with its protective wall, revitalizing fountain, and lush vegetation, was a natural metaphor for the integrity of the virgin's body, and one that is assumed in the description of the *hortus conclusus* as the *domicilium virginitatis* in Herrad's text.[9] This interpretation of the untainted fecundity of the enclosed garden as the body of the virgin lent increasing momentum to the Marian interpretation of the Song of Songs, which had been initiated by Rupert of Deutz.[10] A sermon, wrongly attributed to Bernard of Clairvaux, teaches: "Your most holy womb is for us a garden of delights (*hortus deliciarum*), O Mary, since from it we can gather many flowers of joy."[11]

Enclosure has been interpreted by most historians in a negative light; however, it did have positive associations within medieval spirituality.[12]

Indeed, the wall—the enclosure—is crucial to the definition of a garden since it is the garden's inaccessibility that is the source of its desirability. Indeed, each of the three biblical gardens was characterized by inaccessibility, remoteness, and seclusion, and none more so than the *hortus conclusus*, which was enclosed by an encircling wall and sealed by the gate at which the lover knocks, seeking entrance to his beloved (Song of Songs 5:2, 6). This gate brings to mind that gate which opened onto the Garden of Eden, the gate through which Adam and Eve had been expelled and by which they were prevented from regaining the earthly paradise.[13] Similarly, the heavenly city (presented not so much as a garden as the celestial Jerusalem) was surrounded by a wall and studded with twelve gates (Revelation 21:12). Comito comments that "as Milton knew, it is the fallen world that is a 'fenceless' one"[14]—a helpful reminder that the wall was intended first and foremost to keep sinful humans *out* of the garden, whether that garden was later taken to mean Eden, the monastery, or the virgin's body. The goal of the spiritual life was thus to regain the garden from which sin had barred them entrance. Within the monastery, the professed religious had achieved the closest possible earthly equivalent to the garden of paradise—the garden of the monastic cloister in which, suspended between this world and the next, she could devote herself to contemplation of God.

Indeed, to some, the monastery was not only a garden—literal or figural—but also a compelling symbol of paradise, both the paradise that had been lost and the paradise that was still to be gained.[15] Honorius Augustodunensis argued strongly for the association of the monastery with both the earthly and the heavenly paradise:

Moreover, the cloister represents Paradise, and indeed the monastery is a more secure Paradise than Eden. The fountain in this place of pleasure is the baptismal font in the monastery; the tree of life in paradise is the body of Christ in the monastery. The different fruit trees are the different books of sacred Scripture. Truly the enclosure of the cloister bears the image of heaven, in which the just are segregated from the sinners just as those who profess the religious life are sequestered in the cloister from secular people. Moreover monasteries foreshadow the celestial paradise.[16]

For the Augustinian canon Hugh of Fouilloy, the cloister was a symbol of the heavenly Jerusalem as well as an allegory of the soul; in his *De claustro animae*, he taught that the walls of the cloister symbolized love of God and of one's neighbor, and contempt for the world and for oneself.[17] Although not all monastic writers agreed with Honorius and Hugh,[18] for

Herrad, the monastery as a garden, and the promise of union with God on earth that such an image suggested, was consistent with her spiritual purpose in the *Hortus*. As a type of paradise on earth, the monastic cloister pointed toward the true paradise of heaven. In the same way, the *Hortus deliciarum*—the book as a textual garden within the monastery as a physical and symbolic one—could serve as a signpost for its female readers on their path to the eternal, celestial garden.

Eschatology of the Garden

The three biblical gardens were related to each other by more than the simple facts of their encircling walls and their inaccessibility. As we saw above, they shared a particular spiritual significance as places in which encounters between God and human beings could, and did, occur. These meetings occurred along a historical continuum that was coeval with Herrad's salvation history: humankind's past, present, and future each figured in her presentation, and each could be represented by a particular garden, whether that garden was Eden, the *hortus conclusus* as monastery, soul, church, or virgin, or the heavenly Paradise. The Garden of Eden signified the perfection of humankind's prelapsarian state, but also called vividly to mind the temptation, fall, and man's exile from God. Read against the cautionary example of this first garden, the garden of paradise held forth the promise of humankind's final reconciliation with God, which could be experienced on earth—whether in prayer, study, or flashes of divine illumination—in the metaphorical *hortus conclusus*.

The garden image could also suggest a fourth biblical garden, Gethsemane, the historical garden of Christ's agony, in which Christ, as the second Adam, had made restitution for the transgression of the first man in the Garden of Eden. The allegorical interpretation of Christ, the Son of Man and the true Tree of Life, as the second Adam was a commonplace in medieval thought and was matched by depictions of Mary, the virgin mother, as the second Eve. Connections between Eden and the garden of Gethsemane were often expressed visually in depictions of the crucifixion, in which the cross itself seems to emerge from the tomb of Adam (as in *HD* fol. 150r).[19] The contrast between Mary and Eve is highlighted in the *Hortus* Last Judgment cycle of images (fols. 251v and 253r); while Mary would originally have appeared immediately to Christ's right (before the interpolation of folio 252 disturbed the sequence of the images), Eve is shown on the left at the base of the cross beneath Christ's throne (fol. 253r).[20] The relationship that these images suggests was affirmed in the commonly held belief that the cross had been fashioned from wood taken from the tree of knowledge in the Garden of Eden.[21] This visual and imaginative connection served to underscore the theological principle that the cross had made total satisfaction for Adam and Eve's disobedience in eating the forbidden fruit.

The tree of knowledge was therefore central both to the cautionary account of Eden, the garden of man's sin, and to the salvific message of Gethsemane, the garden of God's grace. It was also evoked in the image of Paradise described by John in Revelation, where he records that he saw the "tree of life" in the heavenly city of Jerusalem.[22] He writes:

Then he showed me a river of the water of life, as clear as crystal, flowing from the throne of God and of the Lamb down the middle of the great street of the city. On each side of the river stood the tree of life, bearing twelve fruits, yielding its fruit every month and the leaves of the tree for the healing of the nations (*ad sanitatem gentium*). And no curse shall be any more. (Revelation 22:1–3)[23]

The eschatological significance of this tree in the context of John's vision is clear. In contrast to the tree of knowledge in Eden, the misuse of which had provided the occasion for death to enter the world, the tree reappears here "for the healing of the nations" and as a promise for the righteous—in verse 14 John declares, "Blessed are those who wash their robes, that they may have the right to the tree of life and may go through the gates into the city." The promise of the ultimate return to Eden, the "right" (*potestas*) as John puts it to the tree of life, is made explicit in the prophecy of Isaiah to Israel: "for the Lord shall comfort Zion: he will comfort all her waste places; and he will make her desert as a place of pleasures, and her wilderness like the garden of the Lord; joy and gladness shall be found therein, thanksgiving, and the voice of praise" (Isaiah 51:3).

The images both of the tree and of the garden suggest, then, an inevitable and infinite cycle of life and death, of germination, growth, blossom, and decay.[24] As such, the very fertility of paradise—evoked in descriptions of the rivers, dew, moisture, and of course, the tree—carries the specter of sin and death, the consequence of disobedience. Within the monastic compound, the twofold signification of the garden, evoking both life and death, could be underscored through the planting of trees in the cemetery, or, conversely, the burial of the dead in orchards, practices that are attested in the Plan of St. Gall. As Meyvaert notes, the combination of trees and tombs could serve as a powerful reminder of sin and the cross, while at the same time offering the promise of the resurrection, when, in the words of Guerric of Igny, "the beauty of a garden will flower forth in the springtime of the resurrection, when their [the just's] flesh will be renewed, and not only will their bones flourish like grass, but the whole just man will blossom like the lily and will shine forever before the Lord."[25] In keeping with the role of the tree in linking heaven with earth, it was sometimes depicted as a ladder, connecting the human with the divine.[26] The salvific potential of the tree as a ladder formed the basis for such tree images as the Ladder of Virtues, which Herrad depicts on folio 215v (plate 5), as well as the *Arbor virtutum*, which provided the structure for Conrad of Hirsau's *On the fruits of the flesh and of the spirit* and which, in turn, inspired Herrad's psychomachia cycle.[27]

The three biblical trees—the tree of the knowledge of good and evil in Eden, the tree of the cross, and the tree of life in Revelation 22:14—like the three (or four, if we include Gethsemane) biblical gardens reinforced the themes of fall and salvation central to the *Hortus*. Furthermore, the recapitulation of the garden and tree themes in John's vision of the heavenly Paradise powerfully reinforced the idea of an eventual return to Eden; heaven, the rest of the just soul, is in John's image not only reconciliation with God (Revelation 22:4 "They will see his face") but also a sort of homecoming, a reclamation of the Paradise that had been lost through sin.[28] The image of the garden, then, served to juxtapose sin with salvation, the paradise that had been lost with the heavenly paradise that might ultimately be regained.

The Tree of Knowledge

Herrad's description of the *Hortus deliciarum* as a garden provided her with the symbolic shorthand to evoke for her readers each of the biblical gardens along with their particular spiritual significance within the theology of salvation. However, her purpose was not simply to bring these gardens to mind but to present a particular account of salvation that incorporated practical and spiritual guidance. To Herrad, salvation history was, after all, more than a topic for impartial theological enquiry, a "history" as we might now understand the term to signify something that has already happened, an action that is complete and in the past. Rather, salvation history was ongoing in Herrad's view and its course, although foretold in

Revelation and hinted at in the words of the prophets, was yet to be completed. For Herrad and the women of her community, as for all professed
monastics and ideally all Christians as well, the unfolding of salvation history—and the place of the individual soul within it—was a topic of crucial
importance.

Examined within the context of her eschatological concerns, Herrad's
emphasis on the garden emerges as more complicated, and more interesting, than it might at first appear. The "garden" that she offers her audience is a garden of pleasures, to be sure. But the garden that she meant to
call to mind was not only sweetness and enjoyment. Within the context of
salvation history, the garden image was a profoundly ambivalent one: as
Adam and Eve were warned, gardens were dangerous places as well as
potentially delightful ones. The danger and the delight of the garden are
epistemologically linked since the pleasure of the garden, which is the
hope of salvation and of union with God, had its origin, and its necessity,
in the sin that was the result of Adam and Eve's failure to negotiate safely
the danger of Eden. So the garden could be both a place of happiness and
pleasure and also one of temptation and danger, as the *Hortus deliciarum*
makes clear: the Ladder of Virtues on folio 215v (plate 5) shows a hermit
tempted away from his rightful goal—the crown of life—by the attractions
of his garden.

The centrality of the garden image as an organizing principle within
Herrad's depiction of salvation history is a function of its ability to invoke
both the separation from God that began in the Garden of Eden and the
reunion with God that would be achieved for the faithful at the end of
time. But the garden is also a warning against the disobedience that was
the source of the Fall, disobedience that was powerfully evoked in the
image of the tree. On the most basic level that disobedience was the failure
to observe God's commands. But the disobedience of Adam and Eve was
only the manifestation of another sin: the wrongful desire for knowledge
that had first prompted Eve to eat the fruit. Knowing humankind's basic
desire for knowledge, the serpent had concluded that Adam and Eve
would be most easily induced to disobey God by the promise of wisdom,
through which they could become "like God." In the *Hortus*, the devil's
temptation and Eve's capitulation are presented in a verse that was most
likely put to music and sung together by the women.[29] The verse, which
appears in a poem immediately following the cycle of images depicting the
Creation, temptation, and expulsion (fol. 17 r–v), tells of how the serpent,

the father of death (*necis pater*) came to Eve "with a terrible expression" (*vultu cum terribili*), and said:

Listen to me, woman, do the things which I shall say
Eat from the fruit prohibited you
So you will be like the Lord, do not doubt this.[30]

The devil's promise in the subsequent verse is even more explicit in its guarantee of what being "like the Lord" would entail:

You will know all things
Whatsoever you demand
Shall be brought to pass in the heavens. (*HD* no. 69)[31]

Here is where the tree imagery is so important. The Book of Genesis records that "The Lord God had planted a paradise of pleasure (*paradisum voluptatis*) from the beginning, in which he placed the man he had formed. And the Lord God brought forth from the gound all kinds of trees, fair to behold and pleasant to eat of. In the middle of the garden were the tree of life and the tree of the knowledge of good and evil" (Genesis 2:8–9). The two trees that are emphasized in this account and that lay at the center of the garden symbolized life and knowledge, specifically, the knowledge of good and evil.[32] The story, then, of humankind's transgression in the Garden of Eden was intricately bound up with knowledge, since it was the illegitimate quest for knowledge (knowledge that would make human beings "like God") that had served as the catalyst for humankind's separation from God. The premise that salvation would entail humankind's return to the garden of paradise—which was frequently conflated with the heavenly paradise—was a powerful factor in shaping the medieval understanding of heaven, as we have seen. The tree of Eden, which reappeared in medieval theology in the wood of the cross, the tree on which Christ was crucified, appears one last time in John's vision of heaven, where it functions as a symbol of healing. The extension of the tree image—which was at once the symbol of the Fall, salvation, and reunion with God—within John's heavenly city suggests the centrality of knowledge—and the rightful use of knowledge—to the progression of salvation history. Ultimately, the recurrence of the tree image suggested that human beings would need a new approach to knowledge in their quest for salvation. Since the illegitimate desire for knowledge had lain at the root of the Fall, it was logical to assume that a corrected approach to knowledge would be essential to the process by which humankind's fallen state might be repaired. In Herrad's presentation, then, salvation was intimately bound up with knowledge within an appropriate spiritual context. Knowledge, the tree, and the garden were intricately, even inextricably, connected both to the Fall and to Herrad's quest for salvation.

Philosophy as Divine Wisdom

Herrad's decision to describe her work as both a garden and a honeycomb is fully comprehensible only within the spiritual framework of her work and its ultimate purpose. The significance of the garden as a place in which the misuse of knowledge could and did have devastating effects exerted a powerful influence throughout her work. However, as Herrad suggested in the *Hortus*, knowledge could also be the path to salvation since, through study, the soul's memory of heaven, its "true" homeland, could be revived.

In her prologue, alongside her depiction of herself as a bee and her presentation of her work as a garden, Herrad offers an unusual piece of information—unusual especially for the late twelfth-century monastic context in which she was working. Describing her work on the *Hortus*, she comments that she "collected from the diverse flowers of sacred Scripture and philosophic writings this book" (*HD* no. 2). Herrad's claim is odd on two levels, first because she rarely uses scriptural sources in her work, although her entire organizational edifice was constructed around biblical events,[33] and second because she claims to have drawn her textual flowers from "philosophic writings." This latter claim is largely unparalleled in the writings of Herrad's monastic contemporaries.[34] Even in the *Hortus*, it is unique; it is repeated neither in the *incipit* to the work (*HD* no. 3), where she limited herself to the scriptural sources that she claims as the basis for the *Hortus*,[35] nor in her introductory poem (*HD* no. 1), which in any case does not discuss the *Hortus* sources.

Precisely what Herrad meant by the term "philosophy" is difficult to determine, especially since she did not include any overtly philosophical works in the *Hortus*. The works of ancient philosophers do not appear in the manuscript, nor did Herrad draw from contemporary works of a philosophical nature.[36] Aristotle is entirely absent and, although Plato and Socrates do appear in the image of *Philosophia* on folio 32r (plate 9), con-

firming at the very least that Herrad knew of them, there is no evidence
to suggest that she knew their work directly.

Stranger still is the apparent ease with which Herrad invokes philosophy as one of her sources, and the equation of philosophic with scriptural
sources that her pairing of them suggests. What can she have intended?

Philosophy and the Arts in Monastic Thought

Herrad's claim to have consulted philosophic sources is most striking
given the intellectual climate in which she was writing. By the late eleventh
and twelfth centuries, philosophy both as a subject for inquiry and also as
a descriptive term occupied a vexed place within monastic thought, a result
not only of uneasiness regarding the arts, and their potential misuse, but
also of anxiety concerning the burgeoning of the scholastic enterprise from
the first half of the twelfth century.[37] Of course Christian attitudes toward
the learning of pagan antiquity had always been complicated; Jerome's
dream, in which he was beaten as a Ciceronian and not a Christian (*Cicero-
nianus es, non Christianus*),[38] was a valuable reminder of the dangers implicit in secular literature. However, both Jerome and Augustine had
largely rationalized their use of pagan literatures through the invention
of what Morrison calls "metaphors of appropriation."[39] Augustine had
suggested that the riches of pagan knowledge could be considered in the
same light as the "Egyptian gold," which had been rightfully taken by the
Israelites when they fled slavery. He argued that pagan authors were the
"unjust possessors" of truth and counseled Christians simply to take from
them the "treasure" of their learning.[40] Jerome added a further metaphor:
pagan learning should be like the woman captured by Israelites, purified
according to the requirements of ritual, and then rightfully kept as a slave
(Deuteronomy 21:10–14).[41] Yet, while both defended the lawfulness of appropriating pagan knowledge, Augustine was careful to add that the
knowledge collected from pagan sources is insignificant compared to the
"knowledge contained in divine scriptures."[42]

Patristic ambivalence concerning the proper use of pagan knowledge
is echoed in the hesitant attitude toward the liberal arts that was adopted
by many medieval authors, whom scholars have often identified as representing a conservative, "monastic" viewpoint. Anxiety, particularly with
regard to dialectic, is generally associated with three eleventh-century figures—Otloh of St. Emmeram, Peter Damian, and Manegold of Lauten-

bach.[43] The concern with which these authors approached the liberal arts extended beyond the basic worry that reading pagan authors might drive easily influenced monks into moral bankruptcy. Indeed, Otloh, the earliest of the three, was content to repeat Augustine's Egyptian gold metaphor in order to justify the Christian adoption of pagan texts.[44] Instead, it was the evil purpose to which knowledge of the liberal arts might be put that troubled him, which is precisely why dialectic provided the focus of his criticisms. Since dialectic sharpened the capacity to argue and persuade, its purpose was to convince even where it lacked truth—that is, to lie.[45] Although Otloh's concerns were fuelled by his association of dialectic with the often injurious lawsuits in which monasteries could become embroiled, for Manegold and Peter Damian, opposition toward dialectic was associated primarily, if not exclusively, with criticism of the imperial party.[46] Opposition to the liberal arts was thus more political and spiritual than intellectual; all three were men of obvious erudition, whose concerns were not so much with the acquisition of learning as with the potentially immoral uses to which it could be put.[47]

Despite their own education in the arts, Otloh, Peter, and Manegold contributed to an intellectual climate in which the perception of the arts was shaded by anxiety concerning their proper use. The denunciation of secular knowledge, and the preference for "untaught wisdom" affirmed by later monastic authors, is most succinctly expressed in Peter Damian's credo, "I reject Plato, prying into the secrets of hidden nature," and his prayer, "May the simplicity of Christ instruct me, and may the true ignorance of the wise break the bonds of my uncertainty."[48] In the same vein, Manegold of Lautenbach condemned the writings of philosophers as containing "much that poses difficulty, little that is of use, and nothing that offers salvation."[49] Although eleventh-century "opposition" to the arts and to philosophy has certainly been overstated, as Resnick and others have argued, the anxiety of these men must call attention, if not to a situation in the late eleventh century in which philosophy posed a real challenge to the primacy of monastic scriptural study, then at least to one in which the liberal arts and philosophy were charged terms.[50]

By the twelfth century, when Herrad was writing, philosophy and the arts were seen in a decidedly equivocal light, particularly by many of the newer monastic orders. Ambrose's warning that "no one can see Christ who has assumed the garment of philosophy or, specifically, the dress of secular wisdom," was reflected in the sense that philosophy could constitute a serious barrier to faith.[51] The trial of Berengar of Tours and also those of Abelard and Gilbert of Poitiers, both spearheaded by Bernard of Clairvaux, are evidence of the prevailing climate of skepticism concerning the uses to which learning could be put, and the theological challenges that philosophy might present.[52] For the author of the *Metamorphosis Goliae* (ca. 1142), the quarrel between Bernard and Abelard was essentially a quarrel between the two types of learning proposed by Leclercq, the one represented by the "philosopher" and the other by the monk: "The throng of those educated by the philosopher cry out in protest: the monk-cowled primate of the monk-cowled tribe, thrice wrapped round in imprisoning tunics, has had silence imposed on so great a prophet."[53] Although it is possible to overstate monastic, particularly Cistercian, opposition to the emerging universities, it is clear that these men felt ambivalent about the application of reason to the understanding of God. In their view, God was to be found not in study, but through experience, as Bernard of Clairvaux argued in a letter to Henry Murdac: "You will find more in forests than in books," he wrote, "Woods and stones will teach you what you are not able to hear from masters."[54]

Those authors who continued to encourage the study of the *artes* in this climate generally warned against mastery of the *artes* as a goal in itself, arguing instead for their propaedeutic value. In his *Dialogue on the Authors*, Conrad of Hirsau presents the acquisition of pagan knowledge, which he likens to "nourishing milk," as a first step toward the deeper truth of sacred understanding, what he calls "solid food":

Seekers after wisdom should regard secular knowledge in such a light that, if they find in it, in its words and ideas, any steps on the ladder of their common progress from which the higher wisdom may be grasped more firmly, these should not be altogether scorned, but the mind exercised on them for just as long as it takes to find what one seeks through the medium of secular knowledge.[55]

Like seasoning for food, which is discarded once its culinary work has been accomplished, Conrad argues that secular studies should be abandoned in favor of sacred learning, as soon as the monk has achieved a basic level of education.[56] Although monastic authors did continue to study the liberal arts, they did so only under certain conditions, as Chenu has observed: "To be sure the monks had cultivated and made magnificent use of the seven secular arts, but only after purging them of their arrogant ways and . . . reducing them to handmaids."[57]

By the later twelfth century, the philosophy that Herrad claims for herself was so contentious that her slightly earlier contemporary, Hildegard of Bingen, chose not to mention it among the works for which she claimed divine understanding in her *Scivias*, although thirty years later, once her prophetic persona had been more securely established, she would claim it in her *vita*.[58] Similarly, in his *Rule* for the Paraclete, Abelard, himself a "philosopher," cautioned the women against the study of philosophy, which he saw as inappropriate to the immediate needs of the female monastery. Although he did not see anything intrinsically dangerous in philosophy, he nonetheless warned that the deaconess need not address herself to "philosophic studies": he writes, "If she is not lettered let her know that she should accustom herself not to philosophic studies nor dialectical disputations but to teaching of life and performance of works."[59] His own confession of faith, written for Heloise some years later, declared his primary allegiance to God, and not to philosophy: "I do not wish to be a philosopher if it means conflicting with Paul, nor to be an Aristotle if it cuts me off from Christ."[60] Even Honorius Augustodunensis, Herrad's most important source, condemned philosophy, associating the first plague (the plague of blood) that had been sent by God against the Egyptians with philosophy and philosophers.[61]

Philosophy in the *Hortus deliciarum*

Herrad's intentions in claiming "philosophic writings" among the sources that she consulted during the course of her work on the *Hortus* may best be understood from an examination of her full-page image of *Philosophia* and the liberal arts (fol. 32r; plate 9). This folio, which is frequently included in studies of medieval education and is one of the many reasons for Herrad's continuing fame, presents a graphic illustration of the relationship between *Philosophia* and the liberal arts—and also between Christian and pagan knowledge—within a precisely organized circular schema.[62]

In the *Hortus* image, *Philosophia* is depicted at the center of two concentric circles surrounded by the personified *artes*, who are identified both by their iconographic devices as well as by short tituli. Of these, perhaps the most striking is *Rethorica*, who is personified as a young woman holding a *stilus* and a *tabula* in one of the very few medieval images of a woman writing.[63] The *artes* are separated from each other by seven columns radiating from *Philosophia*'s central circle such that each occupies her own arch. At the center of the image beneath *Philosophia*'s throne, Socrates and Plato are shown at their writing desks, Socrates to her right and Plato to her left. Both are engaged in the act of writing, and an inscription identifies philosophers as the sages of the world (*sapientes mundi*) and the clerics of the gentiles (*gentium clerici*).[64] At the bottom of the folio, outside the circles defined by *Philosophia*, four seated figures identified as poets and magicians are also shown at their desks. In contrast to Plato and Socrates, who, although not Christian, appear under the aegis of Philosophy, these men appear to derive inspiration from little black birds that are perched on their shoulders.[65] An inscription on the facing page (*HD* no. 124), which is partially duplicated on the image itself, warns against the inappropriate use of knowledge. Recounting how God had scattered men over the face of the earth after Babel, the text adds that some men studied philosophy and were called philosophers—defined here as lovers of wisdom (*amatores sapientie*). However, others, who were blinded in their reason (*ratione cecati*) and inspired by unclean spirits, wrote works of magic and poetry and began to worship idols.[66] The verso of this folio—now lacking—displayed a full-page presentation of Idolatry (fol. 32v), presumably to reinforce the message that idolatry was the wrongful quest for worldly knowledge and must result in separation from God.[67]

The *Philosophia* image is important for reasons that extend beyond the obvious indication that it provides of knowledge of the liberal arts at Hohenbourg. In fact, this image, which is often cited as proof that women at Hohenbourg studied the arts, is not accompanied in the *Hortus* by any texts that might have served as teaching tools within a liberal arts curriculum. Few traditional teachers of the arts are mentioned in Herrad's text. As such, the *Philosophia* image can be taken only as evidence that Herrad's audience was familiar with the liberal arts, rather than as an example of how these arts may have been taught within the community. This caveat does not necessarily detract from the significance of the image or from the indication that it provides of the spiritual and intellectual climate at Hohenbourg. Indeed, the construction of the image, its numerous tituli, and its physical placement in the manuscript—its position within the context of Herrad's presentation of salvation history—shed important light on Herrad's epistemology and her overall purpose in the *Hortus*. Although the image and its accompanying texts have generally been seen as a digression from the main narrative of the Old Testament section of the *Hortus*, the *Philosophia* cycle is in fact an integral part of Herrad's plan to present the hope for salvation (through knowledge) as an antidote to the Fall.[68]

Herrad's *Philosophia* is a composite figure reflecting diverse influences, but ultimately interpreted as a personification of Divine Wisdom. She is at once *Sapientia*, the Divine Wisdom of the Old Testament,[69] Sophia, the Wisdom of God, whom medieval exegetes associated with the second person of the Trinity,[70] and the imposing allegorical figure of Boethius's *Consolation*.[71] She might also be seen as a figure of Mary, the Queen of Heaven, since Mary was increasingly portrayed as a philosopher during the twelfth century; Mary's relationship with the seven liberal arts was depicted on the south tympanum at Chartres.[72] Although the *Hortus* image encompasses each of these possible identifications, Herrad's depiction of *Philosophia*, a secular figure, rather than *Sapientia*, a biblical one, is significant and reflects recent intellectual developments, as Katzenellenbogen comments: "it was, indeed, a bold step when about 1160 Philosophy took over the place of Wisdom."[73] Herrad's *Philosophia* is shown as a queen enthroned; from her breast flow seven rivers, identified by an inscription to her right as the seven liberal arts,[74] but also suggestive of the seven gifts of the spirit, to which the arts were sometimes likened in medieval exegesis. An inscription to her left claims the Holy Spirit as the inventor of the seven liberal arts.[75] The rivers, which also call to mind the rivers of Paradise, suggest the preeminence of *Philosophia*, who, as Sophia of Ecclesiasticus, was the "firstborn before all creation" (Ecclesiasticus 24:5). The four rivers flowing to her right represent the subjects of the quadrivium, the three to her left, the trivium.

The emanation of the rivers from *Philosophia*'s breast explicitly identifies her (along with the Holy Spirit) as the source of the liberal arts, an identification in keeping with Boethius's account of how *Philosophia* banished the Muses—the "harlots of the stage" (*scenicas meretriculas*)—and replaced them with the liberal arts.[76] Like *Sapientia*, who built herself a house of seven columns (Proverbs 9:1), Herrad's *Philosophia* is depicted at the center of an atrium—the perimeter is marked by seven columns, dividing the arcade into seven arches, each occupied by one of the liberal arts.[77] The banner in her hand asserts the divine origins of all wisdom: "All wisdom is from the Lord God" (*Omnis sapientia a Domino Deo est*)[78] and the freedom that comes with learning: "Only the wise are able to do what they desire" (*Soli quod desiderant facere possunt sapientes*), a text taken from Boethius.[79] From her crown, three heads protrude, which are identified as *ethica*, *logica*, and *phisica*, the divisions of learning designed by the Stoics and mistakenly, but repeatedly, attributed to Plato.[80] An inscription in the circle around *Philosophia*'s sphere declares: "I, Philosophy, ruling by

divine art the things that are, divide the subjected arts into seven parts."[81]
Around the outer circle verses set forth in order the stages by which philosophy reveals hidden knowledge and teaches it to her pupils:

These are the practices which the philosophy of the world tracked down
And, once they had been tracked down, she took note of them
And she strengthened them in writing and instilled them in her students.
Through studies, *Philosophia* teaches the seven arts
She inquires into the secrets of the elements and of things. (*HD* Cat. No. 33)[82]

Herrad's presentation of *Philosophia* is not without parallel in medieval art. Several of the *Philosophia* inscriptions appear on a twelfth-century
bronze bowl, which also depicts *Philosophia* together with representatives
of the arts (plate 10). On this bowl, *Philosophia* is shown much as in the
Hortus, at the center, flanked by Plato and Socrates, wearing a triple crown
out of which *ethica, phisica*, and *logica* emerge, and holding a banner inscribed with the phrase "Soli quod [desid]erant facere possunt sapientes."[83] Around her, six bearded figures represent wise men, each
accompanied by a smaller, beardless youth holding a banner inscribed with
the name of the art for which he is famed (*Astronomia* has been omitted).
At the center, *Philosophia* is depicted with a ladder on the front of her
garment—an aspect that is deliberately lacking in the *Hortus* image.[84] Errors are rife, leading Green to describe the inscriptions as "illiterate."[85]
Around the central group of *Philosophia*, Socrates and Plato, a text reads:
"Septem per stu[dia] docet artes Phiolsphia (sic) ec elementorum scr[uta-
t]ur et abdite (sic) rcrum (sic)," a phrase similar to the one that appears in
the *Hortus* image. The remainder of this text appears on the lip of the
bowl: "Hec exercicia que mundi Philo[so]phia Investigavit investig[at]a
notavit [Scr]ipto firmavit alumnis nisinva (sic);" its conclusion is partially
obscured.

The *Philosophia* bowl is part of a collection of some two hundred
engraved bronze bowls, catalogued by Weitzmann-Fiedler, which she argues were used by nuns to wash their hands in a symbolic purification
ritual prior to confession.[86] Given similarities between the *Hortus* miniature and the bowl in layout and text, it is possible that the two derived
from a similar source, possibly the illustrated eleventh-century school-
books that Weitzmann-Fiedler argues inspired the bowls. However, the
similarities should not be pushed too far: Herrad's model is more overtly
christianized than the bowl, despite its moralizing purpose.[87] Although

the two share many of the same inscriptions, Herrad added a biblical inscription (Ecclesiasticus 1:1) in order to promote a Christian reading of the
image as a whole. Where Plato and Socrates had flanked *Philosophia* in the
bowl, they appear beneath her feet in the *Hortus*. Even more clear is Herrad's relegation of pagan learning to the realm outside the divine circles
ruled by *Philosophia*.

Another possible model for the *Hortus Philosophia* image (and possibly also the *Philosophia* bowl) is a diagram of the liberal arts that appears
in a manuscript of Boethius's *De musica*, now in the Newberry Library,
that was probably written at Admont in the early twelfth century (MS F9
fol. 65v). Although the Newberry diagram lacks visual personifications, it
does provide descriptions that may have been intended as a guide for artists; it is possible that these descriptions provided the inspiration for depictions both on the bowl and in the *Hortus*.[88] However, here too, the
connection can be overstretched: the Newberry depiction has fourteen
figures around a central hub occupied by *Philosophia* and two kings. These
fourteen include each of the seven liberal arts together with a related *magister*: Aristotle for Dialectic, Priscian for Grammar, and so on.[89] Although
the circular schematic is similar to that of the *Hortus*, with its central hub
and surrounding arches, the similarities are not conclusive. None of the
inscriptions suggested by the Newberry diagram for the arts appears in the
Hortus, and, as we have seen, Herrad omitted the male *magistri*, depicting
the arts alone, personified as women. On the whole, Herrad's image defies
categorization; as Katzenellenbogen observes the entire *Philosophia* image
comprises "an intricate philosophical system."[90]

For Herrad, *Philosophia* was equated with the Wisdom of God (*Sapientia Dei*). In keeping with her presentation of salvation history, the arts
are shown not as ends in themselves but in a propadeutic role, as guides
for the soul on its path to *Philosophia*, who is Divine Wisdom. However,
the inclusion of Plato and Socrates within the ambit defined by *Philosophia*
is a clear statement of Herrad's position in the debate concerning the
proper use of pagan knowledge, as are the many tituli which accompany
the image. As we saw above, Herrad did not shun pagan knowledge, but
taught that "all knowledge is from God," an idea that is reenforced in an
unidentified text on folio 9v, which states: "Philosophers have examined
all these things through worldly wisdom, which, however, the Holy Spirit
inspired."[91] Instead of warning her audience against the dangers of philosophy, Herrad taught that philosophy was the goal of wisdom, the knowledge of all things both human and divine,[92] and that all knowledge,

properly used, leads to God. A text on folio 30v teaches that the liberal arts are so called because they liberate the soul from its earthly cares and prepare it for knowledge and understanding of its creator (*HD* no.115).[93]

Philosophy, the Fall, and Salvation

Herrad's *Philosophia* image was central to her teaching on the Fall and of the narrative of salvation history by which the entire *Hortus* was organized. According to Boethius and later Christian writers, it was the memory of God that guided human beings toward salvation; however, since memory had been damaged in the Fall, it had to be repaired through study. In Book One of the *Consolation of Philosophy*, Dame Philosophy appears to Boethius, who is sorrowing and alone in his prison cell, and asks him: "do you remember the final purpose of the world, the goal to which the whole order of nature proceeds?" Boethius confesses that although he once knew the answer, in his grief he has forgotten. Finally, Philosophy declares that she has detected the cause of his sadness:

"Now I know," she said, "the further cause of your sickness, and it is a very serious one. You have forgotten your own identity. So I have now fully elicited the cause of your illness, and the means of recovering your health. Forgetting who you are has made you confused, and this is why you are upset at being both exiled and stripped of your possessions."[94]

Philosophy's assessment of Boethius's sadness is founded on Platonic reminiscence, the assumption of the soul's memory of God and its natural desire to seek God based on this memory.

The Neoplatonic model of the soul's exile and return that was implicit in Philosophy's assessment of Boethius's state was easily assumed in the Christian account of salvation.[95] The urgency of man's return to God animated Augustine's writings in particular. In his view, "the soul defiles itself with unchaste love when it turns away from you and looks elsewhere for things which it cannot find pure and unsullied except by returning to you."[96] Memory was crucial to Augustine's hermeneutic of salvation and is a major occupation in Book 10 of the *Confessions*, where he was concerned to discover how men can seek God if they do not have some knowledge of him, or if they did not at one time know who he is.[97] Augustine concludes that men have a residual memory of God, that they can recognize what he calls the "life of blessed happiness" (*vita beata*) when they see it:[98]

See how I have explored the vast field of my memory in search of you, O Lord! And I have not found you outside it. For I have discovered nothing about you except what I have remembered since the time I first learned about you. Ever since then I have not forgotten you. For I found my God, who is Truth itself, where I found truth, and ever since I learned the truth I have not forgotten it. So, since the time when I first learned of you, you have always been present in my memory, and it is there that I find you whenever I am reminded of you and find delight in you. This is my holy joy, which in your mercy you have given me, heedful of my poverty.[99]

According to Augustine's teaching, memory was at once a remembrance of things past, a recognition of things present, and an expectation of things future.[100]

Christian writers inspired by Neoplatonism embraced the idea that the soul, lost and exiled in a fallen world, had forgotten its true purpose; only through knowledge, which would facilitate remembrance of the soul's origin and destination, could it return from exile. Writing in the 1120s, Hugh of St. Victor offered a Neoplatonic image of salvation inspired by Augustine's theory of memory. Contending that man's separation from God means that he no longer knows who he is, Hugh argued that human beings can remember their origin and purpose through the pursuit of knowledge and thereby find reconciliation with God.[101] He writes:

For the mind, stupefied by bodily sensations and enticed out of itself by sensuous forms, has forgotten what it was, and, because it does not remember that it was anything different, believes that it is nothing except what is seen. But we are restored through instruction, so that we may recognize our nature and learn not to seek outside ourselves what we can find within. "The highest curative in life," therefore, is the pursuit of Wisdom: he who finds it is happy, and he who possesses it, blessed.[102]

In Hugh's presentation, learning was essential because of the Fall, man's separation from God, and expulsion from Eden. Similarly, the twelfth-century English scholar Adelard of Bath wrote that "When the soul, then, is oppressed by these bonds in the prison of the body, among all possible remedies there is one by which she can restore herself to herself and bring herself back home: that is, the teachings of this philosophy, and what they call 'the liberal arts'."[103] For Adelard, philosophy was tied to contempt for the world, an idea that is made more explicit when Philosophy declares that her disciples, having been freed from worldly belongings, have access to "true speculation on things."[104]

Ultimately, the significance of Herrad's *Philosophia* image stems from the complex interplay between the image itself and the context in which it is embedded. Whereas the representation of the liberal arts on the façades of twelfth-century churches and on candlesticks during the same period promoted particular interpretations of their function—the "illumination of darkness through rational endeavors," as Katzenellenbogen observes[105]—the placement of Herrad's *Philosophia* image within the schema of the *Hortus* demonstrates her recognition of the importance of knowledge within the framework of Christian history. Of course, the misuse of knowledge was the cause of the Fall, but as Hugh had argued and Herrad's texts and image also suggest, knowledge could be a remedy. Exile from God and reconciliation with him are presented as two parts of the same story in the *Hortus* account of the Creation, which directly precedes the *Philosophia* image.[106] Immediately following the depiction of the temptation and Adam and Eve's expulsion from the garden, Herrad offered her readers the consoling promise of salvation, noting in a rare section from Bernard of Clairvaux's Sermon 96 that the lost paradise had already been restored through Christ (*HD* no. 77).[107] In the same way, Herrad's gloss on the image of Adam and Eve at work reminds her readers that Christ "the true priest," had already absolved Adam from sin and restored him to Paradise by his death (fol. 27r; *HD* Cat. No. 24).[108]

It is within the context of this philosophical framework, and especially in the shadow of Eden, that Herrad's *Philosophia* image makes sense. Deliberately situated at a point in the manuscript following the presentation of the Fall, and the related episodes of the Flood and the Tower of Babel, the *Philosophia* image offered a Christianized paradigm of knowledge in the service of Divine Wisdom. The misuse of knowledge was expressly placed at this juncture in the manuscript: human efforts to reach heaven, epitomized in the building of the Tower of Babel (an image of which appears on folio 27v), had failed, resulting in the confounding of worldly knowledge by God's multiplication of human languages. Babel, which, as Colish notes, was an "act of human presumption against God," was known by John of Salisbury as the "tower of pride"; according to Jerome, it was a symbol of human confusion.[109]

Herrad's inclusion of the *Philosophia* image at this point in her ac-

count of salvation history is a sign that she recognized the essential role
played by knowledge in humankind's recovery of the garden, or, seen another way, in the passage from the garden of Eden to the garden of
heaven. The quest for Wisdom, for *Philosophia*, appears in her account as
an integral stage in salvation history, after the Fall and subsequent confusion. However, Herrad did not embrace philosophy indiscriminately; she
also uses the *Philosophia* image to communicate a message regarding the
proper use of knowledge as a path to Divine Wisdom. According to Herrad, the legitimate quest for knowledge and ultimately also for *Philosophia*,
understood as Divine Wisdom, could lead man back to God, or as Hugh
of St. Victor put it, help him to *remember* his true identity, and to recognize himself.

Accordingly, the *Philosophia* image appears in conjunction with a
group of texts and images that address human attempts to attain knowledge. The Babel image is one example, certainly, but it is followed by a
series of texts that discuss the postdiluvium quest for knowledge in more
general terms. Study is first presented in positive terms: the arts are said to
liberate the soul and philosophy is defined as the knowledge of all things
human and divine (*HD* no. 115). However, a section break is noted after
HD no. 117: "Expliciunt excerpta de philosophia et musica. Incipiunt excerpta quedam de fabulis." On folio 31r the nine Muses are shown, each
in her own small medallion, which together form part of a square, three
medallions to each side. Accompanying texts are explanatory—not con-
demning; however, Herrad never loses sight of the mythical, rather than
moral significance of the Muses. The search for knowledge that followed
the flood is described as having been inspired by evil spirits and by the
blinding of man's reason. Although the two images are clearly presented
as a pair, as Ettlinger noted, the Muses are sharply differentiated from
the *artes*.[110] They lack the moral framework within which the *artes* are
presented—no *Philosophia* figure receives their homage. More important,
they are presented as fables, a foil against which to understand the Christianized *artes*.

As the previous discussion suggests, the purpose of Herrad's image
was not so much to teach the details of philosophy and the liberal arts, as
it has often been thought, but to present the hope of reconciliation with
God in the immediate aftermath of the Fall and to promise that reconciliation was possible, and paradise once more attainable. Philosophy and the
liberal arts had a vital role to play in leading humankind back to God, as
we have seen. That role was essentially to coach the soul to recognize its

true nature and its true purpose—both things that it knew, but that like Boethius, it had forgotten. Hugh of St. Victor put it best in his *Didascalicon*:

This, then, is what the arts are concerned with, this is what they intend, namely, to restore within us the divine likeness, a likeness which to us is a form but to God is his nature. The more we are conformed to the divine nature, the more do we possess Wisdom, for then there begins to shine forth again in us what has forever existed in the divine Idea or Pattern, coming and going in us but standing changeless in God.[111]

The connection that Dame Philosophy drew between Boethius's spiritual sickness and his forgetfulness, like that between Hugh's "stupefied" mind and its forgotten nature, was central to the soteriology of the *Hortus*. Since memory had been damaged in the Fall—the *Hortus* says that it had literally been made infirm and impotent—it needed to be repaired through study. In a text taken from Bernard, Herrad teaches that the hope of reconciliation with God (*spes redeundi ad Patrem*) is created through faith and charity. Moreover, through that hope of reconciliation, memory is raised up (*spes erexit memoriam*) (*HD* no. 81).[112] Herrad pairs this extract with one from a later sermon in which Bernard reminds his hearers that the wisdom that he advocates is not the wisdom of this world but of God—precisely the message that she conveys in her *Philosophia* image (*HD* no. 81 B).[113]

Herrad's ultimate message is that knowledge, like memory, has a moral aspect and that it is in the moral cast of knowledge that humankind's reconciliation—or prolonged exile—is to be effected. Furthermore, the liberal arts, which, as Herrad teaches, "liberate the soul from earthly cares," were explicitly associated in medieval thought with the cultivation of virtue. Philosophy, the progenitor of the *artes* and also their ruler, comprised three categories of learning, *physica*, *ethica*, and *logica*. Within this threefold division, Isidore of Seville had attributed to *physica* the teaching of the quadrivium, to *logica* the teaching of dialectic and rhetoric, and to *ethica* the cultivation of the virtues, ideas that Herrad assumed in the *Hortus*.[114] According to Herrad, ethics serve a moral purpose: either to repel vice or to stimulate virtue (*HD* no. 116).[115] The connection between wisdom and virtue suggested by Isidore's association of ethics with philosophy is clearly expressed in the *Hortus* through an excerpt from Rufinus (*Sapientia comprehendens omnia et virtus qua tota creatura fieri potuit*) (*HD* no. 13). The connection between the liberal arts and the virtues that is implicit in Herrad's presentation was made explicit in the west façade of Notre Dame in Paris. There, the arts were shown together with the virtues in the lower section of the central panel.[116]

Despite similarities between Herrad's presentation of *Philosophia* and that of Hugh of St. Victor, there was, however, a key difference: like Cassiodorus and Augustine, Hugh justifies secular learning as performing a role in the service of theology. Herrad does not make that connection. She never presents *Philosophia* or the liberal arts as handmaidens to theology, which is not mentioned in her image. To be sure, she does not go any farther in the *Hortus* than the *Philosophia* image in her encouragement of secular studies, but neither does she explicitly subordinate secular studies to theology as Hugh, like Cassiodorus, Augustine, and others, was quick to do.

Conclusion: A Garden of Learning

Herrad's interpretation of philosophy as divine wisdom indicates that the *Philosophia* image in the *Hortus* functions more as a symbol of the *need* for proper instruction in the wake of the Fall than as an aid in the transmission of that instruction—it *symbolizes* rather than *is* education. Herrad presumes knowledge of the liberal arts; she does not provide it here. In fact, the discussion concerning the moral aspect of education that the *Hortus* assumes is the sort of discussion that could take place only among a group of highly educated women, women who had already mastered the liberal arts and were in a position to debate the moral worth and purpose of their achievement.

As an account of salvation history, Herrad's *Hortus* was more than a dry narrative—it was a *living* history, the outline of which was known through divine revelation, but the individual outcome of which was not yet certain. Herrad's purpose in the *Hortus* was thus twofold: first, to provide a sketch of salvation history as it had been revealed in the Bible and through the writings of the authorities; and second, to provide guidance for each reader on her path to salvation and to the celestial garden. The garden metaphor furnished Herrad with a device that was appropriate to her audience: as we saw at the outset of the chapter, the garden could denote at once the book, the monastery in which the female readers confronted it, their (in many cases) virginal bodies, and, not least, their souls. The spiritual life of each canoness entailed a passage from one biblical garden (Eden) to another (Paradise)—with spiritual battles (as in the psychomachia cycle, fols. 199v–204r) and temptations (as in the Ladder of Virtues, fol. 215v, and Ulysses and the Sirens, fol. 221r–v) along the way.

Herrad's presentation of salvation history was necessarily a contemporary history, since the women were engaged in spiritual battle even as they read the *Hortus*. Her choice of title was thus influenced by more than the analogue that the garden suggested of the process of compilation; it was equally more than the multiple spiritual interpretations of the *Hortus* within medieval thought. Herrad's garden metaphor had everything to do with her conception of the proper place of learning within salvation. The tree at the center of the Garden of Eden, with its knowledge of good and evil, signified the crucial importance of confronting learning within a moral framework. Any misguided quest for knowledge was doomed to disaster; this was the lesson of Eden. It was equally the lesson of Babel, and of the poets and magicians in the *Philosophia* image, relegated to the exterior of the circle—beyond the "wall" within which *Philosophia*, the arts, and Plato and Socrates were enclosed.

The foregoing discussion of the placement and purpose of the *Philosophia* image in Herrad's presentation of salvation history has demonstrated that the organization of the *Hortus* was not haphazard, but was underpinned by important theological and philosophical assumptions, in this case to do with the salvific significance of knowledge. The similarities between Herrad's approach to knowledge and that of Hugh of St. Victor stand as a powerful reminder that Herrad was working within an Augustinian intellectual context, one that was significantly more receptive to the new learning of the universities than were either the Cistercians or many of the older Benedictine communities. The *Hortus* reflects this characteristic Augustinian intellectual openness. However, by the time that Herrad was writing, even the Victorines were increasingly cautious about secular learning—much more so than they had been in Hugh's lifetime. Of course, Hugh of St. Victor had been cautious too: despite his faith in the propaedeutic merits of the arts, he was critical of contemporary education and especially of those teachers whom he described as "peddlers of trifles."[117] However, by the late twelfth century, criticism of contemporary learning and masters appears to have been rife at St. Victor; Walter of St. Victor asked, "Are there not four labyrinths in France: Peter Abelard, Peter Lombard, Peter of Poitiers, and Gilbert of la Porrée?"[118] Although most Victorine scholars have dismissed Walter as an anomaly, Gibson explains that his view was in fact fairly widespread. She writes that "roads that had once seemed parallel (if distinct) were sharply divergent by the 1170s; and every man had to choose one or the other.''[119] Walter's path was clear; he condemned the new teaching of the schools in no uncertain terms. Although Herrad began her project at this time, she did not join Walter in his condemnation, nor did she separate the knowledge of Peter Lombard from that of the prescholastics, even if she did divorce it from its systematic context. Herrad was bold, both in her presentation of learning as propadeutic to salvation and in her adoption of some of the very texts of which Victorines of her generation were most skeptical.

The singularity of the *Hortus* and, more particularly, of the approach to knowledge that it advocated for women prompt two important observations, the first related to monastic learning in general and the second to the involvement of women in the intellectual renaissance of the twelfth century. Although Herrad's garden title placed her work within a tradition of monastic rather than scholastic composition, the contents of the *Hortus* conflate distinctions between these two types of learning and the *Hortus* as a whole confounds expectations of what monastic reading should look like for professed women. The *Hortus* title suggested that the work should be read within a monastic, spiritual context. But this is the key to its originality; it offers scholastic texts for contemplative reading aimed at the attainment of divine wisdom. Herrad's model suggests that, rather than two separate types of learning, with two different curricula, there may simply have been different ways of reading—one for the school and another for the cloister. As we saw in Chapter 2, the *Hortus* included both traditional Benedictine authors as well as school masters. Both were important to Herrad; only her approach to learning as a path to Divine Wisdom sets her apart from the schools.

Even more interesting is the evidence that the *Hortus* provides for the education of religious women during the twelfth-century renaissance. Katzenellenbogen points out that the representation of *Philosophia* and the seven liberal arts was a fairly recent phenomenon in the twelfth century, and that such representations were tied largely to centers of study and intellectual vitality. At Chartres, the representation of the liberal arts may have been inspired by the work of Thierry of Chartres, chancellor of the school at Chartres and author of the *Heptateuchon*, a guide in which the arts were presented as aids to theological understanding.[120] In the same way, the inspiration behind Herrad's *Philosophia* image was the intellectual vitality of the community at Hohenbourg in the last quarter of the twelfth century.

The singularity of the *Hortus* in terms of women's education is most striking in comparison with the *Speculum virginum*. Where the *Hortus Philosophia* image presented rivers representing the liberal arts, the Mystical Paradise of the *Speculum virginum* encouraged its female audience to drink from rivers representing the Gospels. Peregrinus encourages spiritual rather than secular learning for Theodora: "I wish to set before your eyes, like a painting, an image or reflection of paradise in which the fountain, with its intelligible rivers rushing in their fourfold courses, ministers drink to holy virgins as if to 'doves who dwell beside plentiful streams,' so that they may drink of the Gospel streams and the Church's doctrines . . . and thus steeped in celestial disciplines, they may arrive at the celestial paradise."[121] In his writings for a male audience, Conrad of Hirsau encourages the study of philosophy as a means to "inculcate love of God" and promote contempt for the world, declaring "Let us then serve our king by pursuing liberal studies," with the caveat that the disciple ought to learn his philosophy "in Christ."[122] However, if Conrad was the author of the *Speculum virginum*, his approach was completely different when he directed himself to a female audience. The *Speculum* does not encourage an intellectual approach to God for women as Conrad had for the male audience of the *Dialogue on the Authors*; indeed the prefatory letter with which the *Speculum* was introduced allowed for the possibility that its female recipient might even have difficulty understanding the text: "Scrutinize the faces of your hearts in the mirror I sent, and if you cannot understand all that is written there, it is no small part of knowledge to listen to and love one who does understand."[123]

Despite increasing skepticism toward secular learning during the twelfth century and a spiritual climate in which lack of learning was associated with sanctity for women, not all women were prepared to suppress their love of learning. An anonymous poem in a twelfth-century verse anthology from Bury St. Edmunds preserves for us one woman's rebellion against that type of religion which emphasized for women ignorance of learning. While acknowledging that

It is not for religious women to compose verses,
    Nor ours to ask who Aristotle might be.

The poet affirms her intellectual approach to God:

Great learned writing will not prohibit me from being good,
    learned writing does not prohibit, but allows me to know God.[124]

Although Peter the Venerable praises Heloise for leaving "logic for the Gospel, Plato for Christ, the academy for the cloister," there is evidence that monastic women could devote themselves to both study *and* God.[125] There is evidence, in fact, that Heloise chose both, herself. Mews comments that Heloise's "retirement" from public life at the Paraclete, as Abelard describes it, may have been less for prayer than for study.[126]

   That women did study philosophy is suggested in a poem from the margin of a late eleventh-century manuscript. Although the poet laments the degradation of philosophy, he nonetheless indicates that women were students of philosophy:

Pythagoras is weeping, and you, good Cicero, are weeping too.
    Aristotle the soldier of logic is weeping.

The greatest of all men, both Plato and Socrates, are weeping.
Here is the reason why: they are weeping for philosophy,
    Which once did prosper, flourish, gleam –
But now has become tawdry, now has been reduced to such baseness
    That female hearts even study it.[127]

   It is in this context—the story of women's education during the medieval period—that Herrad's work is most significant. In marked contrast to contemporary works of spiritual formation for women that tended to underscore experience and the body as vehicles for female spirituality, Herrad emphasized the intellectual as a route to the spiritual for the women of her monastery. The texts that she included in the *Hortus* are proof that she wanted to provide them with a sound education—the sort of education that a monk-priest or young student at the schools in Paris might expect, indeed, the sort of education that Abelard himself might have had. The *Hortus* is an example of how women, who were constantly warned against excessive knowledge and whose unique responsibility for the Fall was stressed in literary as well as in visual records, negotiated the acquisition of knowledge.

   A final observation: in describing her book as a garden, Herrad provided for a further iteration of her bee metaphor, since the garden is a place in which bees gather nectar and create honey. The two metaphors—garden and honey—thus represent different, yet connected, processes of study and composition: Herrad's "honey" became a garden for the women of Hohenbourg, who, like her, could also "imitate the bee," gathering nectar from its flowers, as Conrad's poem suggested (*HD* no. 1162). Although Herrad does not make explicit this possibility, the garden that she presented to the Hohenbourg women held the promise of future intellectual work—it was not simply the product of her own learning, but also provided the opportunity for the women to become bees themselves.

6

The Pleasure Garden of Learning: Reading the *Hortus*

Incipit Ortus deliciarum, in quo collectis floribus scriptuarum assidue jocundetur turmula adolescentularum. (*HD* no. 3)

Here begins the *Garden of Delights*, in which the little troop of maidens may be continually delighted by the collected flowers of scripture.

THE OBVIOUS QUESTION IS *why* Herrad had embarked on the *Hortus* project to begin with and, even more curious, how she intended the manuscript to be used. The circumstances at Hohenbourg in the latter half of the twelfth century, the community's recent reform, and its ongoing struggles with its chaplains—at least during Relinde's abbacy—provide one answer: the manuscript was a response to the particular needs of a reformed community of women at a time when the involvement of women in the religious life was increasing dramatically. But context cannot fully explain the genesis of the *Hortus* project. Herrad herself provides a further explanation, writing in her address to the women of Hohenbourg that she had compiled the texts of the *Hortus* first, "to the praise and honor of Christ and the church," and second, "for the sake of your love" (*HD* no. 2).

The first of these objectives is clear enough since, as her organization around the central theme of salvation history suggests, Herrad had designed the entire *Hortus* as a work of praise to God, a celebration of his work in creation, of his grace in redemption, and of his eternal glory in heaven. The manuscript's contents—which lean heavily toward the pastoral—indicate that it was also intended to ensure the perpetuation of legitimate worship at Hohenbourg by providing its audience with orthodox theological training. Ultimately, then, it was not simply the *Hortus* that assured the "praise and honor of Christ and the church," but through it also the community of women as a whole, and Herrad's guidance of it.

The *Hortus* was literally a script for the salvation of each individual soul at Hohenbourg and a means by which the women might come to know God—whether in study as the *Philosophia* image suggested, or in prayer, the singing of hymns, the recitation of the creed, or the contemplation of Christ, risen and enthroned in heaven. Herrad reminded the women that they shared with her the duty, and the privilege, of praising and honoring Christ in a poem that she included in the *Hortus* for them to sing to-gether.[1] "O gracious King," she writes:

O leader of the way,
Supreme Jesus Christ,
Teach our choir
To praise you
By our way of life. (*HD* no. 595)[2]

Herrad's second objective is more curious. What did she mean by her declaration that the *Hortus* had been designed for the "sake of your love"? In the continuation of her prologue, Herrad turns herself fully to the women of Hohenbourg, outlining the encouragement and spiritual repose that she intended them to find in the manuscript:

Therefore, in this very book, you ought diligently to seek pleasing food and to refresh your exhausted soul with its honeyed dewdrops, so that, always possessed by the charms of the Bridegroom and fattened on spiritual delights, you may safely hurry over ephemeral things to possess the things that last forever in happiness and pleasure. (*HD* no. 2)[3]

Herrad's twin motives were thus intricately connected since her attention to the women's "love" was, in the first instance, accomplished through the spiritual emphasis of the manuscript and its presentation of salvation history. Herrad's love for the women was most clear in her concern that they attain salvation, "the things that last forever." As she points out, the *Hortus* provided the locus—both spiritual and intellectual—in which all members of the community could meet with God.

Precisely *how* Herrad's audience should meet God in the *Hortus* is the next question. One of the mysteries of Herrad's prologue is her failure to discuss the manuscript in any real depth, as we have seen, or to provide her readers with instructions for how they should approach the work—how, in short, she intended them to use it. Apart from exhorting them to seek in it "pleasing food" and to "refresh their exhausted souls," Herrad says very little in her prologue to guide her readers in practical terms. However, the last stanzas of her introductory poem take up the question of use directly, at the same time revealing a further dimension of her creation of the *Hortus* for the women's "love"—the pleasure that she hoped that the manuscript would give them. Herrad brings the poem to a close with the following wish:

May this book prove useful
And delightful to you,
May you never cease to ponder it
In your thoughts. (*HD* no. 1)[4]

This stanza sums up the two ways in which Herrad responds to the love of the women: first, through concern for their spiritual souls—her wish that the book should be "useful" in a spiritual sense—and second, through attention to their enjoyment—that it should be "delightful."[5]

The delightfulness of the *Hortus* is readily apparent. The mixture of poetry and prose, dialogue, sermons, and hymns that it presented ensured that it would capture the attention of even the most wayward student. Its folios, glowing with illuminations, can only now be imagined; however, even in the imagining it is clear that they must have been breathtaking. The manuscript was obviously a prized possession at Hohenbourg: although fires repeatedly threatened the monastery—and in 1546 all but destroyed it—the *Hortus* was always rescued from the flames and taken to safety.[6] Only after the fire in 1546, when the monastery was handed over to the care of Premonstratensian canons and the women dispersed, was the precious *Hortus* sent to the palace of the bishop of Strasbourg at Saverne, where it came to the attention of a wider public.

Herrad's intentions for the usefulness of the *Hortus* are less clear. She was evidently not in the least concerned to explain or otherwise delineate the use of her work, whether in her prologue or elsewhere. As a result, we have little sense of how she anticipated that it might be received at Hohenbourg and, lacking any record of the manuscript's use, no firm idea of how it actually was read. In the absence of such information, we can only deduce from the work itself and from the decisions Herrad made regarding its design—the size of its folios, its page layout, the type and density of its glosses, and last, but certainly not least, its illuminations— how it may have been used.[7]

The first clue to the use of the *Hortus* is its size: its folios measured

19.7–20.9 inches by 14.2–14.5 inches, dimensions that exceed those of other works produced around the same time within Augustinian communities in Alsace.[8] The *Guta-Sintram Codex*, which served primarily as a necrology with other largely regulatory texts attached, measured 14 inches by 10.5 inches, and the illustrated Evangeliary of Marbach-Schwartzenthann 10.6 inches by 7.1 inches—both smaller than the *Hortus*, despite their display purpose.[9] The closest comparison to the *Hortus* is to be found in the illuminated Bibles of the twelfth century, many of which shared its dimensions and grandeur.[10] The size of the *Hortus* precludes personal use: Herrad did not design it to be read by individuals, but to be studied and viewed by a group of women together, most likely under the guidance of a *magistra*.[11] The manuscript's cycle of illuminations confirms this conclusion: it was designed to be seen, and not simply read.[12] With its many images and their generous distribution throughout the manuscript, the *Hortus* was a book that was intended for display within the community. The groups of women who gathered around it could examine its images, read and discuss its texts, explore the many cross references that Herrad included, and sing its hymns and neumed poems together.[13]

So how might the *Hortus* have been used at Hohenbourg? We can be confident that Herrad did not intend for it to serve as a reference tool since she eschewed the organizational structure of her sources and omitted from her prologue the time-saving justifications that appear, among others, in Peter Lombard's *Sentences* and Honorius's *Speculum ecclesiae*. Both of these authors presented their works as an alternative to the lengthy process of actually reading the original sources. Peter Lombard promises in his prologue that "it will not be necessary for the seeker to turn through numerous books; for the brevity [of the *Sentences*] offers him, without effort, what he seeks."[14] Other authors, less explicit than Honorius and Peter Lombard in recommending their works as crib notes to the *auctoritates*, nonetheless used time-saving keywords to describe their work; terms such as *summa, brevis, compilare, compilatio,* or *compendium* appear frequently in prologues to works of compilation.[15] Yet Herrad gives no hint of this type of justification—in fact, one gets the distinct sense that she has done everything that she can to *prevent* readers from dipping into the *Hortus*. Although she would have been familiar with the sorts of finding tools that appeared in many of her sources (book divisions, numbered chapter lists at the beginning of a work, headlines, color, letter size, paragraph marks, and marginal indexing symbols), she chose to rely exclusively on biblical order and memory as organizational tools, employing red ink only for the headings that introduce each excerpt.

The layout and organization of the *Hortus* reflect the sort of reading that Herrad intended it to support. Most of the newer finding tools that would have appeared in many of her sources, and especially those from Paris, catered to a different sort of reading than she expected, one that required efficiency, comprehensiveness, and ease of use.[16] Whereas for scholastic readers, who were confronted with an abundance of information, searchability was of the utmost importance, speed was not a monastic virtue. Herrad's organization of the *Hortus* suggests rather the reflective spirit of the *lectio divina*.[17] For her, reading was both study and prayer, as Hugh of St. Victor observed: "the start of learning, thus, lies in reading, but its consummation lies in meditation."[18] Her decision to omit finding tools and to ignore the sorts of time-saving justifications that appear in prologues to her sources indicates that, even though the *Hortus* combined typically scholastic with typically monastic texts, it was ultimately designed to be read within a monastic setting, one in which the supreme goal was not simply knowledge, but more specifically knowledge of God. As Bernard of Clairvaux wrote, echoing the Apostle Paul and expressing the same ideas as Herrad, "we teach not in the way philosophy is taught [*non in doctis humanae sapientiae verbis*], but in the way that the Spirit teaches us: we teach spiritual things spiritually."[19]

Glosses, Scribal Practice, and Education

A further clue to Herrad's intentions for the use of the *Hortus* lies in the rich abundance of its glosses—words, sometimes singly, often as parts of longer phrases, that appear both in Latin and in Middle High German throughout the manuscript and that would have comprised one of the most striking aspects of the layout and presentation of the *Hortus* page. Like the manuscript's images, these glosses serve as a channel through which Herrad could communicate directly with her audience, comment implicitly on the text, and indicate how it should be studied. They appear as notes and explanations on the *Hortus* images, as a web of cross-references linking its diverse texts together, and, most commonly, as marginal and interlinear notes to the *Hortus* texts.[20] These notes, and in particular the marginal and interlinear Latin and German glosses on the

Latin text, have much to reveal concerning the way in which the *Hortus* may have been read at Hohenbourg.

Until recently, it was common to view all glosses as teaching tools and to assume, therefore, that all glossed manuscripts functioned as "class-books" or teaching texts. According to this point of view, the richly glossed folios of the *Hortus* would qualify it as a teaching text, although not, obviously, as a student book on account of its size and luxurious presentation, but rather as a book used by a teacher during the course of instruction. However, the logic of equating "gloss" with "teaching tool" has been seriously questioned in recent years.[21] The old idea that glosses might represent the notes of a teacher preparing to teach a text or of a student trying to understand it can no longer be accepted at face value. Instead, as Lapidge argues, the presence of glosses in a given manuscript may simply reflect the mechanical copying of a scribe from his exemplar.[22] In his view, the fact that glosses often traveled with a text and therefore appear in many different manuscripts must indicate that they were not records of classroom practice. That glossing is frequently not sustained throughout a manuscript mitigates still further the equation of gloss with classbook. As Lapidge concludes, if a scribe lost interest in the gloss shortly after embarking on his work, then the didactic potential of the glosses cannot have been central to their presence in the manuscript.

Lapidge's caution that glosses are not necessarily an indication of the schoolroom has prompted significant discussion concerning the place and purpose of glossed manuscripts, with important implications for our understanding of the *Hortus*. The mere presence of glosses in a manuscript is no longer considered sufficient to designate it as a classbook. Instead, as Wieland argues, certain additional criteria are necessary, the most basic of which is that the glosses should serve the needs of "either students or teachers."[23] Beyond this requirement, he suggests that glosses in class-books must be consistent, they must cover such instructional areas as accent, lexicon, grammar, syntax, and content, and, finally, they must include q: glosses—glosses designed to prompt a teacher to question his students on a certain point (*quare hoc*).[24] The origins of the glosses, in his view, are largely irrelevant. Whether or not they traveled with the texts with which they appear, as Lapidge observes that they might, Wieland points out that their presence in a given manuscript is not necessarily proof of mechanical copying. He argues that such glosses may, in fact, have been copied intentionally from the exemplar, in which case they must represent the scribe's—or teacher's—choice. If, as in the case of the *Hortus*, the teacher and the mastermind of the manuscript project were one and the same, then its glosses must have been specifically chosen to serve a particular purpose, whether they were derivative or, as many of the *Hortus* glosses were, original.[25]

Of the five main types of glosses that Wieland identifies—lexical, grammatical, syntactical, prosodic, and commentary—lexical and commentary glosses are by far the most common in the *Hortus*. A certain number of grammatical glosses also appear; however, there is no record of any that were prosodic or syntactical. This is already interesting since, according to Wieland, grammatical and syntactical glosses are most suggestive of the classbook in that their purpose was to teach Latin. Grammatical glosses clarify parts of speech and identify their forms in a particular sentence.[26] A grammatical gloss might, for instance, supply a word explaining the grammatical property of the lemma. An example of the grammatical gloss appears in Herrad's introductory poem: *Ne vacilles dubia: in.* Here, the gloss *in* makes it clear that *dubia* is ablative so that the line reads "lest you should waver in uncertain faith" (*HD* no. 1 n. 20). Syntactical glosses aid in the interpretation of a sentence by elucidating its structure, linking a noun to the adjective by which it is modified, or a verb to its adverb. Often these glosses appear in the form of dots or other signs, so that a noun and adjective might each share one marker, and a verb and adverb another.[27] The student reading a complex sentence could then easily identify related parts of speech and even render it into a word order more natural to the vernacular. If these glosses did appear in the *Hortus*, the nineteenth-century copyists made no note of them.

Given that grammatical and syntactical glosses do not figure prominently in the *Hortus*, it is likely that the women for whom the manuscript was intended were already competent in Latin. Further support for this conclusion is provided in the manuscript's *Philosophia* image (fol. 32r; plate 9). As we saw in the last chapter, Herrad used this image as a symbol of education in the liberal arts, with which she assumed her audience was familiar, but which she did not explicitly discuss. So although the image was richly glossed, the glosses did not provide the sort of basic information that would have been useful to a student who was confronting the *artes* for the first time—a student who did not already know something either of Plato and Socrates, or of the specific disciplines that the personified *artes* were intended to represent. Herrad used this image as shorthand to evoke a particular curriculum and to present a specific argument concerning the place and purpose of that curriculum in the soul's path to God.

This argument would surely have been irrelevant if the liberal arts did not hold a place in the Hohenbourg curriculum; it would certainly have been meaningless if the women to whom it was addressed did not have the background knowledge necessary to interpret the image as Herrad intended. The fact that the image argues for a progression through the liberal arts toward *Philosophia* suggests that by the time the Hohenbourg women began to study the manuscript, they were already well advanced in their studies.

The preponderance in the *Hortus* of commentary and lexical glosses offers further clues as to the purpose and potential use of the manuscript. These types of glosses do not offer elementary grammatical instruction or help in parsing a Latin sentence, but might instead deepen the reading of a text for those who could already understand its basic message; they support the reading of more advanced students. Commentary glosses, which Wieland defines as "non-prosodic, non-lexical, non-grammatical, and non-syntactical" aid in the interpretation of a text once its basic structure has already been understood.[28] They include interpretative glosses which decode metaphors, clarify the meaning of a lemma through a more specific term, summarize or explain a text's content, provide etymological information, or supply the source of a particular text or idea. A final sort of commentary gloss provides information that might be termed encyclopedic, offering geographical and historical information and explaining unusual terms or objects. In the *Hortus*, these encyclopedic glosses generally derive from the *Summarium Heinrici*, which Herrad used consistently as a reference work throughout her project.

Examples of each type of commentary gloss can be found in the *Hortus*:

Glosses that decode metaphors:

Veri floris: id est Christi (*HD* no. 328 n. 1)

Flos: id est Christus (*HD* no. 328 n. 5)

Glosses that offer greater specificity:

Homo: id est Adam (*HD* no. 544 n. 2)

A judeis gentibus: id est Pilato et militibus ejus (*HD* no. 253 n. 2)

Fluvio transito: id est Jordane (*HD* no. 249 n. 6)

Glosses that summarize or explain content:

Omnes fideles, qui ab inicio mundi futuram passionem Christi crediderunt et exspectaverunt, sanguine et aqua que de latere Christi fluxerunt baptizati et redempti remissionem peccatorem acceperunt. (*HD* no. 543 n. 3, marginal note to a section from Rupert's *De divinis officiis* concerning baptism)

Glosses that provide etymological information:

Propugnacula ejus in jaspides: Propugnacula quod ex his propugnat (*HD* no. 837 n. 7, marginal note; similar gloss at *HD* no. 710 n. 1) [= *Summarium Heinrici*, VII, 2, 82f]

Terminos: termini dicti sunt quod terre mensuram distinguant (*HD* no. 837 n. 9, marginal note) [= *Summarium Heinrici*, V, 20, 441f]

Histrio **spilman**: Dicti sunt histriones quod ab Histria id genus sit adductum, sive quod perplexas historiis fabulas exprimerent quasi hystoriones. (*HD* no. 635, marginal note)

Encyclopedic glosses:

Stratoris: stratores sunt compositores qui regias sellas componunt (*HD* no. 794 n. 12, marginal note)

Hec ex bisso conficitur: bissum **sabe** genus est quoddam lini nimis candidum et molle (*HD* no. 792 n. 28, marginal note) [Cf. *Summarium Heinrici*, IX, 7, 165f]

Basilicam: basilica regalis domus dicitur. Basilice vero divina templa nunc dicuntur, quia ibi omnium regi servitur, sicut olim regum habitacula dicebatur. (*HD* no. 394 n. 3) [= *Summarium Heinrici*, VII, 4, 174–76]

Paranimphos: paranimphus amicus sponsi et sponse, vel **brutebote**. Item paranimphi custodes sive servatores sponse. (*HD* no. 791 n. 21, marginal note)

Glosses that offer source information do appear in the *Hortus*, but are associated primarily with excerpts from the *Elucidarium*; these generally provide only a single name, for instance "Johannes Crisostomus," "Prosper," or "Beda" (*HD* no. 849), and are clearly different from glosses to other texts in the *Hortus*, most of which are introduced either by *id est* or *scilicet.* The singularity of the *Elucidarium* glosses cannot be coincidental, but suggests that they appeared first in the exemplar and were copied directly with the text.[29] Since Honorius used marginal glosses to provide guidance for further study in his *Elucidarium*, this is the most likely conclusion.[30]

The bulk of the *Hortus* glosses simply clarify the meaning of a text, whether by decoding its metaphors, or by providing synonyms, short explanations, or greater specificity to a Latin lemma. However, other types of commentary glosses—the so-called encyclopedic, summary, and etymological glosses—are important in understanding Herrad's method in the construction of the *Hortus.* As the examples listed above indicate, many of these glosses were marginal rather than interlinear, as the vast majority of the *Hortus* glosses seem to have been, and were taken from the *Summarium Heinrici*, a late eleventh-century or early twelfth-century reworking of Isidore's *Etymologies* that was one of Herrad's basic sources. However, unlike her other sources, the *Summarium Heinrici* furnished Herrad not only with texts, but also with the Latin glosses that she added to excerpts from Honorius, Rupert, and others. Their presence in the *Hortus* is a reflection of deliberate scribal and editorial choice and allows some insight into Herrad's working method. Once a particular text had been copied, Herrad (or one of the scribes working with her) searched through the *Summarium* for glosses that would help to explain difficult words, or to identify unfamiliar technical terms. So, for example, when a selection from Honorius's *Speculum ecclesiae* mentioned the destruction of pagan temples and the construction of a Christian basilica, Herrad turned to the *Summarium Heinrici* to find an appropriate gloss to explain what, exactly, a basilica was (*HD* no. 394 n. 3; *Summarium Heinrici*, VII, 4, 174–76).

Herrad also used the *Summarium* as a source for some of the 1,250 or so Middle High German glosses that appear in the *Hortus.* Unlike the Latin glosses that she took from the *Summarium*, all of which are commentary glosses, these German glosses are lexical glosses; each one provides a vernacular equivalent for the Latin lemma, while maintaining the grammatical form of the original term. These glosses, which Curschmann describes as "one of the most pervasive external features of the codex,"[31] locate the *Hortus* firmly within the vernacular culture of Alsace under the Hohenstaufen, highlighting the fact that the women of Hohenbourg were native German speakers who learned Latin only as a second language—as all medieval people who learned Latin did.[32]

As with the bulk of the Latin glosses, the majority of the German glosses appear in interlinear rather than marginal placement, suggesting that they were inserted at the time that the base text was copied. However, their use in the manuscript demonstrates that their presence was anything but mechanical. To be sure, the initial inspiration for the German glosses came from the *Summarium Heinrici*, which was the source for many of them. Some of these were copied along with *Summarium* texts directly into the *Hortus* (e.g., *HD* nos. 24–26), a fact that may initially suggest a mechanical scribe who simply copied text and gloss together without altering either. However, texts from the *Summarium* do sometimes appear in the *Hortus* stripped of their original glosses (e.g., *HD* no. 755), demonstrating that glossing was not an unthinking scribal activity. The Hohenbourg scribe also mined the *Summarium* for German glosses that were inserted into unrelated Latin texts, as she had with its Latin commentary glosses. The intentionality that lay behind this use of the *Summarium* is further demonstrated by the fact that the *Hortus* scribe did not rely on this text as her only source of German glosses, but extended the vernacular glossing of the *Hortus* beyond the terms that she found in it, contributing words that were unique to the area around Hohenbourg. *HD* no. 34, for instance, had no German glosses in the original, but appears in the *Hortus* with *sol: sunne, stella: sterna,* and *sidera: gestirne.* Indeed, as work on the *Hortus* progressed, the scribes began to engage in an increasingly active form of glossing, adding their own German glosses to texts and even to Latin glosses. As they did so, they began to extend the glosses beyond their initial format. Where glosses in the *Summarium,* for instance, are by and large nominal, the glosses toward the end of the *Hortus* are verbal, adverbial, and prepositional.

Although the purpose of these German glosses is somewhat mysterious, one thing is clear: they were not designed primarily to aid in basic Latin instruction or to make the *Hortus* texts available to women who were not already largely proficient in Latin. These glosses were often repetitive and not always illuminating; moreover, difficult words were frequently unglossed while more common terms were glossed, leading Curschmann to argue that they were simply psychological tools that served to make theological material, which might otherwise have seemed irrelevant, more familiar to the Germanic women of Hohenbourg.[33] The inconsistency of the German glosses, their tendency toward repetition, and their apparent simplicity do not necessarily rule out a didactic purpose; however, they would have earned low marks as Latin teaching tools. From her work on classical texts in medieval usage, Reynolds presents an alternate explanation for vernacular glosses, which she calls "translation" glosses, commenting on their "bias towards the everyday" and explaining that since the Latin lemmata were unlikely to have simple Latin synonyms, vernacular glosses were often the easiest and most effective way to explain them. According to her view, "translation is part of a project in the service of Latinity, not in the service of the vernacular."[34]

The purpose of the Latin glosses in the *Hortus* is clearer. As a whole, the types of interpretative glosses that appear in the *Hortus* extend Herrad's allegorical and pedagogical program. Many expand allegorical interpretations and one even offers a definition of allegory: *allegoria est ubi aliud dicitur et aliud significatur* (*HD* no. 792 n. 17). Others present textual refinements in anticipation of potential misunderstanding, as in a gloss to the *Gemma animae*, which differentiates between two similar words: *trames via transversa, trama vel tramis extrema pars vestimenti* (*HD* no. 792 n. 22), or a gloss to a section from the *Speculum ecclesiae*, which specifies the purpose of a word in a sentence: *Sapientia: proprium nomen* (*HD* no. 700 n. 8).[35] Even the apparently random glossing of the *Hortus*—which Lapidge suggests must argue against classroom usage—may in fact signify that the manuscript was used as a guide for the teacher, who needed only occasional reminders of potential lessons or points for discussion, rather than as a schoolbook that would find its ultimate place in the hands of the student.[36] In this case, the book remained in the possession of the teacher, as Wieland suggests in his proposed reconstruction of a lesson within the Anglo-Saxon schoolroom:

The teacher conducts his class mainly in Latin . . . The teacher has a book while the students carry only wax tablets. The teacher dictates from the book, probably clause by clause . . . while the students write down the dictation . . . The teacher then explains the vocabulary, the parts of speech, the syntax, the tropes, and makes general comments on the text; he then dismisses the class, possibly with an injunction to memorize the text on their tablets, or to paraphrase it into prose.[37]

The possibility that the *Hortus* may also have been used in a similar way is strengthened by the appearance of the textual gloss *Hic lege* ("Read here") in the miniatures on folios 3v and 8r, indicating the specific text to be read in conjunction with the image.[38] Like the q: glosses (*quare hoc*), designed to specify places where teachers were to question students on a particular point, the *Hic lege* (or *Lege etiam*) glosses seem to have been intended to prompt the *magistra* to expound on the message of the image on the basis of a linked text. If so, the didactic purpose and immediacy of the q: glosses described by Wieland find a parallel in the *Hortus*, further demonstrating that it was designed, at least in part, for a classroom setting. Suggestions for texts to be read alongside specific excerpts also appear in marginal glosses, as, for instance, the note to a section from the *Gemma animae* calling attention to a reading from the *Sentences* to be found *post sinum Abrahe* (*HD* no. 792 n. 69). A similar note, providing instructions to the reader, appears after a selection from Augustine's *Enchiridion* concerning the resurrection. Here Herrad advises: "Read also in the *Sentences* of Peter Lombard concerning the resurrection of the dead from that place: 'Causa resurrectionis,' until: 'Queri etiam solet an demones.' After this it must be read where the Lord Jesus the just judge of the living and the dead . . ." (*HD* no. 856).[39] The editors of the *Hortus* offer the tantalizing remark that this now-unfinished text continued "with references to other texts in *HD*."[40] Unfortunately the continuation of the text, and with it the continuation of what sounds very much like a teacher's voice, is now lost to us.

It is true that some of the *Hortus* glosses are repetitive, or simplistic, or both. One section of text attributed to "Gregorius," which occupies only eight lines in the *Hortus* edition, is accompanied by a total of nineteen glosses, ten of which refer to the son, eight to the father, and one to the Holy Spirit (*HD* no. 13).[41] An equally simplistic gloss appears for the lemma *celibem*: *id est castam*, a clarification that would seem unnecessary for an audience of professed women, who, if not all virgins, were presumably all chaste (*HD* no. 359 n. 9). However, in most cases the *Hortus* glosses offer useful guidance—the sort of information that a teacher might be expected to give. In one such example, the word *concinnis* is glossed *id est consonantibus vel compositis*, to which a further marginal note offers the following refinement, demonstrating the connection between the participle and the verb, while at the same time offering a range of possible synonyms: *concinno, compono, consono* (*HD* no. 421 n. 3). A similar gloss appears in *HD* no. 257 note 6, where *mancipatur* is glossed *subditur*, which is then further glossed: *mancipio, traho, subdo, quasi manu capio emancipo, manu mitto, id est libertum dono*. A gloss on the word *ibices* offers the same word in the nominative singular and genitive singular: *ibis ibicis* giving the students a sense of how the noun was declined (*HD* no. 145 n. 6).[42] Glosses to *HD* no. 793 (*Sanccimus: sanctio, statuo, decerno*; n. 4) and *HD* no. 792 (*Excubabat: excubo, vigilo, custodio*; n. 5) may have been meant to prompt students to conjugate the verbs. The proximity of these two very similar types of glosses in the *Hortus* makes it unlikely that they were copied from the exemplar, especially since the excerpts with which they appear were taken from two different texts. Rather, their circumstances and similarity make it more likely that these glosses were added by the *Hortus* scribe in anticipation, or reflection, of a classroom exercise.

From these examples, and the many others that appear in the manuscript, it seems clear that the *Hortus* was used as a teaching tool—although not at an elementary level, but at a stage commensurate with the textual and theological sophistication Herrad expected from the women of her community. There are, however, glosses in the manuscript that do cater to students at an earlier stage in their studies, especially those that accompany Herrad's poetic prologue to the *Hortus* and that, of all the glosses in the *Hortus*, can be attributed most securely to her (*HD* no. 1). This poem is one of the most heavily glossed texts in the *Hortus*: its twenty-five stanzas are accompanied by fifty-two Latin glosses, many of which were obviously meant for students just starting their Latin study.[43] Some of these expand on ideas and metaphors that remained implicit in the verse due to the exigencies of poetic meter. These are relatively straightforward: the "terrible enemies" (*diros hostes*) of stanza five, Herrad tells us, are actually demons (*id est demones*, n. 2); the King (*rex*), she adds, is Christ (*Christus*, n. 3). Herrad's gloss on her address to the women of Hohenbourg, described as the "little troop of the bridegroom" in the fourth stanza, is *scilicet tu* (n. 1), indicating that she is addressing the women directly. Interrupting the text with the immediacy of a teacher, Herrad almost seems to be urging the women to wake up and pay attention. Other glosses make elementary grammatical points, providing the subject for a sentence, for instance, *vivens* is glossed *tu* (n. 16), or indicating the mood of the verb by supplying the gloss *ut* (n. 44) for the lemma *inveniar*. Many of her glosses are personal, for instance *tu* (n. 16), *tibi* (n. 50), and *a me* (n. 17), and serve to reinforce the immediacy of the text as an indication of the ongoing relationship between Herrad and the women of her monastery. Still others furnish synonyms for terms that appear in the poem, or expand its metaphors, thereby adding to the Latin vocabulary of the Hohenbourg women.

The glosses in Herrad's opening poem can be contrasted most usefully with those that appear in the penultimate poems in the manuscript, both of which are addressed to the community at Hohenbourg and were probably written by canons who were associated with Hohenbourg in some way. Although the personal touch of Herrad's poem is missing here—the canons do not address the women in the affectionate way that she had—the function of the glosses is similar. In all three cases, the glosses eschew the standard introductory format of *scilicet* and *id est*. Instead, they unfold metaphors that are fairly straightforward spiritual symbols. The "living fountain" (*vivo fonte*) is identified accordingly as the "holy spirit" (*sancti Spiritus*) (*HD* no. 1162 n. 2); the "little sheep" (*ovicule*) are identified as "young women" (*domicelle*) (*HD* no. 1162 n. 3).[44] The glossing of these poems, of which Herrad's is the most heavily annotated, and their immediate relevance to the women of Hohenbourg would have made them ideal access points for young students who were new to the text.

A final observation concerning the function of the glosses in the *Hortus*. Wieland defines a gloss as "any one or more words, letters, and symbols, written in the margin or between the lines of the text, i.e., anything on a page which is not text proper, but which is intended to comment on the text."[45] According to this definition, the *Hortus* glosses may indicate the focus of attention within the manuscript as much as they do the method of instruction that was favored at the community. In fact, the distribution of glossing does reflect the weight that texts were given within the manuscript: the texts from which Herrad cites most often and most extensively are also the most likely to be glossed. Curschmann notes that the "chief 'beneficiaries' " of glossing are, in order, the *Speculum ecclesiae*, the *Gemma animae*, the Old Testament, the *Historia* of Peter Comestor, the *Sentences* of Peter Lombard, the *Elucidarium*, Rupert of Deutz, the pseudo-Clementine *Recognitiones*, and Freculph, which, he says "is in rough proportion to their relative prominence as sources of the *Hortus*."[46] Like the *Hortus* images, Herrad may have used the glosses to draw attention to the texts and ideas that she deemed most important, a further sign that the glossing of the *Hortus* was more than simply an unthinking scribal activity.

"Reading" the *Hortus* Images

A final clue to Herrad's intentions for the *Hortus* is the manuscript's remarkable cycle of illuminations.[47] While images were not uncommon in liturgical texts in the early Middle Ages, and in Bibles during the twelfth century, their presence in a work of theology such as the *Hortus* was a new development.[48] Indeed the visual synthesis of twelfth-century ideas that the *Hortus* presents is one of Herrad's most striking achievements. Yet despite this fact, and the centrality of the images to the physical and spiritual structure of the *Hortus*, Herrad does not mention them, either in her poetic dedication or in her prose prologue. In an earlier chapter I suggested that her silence may have been a result of her refusal to apologize for the manuscript's images, as certain other illuminated manuscripts from the first half of the twelfth century did.[49] Herrad does not invoke the traditional explanation of images as "books for the illiterate." It is now time to explore that suggestion in greater depth.

The origins of the traditional *apologia* for images lay in two letters sent by Gregory the Great to Serenus, bishop of Marseilles, at the end of the sixth century.[50] In the first, written in response to news that Serenus had launched an attack on images in his diocese, Gregory justifies the place of images within Christian society: "For a picture is displayed in churches on this account, in order that those who do not know letters may at least read by seeing on the walls what they are unable to read in books."[51] In a second letter, prompted by continued reports of Serenus's intransigency, Gregory renewed his argument in favor of images: "For it is one thing to adore a picture, another through a picture's story to learn what must be adored. For what writing offers to those who read it, a picture offers to the ignorant who look at it, since in it the ignorant see what they ought to follow, in it they read who do not know letters."[52] Although Gregory's comments were specifically related to the sort of public art that appeared in church wall paintings, his comments were subsequently adopted to justify the use of images within a wide range of contexts, including book art.

The association of images with the illiterate, established by Gregory's letter, gained widespread acceptance in part because it confirmed certain elemental assumptions concerning both images and the unlearned. Excluded from the spiritual understanding of the written word—which was fully available to church men—illiterate men and women were thought to be limited to an understanding of God that was mediated through their senses: through their ears, but also, as Gregory allows, through their eyes. Since images appealed primarily to the senses, they were therefore seen as appropriate to the carnal nature of the illiterate, for whom the written word was wholly inaccessible. This justification did not redeem images for their own sake, but simply allowed their use under certain circumstances. However, for the literate and thus spiritually mature, images remained a form of communication that was not simply unnecessary, but potentially dangerous. The danger that images posed for the spiritually mature was the very reason for their effectiveness with an illiterate audience—images appeal to the bodily senses, provoking an affective and often physicalized response in their viewers. As such, they were seen as obstacles that could impede spiritual progress in the more mature, as much as they might be allowed as dim reflections of the written word for those who were less learned.[53]

Gregory's justification for the role of art—intended originally as an argument in favor of wall paintings, which would have a diverse public audience—left little room for book art, which did not usually command a public audience but was largely confined to small, and most often also literate communities.[54] Possibly in response to the contradiction that was therefore inherent in book art, some illustrated books contain references to the illiteracy of their potential audience, offering the possibility of an unlearned user as a justification for the presence of their images. The Augustinian canon Hugh of Fouilloy invoked the Gregorian equation of pictures as books for the illiterate to justify the images that he included in his illustrated *Aviarum*. In the first of his two prologues, Hugh suggested that the images were intended as a concession for the unlearned lay brothers in his congregation. He writes of his intention "by a picture to instruct the minds of simple folk, so that what the intellect of the simple folk could scarcely comprehend with the mind's eye, it might at least discern with the physical eye; and what their hearing could scarcely perceive, their sight might do so."[55] However, in his second prologue, Hugh acknowledges the fact that his work might also have a "diligent reader" who would wonder at the presence of these visual representations. To this other reader, Hugh writes: "Because I must write for the unlettered, the diligent reader should not wonder that, for the instruction of the unlettered, I say simple things about subtle matters. Nor should he attribute it to levity that I paint a hawk or a dove . . . For what Scripture means to the teachers, the picture means to simple folk. For just as the learned man delights in the subtlety of the written word, so the intellect of simple folk is engaged by the simplicity of a picture."[56] This second prologue and its apologetic address to a "diligent reader" hints at the fact that Hugh's true audience may not have been limited to the lay brothers, but may in fact have included educated readers who were to adopt the stance of illiterate men in their attitude to his work. The illiteracy of his audience, and the related question of the images of the *Aviarum*, was thus a rhetorical trope by which Hugh conveys his hope for the appropriate reception of his work.[57]

There was one audience, however, for whom illiteracy was more than a rhetorical trope, but was rather an expectation, a characterization, and even, in some sense, a spiritual ideal. That audience was women. Since they were understood both medically and spiritually as being more bound to the body than men, women were in many ways the ultimate lay audience. Defined according to the body and the senses, they were characterized as both unlearned and nonreaders. Gregory's *apologia* had a particular bite when applied to a female audience, since it was assumed that women were, by their nature, unable to transcend the physical in order to attain the spiritual, as a male cleric or even lay brother might. This assumption was at the root of the comparison of the anchoress to a bird that appears in the thirteenth-century *Ancrene Wisse*. The author writes: "However high she [the good anchoress] flies, she must sometimes come down to the ground because of her body."[58] The association of women with body, rather than spirit, and with emotion, rather than reason, had important implications for their engagement with the written word. In keeping with their supposedly physicalized natures, women are inevitably figured in medieval texts as "bad" readers, unable to penetrate the literal sense of a difficult text, let alone to unlock its deeper, allegorical meaning. Bound— like Eve—to her female flesh, the woman reader was thought to be excluded from the full, spiritualized understanding of the written word that was so readily available to men.[59]

From the idea of women as bad readers, it was only a short step to depict them wholly as nonreaders and as viewers and listeners instead. Although religious women were often more educated than either they or their biographers wished to admit, they appear in male-authored sources as illiterate, lacking in formal training, and learning by experience and imitation rather than study. Guibert of Nogent's (d. c. 1125) presentation of his mother is a case in point. He describes her as learning "not by sight but by ear" (*non videndo sed audiendo didicerat*) and emphasizes her lack of education.[60] Yet, he declares that she was privy to certain knowledge that she received experientially. In addition to the visions that she received concerning Guibert's career in the church, his mother gave him advice so wise that he comments that "discussing these matters, she might have been thought some eloquent bishop rather than the illiterate woman she was."[61] Here, as elsewhere, women's spiritual knowledge—which was thought to preclude formal training—surpassed that of learned men, reflecting an increasing anxiety among educated men that formal training dulled their ability truly to know God. In this context, lack of formal training became almost a spiritual prerequisite for religious women, since it purportedly allowed them access to experiential spiritual truths, truths denied men. Mulder-Bakker uses Guibert of Nogent's account of his mother's conversion to the religious life to draw certain conclusions concerning women's education. She makes four points: "(a) Women were supposed to acquire knowledge by imitation; they were not supposed to occupy themselves with reading and bookish learning. Even the Psalter they learned by listening to an older voice. (b) The knowledge they gained was therefore a type of wisdom, practical wisdom, which (c) was preserved in the heart. (d) The women then transmitted the knowledge they had acquired by responding modestly but adequately to the questions of visitors seeking guidance for their lives—in any case, the women who became recluses saw this as their task."[62] However, as Mulder-Bakker points out, Guibert's mother "was not nearly as unschooled as Guibert tried to portray her."[63] Why did Guibert strive to present his mother as unlearned, even as he recounts his own flirtation with the liberal arts and above all with the secular poets? The answer is simple: the spiritual ideal for women—and the education that that ideal presupposed—was different for women than for men. For women, "spirituality" largely precluded education—in theory if not in fact.

Women's supposed physicality reinforced their status as nonreaders and, therefore, as hearers or viewers. This connection is most clear in the *Speculum virginum*, a text presented as a dialogue between a male teacher, Peregrinus, and his female pupil, Theodora, in which the woman is constructed as illiterate, regardless of her ability to read.[64] At times Theodora is presented as hopelessly literal-minded, immune to the mystical sense of her teacher's lesson. Toward the end of the dialogue, Peregrinus appears to lose patience with her inability to grasp the true meaning of his teaching, exclaiming: "Your ignorance urges you to tricks, so that you defend what you do not know and do not know what you defend. Very many times you revert to the letter, you who always seem to hesitate in the same mire of heedlessness."[65]

The literal-mindedness that the *Speculum* author sometimes imputed to Theodora reflects the general perception that women were unable to penetrate the mystical or allegorical sense of Scripture because of their bodily nature. However, in the text, Theodora's purported inability to transcend her female body also appears as one justification for the use of images. As we have already seen, images were permissible according to Gregory the Great as "books for the illiterate"; the *Speculum* author invokes Gregory's letter toward the end of book five, where the image of the

Mystical Paradise is introduced.[66] However, the prologue of the *Speculum*, which Powell has shown appears at the beginning of what is now book three, had already established the place of images in the work, linking sight explicitly with its ultimate female audience. The prologue begins with an appeal to the virgin in words taken from Psalm 44:11–12: "Listen, daughter, and see, and bend your ear, and forget your people and your father's house. And the king will desire your beauty."[67] By presenting listening and seeing, the most immediate of the human senses, as the starting point for the ascent of the female soul to God and, more particularly, for the preparation of the Bride for her Bridegroom (in keeping with the influence of the Song of Songs on the text), the *Speculum* author suggested the association of women not only with visual imagery but also with sensuality. The religious contemplation that the *Speculum* encouraged for its female audience was based on experience of God and was reified through the body—initially through women's eyes and ears, but ultimately through their joyful possession of the heavenly marriage bed. From his examination of illustrated prayer books in twelfth-century Germany, Hamburger arrives at a similar conclusion, noting that, "corporeal images proved uniquely suited to the somatic character of female spirituality."[68]

The implications of the *Speculum* for the spiritual instruction of women in the twelfth century are profound and not simply because of the text's assumptions concerning women and visuality. The *Speculum* also adopted the construction of women as learners rather than teachers, found in I Timothy 2:12,[69] positing a male teacher—Peregrinus—and a female pupil—Theodora. Although the *Speculum* author had anticipated that women might not fully understand his text, he assumed that they would nonetheless be able to learn through their male teachers: "if you cannot understand all that is written there [in the mirror, the *Speculum*]," he writes, "it is no small part of knowledge to listen to and love one who does understand."[70] Thus while the work was designed ultimately for a female audience, it was therefore intended for the more immediate use of religious men. Indeed, the *Speculum* was written in response to the particular needs of male pastors, who were called to provide spiritual care—the *cura monialium*—for some of the many women who flocked to the religious life in the early part of the twelfth century. For this reason, Latin manuscripts of the *Speculum*—almost without exception—survive from male, rather than female houses, a fact that has sometimes been interpreted as evidence that men, as well as women, read it for spiritual formation.[71] In marked contrast to the *Hortus*, which gives few explicit

indications concerning its intended reception, the *Speculum* includes images of Peregrinus and Theodora that offer a visual exemplum of its intended use: Peregrinus, the male instructor, holds the text while teaching
Theodora, his female disciple.[72] According to this model, which was to be
replicated by male pastors with the women under their care, the lessons
of the *Speculum* were to be mediated to each woman through her male
instructor, who most likely performed its Latin dialogue with her in the
vernacular as she gazed on its images.[73]

The performative aspect of the *Speculum* is highlighted in the address
that appears at the beginning of book three: "Listen, daughter, and see,
and bend your ear, and forget your own people and the house of your
father. So shall the King desire your beauty." The idealized female audience listens to the voice of the male instructor—who speaks the words of
the Bridegroom—and sees her own spiritual transformation in the mirror
that the *Speculum* offers. The imitative and sensual aspects of the *Speculum*
offer a striking contrast with the *Hortus*. Where the *Speculum* had assumed
women's corporeal nature and attempted to provide spiritual instruction
that was tailored for women's presumed nonreading needs,[74] Herrad assumed a female audience that was literate in Latin and both spiritually and
intellectually capable of understanding complex theological ideas. While
for the *Speculum* author, the vernacular was the appropriate language of
instruction for women—the male instructor would offer a free translation
and explanation for the woman as she gazed on the manuscript's images[75]—nothing in the *Hortus* suggests that instruction at Hohenbourg
took place in the vernacular; as we have seen, the German glosses were
neither extensive nor comprehensive enough to perform a pedagogical
role. Moreover, the Latin grammatical glosses in the *Hortus* demonstrate
instead that some discussions of its contents could also involve drills in
verb conjugation. Finally, where the *Hortus*, like the *Speculum*, may have
been used by a single teacher instructing a group of women, or by a single
lector reading from it as the women looked on,[76] the teacher who held the
Hortus and mediated its message to its ultimate female audience was most
likely a woman and not, as the *Speculum* assumes, a man.[77]

Differences between the two works are reflected in the place of images
in each. Although many of the subjects depicted in the *Speculum* overlap
those that appear in the *Hortus*—evidence of the shared spiritual and intellectual context of south-German reform from which both works originated—the thirteen images of the *Speculum* cycle tend to be more
diagrammatic than those in the *Hortus* and to revolve around a narrower

set of motifs.[78] The majority emphasize spiritual ascent to Christ (who appears in most of the images) and are structured around ladders and trees, and, in one instance, the cross. Since they were thought to link heaven and earth, these motifs, and the ascent to Christ that they permit, bolsters the spiritual purpose of the manuscript as a whole and the theme of individual salvation around which it was organized.[79] So, for instance, while both the *Speculum* and the *Hortus* include depictions of a spiritual ladder, the emphasis in each is markedly different. Herrad's ladder (fol. 215v; plate 5) shows the ascent and temptations of various different groups within Christian society. The lay woman, knight, cleric, monk, nun, recluse, and hermit are each distracted from the ultimate goal: the crown of life. Although Herrad shows a young woman reaching that goal, her inscription indicates that this woman is only a symbol meant to represent the holy and the elect (*HD* Cat. No. 296).[80] The *Speculum* ladder (plate 6), which depicts a similar scene, showcases a single virgin at various points in her ascent, indicating that the author's concern lay primarily with the growth in virtue, not of the Church as a whole, but of the individual virgin. While Herrad's image could be read objectively, as a lesson concerning salvation and temptation, that in the *Speculum* served a more narrow spiritual purpose, inviting the identification of the audience with its female subject.

The lesson of this one comparison can be extended to the visual cycles of both the *Hortus* and the *Speculum*. From Herrad's selection (or design) and placement of the images in the *Hortus*, it is clear that she intended them to function as teaching tools within a theological curriculum and not to promote an individual, spiritual experience or to serve as a devotional apparatus. Few images in the *Hortus* promote the sort of personal spiritual reflection that would be required to class them as devotional aids. Those that might promote personal reflection or provide the focus for contemplation—notably the psychomachia cycle[81]—offer the viewer no opportunity for identification with them. In the case of the psychomachia, it is only the subject of the cycle—spiritual warfare—that would have any real relevance in the Christian life, and not the individual figures it depicted. Even so, each facing page could form the focus for contemplation on the reality of spiritual warfare and the need for constant vigilance, as a gloss on the opening folio reminded the reader: "The life of man on earth is a warfare" (Job 7:1) (*HD* Cat. No. 258).[82]

The typical criticism of images, as we have seen, was that they appealed to the body rather than the spirit, and therefore distracted the soul from higher things. Images, according to this argument, call forth a literal interpretation; indeed that is what was thought to make them so uniquely appropriate to unlettered audiences. However, as we have already seen in previous chapters, the images of the *Hortus* were only infrequently what we might think of as illustrations of the text—which might function as Gregory had intended, as pictures for the illiterate. Instead they tended to present a sophisticated form of visual exegesis, as, for instance, in the two *rotae* that mark the transition from Old to New Testament (fol. 67r–v; plates 11–12). Or they deepen the allegorical reading of a biblical story, as they do throughout the Old Testament section of the manuscript, which presents a typological interpretation of every story, directing the attention of the reader always toward Christ. Herrad did not explicitly warn her audience against the distraction that images might pose for the spiritually immature: she assumed that they were capable of allegorical readings of both image and text. Her teaching is clear in the Leviathan image (fol. 84r; plate 8), which demonstrated the dangers in seeing only the flesh and not the spirit. The Leviathan, deceived by Christ's humanity as it appeared on the cross, failed to see the "hook" of his divinity—the spirit that lay behind the flesh—and was caught. The danger of misinterpreting the cross is equally clear in the depiction of the crucifixion (fol. 150r), where Herrad recalls the Leviathan image through an excerpt from the *Speculum ecclesiae* (*HD* Cat. No. 211). Her message would have been obvious: the crucifixion, although depicted literally in the *Hortus*, had a spiritual and not simply a physical interpretation, a point she made in both image and text.

Herrad's use of images was an extension of the tradition whereby visual aids were used within medieval monastic schoolrooms.[83] Gerbert of Aurillac (d. 1003) provided one of the most famous examples of the use of images and other visual aids in the classroom, several hundred years before the production of the *Hortus*. In addition to the spheres that he designed and built to aid in the teaching of astronomy, Gerbert records how he put together a grammatical chart to help his students. He writes: "last autumn I drew up a diagram of rhetoric on twenty-six leaves of parchment sewed together, and forming in all two columns side by side each of thirteen leaves. It is without doubt a device admirably adapted for the ignorant and useful to the studious scholars in order to help them understand the subtle and obscure rules of rhetoric and to fix these in their memory."[84] Although not all visual aids were as extensive as Gerbert's, diagrams designed to aid in the teaching of the trivium were clearly known in the area around Hohenbourg. The Marbach Schoolbook contains several small-scale diagrams, for instance the various schematic representations of relations between the divisions of learning.[85] The three components of philosophy—*logica*, *ethica*, and *physica*—are given in a schema on folio 73v; this division appears in the *Hortus* in the considerably grander *Philosophia* image. In the Marbach Schoolbook, Socrates and Plato—who are also depicted in the *Hortus Philosophia* image—are listed with Cicero as examples under the subcategory *homo* within a schematic presentation of *substantia*.[86]

Despite the *Speculum* author's rhetorical construction of his female audience as illiterate and his invocation of Gregory the Great's justification of images for the unlettered, the *Speculum* images were no mere illustrations of the text; like Gerbert's teaching aids, they too offered schematic presentations of spiritual frameworks intended as mnemonic tools to support the virgin's reflection and meditation. Virtues and Vices appear as branches on opposing trees; the seven gifts of the Holy Spirit are shown twice, first in the image of the Ancestors of Christ and then again in the depiction of the House of Wisdom; and the Mystical Paradise encompasses the four cardinal virtues and the eight beatitudes, as well as the four rivers of Paradise and symbols of the four evangelists. Like *On the Six Wings of the Seraph*, a mnemonic treatise on penance attributed to Alan of Lille that associated each of the Seraph's six wings with a stage of penance and that was translated into pictorial form in various manuscripts,[87] these images supported the memory work that was essential to devotion. Even so, there are important differences between the *Speculum* and the *Hortus*. As we have seen, images in the *Hortus* were rarely purely diagrammatic, but offered complex theological presentations that not infrequently interpreted or even replaced the text. So although the *Hortus*, like the *Speculum*, includes depictions of the Virtues and Vices, these were shown not within a diagrammatic framework, but were personified as women dressed for a battle that rages across several folios; the narrative structure of the image allowed Herrad to comment implicitly on the dangers of avarice.[88] Similarly, although both manuscripts contain depictions of the House of Wisdom, the *Speculum* House leads to a focus on the seven gifts of the Holy Spirit and features Christ at its center (plate 14), while in the *Hortus*, the House of Wisdom provides the structure for a complex theological argument concerning Philosophy and the seven liberal arts (fol. 32r; plate 9), as we saw in Chapter 5.

In its use of traditionally didactic images such as the *rota*—which, through the geometric perfection of the circle, could represent spiritual perfection, or "divine order"—the *Hortus* formed part of a tradition of teaching through the use of visual images that stretched back to antiquity and in which, as we have seen, the *Speculum virginum* also had a part.[89] However, Herrad's images did not simply present information but could be subject to an extended classroom discussion, with the help of the tituli and inscriptions that she had provided.[90] In the case of the full-page depiction of man as the Microcosm (fol. 16v), Herrad provided a substantial section from the *Elucidarium* in her gloss. The question and answer format of the *Elucidarium* would have been ideally suited to the sort of dialogue between the *magistra* and her pupils to which the image may have given rise.

The role of the *Hortus* images in the classroom at Hohenbourg may provide a final clue concerning Herrad's failure to explain or delineate her intentions for the manuscript. Since the *Hortus* was never circulated outside of the monastery at Hohenbourg, it seems that it was only ever intended for a domestic audience, a conclusion that Herrad's prefatory texts support. In this case, Herrad may have felt that detailed instructions were superfluous; as the work's designer and as the likely teacher of the women of the community, she herself monitored its reception. Moreover, since work on the *Hortus* continued throughout Herrad's life, it was never complete, but was instead subject to continued revision. The continuous revision of the *Hortus* makes most sense if we assume that Herrad used the folios in the course of her teaching at Hohenbourg and then made additions and modifications to its texts and images in response to classroom challenges. Like a beehive, the *Hortus* too was subject to an ongoing process of accumulation as new texts, images, and ideas were added to the existing structure of the work. According to this model, the work was constantly being redefined through its own use, such that its use in fact became the process of composition.

Like Gerbert of Aurillac, who designed teaching aids for classroom use, Herrad too may have developed a file of teaching aids, which she constantly updated and which evolved to meet new needs. That file was the *Hortus*. As an essentially private and constantly evolving dossier of teaching materials, the *Hortus* needed no explanation; Herrad evidently never saw it as complete and never sought to publish it or make it available to a wider public. The fact that the *Hortus* was not originally bound supports this conclusion. The folios of the *Hortus* could have served as Gerbert's diagrams did: as props to a teacher's lesson. In this way, sections of the *Hortus* could be removed from the whole and employed in the service of a particular classroom discussion. Seen as a collection of fascicles, as Morrison proposes, rather than a "book," the *Hortus* and Herrad's intentions for it become clearer.[91] Each subject, or "nucleus" to use Morrison's terminology, could be extracted for teaching, replaced and then built on, as the work evolved. The binding of the *Hortus* fascicles ultimately fixed the manuscript in a way that Herrad may not have intended and that obscured its likely use. The binding of the manuscript prevents the reader, for instance, from appreciating Herrad's great cycle of illuminations depicting the Last Judgment (fols. 247v, 251r–v, 253r–v). Folios that had been designed to face each other have been separated by interpolated leaves, which presumably added to the lesson but were not meant to be anchored at its center.

Images had a very particular pedagogical role to play within the *Hortus*: as mnemonic devices, they served to solidify the manuscript's teachings in the memories of the students at Hohenbourg.[92] Like Honorius Augustodunensis, who encouraged preachers to speak so that "your hearers will think they actually see the events instead of hearing you," and Hugh of St. Victor, who presented his teaching on the ark in the form of an elaborate word image,[93] Herrad recognized the importance of images in the process of memory training, a vital stage in true learning. As Hugh had observed, "the whole usefulness of education consists only in the memory of it, for just as having heard something does not profit one who cannot understand, likewise having understood is not valuable to one who either will not or cannot remember."[94] Honorius's tendency to use word pictures in his sermons was matched by a validation of the senses that appears both in the *Elucidarium*, where he reports that Christ suffered five wounds in order to redeem the five senses from the devil (*HD* no. 319), and in the *Gemma animae*, where he argued for the mnemonic value of images (alongside the traditional "books for the illiterate" argument) in a long text on churches. Herrad included this last text in the *Hortus*: "A picture may be made for three reasons: first, because it is the literature of the laity, second, that the house might be honored with such decoration, and third, in order to bring to mind the lives of those who have gone before" (*HD* no. 789). As Honorius pointed out elsewhere in this same text, sculpture and painting had illustrious histories, having been introduced into churches by Moses and Solomon, respectively.[95]

The modern tendency to view diagrams as aids to verbal or textual understanding is flawed, according to Carruthers, who cautions against the assumption that images were subservient to text. She writes instead

that diagrammatic images "are exercises and examples to be studied and
remembered as much as are the words. Words and images *together* are two
'ways' of the same mental activity—invention. In addition to acquiring a
repertory of words—*dicta et facta memorabilia*—children also gathered
into their memories a repertory of images."[96] The mnemonic purpose of
the *Hortus* images can explain their tendency to depict violent or frighten-
ing events, as, for instance, the bloody battles of the psychomachia cycle,
the gruesome sufferings of souls in hell, or the Massacre of the Innocents
(fol. 98r), where the ground is dotted with severed heads and a knight is
shown driving his sword through the small body of a boy child. These
images make sense since, according to Carruthers, violence was almost a
"mnemotechnical principle."[97]

Herrad does not dwell on the subject of memory training in the *Hortus*, although as we have already seen, her metaphors both for the book
and for herself as its author—the honeycomb and the bee—had specific
meanings within the context of ancient and medieval memory theories.
Herrad's bee metaphor, weighted with implications for her composition
of the manuscript, also communicated her hope for the way in which the
manuscript should be used. In her study of medieval memory, Carruthers
warns that "one should be alert in medieval discussions of honey-bees, for
a trained memory may very well lurk within the meadows and flowers,
chambers, treasure-hoards, and enclosures of the hives/books."[98] The
mnemonic aspect of the *Hortus* is confirmed in the use of images as place
markers in the text, the tendency to represent certain ideas schemati-
cally—as in the *Philosophia* image, the Microcosm, the Ladder of Virtues,
and others—as well as the layout of the page itself. The proliferation of
glosses, images, and texts on folios of varying size would have aided in the
memorization of its message. According to Hugh of St. Victor, the page
layout, color, and design of a book were of critical importance to the
creation of a memory-image. He writes, "it is a great value for fixing a
memory-image that when we read books, we study to impress on our
memory through our mental-image-forming power (*per imaginationem*)
not only the number and order of verses or ideas, but at the same time the
color, shape, position, and placement of the letters, where we have seen
this or that written, in what part, in what location (at the top, the middle,
or the bottom) we saw it positioned, in what color we observed the trace
of the letter or the ornamented surface of the parchment."[99] The *Hortus*
was a book that was designed to be read, studied, and memorized by students over the course of their educational and spiritual lives. Certain parts

of the manuscript, especially the poems, were accompanied by musical notation, evidence that they were sung aloud at Hohenbourg and would have been easily memorized. The memorability of poems may explain why all texts related to Hohenbourg, with the sole exception of Herrad's prose prologue, were written in verse.

Conclusion

As we saw at the outset of this chapter, Herrad's poem at the start of the *Hortus deliciarum* closed with her wish: "May this book prove useful (*utilis*) and delightful (*delectabilis*) to you, may you never cease to ponder it (*volvere*) in your breast (*memoria*)" (*HD* no. 1). Herrad's use of the word *volvere* could also mean that she intended the women of Hohenbourg to "open" the book in their hearts and even to turn it over, examining it literally from every angle. This interpretation—suggestive of the memory training that was equally implied in her bee metaphor—is strengthened by glosses to the poem, which further clarify her meaning. Herrad glosses *volvere* with *pertractare*, a word that suggests the hard work of study and intellectual engagement. More telling is her gloss of *pectore* as *memoria*; what she really meant was that the women should study the *Hortus* in their thoughts and in their memory. With the glosses integrated into the text, Herrad's poem, and her wish for the manuscript's use, might be translated as follows:

May this book be useful
And delightful to you,
May you never cease to study it
In your thoughts and memory. (*HD* no. 1)[100]

Herrad's expectation that the *Hortus* could be studied by the women in their thoughts and memory was not unrealistic. The manuscript as a whole sustains her emphasis on the use of memory as a teaching tool. In its organization, the variety of its contents, its glosses, the integration of text and image within its folios, and, in particular, the preponderance of images as mnemonic devices, the *Hortus* not only enables but actively promotes the pedagogical role of memory.

Herrad's hope that the *Hortus* would be useful and delightful brings us back to the beginning of our inquiry: her declaration that she had designed the manuscript for the sake of the women's love. Obviously, her intention throughout the *Hortus* was not simply that the women would gain an orthodox theological education, but that they would also enjoy it. Her emphasis on the pleasure to be found in the manuscript reflects her own attitude to learning and the attitude that she sought to inculcate in the women of her community. Most important, of course, is her presentation of the manuscript both as a "sweet honeycomb" and a "garden of delights." Herrad also encourages the women to find "pleasing food" in the manuscript and in its "honeyed dewdrops" of learning. Since eating was a metaphor both for reading and for memorization, which was literally the digestion of knowledge, the "pleasing food" that Herrad recommends reinforced the mnemonic aspect of the *Hortus* as a whole.[101] Herrad builds on these two ideas of nourishment and pleasure in her prefatory poem, where she conveys her hope that the manuscript would be both useful (*utilis*) and delightful (*delectabilis*) to the community of women. Although I have translated *utilis* simply as "useful," the word had a specific technical meaning within the context of twelfth-century rhetoric. *Utilitas*, which Minnis and Scott define as the "pedagogic and/or moral usefulness of the work," was one of the six categories of literary analysis included by Boethius in his commentary on Porphyry's *Isagoge*; it was widely adopted in twelfth-century commentaries on, or prologues to, set-texts.[102] Through her choice of the word *utilitas* to describe the *Hortus*, Herrad therefore presented a case both for the work's moral importance and for its place in the Christian curriculum.

Herrad's wish that the *Hortus* should be delightful and the honeycomb metaphor that she uses to describe it did not, however, mean that the *Hortus* would be an easy book to tackle. Ease was not a factor that she considered, just as she avoided time-saving justifications; but this did not detract from the book's appeal. In fact, Augustine explicitly linked the sweetness of knowledge to the difficulty with which it could be attained, depicting the challenges of Scripture as pleasant and useful.[103] In the same vein, Hugh of St. Victor wrote that "honey [is] more pleasing because enclosed in the comb, and whatever is sought with greater effort is also found with greater desire."[104] The knowledge within the *Hortus* was not presented simplistically or with concessions for its female audience; however, since the learning it contained was entirely in the service of Divine Wisdom, the *Hortus* could only ever bring greater satisfaction to its students. According to Hugh for "those who are bent upon the discipline, not of literature, but of the virtues . . . study should not be an affliction but a delight."[105] The honeycomb metaphor of the *Hortus* was no doubt linked to this idea of sweetness within, just as Hugh wrote: "the Sacred Scriptures . . . are most fittingly likened to a honeycomb, for while in the simplicity of their language they seem dry, within they are filled with sweetness."[106]

Reforming Women in the
Garden of Delights

TOWARD THE END OF THE *HORTUS*, Herrad included an image that was
as unique in its vivid and gruesome detail as it is revealing of the spiritual
concerns that motivated her work on the manuscript as a whole. This
image, the full-page depiction of hell (fol. 255r; plate 15), must have been
one of the most distinctive compositions in the manuscript; its distinctiveness was no doubt one reason why it was cut out from the *Hortus* and
sold, only to be reunited with the manuscript before its destruction in
1870. The scene that it presents is visually striking. It is the only image in
the manuscript that was enclosed with a border and one of the few that
was entirely painted, leaving little room for tituli.[1] It is also unusual in its
dark palette. As befits a depiction of hell, the background is black, offering
a sharp contrast to the vivid red of the flames that lick the bodies of
demons and sinners and burn with particular intensity under two pots
marked "Jews" (*Judei*) and "armed knights" (*armati milites*). Human
figures—pale and naked—stand out against their dim surroundings as they
endure a range of punishments. At the top left, a man slices his own belly
open with a knife,[2] while to his left, a woman breastfeeds a serpent, which
is wound around her naked body. A text above their heads repeats the
warning of Isaiah 66:24: "their worm will not die, nor will their fire be
quenched" (*HD* Cat. No. 338).[3] Below these figures, a second woman
devours her child, while a demon riding piggyback on a man piles coins
into his outstretched hands. At the lowest level, Lucifer sits enthroned on
a seat of ravenous beasts, which devour humans and scatter their skulls
beneath his throne.[4] The little form of antichrist is perched on his knee
and beside the two, a man, possibly a usurer in life, is forced by a demon
to consume burning coins. His stomach is swelled with this unwelcome
fruit. Amidst the torments depicted in this scene, one figure stands out: to
the bottom left of the image, a monk is shown being led into hell by a

demon. With his tonsure and habit, this monk is easily identified; a gloss nonetheless labels him as *monachus*. Obviously a new arrival, the monk is one of the few figures who is still clothed and clearly identified in the scene. His punishments have not yet begun, although there is little doubt as to why he has been consigned to hell: in his right hand he clutches a money bag, which is overflowing with coins.

The Hell image showcases two of Herrad's major concerns. First, and most obvious, is her concern with the sin of avarice.[5] Several of the characters in hell are explicitly associated with money, suggesting that their transgressions in life had included avarice. For others, notably the Jews and the knights, the association may be implicit; Jews were thought to be excessively carnal and greedy, while knights were often criticized for selling their services as mercenaries. Taken together, these figures underscore the stern warnings against avarice that appear elsewhere in the *Hortus* and that reflect Hohenbourg's Augustinian affiliation. As a community of Augustinian canonesses, the women of Hohenbourg had renounced private property when they made their profession. The Augustinian Rule warns several times against private property. "Do not call anything your own; possess everything in common," it advises, recalling the words of Acts: "They possessed everything in common," and "distribution was made to each in proportion to each one's need" (Acts 4:32, 35).[6] This advice was highlighted in the Customs of Marbach, which warned canons that they should only use the word *suus* in reference either to their sins or their own parents.[7]

The second concern showcased in the Hell image is linked to Herrad's abhorrence of avarice, but associates it with one group in particular: the clergy. The prominence of the avaricious monk within the Hell scene demonstrates her willingness to criticize contemporary churchmen, not only priests, but also bishops, popes, monks, hermits, and even recluses.[8] Her criticisms constitute one of the most unusual features of the *Hortus*. Like Hildegard of Bingen and Elisabeth of Schönau, who reserved their most scorching criticisms for the clergy, Herrad rarely misses an opportunity to point out the failings of churchmen. Her criticisms tend to focus on the sins of avarice and simony; however, they also include general warnings against the evils of hypocrisy in the religious life. Allusions to false monks, anchorites, and hermits, as well as to false clerics and even popes, are scattered throughout the manuscript.

Although Herrad's criticisms of the clergy are, for the most part, visual rather than textual, one clear indication of her teaching on the failings of the clergy appears in a small booklet toward the end of the manuscript (fols. 309r–14v).[9] Surviving titles from this booklet reflect Herrad's concern with the worthiness of clerics to provide pastoral care, linking performance of the *cura animarum* (care of souls) with submission to a rule and, implicitly, the renunciation of private property.[10] Evidently the booklet was fiercely critical of the unreformed clergy. Arguing for the superiority of the communal life, its texts rail against the perceived degeneracy of the contemporary clergy—their failure to live communally, their misuse of church property, and their extravagant lifestyles. Repeated appeals to the example of apostles (*HD* no. 1134), the "primitive church" (*HD* no. 1143), and the "communal life" (*HD* nos. 1143 and 1150) date it to the early reform period; its strident calls for reform of the clergy locate it even more firmly within the context of the canonical reform of the clergy that appeared first at St. Ruf in 1039 and was subsequently popularized by Hildebrand at the Lateran synod of 1059.[11]

The booklet's presence in the *Hortus* is one of the many mysteries of the manuscript—all the more so since the evidence for it is only fragmentary. As the only booklet mentioned by de Bastard, these folios were not integrated into the main body and most likely represent an interpolation to the manuscript. Yet the topics they addressed were obviously important to Herrad and relevant to the women of Hohenbourg, for whom the provision of appropriate pastoral care continued to be a contentious issue. The first part of the booklet presented a picture of how the clerical life ought to be (*nota qualis esse debeat vita et conversatio clericorum*) (*HD* no. 1132). A second section (*HD* nos. 1135–38) argued that churches should not be viewed as properties to be owned or claimed by individuals, but that only those who scorn belongings (*contemptores proprietatum*) should be chosen for church governance (*HD* no. 1137). One text argued that only regular canons should be trusted with churches "since canons are the followers of the apostles" (*HD* no. 1134); a second declares that "all priests should lead the regular life" (*HD* no. 1142); and a third warns that "none should have the care of souls or the governance of parishes unless he has adopted the communal life in keeping with the custom of the primitive church" (*HD* no. 1143).[12] Two further passages, which were copied more fully, afford an even greater sense of the reform concerns at Hohenbourg. The first extends the argument against church ownership by clerics, charging that the gifts of the faithful—their tithes—ought not to be squandered by churchmen to provide themselves with fine food and drink, to purchase luxurious clothes, or to support their degenerate companions, who stuff themselves with food while the poor go hungry (*HD* no. 1136).[13] The second criticizes canons who appeal to "custom," and in particular the Rule of Aix, in order to defend their luxurious way of life, charging that such canons are not swayed from their excesses even by the fear of God and that they bring scandal to the church by filling it with spectacles (*HD* no. 1155).[14]

Avarice in the Psychomachia Cycle

The concern for the communal life and the renunciation of private property that animates the texts of the booklet is sustained throughout the *Hortus* in Herrad's preoccupation with the evils of avarice. Nowhere is that concern more apparent than in the manuscript's famous psychomachia cycle (fols. 199v–204r), which marks the transition from the life of Christ to the *Ecclesia* section.[15] Spreading across five consecutive openings, the psychomachia cycle presented the spiritual battle waged by all Christians as a grand conflict between the Virtues and Vices, who are depicted as female knights dressed for battle, heavily armed with chain mail, helmets, and weapons.[16] In obedience to Paul's injunction to take up the "sword of the Spirit (which is the word of God)" (Ephesians 6:17), the Virtues carry swords, and the Vices spears. They confront each other across the facing page, with the Vices generally on the verso and the Virtues on the opposing recto. In each scene, a Vice is vanquished by a Virtue. The cycle begins with a mounted Pride (*Superbia*), her sword raised, charging against Humility (*Humilitas*). In the fray that follows, Humility vanquishes Pride; Faith (*Fides*), Idolatry (*Idolatria*); Love (*Caritas*), Envy (*Invidia*); Prudence (*Prudentia*), Vainglory (*Vanagloria*); and so on, with the exception of Anger (*Ira*), who kills herself with her own spear.

Though unquestionably one of the most striking compositions in the *Hortus*, the psychomachia cycle is not unprecedented.[17] The spiritual battle described by Paul was taken up by subsequent authors as a central motif for the Christian life and especially for the struggles inherent in the monastic profession. Of these, the most popular was Prudentius's *Psychomachia* (c. 405), an allegorical poem that dramatized the conflict between virtue and vice.[18] Prudentius elaborated the battle motif suggested in Ephesians, and elsewhere, and combined it with the emerging systematization of virtues and vices in order to present a conflict in which select Vices battled against remedial Virtues. The action that the poem described, and its obvious dramatic appeal, made it a favorite subject for artists, with the result that manuscripts of the poem tended to include a largely standardized series of images illustrating the conflict.[19]

The broad outlines of the *Hortus* psychomachia derived from these standardized images, in combination with Prudentius's poem (which Herrad does not cite). Traditional depictions include the magnificent image of Pride—the only Vice or Virtue to be mounted—riding sidesaddle, seated on a lion's skin, and wearing a turban in place of the helmet worn by the other Vices and Virtues (fol. 199v; Prudentius vv. 178–85). Pride's fall from her horse and subsequent decapitation by Humility are in keeping with Prudentius, as is Indulgence's (*Luxuria*) entry on the bottom of folio 201v.[20] Scattering flowers on the ground as she enters the battlefield in her chariot, Indulgence seduces the opposing Virtues, who are transfixed by her. In the next scene, she is pinned under her chariot, her head crushed by a millstone held by Temperance, who carries a cross (fol. 202v). The gloss, which identifies the stone as Christ, follows Prudentius in reporting that Indulgence's horses had taken flight at the sight of the cross and thrown her under her own chariot (Prudentius vv. 310–43, 407–26; *HD* Cat. No. 276).

Like Pride and Indulgence, Avarice (*Avaricia*) is depicted according to convention: she is dressed in a flowing robe with her waist encircled by copious purses, her hair wild (plate 16). Only her traditional gaping mouth and claw-like hands seem to be absent from the image.[21] Together with her handmaidens (*pedisseque*), Avarice appears in the wake of Indulgence's defeat to gather the loot that had been left behind (Prudentius vv. 454–63). Tripping over each other in their scramble for coins on the ground, the women are depicted in a deranged craze for money. Subsequent scenes follow Prudentius in showing Avarice's downfall at the hands of Liberality (*Largitas*) (who appears as Good Works, *Operatio*, in Prudentius), who reclaims Avarice's ill-gotten goods, seems to kill her with the single thrust of her sword, and then distributes her money to the poor *pro Dei amore* (Prudentius vv. 573–628). The contest between Avarice and Liberality, and Avarice's bloody defeat, constitutes the penultimate battle in the *Hortus* cycle, as it had in Prudentius's poem, and apparently marks the culmination of the psychomachia cycle. It is followed only by a static image of Blasphemy (*Blasphemia*) threatening Fortitude (*Fortitudo*) with her raised spear.

The similarities of the *Hortus* psychomachia to the Prudentius tradition should not obscure differences between the two, some of which reflect the probable influence of a third source, *On the Fruits of the Flesh and of the Spirit*, a text that was most likely written by Conrad of Hirsau.[22] The influence of this text on Herrad's cycle is apparent first in the pairing of the Virtues and Vices in the *Hortus*, which differs from Prudentius, and second in the integration of the seven deadly sins within the psychomachia theme.[23] In the *Hortus*, each battle scene shows a principal Vice squaring off against a principal Virtue, with both supported by lesser Vices and Virtues. *On the Fruits*, which was written within a Benedictine spiritual context in order to warn against pride and to encourage humility, presented two contrasting trees, the first of which had its roots in Pride and produced the fruits of the seven vices and the second, which had its roots in Humility and gave life to the virtues.[24] The ordering of the Vices in the *Hortus* psychomachia follows this schema, underscoring Pride's spiritual importance. Pride's appearance at the outset of the *Hortus* psychomachia inverts the order of Prudentius's poem. Where Prudentius had introduced her only in the middle of the action (v. 178), following the suicide of Anger (vv. 109–54), in the *Hortus* Pride appears at the outset of the psychomachia cycle. Anger's suicide is shown on folio 201r, the opening that follows Pride's triumphal charge. However, Herrad does not maintain the hierarchy of Virtues and Vices presented in *On the Fruits*. Pride does not remain the "chief vice," as Conrad of Hirsau had intended. Instead, as the cycle continues it becomes clear that Herrad was less concerned with pride, the focus of *On the Fruits*, than she was with avarice. Avarice, who appears initially only as one of Pride's seven handmaidens, takes on an increasingly important role throughout the psychomachia cycle and even comes to dominate it by its end. The two final facing pages of the cycle (fols. 202v–4r)—the longest series of images to feature a single figure—are devoted to Avarice.[25]

The displacement of Pride by Avarice as chief vice in the *Hortus* psychomachia is one manifestation of Herrad's position within a debate of particular theological significance to the reformers.[26] Although the Bible delivered a mixed message regarding the chief vice—pride is declared the beginning of sin in Ecclesiasticus 10:15 and love of money as the root of all evil in I Timothy 6:10—until the beginning of the eleventh century, Pride was generally recognized as the most serious of the vices. However, from the eleventh century on, Avarice began to attract increasing attention, moving from fifth place in the hierarchy of vices sometimes even to first. This change was, to a certain extent, a function of economic developments and of growing anxiety concerning wealth. However, as Little concludes, the contest between Avarice and Pride ultimately reflected rising tensions between traditional Benedictine monks and the religious reformers. While monks had abandoned power but not wealth when they entered the monastery and so demonized Pride, the reformers stressed the poverty of the early church and so demonized Avarice.[27]

Herrad's emphasis on avarice in the psychomachia cycle of the *Hortus* demonstrates once again her place within the reform movement and sympathy for its concerns. For Herrad, unlike either Prudentius or the author of *On the Fruits*, Avarice, and not Pride, was the chief vice, a fact that is made clear at the culmination of the psychomachia cycle. The final opening of the cycle presents two corresponding *rotae*—one for a Vice, signifying the devil, and the other for a Virtue, signifying Christ (fols. 203v–204r; plates 17–18).[28] This final battle breaks with both of Herrad's sources, pitching Mercy (*Misericordia*) as the archetypal Virtue against Avarice as the archetypal Vice, a scene that is found neither in Prudentius, nor in the hierarchy of vices established by the author of *On the Fruits*. Avarice's depiction in this final contest underscores Herrad's view of her centrality to the cosmic battle that the cycle as a whole was intended to symbolize. With a handful of coins in one hand and a trident in the other, she is presented as the antithesis of Mercy, whose own message is one of charity and concern for the poor.

In keeping with Herrad's criticism of the clergy, this final depiction of Avarice is implicitly associated with the greed of priests. The trident in Avarice's hand evokes the evil sons of Eli, the High Priest of Israel (I Samuel 2:12–14).[29] Driven by greed, they even went so far as to steal from God—something that the *Hortus* booklet had also accused corrupt priests of doing. Whenever a sacrifice was offered to God, Eli's sons would take a three-pronged fork (a trident), plunge it into the sacrificial pot, and keep for themselves whatever meat they managed to retrieve. The association of Avarice with clerics is further highlighted in Herrad's inscription to the image. Here, Avarice is described as "pursuing gain by guile or force" (*Dolo vel vi sectans lucra*) (*HD* Cat. No. 282), echoing Paul's warning that deacons ought not to pursue riches (*non turpe lucrum sectantes*) (I Timothy 3:8). Avarice's association with the fox, which pulls her chariot, bolsters the ecclesiastical reading of the entire image, bringing to mind the foxes in the garden (fol. 225r), which threaten the church with heresy and schism.

Herrad's decision to pair Avarice (representing the devil) with Mercy (as Christ) in the final confrontation of good and evil evokes John Cassian's observation that the chief vice can have no adversary except God.

However, for Cassian that vice was Pride while, for Herrad, Avarice was the chief vice.[30] In case her readers missed the point, she drove it home with a gloss from Augustine, placed outside the *rota* of Avarice: "What is this madness, to gain riches but to lose heaven?"[31]

Simony and the Cleansing of the Temple

Herrad's preoccupation with avarice, like her reliance on such papal supporters as Rupert and Honorius, and her apparent condemnation, with Hildebrand, of the "stubbornness of private property,"[32] is evidence of her sympathy for the aims of the reform movement. In keeping with this sympathy, avarice was not the only danger against which she warned her readers: simony, the purchase of church office, also appears in the *Hortus* as a threat to the church.[33] The evils of simony and its connection to avarice were showcased in Herrad's full-page image of the Cleansing of the Temple (fol. 238r), an image that constituted one of the most radical elements of her reformist agenda but that is now known primarily through surviving glosses. According to the gospel accounts, Jesus went up to Jerusalem just before the Passover and, filled with righteous anger at the corruption of the temple by merchants, overturned their tables and drove them from the temple court.[34] In John's gospel, which provides the most complete account of the cleansing, this episode follows immediately after the wedding at Cana, where Jesus had performed his first miracle, turning water into wine. However, in the *Hortus*, the Cleansing appeared in the *Ecclesia* section of the manuscript (fols. 199v–240v) and not in the narrative of Christ's life and public ministry (fols. 80v–133v). Herrad's decision to include the Cleansing image in the *Ecclesia* section is the first indication of her interpretive stance: the emphasis in this section is placed squarely on the reality of spiritual warfare in the church and on the need for Christians to defend it from demonic attacks. Instead of contributing to the narrative of Christ's life, Herrad's image of the Cleansing provided the basis for an extended allegory in which the unworthy merchants expelled from the temple were presented as abusers of the contemporary church. The merchants, who in the gospels sell oxen for sacrifice in the temple, appear in the *Hortus* as priests who sell their sermons—a standard Patristic interpretation;[35] Judas, the "worst merchant" (*mercator pessimus*) and a symbol of avarice, is likened to usurers who place their hope in money;[36] and the sheep sellers are like hypocrites, who praise God, in the words of the Pharisee that they are "not like other men" (Luke 18:9–14).[37] Although few details of the Cleansing image have survived, together with glosses that were copied before the destruction of the manuscript, these reveal Herrad's facility with the language, symbolism, and arguments of the Gregorians and testify to her deeply reformist purpose.[38] In every way—from her placement of the image in the manuscript, to her glosses and the connections that she drew between the Cleansing and other biblical episodes—Herrad sought to promote a reformist interpretation of the Cleansing and to suggest the contemporary application of its message.

For Herrad, as for other reformers, simony was not a distinct sin, but rather a form of avarice, a point that she makes visually explicit in the Cleansing image. Notes from the manuscript record that the image included two scenes depicting the leprosy of Gehazi (IV Kings 5), a favorite allegorization both of avarice and of simony.[39] According to the book of Kings, the prophet Elisha had healed Naaman from leprosy, commanding him to bathe seven times in the Jordan River. Once healed, Naaman returned to Elisha and offered him a gift, which he refused. However, Elisha's servant Gehazi pursued Naaman to request silver and clothing, pretending to do so on Elisha's behalf. For his desire to accept material gain in return for the spiritual gift of healing, Gehazi and all his descendents were cursed with leprosy. In the Cleansing image, the connection between avarice and simony was made explicit through the depiction of a leper, representing Gehazi, in conversation with a figure that was most likely intended to represent Simon Magus.[40] The title from a text, presumably from the book of Kings, appeared on folio 237r, immediately before the Cleansing image. By associating Gehazi's desire for "disgraceful gain" (*turpe lucrum*) with his leprosy, this text made clear the link between Gehazi and simony (*HD* no. 814).

The association of avarice with simony and leprosy suggested in the Gehazi connection was reinforced in Herrad's depiction of the three temptations of Christ (fols. 100v–101r). Although these images are missing, notes from the original manuscript indicate that they showed a comical devil attempting to seduce Christ, first by tempting him to make stones into bread in order to assuage his hunger, then by suggesting he throw himself from the pinnacle of the temple in order to test the angels charged with ensuring his safety, and finally by offering him all the kingdoms of the world in return for his worship (*HD* Cat. Nos. 123–25). Although money is not explicitly mentioned in Matthew's account, the two surviving details from the *Hortus* depiction of the third temptation indicate that money played a role in Herrad's explanation of it. These two, one a wide-mouthed bowl and the other an egg-shaped container with a lid, were both shown filled with coins. Her gloss to this image solidified the association of avarice, simony, and leprosy. Drawing from the traditional link between the three temptations of Christ and the three temptations of I John 2:16—"the concupiscence of the flesh and the concupiscence of the eyes and the pride of life"—Herrad connected the third temptation of Christ with the second temptation of I John, the concupiscence of the eyes or avarice, which she calls "the most grave of the greater offences" (*superiorum viciorum est gravissima*).[41] A gloss on the facing page then distinguishes between simony and ihezia (*Gehazia*), which it claims as simply two sorts of avarice,[42] and concludes by linking simony to Jesus' cleansing of the temple:

Not suffering that the house of God should be polluted by such wares, Christ punished this vice alone with a whip made of cords—since He endured the punishments of His own body [with ropes too]—and overturned the stools (*kathedras*) of those selling doves. Therefore those who hold bishoprics (*kathedras*) should not boast unless they administer justice, since they themselves also shall fall. (*HD* Cat. No. 123)[43]

This gloss leaves no doubt as to Herrad's interpretation of the Cleansing scene. Through her explicit equation of the merchants' tables in the gospel account with the bishoprics of the contemporary church, she taught that both were liable to be overturned.

By associating Jesus' actions in the temple of the first century with the particular situation of the twelfth-century church, Herrad entered into a visual form of political allegory, which Robinson defines as "the exposition of a biblical text—in particular, a prophetic text—by reference to current political events."[44] The way in which she presented the image of the cleansing, combining it with relevant texts and linking it to related biblical accounts such as the temptation of Christ, demonstrates her intention to favor a reformist reading of the image. Obviously, Herrad was conversant with the ideas of the eleventh-century reformers, for whom the cleansing was a favorite topic, even though their writings do not appear in the *Hortus*.[45] The cleansing was discussed by Peter Damian, one of the earliest writers to interpret it in a contemporary way, as well as Humbert of Silva Candida, Anselm of Lucca, Bruno of Segni, and even Manegold of Lautenbach. Of these, Bruno of Segni gives the most vivid reformist interpretation of the cleansing, addressing simoniacs directly:

"Jesus entered into the temple and expelled all those who were selling and buying in that place, and he overturned the tables of the moneychangers and the seats of those selling doves." Hear this, Simoniacs, hear this, merchants of wickedness, either cease from your business, or leave the temple. The Lord ejected from the temple not one, or two, but all the merchants and the buyers indiscriminately. He himself overturned the tables of the moneychangers and the seats of those selling doves. You are the moneychangers, you sell doves, you do nothing without money or bribe . . . You are the thieves . . . Therefore leave the house of prayer, which, since you have lived in it, has been made into a den of thieves.

Drawing his invective to a close with a call to action, Bruno writes, "If, therefore, we want to imitate him in this also . . . we must violently expel Simoniacs from the Church."[46]

Commentaries linking the cleansing to the contemporary church were common enough within reform circles, but images of the cleansing promoting a reformist interpretation were not.[47] One exception is the depiction that appears in the eleventh-century *Gospels of Matilda,* a manuscript produced in northern Italy and given by Matilda of Tuscany to the monastery of Polirone.[48] The *Gospels* give the Cleansing (fol. 84r) pride of place as the only image to be accorded an entire page, a singularity that is further emphasized by the frame in which the entire image is presented. Like the *Hortus* Cleansing, which postdates the *Gospels* by a century, the *Gospels* image is inspired by the description provided in John 2:14–17. Its interpretation of this passage, however, was emphatically contemporary. Rough comments that it represents "some of the most radical moral, theological, and political concepts of the Reform."[49] His observation might just as well be extended to the *Hortus.*

Herrad's decision to include the Cleansing image in the *Ecclesia* section of the *Hortus,* rather than in the cycle of Jesus' life, demonstrates that her purpose was to provide an opportunity for elaboration of its reformist implications and, like Bruno of Segni, to encourage appropriate action. Moreover, she ensured that it would be read in a reformist light by situating it immediately opposite two texts discussing usury and simony. Although the first of these was not copied before the destruction of the *Hortus,* the second, a poem by Walter of Châtillon, denounces the flourishing of simony, identifying simoniacs as the precursors of antichrist, the pastors of the church, and thieves of the Eucharist; Walter further condemns both parts of the religious life—the active, represented in the figure of Martha, and the contemplative, in her sister Mary—as being overly occupied with the quest for money (*HD* no. 816).[50]

Hypocrisy in the Religious Life

Herrad's message of reform was not limited to such issues as simony and the abuse of power by high church officials; she also addresses abuses that would be more immediately relevant to the women of Hohenbourg—especially hypocrisy in the religious life. The hypocrite who was shown as the sheep seller in the image of the cleansing is matched throughout the *Hortus* by warnings against false piety, as we have already seen. Criticisms of false piety are most strongly expressed, however, in the Ladder of Virtues (fol. 215v; plate 5), an image that provided an opportunity to warn against distraction from the goal of the true religious life—the *corona vite*. This image comprises the first of two extended discourses on falsehood and hypocrisy within the religious life. In both concept and content it is linked to the psychomachia cycle, since both made visible the unseen spiritual battle inherent in the Christian life. However, the ladder motif, which was based on Jacob's ladder and elaborated by John Klimakos (c. 600), took the human soul as its subject, rather than the abstract vices and virtues; traditional ladder images, such as that in the *Speculum virginum*, depicted the ascent of the individual soul to heaven as she transcended earthly desires.[51] Herrad's approach was slightly different: she generalized the motif in order to comment particularly on the various groups within Christian society. Instead of focusing on the individual spiritual life, her ladder shows the ascent and temptations of figures representing lay men and women, knights, clerics, monks, nuns, recluses, and hermits, each of which is distracted from the crown of life.

The message of the ladder is one of *contemptus mundi* as Herrad explains on folio 221v. Here, she links the series of images that follow the psychomachia cycle and that together introduce the *Ecclesia* section of the manuscript with contempt for the world, explaining that "Solomon and the Wheel of Fortune and the Ladder of Virtues and the Sirens remind us (*admonent nos*) of contempt for the world and love of Christ" (*HD* Cat. No. 299).[52] Her introduction of these subjects in the wake of the violent psychomachia cycle and the presentation in the concluding *rotae* of the final battle between Avarice and Mercy suggests that Herrad saw contempt for the world as a remedy for the particular evil of avarice. The connection between the two is made explicit in an unidentified text concerning the Virtues and Vices that appears between the image of the Ladder of Virtues and that of Ulysses and the Sirens (fol. 221r–v): "piety through contempt of the world excludes avarice" (*HD* no. 750).[53] Honorius's text on the sirens confirms this connection, noting that the siren who sings with a human voice is Avarice, "who sings the songs of this world to those listening" (*HD* no. 756).[54] Herrad seems to imply that her readers should stop their ears like Ulysses against the siren song of the world.

In her own poetry, Herrad warned the women of Hohenbourg against earthly snares and temptations, encouraging them to scorn the world (*Sperne, sperne seculum*) (*HD* no. 1), a theme that is revisited in a short poem advising them to separate themselves from earthly desires, including the desire for release from the world:

To scorn the world, to scorn nothing, to scorn oneself,
To scorn scorning oneself: these are four good things. (*HD* no. 735)[55]

Herrad's final address to the women of the community reiterated the theme of scorn for the world that infused her introductory poem and dedication piece. There she had expressed her wish that they would "safely hurry over ephemeral things to possess the things that last forever in happiness and pleasure" (*HD* no. 2). In her farewell address, Herrad reminded the women to keep their eyes focused on heaven: "Hasten to heaven, after despising earthly dust, that you may be able to see the Bridegroom, who is now hidden" (*HD* Cat. No. 346).[56] In keeping with her message of *contemptus mundi*, Herrad presented the Virgin Mary to her readers as an example for nuns, calling her the *contemptrix mundi* (*HD* Cat. No. 235). Significantly, she also drew the manuscript to a close with a message of *contemptus mundi*. The Hohenbourg folios (fols. 322v–23r; plates 1–2) are followed by poems entitled *Versus de contemptu mundi* (*HD* no. 1164) and *Hec sunt opprobia mundi* (*HD* no. 1165).

The connection between the Ladder image and avarice is clear: those who tumble from the ladder are invariably distracted from their spiritual goal by worldly possessions. Glosses to the image also blend warnings concerning the false appearance of religion, the reality of temptations, and, implicitly, the dangers of hypocrisy. With the exception of the lay woman and the knight, each figure shown climbing the ladder is identified as an example of falseness in his or her station. The false cleric shown toward the bottom of the ladder seems to be almost a caricature of the dissolute clerics castigated in the *Hortus* booklet. Falling off the ladder backward, in defiance of gravity, he is doubled over with his arms outstretched toward his table, which is laden with delicious foods. Less directly in his line of sight, but still among the objects of his desire, are his church and his concubine (*amica*). Counting the church among the material objects of the cleric's desire, Herrad seems to be suggesting that his devotion to the church ranks no higher than his devotion to his table or to his concubine. Her gloss identifies him as a symbol of all false clerics who are "devoted to drunkenness, extravagance, simony and other vices" (*HD* Cat. No. 296).[57] Above the cleric, a monk also falls toward the earthly object of his desire: his large, overfilled money pot. With a money bag in one hand and a purse brimming with coins around his neck, he offers a vivid warning against the love of money, especially within the monastic life. Herrad's gloss points out that the monk is distracted from his performance of the divine office by his covetousness. His treasure—money and personal belongings—is fixed on the earth and there too is his heart.[58] Other depictions include the recluse tempted by the promise of his bed, the hermit by his garden, and the nun by the flattery and seductions of her priest. Only the virtuous person (*persona virtutis*), depicted as a young woman, promises to reach the ladder's summit and its prize, the crown of life. Herrad's gloss points out that this woman—*Caritas*—signifies all the holy and the elect (*omnes sanctos et electos*).[59]

The light-hearted cautionary tone of the Ladder image, with its almost comical portrayal of temptation, is abandoned in the texts and images related to judgment and hell—subjects that were uniquely appropriate for warnings against hypocrisy within the religious life. By this time in the *Hortus*, as well as in the salvation history that the manuscript charts, the spiritual battles that had been depicted in earlier images had either been won or lost and the souls of men and women were bound for heaven or hell. The Last Judgment depicts the moment at which all would be called to give account for themselves. Originally designed as a visual cycle that would extend across two openings, the cycle culminated in a facing-page depiction of Christ in Majesty (fols. 251v and 253r). Martyrs, churchmen, monks, and hermits are pictured to the right of Christ (fol. 251r), while to his left pseudo-popes and pseudo-apostles, false clerics, monks, and hermits cover their faces, weep, and plead as tongues of fire lick their feet (fol. 253v; *HD* Cat. No. 335). The pseudo-pope, false bishops, and clerics are identified in a gloss as those who do not preach in Christ's name, but for a fee, like the merchants selling oxen in the Cleansing image.[60] False hermits and recluses are identified as "those who have dishonored their order with belongings, drunkenness, and other vices."[61] As in the psychomachia cycle, the folios of the Last Judgment cycle are divided into three horizontal registers. In the bottom third, angels are

shown forcing the impious into hell. Figured prominently among the impious are a bishop in his miter and a monk, whose money bag identifies
him as the same monk who will appear some folios later in hell. As with
the fall of Lucifer at the outset of the manuscript, a turn of the page here
too carried the readers from one moment in the narrative to another—in
this case from judgment into hell.

The appearance of the monk with his money bag at three different
points in the *Hortus*—the Ladder image, the Last Judgment, and Hell—
offers yet another sign of the importance that Herrad attached to the renunciation of property and its reverse: avarice. As we have seen, Herrad
was deeply concerned with avarice and the related issues of simony and
hypocrisy, particularly among churchmen. Although the warnings in her
manuscript were clearly intended for a female audience, it is striking that
no woman—with the exception of the allegorical Avarice—is depicted in
scenes cautioning against love of money.

Herrad's emphasis on avarice reveals a larger concern with the state
of the church as a whole, which provides the subject of the *Ecclesia* section
of the *Hortus*. In marked contrast to the primarily historical and narrative
presentation of the life of Christ, this section takes up an allegorical approach, closer to that of the Old Testament section. The church, presented
alternately as Bride, Virgin, and mystical body of Christ, is in every case a
contemporary one. Of all the sections in the manuscript, this one is most
directly concerned with the lives and actions of contemporary Christians.
The first part is devoted entirely to the conflict of virtue and vice within
the soul of individual Christians, opening with the psychomachia cycle and
continuing with an unusual series of texts and images devoted to the life
of Solomon (fols. 204v–15r).[62] The first of these images depicts Solomon,
whose name means *Pacificus*,[63] lying in his bed surrounded by knights.
The contrast to the raging battle of the Virtues and Vices is explicit in
Herrad's glosses to the image: Solomon's bed is identified as the church
and his rest is the described as the peace of the "true Solomon" (i.e.,
Christ) that follows the defeat of devil and of the vices (*HD* Cat. No.
286).[64] In this peaceful interlude the struggle of spiritual battle is only
momentarily forgotten. Despite Solomon's wisdom and his good work in
building the temple (a prefiguration of the church), his own failure to
withstand the temptations of the flesh meant that his story could represent
a warning against the lures of the world, as much as it was—at least in
contrast to the psychomachia—a prefiguration of the true rest that might
be found in Christ. The visit of the Queen of Sheba provides Herrad with

the opportunity to explain that the church is black with persecution, but beautiful in virtue (*Ecclesia nigra est persecutionibus sed formosa virtutibus*) (*HD* Cat. No. 292). The Solomon cycle draws to a close with a folio depicting the Wheel of Fortune on one side (fol. 215r), and the Ladder of Virtues (fol. 215v; plate 5) on the other, followed by a series of images of Ulysses and the Sirens (fol. 221r–v).

The subsequent texts and images of the *Ecclesia* section address the church more directly, outlining the various different groups of which it is composed through a series of excerpts from Honorius's *Sermo generalis* and describing it—its symbolism, ornament, architecture, sacred objects, and ministers—in long excerpts from his *Gemma animae*. Concern for the well-being of the church is expressed in the image of *Ecclesia* (fol. 225v; plate 13), where demons and angels battle on the roof of a physical church, while a queen enthroned within symbolizes the mystical church, and the groups of laypeople, religious figures, and church leaders represent its body.[65] The attacks of the demons on the roof are anticipated on the previous folio, which shows Christ as the bridegroom and *Ecclesia* as his bride in the garden of the Song of Songs. Foxes threatening the vineyard are explicitly identified as heretics and schismatics (*HD* Cat. No. 301). These foxes recall the psychomachia cycle, in which Avarice was represented by a fox (*HD* Cat. No. 282).[66]

To be sure, Herrad does reserve some of her comments concerning wealth for rich laypeople. Her interpretation of Dives and Lazarus (fols. 123r–24r) includes warnings, taken from Honorius, to the wealthy to take care that they not lose the true riches of eternal life. As a text from the *Speculum ecclesiae* points out, some rich people—like Abraham and Job—have been saved, but certain others—like Pharaoh and Nebuchadnezzar—have not (*HD* no. 420). A later section—also from Honorius—encourages the rich to act as "fathers" to the poor (*pauperum patres*) and to support the church, mindful of the fact that they cannot take their wealth with them when they leave this world (*HD* no. 780). However, Herrad's most stinging criticism was always reserved for greedy churchmen, in whom the sin of avarice was compounded by hypocrisy and betrayal of the apostolic example.

Conclusion: The *Cura monialium* and Reform

Herrad's dedication to reform is revealed throughout the *Hortus deliciarum* by the way she selected and combined individual texts, by the manuscript's emphases and organization, and by her thoughtful arrangement of text and image. The *Hortus* as a whole sustained a concern with the central topics of the reform movement—the communal life and the perils of private property, the evil of avarice, and the sin of simony. All of these bore directly on the moral state of the clergy, for whom the communal life had been made mandatory after 1059. Although Herrad was also concerned with the proper authority of the pope and the spiritual state of Christians in general, questions concerning clerical behavior, morality, and education are most prominent in the manuscript.

Herrad's interest in the state of the church, the morality of the clergy, and, in particular, their suitability for the care of souls may, in part, reflect her experience at Hohenbourg during Relinde's abbacy and the early years of her own. At that time, as I have noted, one of the most pressing concerns was to ensure that the women of Hohenbourg would be properly served by priests who had been charged with the *cura monialium* at the community. Having founded two male communities for this purpose—St. Gorgon and Truttenhausen—Herrad might have seen in the *Hortus* a further opportunity to guarantee the quality of pastoral care, using it both to provide her readers with a solid theological education and to instruct them in the qualities that were desirable in a pastor and, by contrast, in those that were to be condemned. The reforming texts and images that Herrad chose to include in the manuscript—the booklet, psychomachia cycle, Cleansing image, and the depictions of the Ladder of Virtues as well as the Judgment and Hell scenes—show that she encouraged her female readers to judge the priesthood and to reject those priests whom they found to be morally or spiritually lacking. The *Hortus* taught the women of Hohenbourg to be critical of the clergy, providing them with a series of related offenses to watch for: failure to renounce private property; love of fine food, drink, and luxurious clothing; and the sale of sermons or other pastoral services—in short, avarice. An excerpt from the *Speculum ecclesiae* observes that priests are the windows of the church through which the light of divinity should shine: "But alas! The land rises above the windows, and the light is not permitted to enter, since the desire for earthly things blinds the mental sight of priests, and therefore the light of divine knowledge shines through them very little in the church" (*HD* no. 251).[67] A similar snippet of dialogue from the *Elucidarium* warns that priests who neither live well nor teach well are like smoke, which smothers the fire and stings the eyes.[68]

The catalogue of potential offenses that Herrad provides is remarkably thorough and consonant with the concerns of reformers generally, with one exception: she does not dwell on the potential sexual transgressions of priests. This is not to say that she was unaware of such possibilities—her Ladder image shows a priest tempting a nun, as well as a cleric who falls toward his *amica*. Nicolaitism, the marriage of priests, was clearly something with which Herrad was familiar, but which she chose not to feature in quite the same way as she did avarice and simony. Although the dominant scholarly picture of reform is one in which pollution fears and accusations of clerical impurity loom large,[69] this is not the picture that emerges from the *Hortus*. In addition to her near total neglect of nicolaitism, Herrad's denunciation of simony is conspicuously lacking in the sexual imagery that was so prevalent among other reformers. Only once, in the Ladder image, does a woman—the priest's *amica*—appear as the object of male avarice. As many have observed, the sexual language of reform tended to demonize women, depicting them as temptresses who brought men to ruin. By avoiding this rhetoric, Herrad excluded from the manuscript the strains of reform that have been seen to vilify women.

Women's interest in reform and their activity as reformers have largely been neglected in scholarship on the topic. However, as Herrad's example demonstrates, women were acutely concerned with the issues of reform. In many ways it is not at all surprising that women, and particularly religious women, should be deeply concerned with the state of the contemporary church. As Moore commented in his study of the origins of reform, "really virulent anticlericalism implies that some importance is attached to the clerical office."[70] Since women were excluded from the priesthood, but were nonetheless dependent on priests to provide them with the sacraments and with pastoral care, the clerical office was a subject of particular interest. It is possible that their exclusion from the ecclesiastical hierarchy and consequent reliance on the priesthood made them even more invested in reform issues than men; their interest in the integrity of the priesthood may have been sharpened by their exclusion from it. The language and imagery of the *Hortus* place Herrad in a tradition of women reformers in the twelfth century, which included such women as Hildegard of Bingen and Elisabeth of Schönau. The thoughtful—and biting—criticism that these women directed at the church and particularly at unscrupulous or immoral clerics gives lie to the idea, often expressed in medieval and even some modern sources, that women were especially vulnerable to bad teachers and, for that reason, more susceptible to heresy. Herrad's one

concern, which the *Hortus* was designed to alleviate, was that the women
of her house have access to solid teaching.

As this chapter has demonstrated, the women of Hohenbourg participated in reform. Moreover, they did so not as they are often depicted, as
byproducts of male ambition or sentiments—the wives and sisters of men
who could no longer protect and support them in the world or the hastily
cast-off wives of recently reformed priests—but rather as thoughtful and
independent coreformers. They were literally reforming women: women
not as the objects of reform, but as reformers themselves.

Conclusion: A Book for Women?

THE *HORTUS DELICIARUM* IS ONE of the few medieval Latin books known to have been written both *by* and explicitly *for* religious women. As such, it is a rare witness to the spiritual priorities and intellectual interests of a female monastic community at the close of the twelfth century. The work as a whole is a product of reform, the reform of Hohenbourg at the mid-twelfth century, but also, and more evident throughout the manuscript, of the broader movement for church reform that had swept Europe since the middle of the eleventh century. Papal primacy, clerical mores, and the state of the church are topics that appear repeatedly in the texts and images of the *Hortus*. It is also, although less self-consciously so, a product of the new intellectual currents of the twelfth-century schools. While the purpose of the *Hortus* was to serve the needs of women within a contemplative setting, it nonetheless included scholastic texts that had been written in the first instance for male university students. As such, it demonstrates that the monastic-scholastic divide posited by some scholars was neither as wide nor as deep as has been thought and, moreover, that women could have access to both traditions. The importance of these observations cannot be overstated: both reform and renaissance are areas in which women are thought to have made little or no mark and from which it is assumed that they were actively excluded.

The *Hortus* indicates that women did involve themselves in the spiritual and intellectual debates that define renaissance and reform. More interestingly, they did so without engaging in the traditionally gendered apologies that are a feature of much medieval women's writing. Since the *Hortus* was written for a female audience, it may be that Herrad saw no need for the sorts of rhetorical strategies that appear in the works of such figures as Hildegard of Bingen and Elisabeth of Schönau; the apologies of these women were intended for a public and largely male audience primed with gendered expectations linking women with lack of education and experiential knowledge of God. The *Hortus* had no such audience. Despite its luxurious presentation and remarkable textual and visual scope, it was essentially a private book, intended only for the women of Hohenbourg. But its singularity is the source of its importance: it allows direct access to the inner spiritual and intellectual workings of a female community, free from the expectations of a male audience and from the often-distorting lens of male biographers and scribes.

The *Hortus* is equally a reflection of the particular intellectual and spiritual context more generally associated with Augustinian canons. It is an important manifestation of the "commitment to educate others" that Bynum identifies as the central aspect of canonical spirituality in the twelfth century.[1] Like Hugh of St. Victor, who wrote for the edification of his community at St. Victor, Herrad's motivation was to add to the teaching by example that her role as abbess ensured, the teaching by word that ordained clerics provided in their preaching. She taught the women of Hohenbourg through the carefully selected and edited words of the *auctores*—men like Honorius Augustodunensis, Rupert of Deutz, and Peter Lombard, whose own writings were in turn heavily reliant on the authorities who had preceded them. This is not surprising, nor should it be seen to compromise Herrad's authorial claim. Since medieval education was based on the study of authoritative texts, compilations were essential to the process of education. As Hathaway remarks, "In the Middle Ages, as in late antiquity, a writer who wished to instruct . . . could not but borrow others' words."[2] Herrad was a teacher who did borrow from the words of other authors, but, according to her metaphorical presentation of herself as a bee, she was also an author. She designed the *Hortus*, determined its spiritual focus and organization, and then selected its texts and images, bringing them together and editing and arranging them according to her clear plan. Her intentionality is evident in every folio of the manuscript: in the texts that she chose, the way she edited them, the words and ideas that she glossed (as well as the way in which she glossed them), her use of images to explain and transform texts, and the page layout that she selected to further the pedagogical and mnemonic purpose of the manuscript as a whole.

In the *Hortus*, Herrad presented learning as an important path to salvation for women. As such, the liberal arts appear neither as dangerous, nor as inimical to faith, but as propadeutic to *Philosophia*, which Herrad identifies as Divine Wisdom. Although the wrongful quest for knowledge in the first garden—Eden—had led to humankind's separation from God,

Herrad presented the rightful search for knowledge in her *Garden of Delights* as an essential stage in the cultivation of virtue and the repair of memory, which would lead ultimately to reconciliation with God in heaven. The traditional ambivalence associated with women and knowledge—a legacy of the fall and of Eve—is absent from the *Hortus*; instead, the liberal arts and *Philosophia* are depicted in the manuscript as women and recommended as appropriate to the book's female audience. In fact, the wrongful quest for knowledge in Herrad's image is identified not with women but with male magicians, who are shown outside the realm of *Philosophia* with black birds hovering above their shoulders.

Herrad's optimism concerning women's capacity for study and knowledge is equally apparent in the way in which she presented the *Hortus*: its texts and images, most of which require a typological or allegorical reading, assume a sophisticated audience well versed in the different levels of scriptural interpretation (these are discussed in *HD* no. 721). The equation of the female reader with the literal, carnal sense of the word, so common in medieval literature, is, like the ambivalence regarding women and knowledge, absent from her work. It is not surprising, then, that the visual cycle of the *Hortus* occasions no comment from Herrad, who evidently saw no need either to offer an apology for the images that might imply an illiterate audience, or to warn the women against their literal misinterpretation.

On the whole, Herrad remained faithful to the central purpose of the *Hortus*: the presentation of salvation history and the ultimate salvation of its audience, who she prays "a thousand times each day" would resist the fleeting pleasures of the world, and its siren song, for the lasting pleasures of the heavenly Jerusalem (*HD* no. 1). Her major concerns reflect this purpose. She encourages *contemptus mundi* (contempt for the world) as a way for the women to maintain their focus on the ultimate goal, the crown of life, she warns of the spiritual warfare in which every soul is engaged, and she cautions against hypocrisy and false piety. Her teaching on the importance of study is consistent with these emphases, since learning, like the *contemptus mundi*, was recognized as a way to separate oneself from the cares of the world. On a practical level, Herrad's warnings against false piety and bad pastors would have helped guide the women of Hohenbourg in their dealings with the canons of St. Gorgon and Truttenhausen.

The *Hortus* offers its readers a presentation of salvation history absent the concessions to a female audience that can be found in contemporary male-authored works for women, such as the *Speculum virginum*. There is no warning against women's scholarship, no particular identification of women with the sins of Eve or with carnality and sensuality, and no sense of women's propensity to the literal interpretation of the text. Indeed, there is very little in the *Hortus* that might mark it specifically as a women's book, and this too is important: the *Hortus* is not gendered female. Although it was clearly intended for a female audience and explicitly dedicated to women, it contains no pointed references to a female readership, beyond those that appear in Herrad's prefatory and concluding materials, and few images and texts that would have concerned women more than men. There is no sense in which Herrad saw the spiritual needs of her female readership as differing in any fundamental way from the potential needs of men within the religious life.[3]

And yet, there is no question that the *Hortus* is a book that was designed for, and also dedicated to, women. As Herrad tells the women of Hohenbourg in her prologue, each image in the *Hortus* and each text had been selected over the course of many long years and brought together for the sake of their love. It is not surprising, then, that the whole sweep of salvation history, from its inception in the creation of the world to its culmination in the attainment of eternal rest—literally from one garden, Eden, to another, Paradise—is framed by texts and images that were specifically related to the monastery and to the women of Hohenbourg. At the beginning of the manuscript, Herrad's poem and prologue emphasize the dedication of the book to them and its relevance to their spiritual journey. At its close, the entire community is again powerfully evoked, this time in image as well as text. The penultimate folios present a full facing-page miniature depicting the legendary foundation of the monastery; these folios also show Hohenbourg's three most prominent abbesses, Odile, Relinde, and Herrad, and the fifty-eight women—forty-six canonesses and twelve novices—who were resident at Hohenbourg at the time that the *Hortus* was produced (fols. 322v–23r; plates 1–2). Although the women are clad in an assortment of bright colors—an indication of their status as canonesses rather than nuns—they are not otherwise visually distinguished.[4] Instead, they appear in uniform rows facing Christ, who addresses them from the opposite page. However, the name of each woman is written above her head so that the entire image has the appearance of a modern class photo. Like the prologue, in which the *Hortus* was dedicated specifically to the women, so too this image served to underscore the communal ownership (and possibly also production) of the manuscript and its relevance to each member of the community. Each woman, on finding her name in the manuscript, would be reminded of its application to her own life, despite the often difficult theological material that it contained. That the entire image was presented with a profusion of greenery—grass, leaves, and trees—rather than the architectural representation of the monastic buildings, might also have reminded the woman as they read the *Hortus* that they themselves were flowers in a monastic garden. Herrad's poetic address to the women underscores this idea:

O snow-white flowers giving forth the scent of virtue,
Always resting in divine contemplation,
Hasten to heaven, after despising earthly dust
That you may be able to see the Bridegroom, who is now hidden.[5]

In addition to these fifty-eight women, two further figures are shown but not named, one at the beginning of the procession of women, the other at the end. By these unnamed women, Herrad might have intended to evoke the eternal community of Hohenbourg women—both those who had come before and those who would come after. The image could have served, then, as a sort of visual necrology—a reminder to pray for past members of the community. At the same time, it was a potent reminder of the continuing cycle of salvation history. Just as Herrad's generation of women journeyed toward Christ, so, too, future women would turn to the *Hortus* for spiritual teaching and guidance as they sought, as Herrad put it, to "navigate through this sea."

In addition to the Hohenbourg community image, which so directly addressed the women, the community was evoked again in the two poems by Conrad and Hugo that appear on the final facing pages of the *Hortus*. The first momentarily shifts the focus from the women themselves to God, addressed alternately as creator and bridegroom: it is a prayer to God, begging his protection for the women and his care for them "in this place of earthly cares" (*spacio seculorum*) (*HD* no. 1162). The second turns to the women once more, addressing them in the imperative with the injunction to rejoice as "daughters of the king" and promising that they will see "God, the King, the True Bridegroom" with their own eyes (*HD* no. 1163). Since these poems appear on the verso of the Hohenbourg image (fol. 323v), they may originally have marked the end of the *Hortus*. However, they are followed now by two further poems on the recto of a half leaf (fol. 324r)—*Versus de contemptu mundi* (*HD* no 1164) and *Hec sunt opprobia mundi* (*HD* no. 1165), which widen the focus of the *Hortus* once

more, returning the reader to the concern with *contemptus mundi* that
had animated Herrad's presentation ever since the emphatic "Scorn, scorn
the world!" of her dedicatory poem.

The presentation of the *Hortus* within a localized frame of texts and
images was designed to underscore the relevance of its materials to the
community of women. As we have seen, the manuscript's German glosses
may, in part, have served a psychological purpose, making the manuscript
as a whole, and its Latin content in particular, more familiar to the German
speaking women of the community. So, too, the Hohenbourg-specific
texts and images at the beginning and end of the manuscript mediated the
theological material that appeared within the *Hortus* to its female audience. The vast majority of the texts that Herrad incorporated into the
Hortus had been written in the first instance for priests and students of
theology. They dealt with such subjects as the celebration of the divine
service, the delivery of a sermon, the spiritual symbolism of the liturgy,
and the teaching of the sacraments to a lay audience and often explicitly
invoked their male audience. Although Herrad generally edited her chosen texts to remove such invocations, in a few instances appeals to male
listeners crept into the *Hortus* so that the women of Hohenbourg would
have found themselves addressed as the original audience of the *Hortus*
texts must have been—as *karissimi*, or even simply, "brothers." Herrad's
frame of Hohenbourg-specific texts and images made it clear that, despite
their explicit attention to the concerns of male priests and students of
theology, the theological texts in the *Hortus* were equally appropriate for
the female audience at Hohenbourg.

In addition to the Hohenbourg frame, there are other indications
that the *Hortus* was intended for a female audience, although none of
these appear as either an apology or a concession. The most striking of
these appears on two folios included in the transitional section after the
ascension had drawn the narrative of Christ's life to a close, yet before the
psychomachia cycle had inaugurated the treatment of *Ecclesia*. These folios explicitly address topics related to religious women: the consecration
of virgins and widows, their clothing, their demeanor, and their specific
relationship to the two exemplary biblical virgins, John the Evangelist and
the Virgin Mary. An image on folio 176v shows a double arcade in which
John and Mary, shown on the left, receive a group of virgins and widows,
who approach from the right (plate 7). Inscriptions explain that the
women wear black as a reflection of their contempt for the embraces of
men (*contemptus amplexus virilis*, HD Cat. No. 235).[6] A gloss notes that

the Virgin Mary had adopted the nun's habit after the ascension, thereby emphasizing her shared vocation with the women, although she appeared here clad in green. The connection between religious women, Mary, and John is highlighted once more in the *Hortus* crucifixion scene (fol. 150r). According to John's gospel (John 19:26–27), Jesus' last words from the cross were directed toward his mother and his concern for her future provision. As he saw Mary standing at the foot of the cross, he therefore entrusted her to John's care, presenting John as Mary's adoptive son and Mary as John's adoptive mother. "Here is your son," he said to Mary, and to John: "Here is your mother."

Although the imitative potential of this scene is not elaborated in John's gospel, medieval men and women regularly interpreted the commendation to John as relating specifically to the care that religious men were to provide for women. Jesus' words from the cross became an injunction, then, to all ordained men to engage in the *cura monialium*, so that care for women could be seen as a central part of the complete *imitatio Christi*. This reading of John's gospel placed the obligation to provide care for women at the very heart of Christianity, by implicating the *cura* in the crucial act of salvation—the crucifixion. Herrad emphasizes the centrality of the commendation to the proper interpretation of the crucifixion, glossing the depiction of Christ's crucifixion in two separate places with the words of Christ's command: "Woman, here is your son," and to John: "Here is your mother" (*HD* Cat. Nos. 211–12). The difficulties that both she and Relinde had experienced in securing priests for the Hohenbourg altar no doubt prompted her emphasis on this episode, and the particular way in which she interpreted it.

Other images in the manuscript may not address women quite so directly, but they do privilege them in subject matter and composition. The Ladder of Virtues (fol. 215v; plate 5) shows only a young woman—a *persona virtutis*—attaining the crown of life. The faithful (*viros ac feminas*) are represented in the *Ecclesia* image by a group of young women, the daughters of Jerusalem, who are shown below *Ecclesia*'s throne on folio 225v (*HD* Cat. No. 302; plate 13). In heaven, virgins are given pride of place, before the apostles, martyrs, confessors, prophets, patriarchs, continent, married, and penitent (fol. 244r; *HD* Cat. No. 317).[7] In the *rotae* marking the transition from Old to New Testament (fol. 67r–v), the figures around the circumference of the first *rota*, each of whom represents some aspect of the old law, are depicted as men. In the second *rota*, which shows Christ as High Priest, the figures surrounding him are all women, representatives of the Virtues. Given this tendency to depict women in the manuscript, it is surprising that there are none in the Bosom of Abraham scene (fol. 263v), which brings Herrad's presentation of salvation history to a close. However, just before this final image, both women and men were numbered among the elect in an image that is now missing (fol. 261r). In this image, Herrad presented an equal number of men and women, the men as a representation of "perpetual youth" (*viri perpetua juventute florentes*) and the women, of eternal beauty and youth (*mulieres eterna pulchritudine et juventute gaudentes*) (*HD* Cat. No. 342). As we have seen, the *Hortus* was also replete with allegorical female figures—the Muses, liberal arts, *Philosophia*, the Virtues (and Vices), *Ecclesia*, and the woman clothed with the sun (as well as the Whore of Babylon).

The optimism regarding women's spiritual potential that infused Herrad's introductory and concluding pieces and that appears in her regular depiction of favorable female subjects does not, however, mean that she entirely avoided the traditionally negative connotations of "woman." The casual misogyny of her sources does creep into her text and there is no evidence that she tried to expunge it, or even that she questioned it. A reference to the "inferior sex" is glossed *mulier* in a text from Rupert's *De divinis officiis* (*HD* no. 538 n. 1). Another text asks why men rather than women are circumcised, since women were punished more for sin than men (*HD* no. 130). The potential of women to bring men to ruin is also stressed several times, most notably in Honorius's Siren sermon, where he explains that sirens have the faces of women, "since nothing alienates the mind of men from God like the love of women" (*HD* no. 756).[8] Herrad's visual depiction of this scene leaves Honorius's interpretation to the side; for her, the sirens represented anything that might distract her audience from their heavenly goal. Still, she did not exclude Honorius's misogynist reading of the story, and even glossed a nearby poem in order to clarify that it was a woman who had brought both Sampson and Solomon to ruin (*HD* no. 754).[9] Finally, although she did not generally associate women with the carnal and men with the spiritual, in her elaboration of the rapture described by Jesus in Luke 17:35, Herrad repeats Honorius's explanation for the gender of the two women at the mill: "The two grinders are described as women not men (*non duo sed due*) since they are raised up not as men to the spirit, but they are moved as women to the carnal."[10]

Morrison draws a stark comparison between the tenor of the *Hortus* as a whole and the instances of casual misogyny that he finds in it, commenting that "amidst the opulence that she commanded and the learning that instructed her mind, and despite the self-confidence represented in the whole enterprise of the *Hortus*, Herrad expressed quite another attitude toward femininity."[11] His judgment is too harsh. Herrad was a product of the twelfth century and it would be anachronistic to expect her to have resisted the gendered stereotypes of her culture entirely. It is true that she could have excised certain comments from her texts; she certainly edited elsewhere as she saw fit in order to incorporate a text or idea into her master plan. But it is too much to say, as Morrison does, that Herrad found "strong negatives" as far as her sex was concerned. The *Hortus* is filled with positive exemplars for the female religious life; as we have seen, Herrad's most stinging criticisms were directed not at women, but at churchmen.

A final way in which Herrad ensured the immediacy of the *Hortus* for her audience was by introducing images of canonesses in many of her depictions of the Christian community. These canonesses were a reminder that the history presented in the *Hortus* was a living history in which each member of its audience was directly implicated; they were visual reminders that each woman at Hohenbourg had a place in salvation history. Canonesses appear among the Christian community to Christ's right in the Tree of his ancestry (fol. 80v),[12] among the faithful bringing grapes for his Mystic Winepress (fol. 241r), and again among the faithful at the Last Judgment (fol. 247v). The women of Herrad's audience could also identify with the daughters of Jerusalem in the *Ecclesia* image on folio 225v (*HD* Cat. No. 302; plate 13), where they are described as *adolescentule*, a term reminiscent of Herrad's description of the women of her community as a *turmula adolescentularum* in her incipit to the *Hortus* (*HD* no. 3). They might equally see themselves in the person of virtue reaching the apex of the Ladder of Virtues (fol. 215v; plate 5) and receiving the crown of life—which, after all, was the ultimate goal of the *Hortus*.

The *Hortus* was a woman's book—designed, constructed, and dedicated by and for women. Its Hohenbourg-specific frame of texts and images and its depictions of women—both allegorical and actual—underscored this fact. Yet, the spiritual concerns that it addressed were universal, as were the methods that Herrad adopted in her teaching. This is not to say that in its origins and inspiration it was not also a "woman's book": the context in which the *Hortus* was written and the factors that both motivated and enabled Herrad's project were clearly specific to women. Reform at Hohenbourg from the middle of the twelfth century threw into sharp relief problems that had simmered in the community for some time—chief among them the need for well-trained and reform-minded priests to provide the *cura animarum*. Although Herrad had founded two houses for canons, who were to perform some services at the Hohenbourg altar, it was clearly desirable that the women of the community not rely exclusively on priests to provide them with spiritual training. The *Hortus* therefore filled two needs at once, providing theological teaching at Hohenbourg while also freeing the women from reliance on sometimes-unreliable male support.

Other female communities faced problems similar to those at Hohen-bourg without producing books comparable to the *Hortus*, a reminder that the *Hortus* project was the product of the particular set of circumstances at Hohenbourg. As the abbess of an independent female community, Herrad commanded more authority and enjoyed greater autonomy than did either Elisabeth of Schönau or Hildegard of Bingen. Both of these women were associated with double communities in which the women were practically and theoretically subordinate to male authority. Never the abbess of the Rupertsberg, Hildegard was only ever a *magistra* whose obedience was owed to the abbot of Disibodenberg. In this environment, Hildegard's and Elisabeth's self-presentation as unlettered prophetesses was both calculated to satisfy a male audience and mediated through a male scribe. Herrad's autonomy as the abbess of an independent community allowed her the freedom to bypass explicitly gendered concerns in her work, even while she exerted her authority among the male foundations associated with her community at Hohenbourg.

The *Garden of Delights* is a critical landmark in the history of women, their education, and their involvement in the religious life of twelfth-century Europe. It demonstrates how a community of women involved themselves in the intellectual and spiritual vitality of the twelfth century. From the cloister, women at Hohenbourg accessed texts from the emerging universities and engaged implicitly in theological and scholastic debates. Their work is evidence of their deep concern for the state of the church, their scathing criticism of unworthy and corrupt churchmen, and their astute negotiation of the political battles between the pope and emperor in the later twelfth century.

Although the *Hortus* is obviously a rich witness to the particular circumstance at Hohenbourg, its significance is not limited to this one community of women: the manuscript challenges the assumption of women's exclusion from the movements of reform and renaissance by which the twelfth century is now largely defined. Although there has been an outpouring of work on medieval women in recent years, much of it has presented them as fringe figures, whose sphere of activity lay outside the mainstream. There has been no recognition of women's engagement in the intellectual currents of the renaissance—with the exception of Heloise, who is a special case for obvious reasons—and very little of their involvement in reform, which is most often depicted as having excluded women and increased clerical misogyny. The *Hortus* provides evidence for women's enthusiastic engagement in both arenas and provides a basis for the study of other female communities, which, while they may not have produced manuscripts on the scale of the *Garden of Delights*, were similarly engaged in the study of the liberal arts, in book production, and in letter writing.

In the debate over medieval women's religious and intellectual experiences, Herrad's significance is twofold. First, she presents a corrective to the traditional view that the participation of women in scholarly endeavors is a development of the modern period. As a text that was written by a woman for the education of women, the *Hortus* is a monument to the role of women in intellectual discourse during the twelfth century. In the second place, Herrad challenges the construction of medieval religious women in much recent scholarship as having experienced God primarily within a separate, feminized sphere of affective spirituality, characterized by visions and physicalized, even erotic, union. As a woman who was not "feminine"—a term that has been used to mean emotional, sensual, and ecstatic—in her approach to God, Herrad was free to read, write, and comment tacitly on the Scriptures through the *Hortus*. Her example suggests the need for a new model for examining religious women in the twelfth century, one that recognizes women's deep involvement in the intellectual and spiritual currents of their age.

Appendix: Latin Texts and Translations

Herrad's Introductory Poem and Prologue

HD NO. I

Rithmus Herradis abbatisse per quem Hohenburgenses virgunculas amabiliter salutat et ad veri sponsi fidem dilectionemque salubriter invitat.

Salve cohors virginum
Hohenburgiensium
Albens quasi lilium
Amans Dei Filium.

Herrat devotissima
Tua fidelissima
Mater et ancillula
Cantat tibi cantica.

Te salutat milies
Et exoptat in dies,
Ut leta victoria
Vincas transitoria.

O multorum speculum
Sperne, sperne seculum,
Virtutes accumula,
Veri sponsi turmula.[1]

Insistas luctamine,
Diros hostes[2] sternere,

[1]scilicet tu.
[2]id est demones.

Te rex[3] regum adjuvat
Quia te desiderat.[4]

Ipse tuum animum
Firmat contra Zabulum,
Ipse post victoriam[5]
Dabit regni gloriam.

Te decent delicie[6]
Debentur divicie[7]
Tibi celi curia,
Servat bona plurima.

Christus parat nupcias[8]
Miras per delicias,
Hunc expectes[9] principem
Te servando virginem.

Interim monilia[10]
Circumdes[11] nobilia,
Et exornet faciem
Mentis purgans aciem.

Christus odit maculas,[12]
Rugas[13] spernit vetulas,
Pulchras[14] vult virgunculas
Turpes[15] pellit feminas.

[3]Christus.
[4]in sponsam.
[5]id est mortem.
[6]scilicet regni celestis.
[7]eternitatis.
[8]in celo.
[9]in isto seculo.
[10]virtutes.
[11]exerceas.
[12]peccata.
[13]crimina anime.
[14]castas.
[15]id est incestas.

Fide cum turturea
Sponsum istum redama,
Ut tua formositas
Fiat perpes claritas.

Vivens[16] sine fraudibus
Es monenda[17] laudibus,
Ut consummes[18] optima
Tui gradus[19] opera.

Ne vacilles dubia[20]
Inter mundi flumina[21]
Verax Deus premia[22]
Spondet post pericula.[23]

Patere nunc aspera,
Mundi spernens prospera,
Nunc sis cruci[24] socia[25]
Regni consors postea.

Per hoc mare[26] naviga,
Sanctitate gravida,[27]
Dum de navi[28] exeas
Syon[29] sanctam teneas.

Syon turris celica,
Bella[30] tenens atria,

[16]tu.
[17]a me.
[18]finias.
[19]ordinis.
[20]in fide.
[21]impedimenta.
[22]tibi.
[23]mundi.
[24]Christi.
[25]duram sustinens.
[26]mundum.
[27]plena.
[28]corpore.
[29]id est urbem celestem.
[30]pulchra.

Tibi fiat statio,[31]
Acto[32] vite spacio.

Ibi[33] rex virgineus[34]
Et Marie Filius[35]
Amplectens te redamet
A merore[36] relevet.

Parvipendens omnia
Temptatoris[37] jacula,
Tunc gaudebis[38] pleniter
Jubilando [39] suaviter.

Stella maris fulgida,[40]
Virgo mater unica,
Te conjungat Filio
Federe[41] perpetuo.

Et me tecum trahere
Non cesses precamine,
Ad sponsum[42] dulcissimum[43]
Virginalem Filium.

Ut tue victorie,
Tue magne glorie,
Particeps inveniar[44]
De terrenis[45] eruar.

[31]requies.
[32]finito.
[33]in Syon.
[34]Christus.
[35]Christus.
[36]hujus seculi.
[37]diaboli.
[38]in Syon.
[39]canticum agni.
[40]Maria.
[41]amore.
[42]Christum.
[43]scilicet.
[44]in celis. ut.
[45]de periculis.

Vale casta contio,
Mea jubilatio,
Vivas sine crimine[46]
Christum semper dilige.

Sit hic liber utilis,
Tibi delectabilis
Et non cesses volvere[47]
Hunc[48] in tuo pectore.[49]

Ne more strucineo
Surrepat[50] oblivio,
Et ne viam[51] deseras
Antequam pervenias.[52]

Amen amen amen
Amen amen amen
Amen amen amen
Amen amen amen.

HD NO. I

The poem of the abbess Herrad, in which she lovingly salutes the Hohenbourg virgins and with good wishes invites them to faith and love of the
true bridegroom.

Hail, virgin band
Of Hohenbourg,
Who, white as the lily,
Love the Son of God.

Herrad,
Your most devoted and faithful

[46]in hac vita.
[47]pertractare.
[48]librum.
[49]memoria.
[50]tibi.
[51]Christum.
[52]ad illum.

Mother and little handmaid,
Sings songs for you.

She greets you a thousand times
And prays each day
That, in happy victory,
You shall overcome all things that pass.

O mirror of many,
Scorn, scorn the world!
Pile up virtues,
Little troop of the true Bridegroom.

Persevere in the struggle
To overthrow the terrible enemies
The King of kings aids you
Since he longs for you.

He himself strengthens your soul
Against Zabulon
After death, which is our victory,
He himself will give you the glory of his kingdom.

The delights of the celestial kingdom become you
The riches of eternity are your due
For you, the heavenly court
Reserves many blessings.

Christ prepares a wedding
Wonderful in delights,
May you await this prince
By keeping yourself a virgin.

Meanwhile, gird yourself
With noble necklaces
And let Christ adorn each face
Purifying the mind's power,

For he hates the blemishes of sin
And scorns the aged wrinkles of a guilty soul,

His desire is for beautiful little maidens
Ugly women he drives away.

With faith like a dove,
Love your Bridegroom in return
So that your beauty
May become an everlasting brightness.

You who are living without deceit
Be admonished by my praises,
That you may complete the best works
Of your rank.

But lest you should waver with uncertain faith
Amidst the streams of this world,
A truthful God pledges rewards
After the dangers are past.

Suffer bitterness now
Despising the fortunes of the world
Be now a partner in Christ's cross,
And thereafter sharer in his kingdom.

Navigate through this sea
Pregnant with holiness,
When you leave this mortal vessel
May you attain holy Syon.

Syon of the celestial battlements
With its beautiful courts
May it be your home, your rest,
When life's course has been run.

There in Syon, may the Virgin King,
Christ, the Son of Mary,
Return your love and, embracing you,
Comfort you from the grief of this world.

Then counting as little
All the darts of that tempter the Devil,

You will be filled with delight
Sweetly chanting the song of the Lamb.

Then may Mary, the sea's shining star,
The only virgin mother,
Join you to her son
With a perpetual pledge of love.

And may you never cease to pull me with you
By your prayers
To Christ, the sweetest Bridegroom,
The Son of the virgin.

So that I may be found a sharer
In your victory and great glory,
Let me be rescued
From earthly peril.

Farewell chaste assembly,
My joy,
May you live without reproach
And always cherish Christ.

May this book be useful
And delightful to you
May you never cease to study it
In your thoughts and memory.

Lest like an ostrich
Forgetfulness should steal upon you
And you should forsake the way
Before you have reached Christ.
Amen.

HD NO. 2

Item prosa per Herradem abbatissam predictis virgunculis causa exhortationis composita.

Herrat gratia Dei Hohenburgensis ecclesie abbatissa licet indigna dulcissimis Christi virginibus in eadem ecclesia quasi in Christi vinea Domini
fideliter laborantibus, graciam et gloriam, quam dabit Dominus. Sanctitati
vestre insinuo, quod hunc librum qui intitulatur Hortus deliciarum ex diversis sacre et philosophice scripture floribus quasi apicula Deo inspirante
comportavi et ad laudem et honorem Christi et Ecclesie, causaque dilectionis vestre quasi in unum mellifluum favum compaginavi. Quapropter in
ipso libro oportet vos sedulo gratum querere pastum et mellitis stillicidiis
animum reficere lassum, ut sponsi blandiciis semper occupate et spiritalibus deliciis saginate[1] transitoria secure percurratis et eterna felici jucunditate possideatis, meque per varias maris semitas periculose gradientem
fructuosis orationibus vestris a terrenis affectibus mitigatam una vobiscum
in amorem dilecti[2] vestri sursum trahatis. Amen.

HD NO. 2

A letter by Herrad, abbess to the aforementioned virgins, composed for
the sake of their encouragement.

Herrad, by the grace of God, abbess, although unworthy, of the church
of Hohenbourg, to the sweetest virgins of Christ faithfully working at
Hohenbourg as though in the vineyard of the Lord Christ, be grace and
glory, that the Lord will give. I make it known to your holiness, that, like
a little bee inspired by God, I collected from the various flowers of sacred
Scripture and philosophic writings this book, which is called the Hortus
deliciarum, and I brought it together to the praise and honor of Christ
and the church and for the sake of your love as if into a single sweet honeycomb. Therefore, in this very book, you ought diligently to seek pleasing
food and to refresh your exhausted soul with its honeyed dewdrops, so
that, always possessed by the charms of the Bridegroom and fattened on
spiritual delights, you may safely hurry over ephemeral things to possess
the things that last forever in happiness and pleasure. And now as I pass
dangerously through the various pathways of the sea, I ask that you may
redeem me with your fruitful prayers from earthly passions and draw me
upwards, together with you, into the affection of your beloved. Amen.

[1] id est inpinguate.
[2] Christi.

Inscriptions on the Hohenbourg Image

o
Vos quas includit,   frangit, gravat, atterit, urit,
in terris
Hic carcer, mestus,   labor, exilium, dolor, estus;
in celis
Me lucem, requiem, patriam,   medicamen et umbram,
Querite, sperate,   scitote, tenete, vocate.

O
You whom prison confines,
Sorrow breaks,
Labor burdens,
Exile and grief wear down,
And passion burns here on earth;
Seek me as light,
Hope for me as rest,
Know me as your homeland,
Hold me as balm,
Call me as cooling shade
In heaven.

O pie grex,   cui celica lex   est, nulla doli fex;
Ipse Syon mons   ad patriam pons,   atque boni fons;
            est
Qui via, qui lux,   hic tibi sit dux,   alma tegat crux.
            castitatis   eternitatis   Christus
Qui placidus ros,   qui stabilis dos,   virgineus flos
            grex
Ille regat te   commiserans me,   semper ubique;   amen.

HD FOL. 322V; HD CAT. NO. 345

O pious flock to whom the heavenly law is given, in whom there is no
    residue of deceit;
He is the mount of Syon, the bridge to paradise, and the fount of good;
May he who is the way of chastity, the light of eternity, Christ, be your
    leader;
May the gracious cross protect you.
O flock, may he who is the peaceful dew, the stable dowry, the virginal
    flower, guide you,
Having mercy on me, always and everywhere. Amen.

HD FOL. 323R; HD CAT. NO. 346

Esto nostrorum   pia merces Christe laborum.
Nos electorum   numerans in sorte tuorum.

HD fol. 323r; HD CAT. NO. 346

O Christ, be the gracious reward of our labors.
Count us in the number of your elect.

HD FOL. 323R; HD CAT. NO. 346

O nivei flores   dantes virtutis odores,
Semper divina   pausantes in theoria,
Pulvere terreno   contempto currite celo,
celo
Que nunc absconsum   valeatis cernere sponsum.

HD fol. 323r; HD CAT. NO. 346

O snow-white flowers giving forth the scent of virtue,
Always resting in divine contemplation,

Hasten to heaven, after despising earthly dust
That you may be able to see the Bridegroom, who is now hidden.

Poems Dedicated to Hohenbourg, by Conrad and Hugo

*The authors' names are given in acrostics: *H[oh]enburgensib[us] C[on]-
radus* and *Hugo Sacerdos*

HD no. 1162

Rithmus de monte Hohenburc.

Hoc in monte[1]   vivo fonte[2]
Potantur ovicule,[3]
Esum[4] vite   sine lite
Congestant apicule.

Nectar clarum   scripturarum
Potant liberaliter,
Bibant,[5] bibant,[6]   vivant,[7] vivant
Omnes eternaliter.

Vultus harum[8]   lumen carum
Habent datum celitus,
Reginarum   hos[9] sanctarum
Credas[10] esse penitus.

Genus tale   speciale
Genus Christo proximum

[1]Hohenburc.
[2]sancti Spiritus.
[3]domicelle.
[4]doctrinam.
[5]hic.
[6]in futuro.
[7]nunc et semper.
[8]ovicularum.
[9]vultus.
[10]o aliquis.

Est commune   tibi une[11]
Fructum[12] portans maximum.[13]

Nevum nescit   nam ignescit
Celibatus gloria,
Semper mentem   gemiscentem
Dat[14] sponsi memoria.

Illum[15] spectat   vix exspectat
Ut remoto speculo,
Bone spei[16]   faciei[17]
Contempletur[18] oculo.[19]

Cetus iste   nichil triste,
Nichil levum doleat,
Rectitudo,   sanctitudo
Sempter (sic) hinc redoleat.

Aula Dei   virginei
Chori sunt et thalamus,
Dictat namque   sic utrumque
Cito scribens calamus.[20]

Verus sponsus   nunc absconsus,
In celi palacio,
Servet, regat,   has protegat
Seculorum spacio.

Ut sodales   virginales
Vivant sine crimine,

[11]o Deus.
[12]virginitatis.
[13]centesimum.
[14]illis.
[15]sponsum.
[16]que nunc est.
[17]quod nondum est.
[18]summum bonum, id est sponsum.
[19]sicuti est in regno.
[20]Spiritus sanctus.

Sub Messya   cum Maria,
Virgines cum virgine.

HD NO. 1162

A poem concerning Hohenbourg.

On this mountain of Hohenbourg, the little sheep
Drink from the living fountain of the Holy Spirit,
The little bees gather
The nourishing doctrine of life, without strife.

They drink freely
The clear nectar of the Scriptures,
May they drink now, may they drink in the future,
May they live now and always, may they all live eternally.

The faces of these little sheep
Possess a precious light given from Heaven,
You would think that these faces
Are really those of holy queens.

Such a race, a beloved race,
A race close to Christ,
Is shared with you alone, O God,
A race yielding the greatest fruit of virginity.

But the glory of celibacy knows no stain
Fot it shines like a fire,
The memory of the bridegroom
Always grants a penitent mind.

Memory gazes toward him, waiting with difficulty
So that when the present mirror
Of good hope is removed,
He may be contemplated face to face.

May this crowd of women suffer neither sadness,
Nor harm,

May uprightness and holiness
Always be fragrant from this place.

In the court of God
Are virginal choirs and a wedding chamber,
For the quill of the holy spirit, writing quickly
Composes both in this way.

May the true bridegroom, who is now hidden
In the palace of heaven,
Preserve, rule, and protect these women
In the place of earthly cares.

So that the virginal companions
May live without reproach
Along with Mary at the foot of the Messiah,
Virgins with the Virgin.

HD NO. 1163

Item rithmus de monte Hohenburc.

Hunc ad montem,   vite fontem,
Derivavit gracia,
Ubertatis,[1]   castitatis[2]
Irrorans solatia.

Gaude leta   cantu sueta
Gaude cohors virginum,
Ordo cujus   ornat hujus
Secli domicilium.

Sacer[3] cultus,   simplex vultus,
Casta mens et humilis,

[1] in rebus.
[2] in corporibus et animabus.
[3] ecce ostensio ordinis.

Amatori,   servatori,
Christo est amabilis.

Cantus suavis,   gestus gravis
Motus pudicicie,
Eternalis   absque malis
Signa sunt leticie.

Regis nate   sic ornate
Sunt ab intus singule,
Dant fimbrias   tunc aureas
Nunc absconse gemmule.

O spes certa   que aperta
Licet sit in speculo
Sponsum Deum   regem verum
Videbitis[4] oculo.

HD NO. 1163

Another poem concerning Hohenbourg.

Grace has flowed down
To this mountain, the fountain of life,
Bringing the comforts of bounty and of chastity,
Sprinkling them like dew.

Rejoice, happy virgin band, accustomed to singing
Rejoice, virgin band,
Whose way of life adorns
The dwelling place of this world.

Sacred worship, a simple face,
A pure and humble mind,
These are delightful to Christ,
The Lover, the Saviour

[4]sponse.

Sweet song, sober bearing,
The gesture of chastity,
These are signs of eternal happiness
Without wickedness.

Daughters of the King, each one
Thus inwardly adorned,
The precious little jewels, now hidden,
Will give you golden fringes at that time.

O certain hope, which has been revealed,
Although it is in a mirror,
You, the brides, will see the bridegroom
God the true King, face to face.

Poems Possibly Written by Herrad

HD NO. 374

De primo homine. Rithmus.[1]

Primus parens hominum
Lumen cernens coelicum,
Ita fuit conditus
Coetus ut angelicus,
Consors esset illius
Ac foret perpetuus.

Serpens hunc deceperat
Pomum quod gustaverat,
Fuerat quod vetitum
Et sic vicit miserum
Statim pulsus patria
Pulchra liquit atria.

[1] id est numerus.

Flebilis miserrimum
Ruit in exilium,
Plagis est impositus
Diris de latronibus
Quos infelix incidit
Patria dum excidit.

Hunc et spoliaverant
Semivivum liquerant;
Cui subvenit gratia
Ille de Samaria,
Stabulo induxerat
Curam ejus egerat.

Ejus sanans vulnera
Solita clementia,
Sic nos pius Dominus
Eruit de faucibus
Colubri nequissimi,
Hostis invidissimi.

Qui humani generis
Gaudet de miseriis,
Cruciatu pascitur,
Poenae pater dicitur:
Visu est horribilis
In omni terribilis;

Nullis flecti precibus
Potest crudelissimus.
Si in malo opere
Quemquam sentit vivere
Hunc dolose decipit
Servum sibi eligit.

Servis suis praemia,
Dabit amarissima,
Illos quando tartarum
Mergit in sulphureum.

Ejus aula sordida
Multa habet tristia.

Ibi errant animae,
Dolor adest undique
Gemitu moerentium
Et luctu dolentium
Domus tota personat,
Ipse poenas ordinat.

Orcus sedens solio
Ignis pice fumido,
Visus ejus horridus
Dolor est aestuantibus;
Pro diversis viciis
Poenas tradit singulis.

Potentes potentibus
Committit tortoribus.
Ibi sunt angustiae
Et multe miseriae,
Ibi poenitentia,
Sine indulgentia.

Vae, vae lamentabiliae
Clamant semper animae;
Verba dant precantia
Nec auxiliantia
Post calorem nimium
Aquas intrans nivium.

Nulla tamen anima
Nisi carnis famula
Pertimescat tartarum
Et regem tartareum,
Quae internis tenebris
Carne jacet debilis.

Habet post delicias
Hec aeternas tenebras

Ibi fletus luminum
Et est stridor dentium,
Clamor hic plorantium,
Dolor ululantium.

Judex hic tartareus
Gaudens cruciatibus
Mala nostra trutinat,[2]
Poenam et remunerat,
Ne nos hoc voragine
Versaremur misere,

Deus quaerens venerat
Ovem quam prodiderat,
Et qui legem dederat
Legi se subdiderat,
Et pro his quos condidit
Mortem diram subiit.

Nobis sic compatiens
Dederat omnipotens
Liberum arbitrium
De vitandi tartarum,
Vitia si spernimus
Et si bona facimus.

Nil nocebit animam,
Veniet ad gloriam
Et debemus Dominum
Et amare proximum;
Haec praecepta gemina
Ducunt ad coelestia,

Et per portam ferream
Dant ad urbem semitam,
In qua lux justitia
Et est vox laetitia,

[2]wiget.

In qua gaudent agmina
Requie perpetua.

Est vere floridior
Et sole splendidior
Mellis habet flumina,
Dulcis aurae flamina;
Dicta pacis visio,
Ornatu angelico,

Est exstructa civitas,
In qua est jocunditas;
In tam dulci patria
Nulla erunt taedia,
Ibi exsultatio,
Ibi delectatio.

Inenarrabilia
Ibi dantur gaudia
Quae paravit Dominus
Sese diligentibus;
Festinemus ingredi
Civitatem Domini.

Fugiamus exilio
Ut nos Dei filio
Jungamus feliciter
Et perpetualiter;
Hoc concedat omnibus
Seculorum Dominus
Qui per cuncta tempora
Regnat summa gloria. Amen.

HD NO. 374

A poem concerning the first man.

Man's first parent
As he gazed upon the heavenly light

Was created
Just like the company of angels,
He was to be the consort of angels
And to live forever.

The serpent deceived that wretched man
The apple that he tasted
Was the forbidden one,
And so that serpent conquered him
And immediately, expelled from paradise,
He left those beautiful courts.

The lamentable man
Tumbled into most miserable exile
Trapped in the snares of dread bandits.
He came upon them,
That unlucky one,
As he left paradise.

They robbed him
And left him half-dead.
But, by grace, that one from Samaria
Ministered to him.
The Samaritan led him to lodging
And took care of him.

Healing his wounds
With his wonted kindness,
In the same way, our loving Lord
Rescued us from the jaws
Of that most wicked snake,
That most hateful enemy.

The one who delights
In the miseries of the human race,
Who feasts on torture,
Is called the father of punishment.
He is horrible to see,
Terrifying in every way.

By no entreaties can
The cruelest one be swayed.
If he senses that anyone
Is living wickedly
He ensnares such a man craftily
Choosing him to be his slave.

To his slaves
He will give most bitter rewards
When he plunges them
Into fire and brimstone.
His squalid palace
Contains many miseries.

There souls wander
And trouble appears on every side;
The whole house resounds
With the moaning of those who sorrow
And the laments of those who grieve;
These penalties he sets out.

The god of hell sits on the throne
Which smokes with pitch-black fire;
His face is horrifying.
There is pain to those who are burning
For different vices
He hands down his punishment to each.

The powerful
He entrusts to powerful torturers
In that place where dire straits are
And many miseries
And penitence
Without leniency.

Woe, woe!
The mournful souls always shout
They utter words of prayer,
But there is no succor;

After the excessive heat
They plunge into icy waters.

But there is no soul
Except a servant of the flesh
That should fear the underworld
And the king of hell.
Such a one lies dead in inner darkness
Weakened by the flesh.

After the delights of the world
This soul has an eternal night
In which there shall be weeping
And gnashing of teeth
The shouts of those lamenting
And the sorrow of those shrieking.

The infernal judge,
Rejoicing at the terrible sufferings,
Weighs our evil deeds
And repays us with punishments.
But lest our wretched selves
Be tossed in this abyss

God came seeking the sheep
That he had lost,
And he who had given the law
Put himself under it,
So that for those whom he created
He suffered a most horrible death.

Suffering in this way with us,
The omnipotent one
Gave free will,
To avoid hell,
If we scorn vices
And if we do good.

Nothing will harm our soul;
It will come into glory,

And so we ought to love God
And our neighbor.
These twin precepts
Lead to heaven.

And through the iron gate
They supply the path to the city
Whose light is justice
And whose voice is gladness,
In which the throngs rejoice
In peace everlasting.

It is more full of flowers than the spring,
More splendid than the sun;
It has rivers of honey
And sweetly-smelling breezes;
It is called the vision of peace,
In the beauty of angels.

There is a city built
In which there is joy;
In such a sweet country
There will be no weariness,
But exultation
And delight.

Indescribable
Joys are given there,
Which the Lord prepared
For those who love him;
Let us hasten to enter
Into the city of God.

So let us flee from exile
That we may happily
And perpetually
Join ourselves to the Son of God.
May the Lord of the ages
Grant this to all,

He who rules through all time
With utmost glory. Amen.

HD NO. 595

Rithmus de Domino nostro Jhesu Christo.

O Rex pie,
O Dux viae,
Jesu Christe optime,
Nostrum chorum
Laudes morum
Doce tibi promere.

Ut concordes
Mentis sordes
Tua ope celica
Expurgemus
Et mundemus
Cordis nostris intima.

Ut psallamus
Et solvamus
Vota nostra plenitus,
Spe sincera
Vita vera
Te colentes jugitus.

Tu fons vitae
Manans rite
In purgata pectora
Rigas mentem
Sitientem
Sancta per carismata.

Tu solamen
Et levamen
Pro te tribulantibus

Onus leve,
Hujus suave
Bene laborantibus.

Flos virtutis,
Spes salutis,
Honor ineffabilis,
Pulchritudo,
Sanctitudo
Est inestimabilis.

Te sitire
Et te scire
Fac nos in hac nebula
Sic curramus
Ut spernamus
Mundi hujus flamina.

Ut secure
Viae durae
Linquamus pericula,
Et mox lete
Ac quiete
Coeli dones praemia.

HD NO. 595

A poem concerning our Lord Jesus Christ.

O gracious King,
O leader of the way,
Supreme Jesus Christ,
Teach our choir
To praise you
By our way of life.

So that as one
We may expel filth

From our minds
With your heavenly help
And cleanse
The recesses of our hearts,

That we may sing Psalms
And fulfill
Our vows completely,
With sincere hope
And true life,
Perpetually worshipping you.

You are the fount of life,
Duly flowing
Into purified hearts;
Through your holy gifts of grace
You moisten
The parched spirit.

You are solace
And comfort
For those in tribulation for your sake.
His burden is a light
And pleasant one
For those who labor well.

You are the flower of virtue,
The hope of salvation,
Honor unspeakable.
Your beauty,
Your holiness,
Are inestimable.

Make us thirst for you
And know you
In this mist.
Thus let us hasten
To scorn
The blasts of this world,

So that carefree,
We may leave behind
The dangers of the hard road
And soon happily and peacefully
You will bestow on us
The rewards of heaven.

Abbreviations

AD   *Alsatia aevi Merovingici, Carolingici, Saxonici, Salici, Suevici diplomatica.* Ed. Johann Daniel Schoepflin. 2 vols. Mannheim: Ex Typographia Academica, 1772–1775.

ADBR   Archives Départémentales du Bas-Rhin.

CCCM   *Corpus christianorum: continuatio medievalis.*

CCSL   *Corpus christianorum: series latina.*

CGS   *Guta-Sintram Codex*, Bibliothèque du Grand Séminaire de Strasbourg, MS 37.

CSEL   *Corpus scriptorum ecclesiasticorum latinorum.*

HD   Herrad of Hohenbourg. *Hortus deliciarum.* Ed. Rosalie Green, Michael Evans, Christine Bischoff, and Michael Curschmann. 2 vols. London: Warburg Institute, 1979.

MGH   *Monumenta Germaniae Historica.*

     Conc.   *Concilia.*

     DDRG   *Diplomatum regum et imperatorum Germaniae.*

     Libelli   *Libelli de lite imperatorum et pontificum saeculis XI et XII conscripti.*

     Necr.   *Necrologia Germania.*

     SS   *Scriptores.*

     SSRG   *Scriptores rerum Germanicarum.*

     SSRM   *Scriptores rerum Merovingicarum.*

NSD   S. A. Würdtwein, *Nova subsidia diplomatica.* 14 vols. Heidelberg: T. Goebhardt, 1781–1792.

PL   *Patrologiae cursus completus: series latina.* Ed. J.-P. Migne. 221
          vols. Paris: Migne, 1841–1864.

SBOp   Bernard of Clairvaux, *Sancti Bernardi Opera.* Eds. J. Leclercq,
          C. H. Talbot, and H. M. Rochais. 8 vols. Rome: Editiones Cist-
          ercienses, 1957–1998.

SV   *Speculum virginum.*

Notes to Citations

Translations are the author's own, unless otherwise noted.

Biblical citations refer to the Vulgate.

Hortus deliciarum: Notes follow the 1979 reconstruction of the *Hortus deliciarum* in designating texts from the *Hortus* (vol. 2) as "*HD* no." Citations from the *Commentary* (vol. 1) are designated by the author's name followed by "*HD*" and the page number. Descriptions of miniatures from the *Hortus* appear as "*HD* Cat. No." Folios refer to the *Hortus* (vol. 2), unless otherwise noted. In texts from the *Hortus*, parenthetical words reflect interlinear and marginal glosses in the original manuscript; Middle High German glosses are shown in bold type.

Notes

Introduction

1. Green, *HD* 17.

2. The most important of these were Christian Moritz Engelhardt, who made the first complete study of the *Hortus*; Comte Auguste de Bastard, to whom the manuscript had been on loan in Paris for a period of about ten years; and Baptiste Petit-Gérard, whose mid-nineteenth-century tracings of the *Hortus* are now in the Oeuvre Notre-Dame in Strasbourg. Sources for the 1979 reconstruction of the *Hortus* are listed in Evans, *HD* 4–5, and discussed in Green, *HD* 17–18.

3. Herrad of Hohenbourg, *Hortus deliciarum*; ed. Green, Evans, Bischoff, and Curschmann.

4. Sit hic liber utilis,
   Tibi delectabilis
   Et non cesses volvere (pertractare)
   Hunc (librum) in tuo pectore (memoria). (*HD* no. 1)

5. Heloise, *Epist.* 6; ed. Muckle, 242; trans. Radice and Clanchy, 94. For discussion of this letter, see Georgianna, "In Any Corner of Heaven."

6. Abelard, *Epist.* 8; ed. McLaughlin, 243; trans. Radice and Clanchy, 131. On Abelard's optimism concerning women's spiritual potential, see Blamires, "*Caput a femina, membra a viris.*"

7. Perhaps not surprisingly, Abelard's rule was never put into effect in Heloise's community. Newman commented that "Abelard's insistence on mutual service left the lines of authority muddled, making his rule unworkable in practice." "Flaws in the Golden Bowl," 27. Clanchy calls Abelard's *Rule* "worse than useless as a working document." *Abelard*, 222.

8. For discussion of the authorship of the *Speculum virginum*, see Mews, "Virginity, Theology, and Pedagogy," 16–20; and *SV*, ed. Seyfarth, 37*–42*.

9. *SV, epistula*; ed. Seyfarth, 2; trans. Newman, 270.

10. Bernards, *Speculum virginum*, 12.

11. Coakley writes, for instance, of the friars' "admiring fascination with the women." Coakley, "Gender and the Authority of Friars," 449; see also Coakley, "Friars, Sanctity, and Gender."

12. On the difficulties involved in interpreting texts written by men about holy women, see the essays in Mooney, *Gendered Voices.*

13. See, for instance, Clark's study of Elisabeth of Schönau's relationship with her brother, Ekbert. Clark, *Elisabeth of Schönau*, 50–67; and Clark, "Repression or Collaboration?"

14. Hollywood, *The Soul as Virgin Wife*, 29.

15. For discussions of the various ways in which gender and the rhetoric of inferiority were used by women as a means to claim authority, see Newman, "Hildegard of Bingen: Visions and Validation."

16. Poor, *Mechthild of Magdeburg*, xi.

17. Poor, xiii.

18. For the ways in which attention to gender can "provide new perspectives on old questions," see Scott, "Gender: A Useful Category of Historical Analysis," 1075. However, Scott cautions that "slippage . . . often happens in the attribution of causality: the argument moves from a statement such as 'women's experience leads them to make moral choices contingent on contexts and relationships' to 'women think and choose this way because they are women'" (1065). The unproblematic association of women with behaviors deemed "feminine" is one such slippage, which obscures a wide range of potential choices and behaviors available to both men and women.

19. Newman, *Sister of Wisdom*, xix.

20. For theories of decline for religious women after the mid-twelfth century, see Elkins, *Holy Women of Twelfth-Century England*, 105–60; Johnson, *Equal in Monastic Profession*, 248–66; and Venarde, *Women's Monasticism and Medieval Society*, 133–69, although Venarde recognizes a period of monastic expansion for women during the mid-thirteenth century.

21. This is a central thesis of McNamara's *Sisters in Arms*.

22. The term "double monastery" is imprecise, since, as Elkins and Gold point out, all female monasteries were "double" to some extent, in that women relied on chaplains to provide them with sacramental services. For criticisms of the term "double monastery," see Elkins, xvii–xviii; and Gold, *The Lady and the Virgin*, 101–2.

23. The model of male opposition to the pastoral care of women is underscored in the work of Grundmann, who outlined Franciscan and Dominican efforts to avoid the *cura monialium* during the thirteenth century. His model has since been widely accepted. See Grundmann, *Religious Movements in the Middle Ages*, 89–137. Significant exceptions are provided in Elkins, 45–60, 78–91; and, for the later period, Hamburger, *The Visual and the Visionary*.

24. On the difficulties in defining reform, see Tellenbach, *The Church in Western Europe*, 157–84. On reform in general, see Constable, "Renewal and Reform in the Religious Life"; Constable, *The Reformation of the Twelfth Century*; Ladner, "Terms and Ideas of Renewal"; and Blumenthal, *The Investiture Controversy*.

25. Schulenburg writes: "the reform movements of the period, for example the Carolingian, Cluniac, and Gregorian reforms, placed an increased emphasis on the regularization of monastic life, on celibacy with an exaggerated fear of female sexuality and threat of moral contagion, which resulted in a full-blown misogynism." Schulenburg, "Gender, Celibacy, and Proscriptions of Sacred Space," 370. Herlihy writes that "the reformers were intent on placing distance between the now-celibate clergy and women. One casualty of their policies was the double monastery." Herlihy, "Did Women Have a Renaissance?" 8. See also McNamara,

"The 'Herrenfrage'"; and McNamara, "Women and Power Through the Family Revisited."

26. For the dominance of purity concerns in scholarly assessments of reform, see, for instance, Elliott, *Fallen Bodies* and the essays edited by Frassetto: *Medieval Purity and Piety.* Leyser suggests a reevaluation of the pollution language of reform in "Custom, Truth, and Gender in Eleventh-Century Reform."

27. Concerning the Cistercian response to women, see Thompson, "The Problem of the Cistercian Nuns"; and the revision of early Cistercian women's history provided by Berman, "Were There Twelfth-Century Cistercian Nuns?" Referring to the earlier period, Venarde commented that the tendency to study nuns "in the context of the subject position of women" has resulted in an "unduly gloomy picture." Venarde, *Women's Monasticism,* 13 and 14, n. 19.

28. For a collection of primary sources highlighting women's involvement in reform, see *Women and Monasticism in Medieval Europe,* trans. Berman.

29. See Haskins, *The Renaissance of the Twelfth Century; Renaissance and Renewal in the Twelfth Century,* ed. Benson and Constable; and, for a critical reappraisal of the term "renaissance," Jaeger, "Pessimism." For a brief survey of the intellectual vitality of the schools during this period, see Luscombe, "Masters and Their Books."

30. Strasbourg, Bibliothèque du Grand Séminaire, MS 37; hereafter *CGS.* The manuscript has been reproduced in a facsimile edition with an accompanying volume of commentary; ed. Weis. For discussion of Guta's collaboration with Sintram, see Griffiths, "Brides and *Dominae.*"

31. In the earlier period, communities of canonesses had served as centers of education, providing training for young noblewomen, whether or not they intended to embrace the religious life. Heinrich, *The Canonesses and Education.*

32. See Lewis's discussion of learning within fourteenth-century German sister-books. Lewis, *By Women, For Women, About Women,* 263–83.

33. On Helfta, see Bynum, "Women Mystics in the Thirteenth Century." On Unterlinden, see Lewis, *By Women, For Women, About Women,* 13–15.

34. Heinrich von Nördlingen, *Letter* 35, 40; trans. Corsini, 196–97, 214–15.

35. Poor notes that Beatrice of Nazareth and Hadewijch chose to write in the vernacular, even though they were presumably literate in Latin. Poor, 24–25.

36. This fact complicates attempts to draw conclusions concerning her broader significance. No other nun, as far as we know, produced a work of the scale and intellectual sophistication of the *Hortus.* Indeed, as scholars have observed repeatedly in recent years, there are few extant Latin texts written by women during the twelfth century.

37. Newman, "Visions and Validation," 169.

38. Dronke, *Women Writers of the Middle Ages,* vii. Joan Ferrante similarly observed: "What we do not have is a comprehensive study of the education available to women; we must piece together allusions in letters and lives and romances with passages from monastic rules, and supplement them with the writings of the women whose work is extant, in order to deduce what they must have been taught and where." Ferrante, "The Education of Women in the Middle Ages," 9.

39. Marignan expressed doubts that "cette encyclopédie, qui a réuni toutes

les conaissances de l'extrême fin du XIIe siècle, soit due à une femme." Marignan, *Étude sur le manuscrit de l'Hortus deliciarum*, 4.

40. Bischoff, "Die Kölner Nonnenhandschriften"; McKitterick, "Nuns' Scriptoria in England and Francia in the Eighth Century"; McKitterick, "Women and Literacy in the Early Middle Ages"; and Beach, *Women as Scribes*.

41. Hotchin, "Women's Reading and Monastic Reform."

42. El Kholi, *Lektüre in Frauenkonventen*; Bodarwé, *Sanctimoniales litteratae*.

Chapter 1. Reform and the Cura monialium at Hohenbourg

1. Frederick's diploma can be found in *Die Urkunden Friedrichs I.*, ed. Appelt, MGH DDRG 10.1, no. 45. Apart from this brief mention, there is no other record of Frederick visiting Hohenbourg, although he did stay at nearby Ehenheim in 1178, at which point he issued several confirmations for the monastery. For Frederick's 1153 visit, see Simonsfeld, *Jahrbücher des deutschen Reiches*, 150; and Opll, *Das Itinerar Kaiser Friedrich Barbarossas*, 144. On Frederick's activities within Alsace, see Mariotte, "Les staufen en Alsace."

2. "Relatum est, qualiter Fredericus dux, pater Frederici imperatoris, ecclesiam, que dicitur Hohenburc . . . per indiscretam rerum invasionem disturbaverit et usque ad tempus filii sui Frederici imperatoris pene destructam reliquerit. Ipse vero Fredericus Romanorum imperator divina gratia instinctus, pro tam miserabili patris dilecto graviter doluit, et eterni regis gratiam reconciliare volens, prefatam ecclesiam consilio spiritalium personarum restaurare elaboravit, et sicut ab eis didicit religiosam et idoneam personam nomine Relint eidem ecclesie prefecit." ADBR, G 28 (2) (1185); AD I, no. 335.

3. On the early history of the community, see Pfister, *Le duché Mérovingien d'Alsace*; the revised arguments in Pfister, "La légende de sainte Odile"; and the more recent analysis of Büttner, "Studien zur Geschichte des Stiftes Hohenburg." A thirteenth-century document places the foundation of Hohenbourg in 738. ADBR, G 1613 (8). However, the oldest reference to Hohenbourg appears in a donation of 783. See n. 78.

4. *Vita Odiliae*; ed. Levison, MGH SSRM 6, 24–50.

5. On Hohenbourg's early rule, see Burg, "Quelle règle"; and Barth, *Die Heilige Odilia*, 49. Concerning the *Institutio sanctimonialium*, see n. 30.

6. The false diploma of Louis the Pious is AD I, no. 132. A twelfth-century copy of the false *Testament of St. Odile* is preserved as ADBR, G 1 (1) (708); AD I, no. 24. Ebersheim's chronicle is *Chronicon Ebersheimense*; ed. Weiland, MGH SS 23, 427–53.

7. Leo's first visit is recorded in the *Annals of Marbach*: "Anno Domini MXLV Dedicatum est monasterium Hohenburch in honore beate Marie virginis a venerabili Brunone Leucorum episcopo, postea apostolico." *Annales Marbacenses*; ed. Bloch, MGH SSRG 9, 28.

8. ADBR, G 12 (1050); AD I, no. 209. For a discussion of the partial falsifi-

cation of this bull, see Büttner, "Studien," 118–28. Leo IX describes Hohenbourg as "prefatam ecclesiam, quam velut incultam invenimus."

9. In his bull for Hohenbourg, Leo IX noted: "parentum nostrorum semper inibi devote famulantium et in Christo quiescentium debita constrinxit recordatio." ADBR, G 12 (1050); AD I, no. 209. Leo's biography mentions his composition in honor of St. Odile. *Vita Leonis noni*, I, 15; ed. Parisse and trans. Goullet, 54–55.

10. Mantz, *Le mur païen*; Pétry and Will, *Le Mont Sainte-Odile*; and Wilsdorf, "Les très anciennes forteresses." Mantz notes that the wall extended for more than 10 kilometers and enclosed a space of about 118 hectares (40). Pétry and Will estimate the original height of the wall at 3–4 meters, as opposed to its current height of 1.6–1.8 meters (43).

11. A thirteenth-century diploma of William of Holland restored to Hohenbourg several of the properties that had purportedly been usurped by Duke Frederick II at the time of his "invasion," including the much-coveted *salhof* of Obernai. Discussed in Pfister, *Le duché Mérovingien*, 88 n. 3.

12. Meister emphasizes Frederick's devastation of Hohenbourg; Meister, *Die Hohenstaufen im Elsass*, 46. However, Büttner warns against too wide an interpretation of Lucius's remarks; Büttner, "Studien," 132–33. Schmidt interprets Lucius's bull as evidence for Frederick's miscarriage of his role as advocate; Schmidt, *Herrad de Landsberg*, 5. Concerning Duke Frederick's military activity in Alsace, see Otto of Freising, *Gesta Friderici I. imperatoris*, I, 12–14; ed. Waitz, MGH SSRG 46, 27–30; trans. Mierow, 45–47.

13. In a charter dated 1179, Duke Frederick V referred to himself as "Elizatii Dux, Hohenburgensisque Ecclesiae advocatus." NSD 10, no. 31. In 1181, Frederick again referred to himself as "Elisatie Dux, Hoenburgensis Ecclesiae advocatus." NSD 10, no. 35. ADBR, G 28 (1) (1181); AD I, no. 328. On the importance of advocacy in Alsace, see Dubled, "L'Avouerie des monastères." Concerning advocacy in general, see Constable, *Reformation*, 249–56.

14. Otto of St. Blasien, *Continuatio*; ed. Wilmans, MGH SS 20, 326. The capture of Sibylle is also mentioned in the *Annals of Marbach*, although her imprisonment at Hohenbourg is not. *Annales Marbacenses*; ed. Bloch, MGH SSRG 9, 65. For the names of Sibylle's daughters, see Wagner, *Untersuchungen*, 82 n. 53. If the "Sibilia" on folio 323r of the *Hortus* is the exiled Queen, then this folio must have been painted after 1194, the first year of Sibylle's imprisonment at Hohenbourg. For the circumstances of Sibylle's exile from Sicily, see Matthew, *The Norman Kingdom of Sicily*, 285–93; Clementi, "The Circumstances"; and Fröhlich, "The Marriage of Henry VI."

15. In addition to the named canonesses and *conversae*, two unnamed women appear in this image. Most likely, as Green suggests, they were intended to represent past and future members of the community of Hohenbourg. Graf offers a different interpretation, one that emphasizes the symbolic importance of the number sixty: she links the sixty women pictured here (fifty-eight plus two) to the sixty queens mentioned in the *Song of Songs*. Graf, *Bildnisse schreibender Frauen*, 72.

16. "Rilinda venerabilis Hohenburgensis ecclesie abbatissa tempore suo ejus-

dem ecclesie queque diruta diligenter restauravit et religionem divinam inibi pene destructam sapienter reformavit." *HD* Cat. No. 345.

17. *Necrologium Zwifaltense*; ed. Baumann, MGH Necr. 1, 258, no. 22. *Necrologium Monasterii S. Arbogasti*; ed. Grandidier, 171. The necrology of Truttenhausen gives neither the day nor the year of Relinde's death, simply noting "Rilindis abbatissa in Hoenburg" among the sisters of Hohenbourg and Niedermünster. "Das Jahrzeitbuch des Chorherrenstifts Truttenhausen," 20.

18. Grandidier suggested that Relinde became abbess in 1154, a date which he probably drew from Frederick's visit to the monastery in the previous year. Grandidier, *Oeuvres historiques inédites*, II, 291.

19. My review of the literature concerning Relinde's origins follows Will, "Les origines de l'abbesse Relinde de Hohenbourg." The connection between Relinde of Hohenbourg and Relinde of Admont was restated by Radspieler, "Regilind aus Admont."

20. "Bergense cenobium per Admuntenses sub domina Regillinde abbatissa ad spiritalem ordinem reformatur." *Annales Admontenses*; ed. Wattenbach, MGH SS 9, 582.

21. In the eighteenth century, Ziegelbauer conflated the two Relindes identified by Bruchius, suggesting that this conglomerate Relinde died on April 4, 1169. Ziegelbauer, *Historia rei litteraria O.S.B.*, III, 508–9.

22. Peltre, *La vie de Ste Odile* (no page numbers).

23. Curschmann argues that the *Hortus* is related to three vernacular collective manuscripts from Vienna, Milstatt, and Vorau; he notes that Bavarian influences at Hohenbourg can also be seen in the language of the German glosses and the style of the *Hortus* images. "Texte-Bilder-Strukturen," 385–92. Cames, too, stresses the Bavarian connection. *Allégories et symboles*, 130–41.

24. The names of the Hohenbourg women, which are included in the depiction of the community on folio 323r (plate 2), are another clue to a possible Bavarian link. For a discussion of these names, see Wagner, 68–69. Radspieler cites these names as evidence for the disputed Bergen connection (37); Will disagrees ("Les origines," 12 n. 47).

25. Will, "Les origines," 7.

26. ADBR, G 28 (2) (1185); AD I, no. 335.

27. Will, "Les origines," 5, 11.

28. See n. 93.

29. "Ipsam ecclesiam ad honorem Dei prudenter et honorifice reformavit, omnemque divine legis religionem ac canonice discipline rigorem secundum regulam beati Augustini inibi pleniter informavit." Concerning Burchard's role, Lucius commented, "Auxilio et consilio Borcardi Argentinensis episcopi." ADBR, G 28 (2) (1185); AD I, no. 335. For the role of bishops in introducing canonical reform, see Weinfurter, "Reformkanoniker und Reichsepiskopat."

30. Concerning the *Institutio sanctimonialium*, see Schilp, *Norm und Wirklichkeit*. The basic work on canonesses is still Schäfer, *Die Kanonissenstifter*; see also the essays in Crusius, ed., *Studien zum Kanonissenstift*. Other important studies include Siegwart, *Die Chorherren- und Chorfrauengemeinschaften*; Hein-

rich; Leyser, *Rule and Conflict*, 63–73; Parisse, "Les chanoinesses dans l'Empire"; and Parisse, "Les femmes au monastère."

31. A clue to the origins and social standing of the women of Hohenbourg in the twelfth century lies in the names provided on folio 323r, the group portrait of the women who were resident at the community during the time of Relinde and Herrad. Wagner argues that the majority had come from noble Swabian families, repeating the claim that Relinde was a relative of Barbarossa and Herrad a member of the Landsberg family (66–69). In general, however, Augustinian communities appealed to ministerials. As Tenxwind's letter to Hildegard demonstrates, Augustinian reformers opposed the special treatment of noble women within the monastery. *Epist.* 52; ed. van Acker, CCCM 91, 125–27; trans. Baird and Ehrman, I, 127–28. For discussion, see Haverkamp, "Tenxwind von Andernach und Hildegard von Bingen."

32. For scholarship within communities of canonesses, see Heinrich; Bodarwé, *Sanctimoniales litteratae*, 75–86; Wemple, *Women in Frankish Society*, 175–88; and Van Winter, "The Education of the Daughters of the Nobility." Based on his study of their libraries, Kottje argues that canonesses were more intellectually engaged than canons. Kottje, "*Claustra sine armario?*"

33. "Tunc omnes unanimiter responderunt, se regularem velle conversationem habere. Illa autem cum humilitate et mansuetudine dixit eis: 'Scio enim, carissimae sorores et matres, vos promptissimas esse ad omnia aspera et dura pro Christi nomine toleranda; sed timeo, nos, si regularem vitam elegerimus, maledictionem a successoribus nostris incurrere, quia iste, ut scitis, locus valde incompetens et laboriosus est regulari vitae, adeo ut nec aqua nisi cum magno labore hic adipisci possit. Unde mihi videtur, si vestrae placuerit almitati, melius esse, ut in canonico habitu consistatis.' Tunc omnes secundum illius verba elegerunt canonicam regulam, in qua usque hodie in supradictis monasteriis degentes praecedentium normam sequendo perseverant." *Vita Odiliae*, 16; ed. Levison, MGH SSRM 6, 46.

34. Although most scholars agree that the *vita* was written at Hohenbourg, they have tended to assume a male author, with the exception of McKitterick. McKitterick, "Women and Literacy," 28. See Pfister, "La légende," 92–99, where he discusses the intellectual influences evident in the *vita* and touches on the question of authorship.

35. Hohenbourg was not alone in its probable opposition to reform. Based on his study of the *Bamberg Rule Book* (in which both Caesarius and Benedict appear), Cohen suggests the possibility of opposition to reform among the canonesses of Niedermünster, most of whom, having come from noble families, were in a position to resist change. Cohen, *The Uta Codex*, 17.

36. Canon 26 declared: "We decree that the pernicious and detestable custom which has spread among some women who, although they live neither according to the rule of blessed Benedict, nor Basil nor Augustine, yet wish to be thought of by everyone as nuns, is to be abolished. For when, living according to the rule in monasteries, they ought to be in church or in the refectory or dormitory in common, they build for themselves their own retreats and private dwelling places where, under the guise of hospitality, indiscriminately and without any shame they receive guests and secular persons contrary to the sacred canons and good morals.

Because everyone who does evil hates the light, these women think that, hidden in the tabernacle of the just, they can conceal themselves from the eyes of the Judge who sees everything; so we prohibit in every way this unrighteous, hateful and disgraceful conduct and forbid it to continue under pain of anathema." Lateran II, canon 26; *Decrees of the Ecumenical Councils*, ed. and trans. Tanner, I, 203.

37. The council of Rheims required that "sanctimoniales, et mulieres quae canonicae nominantur et irregulariter vivunt, juxta beatorum Benedicti et Augustini Regulam vitam suam in melius corrigant et emendent." PL 105, 645.

38. The basic introduction to the canons is still that of Dereine, "Chanoines." Other useful studies are Dickinson, *The Origins of the Austin Canons*; Becquet, *Vie canoniale*; Châtillon, *Le mouvement canonial*; Siegwart, *Chorherren*; Parisse, "Les chanoines réguliers en Lorraine"; and Parisse, "Être moine ou chanoine." For communities of canons in Germany, see Weinfurter, "Neuere Forschung."

39. On the language of the reformed canons—specifically references to the communal life, the Rule of Augustine, and regular canons—see Dereine, "Vie commune." On the language of reform in general, see Constable, *Reformation*, 125–67. The author of the *Libellus de diversis ordinibus et professionibus qui sunt in aecclesia* writes: "Having examined these matters carefully, you will understand that the name secular does not stem from the fact that many of them live secular lives, but they are called seculars suitably because they must direct and instruct the men of the world among whom they live. They will do well, then, if they live communally, if they cut off superfluous things from their lives, and then they will properly be called canons, that is regulars." *Libellus de diversis ordinibus*, ed. and trans. Constable and Smith, 98–99.

40. For references to the Rule in conciliar legislation, see Dickinson, 64. For a listing of Augustinian foundations, see Wendehorst and Benz, "Verzeichnis der Stifte. " For communities in Alsace, see Mathis, "Les prieures monastiques et canoniaux d'Alsace."

41. For disputes between monks and canons, see Chenu, *Nature, Man and Society*, 202–38; and, for the major authors of the polemical literature, Dereine, "L'élaboration du statut canonique," 558–59.

42. Bynum, "The Spirituality of Regular Canons," 57 and *Docere verbo et exemplo*.

43. On the community and school at St. Victor, see Sicard, *Hugues de Saint-Victor*; Ehlers, "Das Augustinerchorherrenstift St. Viktor"; Châtillon, "La culture de l'école de Saint-Victor"; Fassler, *Gothic Song*; Jaeger, *The Envy of Angels*, 244–68; Smalley, *The Study of the Bible*, 83–111; and the essays in Longère, ed., *L'abbaye parisienne de Saint-Victor*.

44. Marbach was founded near the present-day village of Obermorschwihr, southwest of Colmar. For Marbach's importance as a reform center, see Siegwart, *Die Consuetudines des Augustiner-Chorherrenstiftes Marbach*; and Semmler, "Klosterreform und Gregorianische Reform." For the Marbach liturgy, see Wittwer, "Quellen zur Liturgie."

45. The *Annals of Marbach* identifies Burchard simply as a "militaris" and "illustris vir." *Annales Marbacenses*, ed. Bloch, MGH SSRG 9, 37. Concerning

Manegold of Lautenbach, see Ziomkowski, "Introduction," 15–31; and the older account of Châtillon, "Recherches critiques."

46. Richard writes that "during this time Manegold the philosopher began to flourish in the German land; he was learned beyond all his contemporaries in letters divine and secular. His wife and daughters also flourished in the religious life, having an impressive knowledge of the Scriptures; and his aforesaid daughters taught their own students." Richard of Poitiers, *Chronicon*; ed. Waitz, MGH SS 26, 78; trans. Ziomkowski, 129–30. Ziomkowski suggests that Richard's description of Manegold's *filie* may have been in error for *filii*. See Ziomkowski, 27–31 for discussion.

47. Manegold, *Liber ad Gebehardum*; ed. Francke, MGH Libelli 1, 300–430.

48. Manegold, *Liber contra Wolfelmum*, 23; ed. Hartmann, 99; trans. Ziomkowski, 64.

49. Haaby, *Stift Lautenbach*, 22–38; Mois, *Das Stift Rottenbuch*, 99–106. The *Annals of Marbach* note: "Anno Domini MXCIIII. Magister Manegoldus adiutorio domini B[urchardi] Marbacense monasterium a fundamentis construere cepit seque unum canonicorum eorundem communiter viventium esse voluit." *Annales Marbacenses*; ed. Bloch, MGH SSRG 9, 38. Bernold of Constance also lists Manegold's arrival in 1094: "Hoc tempore magister Manegoldus de Liutenbach monasterium clericorum apud Marhbach instituere cepit, seque unum eorumdem clericorum communiter et regulariter viventium esse voluit." *Chronicon*; ed. Robinson, 404.

50. Concerning Bernold's role as a supporter of the Gregorian cause in southern Germany, see Robinson, "The Bible in the Investiture Contest"; Robinson, "The Friendship Circle"; and Cowdrey, *Pope Gregory VII*, 265–70.

51. Bernold, *Chronicon*; ed. Robinson, 382–84.

52. Urban's favor demonstrates Manegold's importance to the reformed papacy. In general only the pope had the power to grant absolution, a point that Gregory VII had made more than clear. Tellenbach, 239–40.

53. Bernold, *Chronicon*; ed. Robinson, 408; trans. Ziomkowski, 120.

54. Bernold, *Chronicon*; ed. Robinson, 426; trans. Ziomkowski, 120. Manegold's devotion to the papacy was not in the least diminished by his imprisonment. Immediately following his release, sometime in or around 1103, he approached Paschal II requesting papal protection for Marbach, a move that suggests his desire to ward off, or at the very least to discourage, further conflicts with the secular authorities. Paschal's bull of August 2, 1103, was issued in response to Manegold's petitions (*charissimi filii Manegaldi vestri praepositi petitionibus*), suggesting that he was indeed free and at Marbach by this time. PL 163, 116.

55. The Marbach customs are edited in Siegwart, *Consuetudines*, 101–261. Siegwart addresses the question of Manegold's role in their codification in *Consuetudines*, 18–24.

56. There are two extant necrologies for Marbach, the first dating from 1154 and included in the *Guta-Sintram Codex* (pp. 16–158), and the second from 1241. The text of the 1154 necrology, which Marbach shared with Schwartzenthann, is reproduced in *Le Codex Guta-Sintram*, ed. Weis, II, 81–113. For the 1241 necrology,

see *Necrologium conventus Marpach*, ed. Hoffman, 173–222. The two necrologies are discussed in Weis, "Die Nekrologien."

57. Manuscript evidence for the spread of Marbach's liturgical practice is presented by Wittwer.

58. For Marbach's service to women, see Griffiths, "Brides and *Dominae*." For women in Hirsau communities, see Küsters, "Formen und Modelle religiöser Frauengemeinschaften"; Hotchin, "Female Religious Life"; and Gilomen-Schenkel, "'Officium paterne providentie' ou 'Supercilium noxie dominationis'," 368.

59. Weis, "Die Nekrologien," 64.

60. "A congregatione dominarum Marbacensium." *Annales Marbacenses*, ed. Bloch, MGH SSRG 9, 40. Concerning Marbach's influence on the development of the double monastery, see Gilomen-Schenkel, "Engelberg, Interlaken und andere autonome Doppelklöster."

61. Heloise, *Epist.* 6; ed. Muckle, 242; trans. Radice and Clanchy, 94.

62. For the Latin texts and English translations of this letter, and Augustine's rule for monks, see Lawless, *Augustine of Hippo*, 74–118.

63. For arguments supporting the priority of the masculine version of the rule, see Lawless, 135–48. Both Brooke and Parisse repeat the idea that Augustine's Rule was written for women. Brooke, *The Monastic World*, 21; Parisse, "Les chanoinesses dans l'Empire," 111.

64. Verheijen details the history of the idea that the rule was written first for women: Verheijen, *La Règle de saint Augustin*, II, 19–70. At least two twelfth-century texts reflect this view. The first is an early twelfth-century letter from Gualtier, bishop of Maguelonne, in which he writes that Norbert of Xanten believed that the rule was written for women. For the text of this letter, see Dereine, "Saint-Ruf et ses coutumes," 170–74. The second appears in Idung of Prüfening's *Dialogue of Two Monks*, where the Cistercian argues that the Augustinian Rule had been written for women. Presumably Idung had seen a feminine version of the rule at some point and assumed that it reflected Augustine's original text. *Dialogus duorum monachorum*, II, 56; trans. O'Sullivan, Leahey, and Perrigo, 95.

65. For discussion of the dedication page, see Griffiths, "Brides and *Dominae*."

66. "Dulcis, amanda, pia, spes nostra, beata Maria, affectu matris, nos nostra simul tuearis." *CGS*, p. 9.

67. "Scriptis, figuris [changed by a later hand to *picturis*], ope sumptibus, arte figuris, hoc exornastis opus ambo, michique dicastis; ambos ergo pari faciam requie sociari." *CGS*, p. 9. While the image suggests a degree of equality, Sintram nonetheless occupies a place of greater favor to the right of the Virgin, while Guta, to the left, is in a less prominent position.

68. Weis, "Die Nekrologien," 58.

69. Pages are as follows: Necrology (pp. 16–158), Homilary (pp. 107–64), Rule of St. Augustine (pp. 167–74), commentary on the rule, entitled *Expositio in Regulam beati Augustini* (pp. 175–223), and Customs of Marbach (pp. 224–82).

70. Abelard, Sermon 30, *De eleemosyna pro sanctimonialibus de Paraclito*; ed. Granata, 54–59.

71. Canon 27 declared that, "In the same way, we prohibit nuns to come

together with canons or monks in choir for the singing of the office." Lateran II, canon 27; *Decrees*, ed. and trans. Tanner, I, 203. For the architectural and liturgical arrangements that this legislation required, see Golding, *Gilbert of Sempringham*, 126–32; Sorrentino, "In Houses of Nuns, in Houses of Canons"; and Simmons, "The Abbey Church at Fontevraud."

72. Golding, "Hermits, Monks and Women," 138; Leyser, *Hermits and the New Monasticism*, 50; and Hotchin, "Female Religious Life," 70–71. Milis dates the absolution of women's communities closer to 1200. Milis, *L'Ordre des chanoines réguliers*, 516–17.

73. Steinbach was known as Schönensteinbach from the thirteenth century onward. Winnlen, *Schönensteinbach*. Concerning Lucelle, see Chèvre, *Lucelle*. For a recent approach to the question of Cistercian nuns, see Berman, "Were There Twelfth-Century Cistercian Nuns?"

74. Dietler, *Chronik des klosters Schönensteinbach*, 29–31, 35–36.

75. For discussion, see Hamburger, *St. John the Divine*, 165–66; Hamburger, "Brother, Bride and *alter Christus*," 306–7.

76. Concerning Sempringham, see Golding, *Gilbert of Sempringham*, 89. For Fontevrault, see Kerr, *Religious Life for Women*, 52; and, more generally, Gold, "Male/Female Cooperation."

77. "Venerabilis abbatissa Rilindis, que canonice religionis ordinem in hohenburc restituit. ad nos veniens. hoc fideliter impetravit. ut in orationibus et in ceteris obsequiis. talia pro sanctimonialibus defunctis hohenburgensibus suffragia faciamus. sicut pro nostris sororibus facere solemus. Ipse vero quia pauciores nobis habent sacerdotes. ut orationes elemosinis restituant. XXX. prebendas pauperibus in obitu cuiuslibet defuncti canonici fratris nostri dare promiserunt." *Necrologium conventus Marpach*, ed. Hoffman, 180.

78. For a description of this document, see Wagner, 72 n. 3. Relinde's charter appears in a twelfth-century hand on one side of a piece of parchment, followed by a list of revenues in three different hands. On the verso, two documents appear: the first, the charter of abbess Adala, dated 783 (text provided in Wagner, 72 n. 3), and the second, an undated donation from a certain Heinricus (text provided in Wagner, 73 n. 7). The text of Relinde's charter is provided in Wagner, 75 n. 25.

79. Siegwart, *Chorherren*, 267–68. Weinfurter questions the use of the term "daughter house" to describe Ittenwiller. Weinfurter, "Reformkanoniker und Reichsepiskopat," 177 n. 103.

80. Of those houses whose adoption of the Marbach customs can be dated (Siegwart, *Consuetudines*, 80–83), Interlaken, Ölenberg, Rottenbuch, Bernried, Ravengiersburg, Reichersberg, Schwarzenthann, Konstanz-Kreuzlingen, Schönensteinbach, and Truttenhausen either had female members, close contact with female communities, or engaged in service to women. Marbach was also connected to Springiersbach and Frankenthal. Siegwart, *Consuetudines*, 81.

81. Two other manuscripts are thought to have been the product of collaboration between the two monasteries. The first was an Evangeliary, now at Laon, that was produced toward the end of the twelfth century (Laon, Bibliothèque Municipale, MS 550); the second, a manual for teaching Latin, now in Nuremberg (Nuremberg, Germanisches Nationalmuseum, MS 27773). Both contain explicit

references to both Marbach and Schwartzenthann. See Walter, "L'Évangéliaire de Marbach-Schwarzenthann"; and Wattenbach, "Eine alte Grammatik." Cames suggests the association of a further manuscript with the Marbach atelier on the basis of stylistic similarities with the Laon lectionary. Cames, "Un nouveau fleuron," 52.

82. The exact date at which *Beati pauperes* was inserted into the *Guta-Sintram Codex* is not known, although it probably occurred between 1154 and the 1180s. Griffiths, "Brides and *Dominae*," 80. Abelard's sermon 30 was obviously known prior to the insertion of *Beati pauperes*.

83. Hildegard, *Epist.* 10; ed. van Acker, CCCM 91, 23–24; trans. Baird and Ehrman, I, 45–46.

84. Heloise, *Epist.* 6; ed. Muckle, 253; trans. Radice and Clanchy, 111. See my discussion of Heloise's concerns and Abelard's response in Griffiths, " 'Men's Duty to Provide for Women's Needs'."

85. The *Vita Odiliae* mentions two chapels: one dedicated to the Virgin Mary and a second dedicated to John the Baptist. *Vita Odiliae,* 22; ed. Levison, MGH SSRM 6, 49. Louis the Pious's 837 charter lists the monastery as consecrated to the Virgin and St. Paul; AD I, no. 97. Pétry and Will note that in the latter half of the twelfth century five new chapels were built at Hohenbourg in addition to the work of reconstruction that was carried out on the three existing sanctuaries, dedicated to the Virgin Mary, John the Baptist, and St. Peter, respectively. Pétry and Will, *Le Mont Sainte-Odile*, 93–94.

86. ADBR, G 12 (1050); AD I, no. 209. The bull, which was issued following Leo's second visit to Hohenbourg, records his consecration of the community's church some five years earlier and confirms many of its land holdings.

87. For what follows, I am indebted to Büttner's analysis of Leo's bull. Büttner, "Studien," 118–28.

88. The additions were also designed to guard against a bad abbess, a stipulation that Büttner observes reflects the spirit of Hirsau monasticism. Büttner, "Studien," 126.

89. ADBR, G 31 (1196); ed. De Sainte-Marthe, revised Piolin, *Gallia Christiana*, V, 490–91.

90. "Eodem quoque anathemate percussus existat, si quis ebdomadariorum sive aliorum sacerdotum Hohenburgensem ecclesiam contentione vel rebellione gravare audeat. Ipsi etiam ebdomadarii nil in monte preter domos necessarias ab abbatissa pro beneficio eis concessas possideant. Amen." ADBR, G 12 (1050); AD I, no. 209.

91. The chronicle records the agreement: "Ut in cunctis spiritalibus et consilio et auxilio eis preesset, ea scilicet conditione ut in summis festivitatibus, in nativitate Domini videlicet et in pascha et in pentecostes, de Noviento presbiter unus ac diaconus et subdiaconus ibi missas celebrarent et ancillas Christi communicarent; abbas vero ipse in nativitate sancte Marie inibi missarum solempnia compleret." *Chronicon Ebersheimense*; ed. Weiland, MGH SS 23, 437–38. For a discussion of Ebersheim's forged charters, see Hirsch, "Die Urkundenfälschungen."

92. See n. 6. These lands were at Kuenheim, Gundolsheim, Réguisheim, Ruelisheim and Baldersheim. Pfister emphasizes the overlapping land claims as

evidence for Hohenbourg's troubled relationship with Ebersheim during the twelfth century. Pfister, *Le duché Mérovingien*, 81. Dubled notes that there is no reason why both houses could not have held lands in the same localities, suggesting that Ebersheim's false donation may also have been intended to restrain the aggression of episcopal and secular powers. Dubled, "L'Avouerie des monastères," 46. Büttner does not go so far as to discount the conflicting land claims, but neither does he emphasize this disagreement, describing Hohenbourg's false diploma of Louis the Pious as nothing more than an imperfect blow against the claims of Ebersheim. Büttner, "Studien," III. Instead, he focuses on Hohenbourg's relationship with the chaplains on the mountain. For a bibliography of works relating to the forgeries of Ebersheim, see Dubled, "L'Avouerie des monastères," 45 n. 204.

93. Herrad's foundation of St. Gorgon is attested in a charter that she issued in 1178. Although the original is lost, the content has been preserved (NSD 10, no. 25). The foundation was approved in 1178 by Frederick Barbarossa (ADBR, G 23 (1178); *Die Urkunden Friedrichs I.*, ed. Appelt MGH DDRG 10.3, 767), by his son Frederick V, Duke of Alsace (NSD 10, no. 31), by Pope Lucius III (NSD 10, no. 38), and by Henry, bishop of Strasbourg in 1183 (*Confirmatio Henrici Episcopi Argentinensi*, in Peltre, *La vie de Ste Odile*).

94. Herrad's foundation charter for St. Gorgon stipulates that: "Ut praedictus abbas et successores ipsius fraterna visitatione, quotiescumque voluerit et exoccupatus fuerit Hohemburgensem Ecclesiam visitet, et in festo sanctae Odiliae et in dedicatione Capellae ejus, et in nativitate S. Mariae ad eandem Ecclesiam, nisi infirmitate corporis praeventus, vel aliquo Ecclesiae suae negotio fuerit occupatus, missam sollemnem annuatim celebrare veniat . . . unum etiam ex Canonicis suis qualemcunque voluerit, et quem ad hoc idoneum perspexerit, sacerdotem ebdomatarium in Hohemburgensi Ecclesia constituet Insuper et alium sacerdotem idoneum, qui cottidie privatim ad altare sanctae Odilae missam celebret, qualemcunque voluerit, semper praevidebit." NSD 10, no. 25.

95. Herrad's foundation charter for Truttenhausen is no longer extant; no copy has been preserved. However, it was confirmed by Duke Frederick V in 1181 (G 28 (1) (1181); NSD 10, no. 35) and then by Pope Lucius III in 1185, who placed Truttenhausen under the protection of the Holy See: "Locum ipsum sub beati Petri et nostra protectione suscipimus" (ADBR, G 28 (2) (1185); AD I, no. 335). The number twelve was symbolic; Duke Frederick V's confirmation for Truttenhausen allows that the community should house "twelve canons or rather as many as the resources of that place should permit" ("Duodecim canonici, vel tot quot facultas ipsius loci permiserit"). NSD 10, no. 35.

96. "Statutum est itidem, ut quilibet prepositus in Trutenhusen cum voluerit, Hohenburgensem ecclesiam visitet, et missarum sollempnia secundum ordinem ipsius ecclesie celebret, ac duos ex canonicis suis religiosos et ydoneos ebdomadarios in Hohenburc semper constituat servituros. Quod si predicti sacerdotes aliquando commutandi fuerint, praepositus absque ulla contradictione abbatisse libere eos ad claustrum revocans, alios ydoneos restituere curet, qui de monte absque licentia abbatisse non recedentes, divina officia absque ullo gravamine secundum consuetudinem Hohenburgensis ecclesie celebrare non recusent. In

purificatione quoque sancte Marie et in die palmarum et in coena Domini et in nativitate ac decollatione sancti Joannis baptiste et in assumptione sancte Marie et in festivitate sancti Michaëlis et omnium sanctorum ad monasterium Hohenburgense, si inevitabilis causa non impediat, missam sollempnem celebraturus annuatim veniat, et etiam in festo sancte Odiliae ac in capelle ejus dedicatione et in nativitate Domini missam diurnam priorem celebret." ADBR, G 28 (2) (1185); AD I, no. 335.

97. Herrad's foundation charter for St. Gorgon states: "a manu Hohemburgensis Ecclesiae abbatissae absque ulla contradictione primo aditu per librum gratis recipiat." NSD 10, no. 25. Lucius III's confirmation of Herrad's foundation at Truttenhausen notes that, "et ipse electus investituram prepositure de manu Hohenburgensis abbatisse absque ulla contradictione primo aditu per librum gratis accipiat." ADBR, G 28 (2) (1185); AD I, no. 335.

98. Duke Frederick V refers to Günther as "ejusdem ecclesie ministerialis" in his confirmation of Truttenhausen. NSD 10, no. 35.

99. Lucius III records, "construxit primum ibi capellam ad honorem Dei ac memoriam beate Marie semper virginis et curtem cum ceteris edificiis, donec construeretur ibi major ecclesia, id est monasterium in memoriam beati Nicolai, cum claustralibus officinis, videlicet cum hospitali pauperum et hospicio adventientium hospitum." ADBR, G 28 (2) (1185); AD I, no. 335. Günther of Vienhege appears as witness to several charters during Herrad's abbacy: ADBR, G 22 (1178); ADBR, G 33 (1196); ADBR, G 1219 (2); and ADBR, G 1229 (1b).

100. "Errat abbatissa fundatrix huius loci." "Das Jahrzeitbuch des Chorherrenstifts Truttenhausen," 20. Günther is remembered as "cooperator fundacionis" (23).

101. "Henricus frater abbatisse fundatricis huius loci." "Das Jahrzeitbuch des Chorherrenstifts Truttenhausen," 23.

102. "Ut ad honorem Dei et Hohenburgensis cenobii, per laborem suum prepositura ibi canonicorum regularium fundaretur, qui secundum beati Augustini regulam et consuetudinem Marbacensis ecclesie instituti et permanere deberent." ADBR, G 28 (2) (1185); AD I, no. 335.

103. On relations between Hohenbourg and Étival, see Idoux, "Relations d'Étival," 70–92.

104. Herrad's charter records that she wished to establish "inter Stivagiensem atque Hohemburgensem Ecclesiam Caritatis vinculum." ADBR, G 1216; NSD 10, no. 25.

105. See Idoux, 6–42; Büttner, "Kaiserin Richgard"; and MacLean, "Queenship, Nunneries."

106. Étival's adoption of the Augustinian Rule and affiliation with Prémontré is noted in a bull of Eugene III (1147). PL 180, 1274–78.

107. Parisse, "Les chanoines réguliers en Lorraine," 379.

108. Étival's willingness to engage with Herrad demonstrates that the model of Premonstratensian opposition to women in the latter half of the twelfth century may not hold in every case. In particular, this model may be inappropriate for the German scene, as Wolbrink argues. Wolbrink, "Women in the Premonstratensian Order." Even so, Étival did not always treat women's communities well: in 1126

Honorius III demanded that the monastery restore goods that it had seized from Niedermünster. NSD 13, no. 73.

109. ADBR, G 22 (1178); NSD 10, no. 26.

110. ADBR, G 1219; *Die Urkunden Friedrichs I.*, ed. Appelt, MGH DDRG 10.3, 769.

111. Berthold's gift is recorded in: ADBR, G 1229 (1b); Pfister, *Le duché Mérovingien*, 169, VIII. Burckhard's gift is recorded in: ADBR, G 1229 (1c); Pfister, *Le duché Mérovingien*, 170, X.

112. The first of these charters records that Elisabeth of Rodesheim, with her sister Irmburge and Irmburge's son, gave part of a vineyard at Rodesheim to Hohenbourg. ADBR, G 1219 (1); Pfister, *Le duché Mérovingien*, 170, IX. A second charter records a similar gift from Luikart, daughter of Walther of Schadeloch. ADBR, G 1229 (1a); Pfister, *Le duché Mérovingien*, 169, VII.

113. "Censum quem debuit ecclesie in Hohenburc de decimatione in Tutelnheim." ADBR, G 1229 (1d); Pfister, *Le duché Mérovingien*, 171, XII.

114. "Eadem quippe officia debet villicus abbatisse perpetuo jure illis hominibus concedere, quos electio villanorum ad hec convenientes et providos deliberaverit." ADBR, G 33 (1196); NSD 10, no. 27.

115. "Tres agros . . . quos abbatissa Herrat justo judicio ab eo requisivit et ecclesie Hohenburc restituit." ADBR, G 1229 (1); Pfister, *Le duché Mérovingien*, 169, VI.

116. "Quodsi prepositus et canonici sui hec privilegii decreta neglexerint, ecclesiamque Hohenburgensem irrationabili gravamine inquiete perturbaverint, abbatissa et conventus eis prebendas ac beneficia ad praebendas pertinentia subtrahant et aliunde sibi sacerdotes quos voluerint quietos et religiosos provideant. Isti vero officia in missarum sollempniis prius sibi concessa, amplius in monte Hohenburc nisi permissione abbatisse et conventus sicut et alieni celebrare non audeant. Simili quidem modo si Stivagiensis abbas, et canonici sui Hohenburgensem ecclesiam per injustam contradictionem contentiose impugnaverint, nec privilegii sui statuta, a manu Hohenburgensis abbatisse data, mansuete obtemperando, observaverint, locus sancti Gorgonii cum omnibus appendiciis suis, quem quilibet Stivagiensis abbas ab Hohenburgensi abbatissa accipere debet, ceteraque beneficia de Hohenborc suscepta eis subtrahantur, aliique sacerdotes ydonei pro libitu abbatisse et conventus aliunde eligantur. Ipsi autem amplius in monte Hohenburc missarum sollempnia quemadmodum alieni nisi permissione abbatisse, celebrare non audeant." ADBR, G 28 (2) (1185); AD I, no. 335.

117. See n. 89.

118. See ADBR, G 1219 (1); Pfister, *Le duché Mérovingien*, 170, IX and ADBR, G 1229 (1a); Pfister, *Le duché Mérovingien*, 169, VII.

119. "Das Jahrzeitbuch des Chorherrenstifts Truttenhausen," 17–21. See, for example, among the "fratres huius domus," "Giselburg conversa hic," "Gerina conversa hic," "Gotelindis conversa," "Adelheidis conversa," "Hiltegundis conversa," and others.

120. Hotchin, "Female Religious Life," 71.

121. Hildegard appears only once as *abbatissa*, in a charter issued by Frederick

Barbarossa for the Rupertsberg in 1163. *Die Urkunden Friedrichs I.*, ed. Appelt, MGH DDRG 10.2, no. 398.

Chapter 2. The Hortus deliciarum*: A Book for Reform and Renaissance*

1. Canon 27 declared: "We therefore strictly order bishops carefully to prepare those who are to be promoted to the priesthood and to instruct them, either by themselves or through other suitable persons, in the divine services and the sacraments of the church, so that they may be able to celebrate them correctly. But if they presume henceforth to ordain the ignorant and unformed, which can indeed easily be detected, we decree that both the ordainers and those ordained are to be subject to severe punishment." Lateran IV, Canon 27; *Decrees*, ed. and trans. Tanner, I, 248.

2. Poor notes that, during the fifteenth century, the exigencies of reform and the shortage of priests to provide for the *cura monialium* likewise produced a climate in which women participated in the production of devotional books designed to provide religious instruction and, in particular, to substitute for sermons, which were in short supply. Poor, 138.

3. "Quasi apicula Deo inspirante comportavi et ad laudem et honorem Christi et Ecclesie, causaque dilectionis vestre quasi in unum mellifluum favum compaginavi." *HD* no. 2.

4. Daly, "Peter Comestor," 67. Sylwan argues for a dating between 1168 and 1175. Sylwan, "Petrus Comestor, *Historia Scholastica*," 347. On the dissemination of the *Historia*, see Sylwan, 347–49 and Karp, *Peter Comestor's* Historia scholastica, 225–38. On Peter Comestor, see also Morey, "Peter Comestor"; and Luscombe, "Peter Comestor." The *Historia scholastica* is PL 198, 1053–1722.

5. "Facta est hec pagina anno MCLXXV." *HD* no. 1160. A second date appears in the prose introduction to a poem in which each word was designed to signify one year since the birth of Christ. *HD* no. 1161. The introduction announces: "si autem ab aliquo queratur quo tempore factum sit, anno millesimo centesimo quinquagesimo nono ab incarnatione Domini." *HD* no. 1161. Since it is unlikely that this poem was composed specifically for inclusion in the *Hortus*, the stated date of 1159 can be ignored. Bischoff, *HD* 12.

6. Sylwan notes that the earliest dated manuscript of the *Historia scholastica* was copied at Corbie in 1183. Sylwan, 347. Herrad's copy of the *Historia* was apparently already titled "Scolastica hystoria" (*HD* no. 172), a fact that indicates that it was not one of the earliest manuscripts of the work. According to Sylwan, Peter did not give his work this title, since he could not have known how it would be read in the schools, but rather the title was attached to it by others who recognized its utility, possibly after Lateran III had called for training of poor clerics. Dissemination of the *Historia* increased rapidly in the 1180s, at which time commentaries and glosses on it began to appear. Sylwan, 347–49.

7. Since Lucius died in 1185, Green suggests that the manuscript must have been largely completed in the decade between about 1175 and 1185. Green, *HD* 25.

8. These notes appear as footnotes to *HD* no. 1156.

9. On the schism and the papacy of Alexander III, see Laudage, *Alexander III. und Friedrich Barbarossa*; Gilchrist, "The Gregorian Reform Tradition"; Madertoner, *Die zwiespältige Papstwahl*; Baldwin, *Alexander III*; and Pacaut, *Frédéric Barberousse* and *Alexandre III*. For a contemporary record of the schism, see *Boso's Life of Alexander III*; ed. and trans. Ellis.

10. ADBR, G 1229 (1d); Pfister, *Le duché Mérovingien*, 171–72, XII. The presence of Walter of Châtillon and Geoffrey of St. Thierry in the *Hortus* indicates that revisions and additions to the manuscript may have continued until Herrad's death sometime after 1196, even though the bulk of it had most likely been completed by about 1185. Since the interpolation on folio 176v "shows the hand of the master artist," Green concludes that, "It is therefore obviously wrong to assume a long time lapse before some interpolations were executed." Green, *HD* 32. The dating and purpose of interpolations are discussed further in Chapter 4.

11. Green discussed the possibility that the *Hortus* was a collaborative work. *HD* 24–25. For Radspieler, Relinde was more than a possible architect of the *Hortus* project; he claims her as the author of several of the manuscript's poems as well.

12. "Congregatio religiosa temporibus Relindis et Herradis abbatissarum in Dei servicio in Hohenburc caritative adunata." *HD* Cat. No. 346.

13. Relinde's poem is in the shape of a cross and Herrad's of a scroll. Relinde's poem, *O pie grex*, is explicitly attributed to her and addressed to the women: *Relindis Hohenburgensi congregationi*. *HD* Cat. No. 345. Herrad's poem, *O nivei flores*, encourages the women of Hohenbourg to maintain their purity of mind and body, scorning the things of the world so that they might be able to present themselves spotless at last before the heavenly Bridegroom. *HD* Cat. No. 346.

14. The Hohenbourg image must have been one of the finishing touches to the manuscript; indeed, if the Sibilia who is represented among the *conversae* can be identified with the deposed queen Sibylle of Sicily whom Henry VI had imprisoned at the monastery, then it must date to the period after her arrival at Hohenbourg in 1194.

15. "Herrat Hohenburgensis abbatissa post Relindam ordinata ac monitis et exemplis ejus instituta." *HD* Cat. No. 346.

16. Odile's *vita* records that her mother, Berswinde, was related to Leodegarius. *Vita Odiliae*, 2; ed. Levison, MGH SSRM 6, 38.

17. Photos of the second and third faces of the stone appear in *HD* figs. 349, 350.

18. Haupt, *Das hohe Lied*, xx–xxiv.

19. Bischoff, *HD* 12. Green disagrees; *HD* 24 n. 20.

20. "Quod papa sit summus et imperator sub ipso . . . Caesar ergo suscipit usum temporalem ab eo, qui possidet curam pastoralem." Walter of Châtillon, *Carmina II*; ed. Boehmer, MGH Libelli 3, 558–60.

21. Kempf, "Ein zweiter 'Dictatus papae'?" 139. Kempf argues against Mordek's earlier dating of the text. Based on what he saw as similarities with *Dictatus papae*, on which he argued *Proprie auctoritas apostolice sedis* relied, Mordek had

dated *Proprie auctoritates* between 1075 and 1085 and proposed the papal court as its place of composition. Mordek, "Proprie auctoritates apostolice sedis," 113–14.

22. The earliest of these is dated c. 1123/4; it may have been produced in a scriptorium in Pistoia (now Archivio capitolare del duomo, C. 135). A second is from the Benedictine monastery of Mont St. Michel (now Avranches Bibl. Municipale 146). The folio containing the *Auctoritates apostolice sedis* is dated to c. 1130. See Jacqueline, "A propos des *Dictatus papae*"; and Mordek, 108. A third manuscript, Monte Cassino cod. 216, is dated to the late twelfth century. Wojtowytsch, "Proprie auctoritates apostolice sedis," 619. The final manuscript, from the fifteenth century, is Venice Biblioteca Marciana, Lat. IV. (2301).

23. Robinson argues that support for the emperor was partly due to the disaffection among German prelates, who saw the reformed church as diminishing their own office. Robinson, *Papacy*, 398–524. The papacy itself had also changed; Gilchrist notes differences between the papacy of Alexander III and that of Gregory VII: "The Gregorian Reform Tradition." For the support of the bishops of Salzburg, see Robinson, *Papacy*, 460. After Victor IV's death in 1164, Hillin of Trier also gave his allegiance to Alexander; Hilpisch, "Erzbischof Hillin von Trier."

24. The incorporation of Steinbach to Marbach was confirmed by a papal bull issued by the anti-pope Victor IV in April 1159. Dietler, 31–33.

25. Constable notes that this period, which he identifies as the "fourth and final period [of reform], from 1130 to 1160," was characterized by "an intense concern with the nature of religious life and personal reform of all Christians." Constable, *Reformation*, 4.

26. Bernard of Clairvaux, *Sermones super Cantica canticorum*, 33; *SBOp* I, 244; trans. Walsh, II, 157–58.

27. See Büttner, "Die Beziehungen." Concerning Hildegard's relationship with Frederick Barbarossa and her reform stance, see Kerby-Fulton "Prophet and Reformer"; Kerby-Fulton, "A Return to 'The First Dawn of Justice'"; Mews, "Hildegard, Visions and Religious Reform"; Mews, "From *Scivias* to the *Liber Divinorum Operum*"; and Kienzle, "Defending the Lord's Vineyard." Newman describes Hildegard's relationship with Barbarossa as "double-edged"; *Sister of Wisdom*, 13.

28. Newman, *Sister*, 11. Hildegard's letter to Frederick is *Epist.* 312; ed. van Acker and Klaes-Hachmöller, CCCM 91B, 72–73; trans. Baird and Ehrman, III, 112. Frederick refers to Hildegard's visit in a letter written in the later 1150s: *Epist.* 314; ed. van Acker and Klaes-Hachmöller, CCCM 91B, 74–75; trans. Baird and Ehrman, III, 113–14.

29. *Die Urkunden Friedrichs I.*, ed. Appelt, MGH DDRG 10.2, no. 398.

30. "Sed quia Ecclesia divisa erat, vocem hanc subtraxi." Hildegard, *Epist.* 15r; ed. van Acker, CCCM 91, 44; trans. Baird and Ehrman, I, 60. In a sermon that Hildegard delivered at Trier in 1160, she identified the beginnings of the "womanish time" in which she lived with the reign of Henry IV, to whom she referred simply as a "certain tyrant." *Epist.* 223r; ed. van Acker, CCCM 91A, 491; trans. Baird and Ehrman, III, 19. However, in her so-called Mainz prophecy (1163), she described Frederick as "the one who sits upon the black horse" of Apocalypse

6.5; *Epist.* 169r; ed. van Acker, CCCM 91A, 379; trans. Baird and Ehrman, II, 124. Concerning Hildegard's Trier sermon, see Newman, *Sister*, 27–28; for her sense of the present as a womanish age, see Newman, *Sister*, 238–49.

31. It may be at this time that Hildegard spoke out, castigating Frederick in a letter as a "little boy" and a "madman" (*velut parvulum et velut insane viventem*). *Epist.* 313; ed. van Acker and Klaes-Hachmöller, CCCM 91B, 74; trans. Baird and Ehrman, III, 113. Van Acker and Klaes-Hachmöller date this letter to 1152/3; however, Dronke and Newman claim it as a product of Hildegard's distress at the continuation of the schism in 1164. Dronke, *Women Writers*, 149; Newman, *Sister*, 13; and Newman, "Introduction," 15. For a discussion of the evolution of Hildegard's apocalyptic thought, see Mews, "From *Scivias* to the *Liber Divinorum Operum*."

32. Hildegard, *Epist.* 10; ed. van Acker, CCCM 91, 24; trans. Baird and Ehrman, I, 45.

33. Hildegard, *Scivias* III, 11, 25; ed. Führkötter and Carlevaris, CCCM 43A, 589–90; trans. Hart and Bishop, 501–2. While Newman interprets this image as the attempted rape of *Ecclesia* (Newman, *Sister*, 245), Kerby-Fulton sees it as a sign of Hildegard's early criticism of the church (Kerby-Fulton, "Prophet and Reformer," 83).

34. See especially Hildegard's letter to Werner of Kirchheim. *Epist.* 149r; ed. van Acker, CCCM 91A, 333–37; trans. Baird and Ehrman, II, 92–94.

35. Kerby-Fulton, "Prophet and Reformer," 80.

36. Elisabeth of Schönau, *Epist.* 4; ed. Roth, 140; trans. Clark, 237.

37. Elisabeth of Schönau, *Liber viarum Dei*, 15; ed. Roth, 113; trans. Clark, 195. Elisabeth also spoke out against the clergy in the middle of matins. *Liber visionum primus*, 69; ed. Roth, 33; trans. Clark, 86–87.

38. Clark cautions against assuming that Elisabeth was influenced by Rainald through Ekbert; Clark, *Elisabeth of Schönau*, 122.

39. To be sure, issues had not been entirely clear in the early reform period. As Semmler cautions, monastic reform and allegiance in the battles of the investiture controversy did not necessarily overlap. Even Hirsau sent a monk to reform the pro-imperial monastery of Komburg in 1090, during the most intense period of the investiture controversy, and the Augustinian foundation of Hördt was established through the support of the bishop of Speyer, who remained loyal to Henry IV. Semmler, "Klosterreform und Gregorianische reform," 170–71. The "Kaiserbild," which appears in a manuscript thought to have been produced at Marbach, further complicates the picture of reforming attitudes toward secular power. Reinhardt, "Eine Handschrift des 12. Jahrhunderts," 10, 14.

40. "Doctores et magistri tuba iustitie canere nolunt." Hildegard, *Epist.* 223r; ed. van Acker, CCCM 91A, 490; trans. Baird and Ehrman, III, 18. Concerning Hildegard's preaching, see Kienzle, "Defending the Lord's Vineyard"; and Kienzle, "Operatrix in vinea Domini."

41. For Hildegard's sermon at Cologne, see Hildegard, *Epist.* 15r; ed. van Acker, CCCM 91, 34–44, plus appendices, 44–47; trans. Baird and Ehrman, I, 54–65. Concerning the activities of Cathars in Cologne during the mid-twelfth

century, see Moore, *The Origins of European Dissent*, 168–96; and for Hildegard's response, Kienzle, "Defending the Lord's Vineyard."

42. Hildegard, *Epist.* 149r; ed. van Acker, CCCM 91A, 334; trans. Baird and Ehrman, II, 92.

43. Elizabeth of Schönau, *Liber tercius visionum*, 25; ed. Roth, 76; trans. Clark, 145.

44. Christus parat nupcias (in celo)
    Miras per delicias,
    Hunc expectes (in isto seculo) principem
    Te servando virginem. (*HD* no. 1)

45. Christus odit maculas (peccata),
    Rugas (crimina anime) spernit vetulas,
    Pulchras (castas) vult virgunculas
    Turpes (id est incestas) pellit feminas. (*HD* no. 1)

46. Patere nunc aspera,
    Mundi spernens prospera,
    Nunc sis cruci (Christi) socia (duram sustinens)
    Regni consors postea. (*HD* no. 1)

47. Et me tecum trahere
    Non cesses precamine,
    Ad sponsum (Christum) dulcissimum (scilicet)
    Virginalem Filium.

    Ut tue victorie,
    Tue magne glorie,
    Particeps inveniar (in celis. ut)
    De terrenis (de periculis) eruar. (*HD* no. 1)

48. "Meque per varias maris semitas periculose gradientem fructuosis orationibus vestris a terrenis affectibus mitigatam una vobiscum in amorem dilecti vestri sursum trahatis." *HD* no. 2.

49. The allegory of the sea as the world, and the Christian soul traversing it, was a favorite with Honorius, who used the idea in his famous Siren sermon (see *HD* no. 756). It was derived from Augustine, who describes the ark as "a symbol of the City of God on pilgrimage in this world, of the Church which is saved through the wood on which was suspended 'the mediator between God and men, the man Jesus Christ'." *City of God*, XV, 26; ed. Dombart and Kalb, CCSL 48, 493; trans. Bettenson, 643. For Ambrose too, the boat was a symbol for the church: "For why was a boat chosen for Christ to sit in instructing the crowds unless it is because the boat is the Church which navigates easily in this world, at full sail with the Lord's cross and in the wind provided by the Holy Spirit." *De virginitate*, 119; ed. Gori, 94–96; trans. Callam, 58. The spiritual boat was also a favorite symbol within Victorine thought, stemming from Hugh's writings on Noah's ark. See Zinn, "*De gradibus Ascensionum*"; Zinn, "Hugh of St. Victor, Isaiah's Vision, and *De arca Noe*"; and Sicard, *Diagrammes médiévaux*. The idea of the "boat" as the human body appears in Herrad's introductory poem, where *navi* is glossed *corpore*. *HD* no. 1 n. 28.

50. Per hoc mare (mundum) naviga,
    Sanctitate gravida (plena),
    Dum de navi (corpore) exeas
    Syon (id est urbem celestem) sanctam teneas. (*HD* no. 1)

51. Stella maris fulgida (Maria),
    Virgo mater unica,
    Te conjungat Filio
    Federe (amore) perpetuo. (*HD* no. 1)

52. Esto nostrorum   pia merces Christe laborum.
    Nos electorum   numerans in sorte tuorum. (*HD* Cat. No. 346)

53. Honorius, *De luminaribus ecclesiae*; PL 172, 232–34. Honorius's biography is proposed in Flint, *Honorius Augustodunensis*, 95–128. See also the essays reprinted in Flint, *Ideas in the Medieval West*; Sanford "Honorius, *Presbyter* and *Scholasticus*"; Dietrich, *Eruditio sacra*; and Fulton, *From Judgment to Passion*, 247–88.

54. Honorius, *Quod monachis liceat predicare*; ed. Endres.

55. Honorius chose to call his work the *Elucidarium*, as he writes in his prologue, since the work was designed to elucidate obscure things. "Titulus itaque operi, si placet, Elucidarium praefigatur, quia in eo obscuritas diversarum rerum elucidatur." *Elucidarium*, Prologus; ed. Lefèvre, 359. On the *Elucidarium*, see also Gottschall, *Das "Elucidarium."*

56. Flint comments that "the Elucidarius began, then, as an up-to-the-minute teaching text for the encouragement and instruction of that improved priesthood for which it fought." She lists it among Honorius's "polemical" works, describing it as "arguably the most revealing and important of all Honorius's writings." However, she notes that Honorius's reforming enthusiasm was limited to the lower echelons of the church hierarchy: "the upper levels of the reform (pope versus emperor, the investiture of bishops, royal authority versus sacerdotal) receive no attention." Flint, *Honorius Augustodunensis*, 131, 129, 130.

57. Gurevich writes that Honorius "set himself the goal of popularizing theological principles by instructing those priests who were in direct contact with the faithful." Gurevich, "The Elucidarium," 153.

58. "Quidam enim vestrum de longe huc venerunt et longum iter domum habebunt. Aliquibus autem forsitan sunt domi hospites, aut infantes plorantes." Honorius, *Speculum ecclesiae*; PL 172, 855; ed. in Sanford, 412.

59. Reform was central to Honorius's life and work. As Flint concludes, "I now suspect that the serving of the Benedictine Order, in its pursuit of influence in the reformed church, formed the focus of Honorius's whole productive life." Flint, "The Place and Purpose," 97.

60. "Hoc igitur speculum omnes sacerdotes ante oculos Ecclesiae expendant, ut sponsa Christi in eo videat quid adhuc Sponso suo in se displiceat, et ad imaginem suam mores et actus suos componat." Honorius, *Speculum ecclesiae*; PL 172, 815.

61. Cited in Sanford, 412.

62. According to Mâle, Honorius's work provided "one of the perennial sources of inspiration for medieval art." *The Gothic Image*, 105. Honorius's com-

mentary on the Song of Songs was meant to be accompanied by four allegorical images of the brides of Solomon; however, his role in designing the image cycle is unclear. See Curschmann, "Imagined Exegesis," 153–60. His *Clavis physicae* was also often illustrated. Pächt, *Book Illumination*, 158.

63. For the influence of Honorius on the images of the *Hortus*, see Gillen, *Ikonographische Studien*, 66–69; and Cames, *Allégories et symboles*, 3.

64. In addition to these, the unique depiction of the Dream of Procula (fol. 143r) is glossed with a text from the *Elucidarium* and the suicide of Herod (mentioned in the image of the Massacre of the Innocents on folio 98r) may also have been inspired by a section from the *Speculum ecclesiae*, which appears on folio 96v (*HD* no. 352). These two images are discussed in Cames, *Allégories et symboles*, 43–45.

65. As Colish writes, "In no sense does Honorius seek to alert his readers to the theological controversies of the day . . . his aim is not to provoke inquiry but to lay questions to rest." Colish, *Peter Lombard*, I, 41. Flint writes that in Honorius's writings "complexity is always subordinated to simplicity; and simplicity becomes therefore the outstanding characteristic and the all pervasive one." Flint, "Place," 109.

66. See van Engen's biography of Rupert; *Rupert of Deutz*.

67. "Haec vero sacramenta celebrare et causas eorum non intelligere quasi lingua loqui est et interpretationem nescire." Rupert, *Liber de divinis officiis*, Prologus; ed. Haacke, CCCM 7, 5. On the *De divinis officiis*, see van Engen, 58–67.

68. van Engen, 65.

69. More than forty manuscripts of this work survive, all of them from the Empire. Rupert, *Commentaria in Canticum canticorum*; ed. Haacke, CCCM 26, xv–lx.

70. For a catalogue of surviving Honorius manuscripts, see Flint, *Honorius Augustodunensis*, 159–75.

71. Flint, "Place," 118. Even so, Flint notes that no early manuscript of Honorius can be associated with Hirsau itself. Flint, *Honorius Augustodunensis*, 156.

72. Flint, "Place," 118.

73. From her study of the textual transmission of the *Elucidarium*, Flint concluded that "books containing the *Elucidarius* seem . . . to be for the most part 'pastoral' books, codices made up . . . to serve the needs of a man or community with a care of souls." Flint, "Place," 113; on the use of the *Elucidarium*, see also Gottschall, 30–35. For the dissemination of the *Elucidarium* during the twelfth century and a list of surviving manuscripts (without place of origin) of the work, see Gottschall, 25–34, 297–306. Flint adds seven manuscripts to Gottschall's list; Flint, *Honorius Augustodunensis*, 162. Her list of twelfth-century manuscripts of the *Elucidarium* does include place of origin; Flint, "Place," 120–22.

74. Silvestre concludes that Rupert's works were copied in at least 427 manuscripts, of which 266 are extant, and 145 from the twelfth century. Silvestre, "Les Manuscrits des Oeuvres de Rupert," 289. Haacke lists some 68 extant manuscripts and fragments of *De divinis officiis* plus references in 31 library catalogues. *Liber de divinis officiis*, ed. Haacke, CCCM 7, xvii–xlii; Haacke, "Nachlese" and "Überlief-

erung," which is accompanied by a map plotting communities from which manuscripts of Rupert's work have survived.

75. Bauerreiss, "Honorius von Canterbury"; Fulton, 297–98; Flint, *Honorius Augustodunensis*, 110–13; and van Engen, 333.

76. Rupert, *Altercatio monachi et clerici, quod liceat monacho praedicare*; PL 170, 537–42; for Rupert's defense of the Benedictine right to preach, see van Engen, 323–34. Honorius, *Quod monachis liceat predicare*; ed. Endres.

77. Brasington, "Religious Reform and Legal Study," 189. See also Brasington, "*Recte docens vel credens.*" For discussion of the manuscripts of the *Panormia* and its influence, see Fournier and Le Bras, eds., *Histoire des collections canoniques*, II, 85–99; and Fransen, "La tradition manuscrite de la *Panormie.*" On Ivo's place within the development of canon law, see de Ghellinck, *Le mouvement théologique*, 445–55.

78. El Kholi discusses each author known at a female community and provides a list of works that she suggests may have formed part of each community's library holdings. El Kholi, *Lektüre in Frauenkonventen*, for Honorius (138–42), Rupert (234–40), and Ivo (169). Honorius was known at Neuss/St. Quirin, Lippoldsberg, Altomünster, and Hohenbourg. Rupert was known at Lamspringe, Lippoldsberg, Hohenbourg, and Shäftlarn; he may also have been known at Steterburg, Huysburg, Admont, and St. Lambrecht. Twelfth-century manuscripts of Rupert's *De diviniis officiis* survive from Lamspringe (Wolfenbüttel, HAB, Helmst. 510 (557)) and Shäftlarn (Munich, Bayerische Staatsbibliothek, MS Clm 17116). *De diviniis officiis* was also listed in Steterburg's twelfth-century catalogue (239). El Kholi finds only one twelfth-century manuscript of Honorius's *Elucidarium* from a female community: Vienna, Österreichische Nationalbibliothek, 1999 from Neuss/St. Quirin (138). Neither Honorius's *Speculum ecclesiae* nor Ivo's *Panormia* appears to have been known within a women's community apart from the evidence of the *Hortus* (141, 169).

79. Beach, *Women as Scribes*, 65–103.

80. She writes that "the impact of the house's large book collection on the devotional and intellectual life of the monastery's women was probably small, in spite of their important role in its production." Beach, *Women as Scribes*, 117.

81. Beach, *Women as Scribes*, 124–25.

82. For a reconstruction of the nuns' library at Admont, see Beach, *Women as Scribes*, 79–84.

83. Beach, *Women as Scribes*, 84. Mews suggests that both men and women shared in the library holdings at Zwiefalten. Mews, "Monastic Educational Culture Revisited," 191.

84. El Kholi; Bell, *What Nuns Read*; and, concerning limitations on women's reading, Blamires, "The Limits of Bible Study for Medieval Women." For the later medieval period in Switzerland, see Hamburger, "Women and the Written Word." For the reading of nuns at the English community at Syon in the later period, see Hutchison, "What the Nuns Read." A booklist from Essen presents a different picture of women's reading; these books were nonliturgical. Düsseldorf, Universitäts- und Landesbibliothek, MS B4; discussed in Bodarwé, *Sanctimoniales litteratae*, 206–9. See also Karpp, "Bemerkungen zu den mittelalterlichen Hand-

schriften." Wemple too notes the breadth of women's education in the early Middle Ages. She writes that "libraries of Frankish convents were not limited to volumes of the Bible, psalters, and missals. The nuns also had access to commentaries on the scriptures, saints' lives, religious poetry, sermons, patristic writings, penitentials, and books of medicine." Wemple, *Women in Frankish Society*, 179. However, she argues that the Carolingian renaissance marked the end of educational opportunities for women.

85. From his study of records of book ownership at medieval English nunneries, Bell concludes that "slightly more than half are primarily liturgical." Bell, 34. Parisse makes a similar observation in his study of medieval nuns: "les religieuses sont surtout les contemplatives, et elles ne s'adonnent pas vraiment à l'étude." Parisse, *Les Nonnes*, 166.

86. On the community at Lippoldsberg, see Hotchin, "Abbot as Guardian and Cultivator of Virtues" and "Women's Reading and Monastic Reform."

87. *Chronicon Lippoldesbergense*; ed. Arndt, MGH SS 20, 556–57.

88. In letter 35, Sindold writes to N., sending parchment, ink, and silk and giving her instructions for the works that he wants copied. *Die Reinhardsbrunner Briefsammlung*, no. 35; ed. Peeck, 34–36.

89. "Si eundem Hugonem habetis, per presentium portitorem ad breve tempus, ut noster ex hoc corrigatur, mihi transmittatis utque Rupertum de divinis officiis ex vestro exemplari aliquam sororum mearum vel aliam me pergamenum tribuente scribere concedatis." *Die Reinhardsbrunner Briefsammlung*, no. 10; ed. Peeck, 10.

90. For the influence of Rupert on Hildegard, see Arduini, *Rupert von Deutz*, 308–24.

91. The Parisian connection is strengthened by the presence of a text (*HD* no. 523) from the *Summa de ecclesiasticis officiis* (c. 1160–1163) of John Beleth, who was rector of the university of Paris. Bischoff, *HD* 54.

92. Colish, *Peter Lombard*, I, 33.

93. Daly, 71 and Morey, 6.

94. Alexander of Hales introduced the *Sentences* as the starting point for theological lectures at Paris between 1223 and 1227. Minnis, "Late-Medieval Discussions of *Compilatio*," 394.

95. Southern, *Scholastic Humanism*, II, 143.

96. Scholastic texts were rarely found in women's libraries. El Kholi notes that Peter Lombard was known at three women's communities (Hohenbourg, Dünnwald, and Lindau) (208–10), while Peter Comestor was apparently only known at Hohenbourg (207–208).

97. Even so, Colish refers to Honorius and Rupert of Deutz as "the first systematic theologians of the twelfth century." Colish, *Peter Lombard*, I, 41.

98. For Rupert of Deutz's quarrels with schoolmen, see van Engen, 191–215, although van Engen points out that "in the second decade of the twelfth century Rupert's work was perceived as no less innovative and suspect than that of the schoolmen" (10). For a study of "old" versus "new" learning, see Jaeger, *Envy*; and, for monastic opposition to the schools, Ferruolo, *The Origins of the University*, 47–92.

99. For Peter Comestor's glossing of the Lombard, see Luscombe, "Peter Comestor," 110. It was not uncommon for canons at Notre Dame to retire to St. Victor, as for instance Adam of St. Victor may have. Fassler, "Who Was Adam of St. Victor?," 265–66.

100. An account of the Lombard's life is found in Colish, *Peter Lombard*, I, 15–32. Whether or not Peter Lombard took up residence at St. Victor when he arrived in Paris is not clear, although the Victorine influence on his work is marked. Colish, *Peter Lombard*, I, 18–20.

101. For the Victorine influence on Peter Comestor, see Luscombe, "Peter Comestor," 110–12. Daly disagrees (68–70).

102. Hugh writes that "The foundation and principle of sacred learning, however, is history, from which, like honey from the honeycomb, the truth of allegory is extracted." *Didascalicon* VI, 3; ed. Buttimer, 116; ed. Taylor, 138. For discussion, see Smalley, 178–80; and Zinn, "*Historia fundamentum est*." Southern notes that "it was Hugh's most original contribution to systematic theology to see the whole subject as a chronologically ordered study of the historical process which displays God's purposes over the centuries from the Creation to the Last Judgment." *Scholastic Humanism*, II, 62. See also Gorman, "Hugh of St. Victor"; Sicard, *Hugues de Saint-Victor*; and Smalley, 83–111.

103. "Causa suscepti laboris fuit instans petitio sociorum, qui cum hystoriam sacrae scripturae in serie et glosis diffusam lectitarent, brevem nimis et inexpositam, opus aggredi me compulerunt, ad quod pro veritate hystoriae consequenda recurrerent." *Historia scholastica*, prologue; ed. Sylwan, 379. Luscombe writes that, "Peter Comestor was in effect fulfilling Hugh's wish for a continuous and comprehensive commentary which took the form of an *historia*." Luscombe, "Peter Comestor," 119.

104. Smalley, 179.

105. Zinn, "*Historia fundamentum est*," 137.

106. On the idea of a "monastic theology," see Leclercq, *Love of Learning*, 191–235; Leclercq comments that "the difference between scholastic theology and monastic theology corresponds to the differences between the two states of life: the state of Christian life in the world and the state of Christian life in the religious life" (196). Leclercq has addressed the "plurality" of medieval theologies again in "The Renewal of Theology," and more recently in "Naming the Theologies."

107. For reappraisals of Leclercq's model, see Mews, "Monastic Educational Culture Revisited"; Head, "'Monastic' and 'Scholastic' Theology"; and van Engen, 9–10.

108. Colish, *Peter Lombard*, I, 25. Leclercq argues that although monks did not disdain to copy scholastic texts, which might provide them with "patristic texts and doctrine," they preferred the works of Anselm of Laon, William of Champeaux, and Hugh of St. Victor, "regular canons whose cloistered existence is like that of the monks, and whose doctrine is 'strictly patristic'." Leclercq, *Love of Learning*, 183.

109. For a listing of manuscripts from Zwiefalten's library, see *Handschriftenerbe des deutschen Mittelalters*, ed. Krämer, I, 866–72. See also *Die Handschriften des klosters Zwiefalten*, ed. Löffler; and *Katalog der illuminierten Handschriften*

der Württembergischen Landesbibliothek Stuttgart, II (Die Romanischen Handschriften), 1 (Provenienz Zwiefalten), ed. von Borries-Schulten.

110. Mews, "Monastic Educational Culture Revisited," 183.

111. Cohen-Mushlin, "The Twelfth-Century Scriptorium," 99–100.

112. El Kholi, 306.

113. Weis, "Le premier cahier du codex," 57 n. 7. Other women's communities also benefited from gifts of books. Conrad, a deacon of Metz, gave a copy of Gregory's *Moralia in Job* to the abbess Ermentrudis (ca. 995–ca. 1030). Hamburger, "Women and the Written Word," 137. The manuscript is Zentralbibliothek Zurich, Ms. Car. C. 27. Wemple notes that a gift of property, including several books, was made to the monastery of S. Maria da Fontanella by a priest named John at the end of the tenth century. Wemple, "Female Monasticism," 299.

114. Kottje, "Klosterbibliotheken"; Heinzer, "Buchkultur und Bibliotheksgeschichte."

115. Book lending and borrowing were common within medieval intellectual life: Smith, "Lending Books"; Dolbeau, "Quelques aspects des relations"; Gambier-Parry, "Lending Books." Few lending lists have survived from medieval libraries; however, Flint comments on the existence of a twelfth-century Salzburg codex that records loans of Honorius's work; Flint, *Honorius Augustodunensis*, 156. See also Gorman, "A List of Books." McKitterick notes that women are listed as borrowers in lists from Cologne and Weissenburg; McKitterick, "Women and Literacy," 41. Concerning lay borrowers from ecclesiastical libraries, see McKitterick, *The Carolingians*, 261–66.

116. For a brief history and discussion of the Marbach library, see *Catalogue général des manuscrits des bibliothèques publiques de France*, 56, xxiv–xxvi. Walter places the Marbach library amongst the important libraries of the Middle Ages. Walter, "Les miniatures du Codex Guta-Sintram," 4.

117. A description of Colmar MS 128 is provided in de Santis, ed., *I Sermoni di Abelardo*, 12–18.

118. The authenticity of works attributed to Hildebert has been examined by Scott: *Hildeberti Cenomannensis episcopi Carmina minora*, ed. Scott. See also von Moos, *Hildebert von Lavardin*, 359–77.

119. Concerning the identity of Adam, see Fassler, "Who Was Adam of St. Victor?"; and Fassler, *Gothic Song*, 206–10. Fassler warns that "we will probably never know for certain which Parisian sequence texts are actually by Adam." Fassler, "Who Was Adam of St. Victor?" 235 n. 12. The two Victorine sequences in MS Colmar 187 are "Quam dilecta," a sequence for the dedication of the church, which Fassler notes appears only in the mid-twelfth century and which can be found with variations at both St. Victor and Notre Dame, and "Rex Salomon," also for church dedications. Fassler notes that "Rex Salomon" is melodically linked to "Quam dilecta"; although it was already mentioned at St. Victor by the mid-century, it too is connected to both Notre Dame and St. Victor. For "Quam dilecta," see Fassler, *Gothic Song*, 118, 159, and 183 n. 24 and for "Rex Salomon," see 326–28.

120. Concerning the Evangeliary, see Walter, "L'Évangéliaire de Marbach-Schwarzenthann."

121. *Die lateinischen mittelalterlichen Handschriften*, ed. Hilg, II, 33–36.

122. Gilbert, *The Commentaries on Boethius*, ed. Häring. For a description of the manuscript, see *Die lateinischen mittelalterlichen Handschriften*, ed. Hagenmaier, MS. 367. On Gilbert, see Marenbon, "Gilbert of Poitiers."

123. For discussion of the sources and authorship of the *Marbach Annals*, see Schmale, *Deutschlands Geschichtsquellen*, I, 120–24. The *Annals* appear in a thirteenth-century manuscript: Codex Jena Bose q. 6, fols. 123–50. They are a composite piece drawn from a wide variety of different sources, including the *Chronicle* of Bernold of Constance, the *Liber historiae Francorum*, Einhard's biography of Charlemagne, the *Legenda Karoli* of 1166, Turpin's *Chronicle*, the *Vita Hludovici* of Thegan, the *Historia miscella*, the *Gesta Treverorum*, and various saints' lives.

124. Among the texts included in the *Guta-Sintram Codex* are an anonymous commentary on the Augustinian Rule, the *Expositio in Regulam beati Augustini*, a text that has often been attributed to Hugh of St. Victor, and a homeliary composed largely of extracts from Paul the Deacon. Châtillon, "Un commentaire anonyme de la Règle de saint Augustin"; and Étaix, "Les homélies capitulaires."

125. Bischoff, *HD* 46.

126. Häring, "Introduction," 4. Peter Lombard also criticized Gilbert, although not by name.

127. Häring comments on a group of manuscripts linked to the "Basel family," in which marginal annotations alternately point out errors in Gilbert's thinking, or praise him. "Introduction," 39–40. He concludes that "at least in the monastic communities of Austria Gilbert's teaching was carefully examined," and that "even in far-away regions of Austria Gilbert was not without friends" (42).

128. Häring, "Handschriftliches zu den Werken Gilberts." Häring comments that "the manuscript tradition of Gilbert's commentary reflects a lively hidden interest in his teaching despite strong adversary currents." "Introduction," 36.

129. Reinhardt, 8. Basel Universitätsbibliothek, O.II.24, fols. 14r and 92v.

130. See Griffiths, "Brides and *Dominae*."

131. For discussion of this text, see Engels, "*Adtendite a falsis prophetis*."

132. *HD* nos. 77, 81, 96, 508, 509, 759.

133. *Catalogue général des manuscrits des bibliothèques publiques de France*, 56, xxv.

134. "Augustinus lumen mundi et sal terre, vas sincerum doctrine catholice, ingens margaritarum, gemmis insignitum vite apostolice, quam secutus instauravit, et scripta posteris utiliter conservavit." *HD* no. 766.

135. Autenrieth, "Einige Bemerkungen," no. 33; Bischoff, *HD* 58 n. 113.

136. Fassler, *Gothic Song*, 93, 103.

137. On the intellectual connections between Abelard and Hugh, see Luscombe, *The School of Peter Abelard*, 183–97; and Stammberger, "*De longe veritas videtur diversa iudicia parit*." For manuscripts of Abelard's works in the library at St. Victor, see Ouy, ed., *Les manuscrits de l'abbaye de Saint-Victor*, I, 310.

138. Fire destroyed much of the Étival library in year XI and, as elsewhere, the community's manuscripts were pillaged or destroyed through poor treatment; Gasse-Grandjean, *Les livres*, 187–88. See also Benoit, "L'abbaye d'Étival" and Georgel, *L'abbaye d'Étival*, viii–x. In the immediate aftermath of the French Revo-

lution, the monks divided the monastery's manuscript holdings amongst themselves; by this time, many manuscripts had already been lost. In 1802–1803, the few manuscripts remaining at Étival were removed from the monastery to the library at Saint-Dié. *Catalogue général des manuscrits des bibliothèques publiques de France*, 3, 477–505, nos. 6, 31, 35, 71. On the library at Saint-Dié, see Baumont, "Notice historique." Certain manuscripts from Étival can also be found in the Grand Séminaire at Nancy; Benoit, 85–87.

139. These catalogues are listed in Gasse-Grandjean, 221.

140. Bischoff, *HD* 55.

141. Gasse-Grandjean, 73. Although the two communities were not directly connected during Herrad's abbacy, Moyenmoutier did have land at the foot of Mont Sainte Odile. Pfister, "La légende," 99.

142. Autenrieth suggests that Godescallcus should be connected with Hohenbourg. Autenrieth, 310. Whether or not they are the same person, there are some sequences by an author of this name (Godeschalkus) in PL 141, 1323–34.

Chapter 3. A Bee in the Garden of the Lord

1. For a discussion of the poems of the *Hortus* and their likely authorship, see Autenrieth. In addition to these, Autenrieth suggests Herrad's authorship for *Beata illa patria*, a poem that appears in a miniature of the celestial court on folio 244r (*HD* Cat. No. 317); Autenrieth, no. 33. However, as we saw in the last chapter, *Beata illa patria* is the fourth stanza of *Interni festi gaudia*, a sequence common to Augustinian houses in the twelfth and thirteenth centuries; it is not Herrad's. It is still possible that *De primo homine* (*HD* no. 374) and *Rithmus de Domino* (*HD* no. 595) were hers, especially since they share with *Salve cohors virginum* (*HD* no. 1) a similar structure—both rhythmical and syllabic—and certain similarities in content; however the attribution must remain tentative.

2. For a review of medieval women and the question of "authorship," see Summit, "Women and Authorship," and Poor.

3. Green observes that the images of the *Hortus* look "less like the encyclopaedia we have come to expect than like a single great design constructed around the life of Christ." *HD* 24. She cautions: "If we are to continue to refer to HD as an encyclopaedia it must be with a sense of the limits of the term as it can be applied to the pictorial material." *HD* 29.

4. Barthes, "The Death of the Author"; and Foucault, "What Is an Author?"

5. The foundational study of medieval concepts of authorship and authority is Minnis, *Medieval Theory of Authorship*. See also Chenu, "*Auctor, actor, autor*"; Häring, "Auctoritas"; Zimmerman, ed., *Auctor et auctoritas*; Miller, *Poetic License*; Obermeier, *The History and Anatomy*; and Meier, "*Ecce auctor*," which focuses on the authorship of medieval encyclopedias. For connections between memory and authorship, see Carruthers, *The Book of Memory*, 189–220.

6. Despite her sense of herself as author of the *Hortus*, Herrad does not

include an author portrait in the manuscript, in contrast to other medieval "compilers." Meier, "*Ecce auctor*," 349–50.

7. On medieval prologues, see Hamesse, ed., *Les prologues médiévaux*, with chapters devoted to the prologue in various different literary genres. The contents and evolutions of prologues to the authorities (variously described as *accessus, materia, ingressus* or *introitus*, according to the specific discipline) are discussed in Minnis, *Medieval Theory of Authorship*, 9–72; and Hunt, "The Introduction to the 'Artes'." Herrad's prologue is discussed in Luff, *Wissensvermittlung*, 119–28 and her use of the bee image, 134–40.

8. The word that Herrad uses, *diversa*, could also mean "conflicting," thus suggesting that she offers a reconciliation of conflicting viewpoints.

9. "Herrat gratia Dei Hohenburgensis ecclesie abbatissa licet indigna dulcissimis Christi virginibus in eadem ecclesia quasi in Christi vinea Domini fideliter laborantibus, graciam et gloriam, quam dabit Dominus. Sanctitati vestre insinuo, quod hunc librum qui intitulatur *Hortus deliciarum* ex diversis sacre et philosophice scripture floribus quasi apicula Deo inspirante comportavi et ad laudem et honorem Christi et Ecclesie, causaque dilectionis vestre quasi in unum mellifluum favum compaginavi." *HD* no. 2.

10. Herrad describes her prologue as: "Item prosa per Herradem abbatissam predictis virgunculis causa exhortationis composita." *HD* no. 2. The verb that she chooses to describe her work, "componere," can mean to construct or build, to put together, arrange, compile, or compose—words that draw on the original idea of composition as creative compilation and synthesis. The prologue recalls the language and form of a letter, although Herrad describes it as a *prosa* rather than an *epistola*.

11. "Rithmus Herradis abbatisse per quem Hohenburgenses virgunculas amabiliter salutat et ad veri sponsi fidem dilectionemque salubriter invitat." *HD* no. 1.

12. Herrat devotissima
Tua fidelissima
Mater et ancillula
Cantat tibi cantica. (*HD* no. 1)

13. Honorius, *Elucidarium*, Prologus; ed. Lefèvre, 359.

14. Rigg defines a florilegium as a "collection of excerpts" and notes that even the term "excerpt" connotes, in its original meaning, the picking of flowers. Rigg, "Anthologies and Florilegia," 708.

15. For a study of authorial self-presentation in florilegia, see Rouse and Rouse, "Florilegia of Patristic Texts" and Hamesse, "Les florilèges philosophiques du XIIIe siècle." On florilegia in general, see Rigg, "Anthologies and Florilegia"; and Moss, *Printed Commonplace-Books*, 24–39. Concerning monastic florilegia, see Leclercq, *Love of Learning*, 182–84.

16. *Liber florum*, Prologue; ed. Hunt, 138–39; trans. in Rouse and Rouse, "Florilegia of Patristic Texts," 177.

17. "Hec sunt excerpta de quodam libro qui dicitur Itinerarius Clementis, in quo libro quedam capitula a katholicis sunt recepta, quedam dampnata." *HD* no. 1125.

18. "Ne id opus quasi sine auctore putaretur apocrifum, unicuique senten-
ciae per singulas capitulatim virtutes suum scripsi auctorem." Defensor, *Liber scintillarum*, Prologus; ed. Rochais, CCSL 117; trans. in Rouse and Rouse, "Florilegia
of Patristic Texts," 172. The Rouses note that there is "a quite apparent concern
that the authority or authenticity of the excerpts, and hence of the collection itself,
be established. It is for this reason that the names of the authors and books that
provided the excerpts are noted, each by each, and often a list of 'works consulted'
is affixed to the *florilegium*, either before or after" (172). The *Hortus* contains no
list of "works consulted."

19. Peter Lombard, for instance, writes: "Non igitur debet hic labor cui-
quam pigro vel multum docto videri superfluus, cum multis impigris multisque
indoctis, inter quos etiam et mihi, sit necessarius. . . ." *Sentences*, Prologus; ed.
Brady, I, 4. Cf. Augustine, *De Trinitate*, III, *Prooemium*, 1; ed. Mountain, CCSL
50, 127.

20. See, for instance, Newman, "Visions and Validation" and Obermeier,
251–64. Summit writes that "alienation . . . defined 'women's writing' in the
medieval and early modern periods." *Lost Property*, 11.

21. "In hoc autem tractatu, non solum pium lectorem, sed etiam liberum
correctorem desidero, maxime ubi profunda versatur veritatis quaestio: quae uti-
nam tot haberet inventores quot habet contradictores!" Peter Lombard, *Sentences*,
Prologus; ed. Brady, I, 4. Cf. Augustine, *De Trinitate*, III, *Prooemium*, 2; ed.
Mountain, CCSL 50, 128.

22. Marignan's doubts were based on the high regard in which he held the
manuscript and his skepticism that a woman could have had access to the sort of
knowledge that such an intellectual tour de force would have required. He
doubted that "cette encyclopédie, qui a réuni toutes les conaissances de l'extrême
fin du XIIe siècle, soit due à une femme." Marignan, *Étude sur le manuscrit*, 3–4.
Earlier scholars were similarly unwilling to allow Hildegard of Bingen credit for
her works; Newman notes that some scholars imagined "a male ghostwriter behind her mask." Newman, " 'Sibyl of the Rhine'," 1.

23. Concerning the medieval encyclopedia tradition, see Meier, "Grundzüge
der mittelalterlichen Enzyklopädik"; Meier, "Organisation of Knowledge and Encyclopaedic *Ordo*"; Twomey, "Medieval Encyclopedias"; Ribémont, "On the
Definition of an Encyclopaedic Genre"; Becq, ed., *L'Encyclopédisme*; and de Gandillac, Fontaine, Châtillon, and Lemoine, eds., *La Pensée encyclopédique*.

24. Fowler observes, "it must be apparent by now that the true genre [of the
encyclopedia] does not have a single physical form . . . Encyclopaedism is the
genre, not the encyclopaedia." Fowler, "Encyclopaedias," 22–23.

25. Medieval authors—from the twelfth century onward—used such terms
as *speculum* or *summa* to describe their "encyclopedic" works. See Fowler, 27–29.
Herrad's title and floral imagery place the work, at least superficially, among florilegia, although the enormous breadth and textual diversity of the *Hortus*, not to
mention its sophisticated organization, distinguish it from florilegia, which tend
to be more limited in scope, contents, and purpose. By the twelfth century *flores*,
and related terms, were commonly used to describe compilations of selected extracts, often, although not exclusively, from a single author.

26. As Ribémont writes, "to what extent were medieval encyclopaedists conscious of writing a text belonging to a definite genre? If they were, the historian has to try to determine—in terms of their terminology, conceptions, etc.—what the set of constants followed by every author may have been." Ribémont, 47.

27. Herrad refers to the *Summarium* throughout as the *Gemma aurea*. Curschmann has demonstrated that the codex that she consulted must have opened with an *ars dictaminis* entitled the *Gemma aurea*, which she assumed was the first chapter of an entire work by that name. Curschmann, *HD* 67.

28. "Nam ex meo pauca vel quasi nulla; ipsorum igitur est autoritate, nostrum autem sola partium ordinatione." Vincent of Beauvais, *Libellus totius operis apologeticus*, 3; ed. Lusignan, 119.

29. Cited in Minnis, *Medieval Theory of Authorship*, 94. For a discussion of textual reuse and concepts of authorship, see the section entitled: "Faire du neuf avec de l'ancien: citations, remplois, appropriations," in Zimmerman, 219–79.

30. "In labore multo ac sudore volumen Deo praestante compegimus ex testimoniis veritatis in aeternum fundatis, in quatuor libris distinctum." Peter Lombard, *Sentences*, Prologus; ed. Brady, I, 4.

31. "Brevi volumine complicans Patrum sententias, appositis eorum testimoniis, ut non sit necesse quaerenti librorum numerositatem evolvere, cui brevitas collecta quod quaeritur offert sine labore." Peter Lombard, *Sentences*, Prologus; ed. Brady, I, 4.

32. Concerning Chaucer, see Summit, "Women and Authorship," 92.

33. Summit, "Women and Authorship," 91. For a discussion of medieval women's authorship with a particular emphasis on the work of Mechthild of Magdeburg, see Poor. As Poor notes, authorship is only attributed to medieval women "insofar as their agency (rational, active authorship) is downplayed." Poor, 15.

34. Summit, "Women and Authorship," 93.

35. Nichols argues that even copying can be creative: "In the act of copying a text, the scribe supplants the original poet, often changing words or narrative order, suppressing or shortening some sections, while interpolating new material in others"; "Introduction: Philology in a Manuscript Context," 8.

36. On Clemence, see *Virgin Lives and Holy Deaths*, trans. Wogan-Browne and Burgess, xix–xxxv.

37. The literature on this subject is enormous. For a general introduction see Misch, *Apis est animal, apis est ecclesia*, 10–33; and Cook, "The Bee in Greek Mythology." For the bee (and other insects) as a metaphor for people in literature ranging from antiquity to the present, see Hollingsworth, *Poetics of the Hive*.

38. On medieval memory, see Carruthers, *Book*; Carruthers, *The Craft of Thought*; and Carruthers and Ziolkowski, eds., *The Medieval Craft of Memory*. For the association of bees with learning, see Morgan, *Literate Education*, 262–70.

39. On ancient memory houses, see Bergmann, "The Roman House as Memory Theater."

40. For an examination of *imitatio* as a literary model in the Renaissance, and the use of Seneca's apian metaphor, see Greene, *The Light in Troy*; and Fullenwider, "Das *Mellificium*."

41. Seneca, *Epist.* 84, 5; ed. Gummere, II, 278 (I have used Moss's transla-

tion; Moss, 12). Greene calls the 84th letter "one of the most interesting discussions of imitation ever written." Greene, 73.

42. Horace describes himself as a bee as he collected the material for his verses. *Ode*, IV, 2, 27–32; ed. Quinn, 95; trans. Shepherd, 175. The foundational treatment of the apian metaphor for *imitatio* and composition is von Stackelberg, "Das Bienengleichnis."

43. Seneca, *Epist.* 84, 4; ed. and trans. Gummere, II, 278–79.

44. Hathaway, "*Compilatio.*"

45. For discussion of the vocabulary of authorial activity, see Bourgain, "Les verbes."

46. *Liber florum*, Prologue; ed. Hunt, 139; trans. in Rouse and Rouse, "Florilegia of Patristic Texts," 176.

47. Pigman explores the tension between the two implications of Seneca's bee metaphor: mere collection of materials and the transformation of these into a new creation. Pigman, "Versions of imitation," 4–7. However, Greene notes that "Seneca's dominant analogies, mellification and digestion, stress a process of transformation." Greene, 73.

48. For a comparison of Macrobius and Seneca, see Pigman, 5–7. Pigman notes that "Macrobius is concerned with organization, not with transformation" (6). Similarly, Moss comments that "what interests Macrobius is the relation of the gathered parts to the whole, not the problem of how the new author is to make his borrowings his own." Moss, 14. For Macrobius's use of the term *compilo*, see Hathaway, 24.

49. Macrobius, *Saturnalia*, Praef., 4; ed. Willis, 2; trans. Davies, 26–27. Macrobius also likens the unity of a choir—composed of many voices but producing a single sound—to the gathering of individual sources into a single, final product.

50. "Huic nimirum adhuc puerulus Aegil, de patria transportatus, honorifice a parentibus praesentatur. Quem paterna pietate blanditiis delinitum scolae congregationi, ubi lex divina iugi exercitatione discitur et docetur cum summa industria, causa litterarum sociare mandavit. Qui mox, divina gratia ministrante, in tantum proficiebat cotidie in meditatione Sanctarum Scripturarum, ut etiam apes esurientes in colligendis floribus imitari videretur." *Vita Eigilis abbatis Fuldensis*, ed. Wattenbach, MGH SS 15.1, 223.

51. Carruthers, *Book*.

52. Carruthers writes that "composition starts in memorized reading." *Book*, 191. Fulton argues for the recognition of Honorius Augustodunensis as an author, commenting that, "if by modern standards of composition Honorius's work appears somewhat derivative, by medieval standards it is entirely his own—at least, that is, in the only way that mattered, namely, that he had taken what he read, divided it up into memorable 'gobbets,' 'located' those gobbets in his memory with appropriate images and, on the basis of those images, retrieved only what he needed to 'invent' his own work." Fulton, 261. As one of Herrad's major sources, Honorius was then also subjected to her own memorial and authorial process: his works were divided, reorganized, and mediated through images that she chose to explicate them.

53. Cited in Ziolkowski, "A Bouquet of Wisdom and Invective," 21.

54. "Magnarum esse virium clavam Herculi extorquere de manu." Jerome, *Hebraicae quaestiones in libro Geneseos*, Preface; ed. de Lagarde, CCSL 72, 1.

55. Quintilian, *Institutiones oratoriae*, I, 10, 7; ed. Cousin, I, 132; trans. in Carruthers, *Book*, 37.

56. Virgil, *Georgics*, IV, 219–21; ed. Mynors, lxxx. Aristotle had emphasized the prudence of the bee. *History of Animals*, 623b–27b; ed. and trans. Balme, 335–67. For discussion, see Guldentops, "The Sagacity of the Bees."

57. "At Platoni cum in cunis parvulo dormienti apes in labellis consedissent responsum est singulari illum suavitate orationis fore. Ita future eloquentia provisa in infante est." Cicero, *De divinatione*, I, 78; ed. Pease, 228–29. Miraculous bee feeding was also associated with Homer, Hesiod, Pindar, Sophocles, Virgil, and Lucan, as well as others.

58. Plutarch writes: "The bee by nature finds the smoothest and best honey in the most bitter flowers and sharpest thorns; so children, if they are properly educated in poetry, will learn somehow to extract something useful and helpful even from works which are suspected of being immoral or inappropriate." Cited in Morgan, 262.

59. The classic work is Misch. See also Hassig, *Medieval Bestiaries*, 52–61; and Wimmer, *Biene und Honig*.

60. Honey symbolism is reviewed by de Lubac, *Medieval Exegesis*, 162–77.

61. "Favus Scriptura est divina melle spiritualis sapientiae repleta." Rhabanus Maurus, *De universo*, 22, 1; PL 111, 594.

62. In his *De virginibus*, Ambrose likens the virgin to a bee and the dew that sustains her to the word of God. This image draws on the ancient idea (discussed by Seneca) that honey was dew that bees simply gathered from flowers. *De virginibus*, I, 8.40; ed. Gori, 140; trans. Ramsey, 84.

63. Knowledge of Seneca's *Letters* reached its peak during the twelfth century. However, the letters were known in two parts, which circulated separately: letters 1–88 and letters 89–124. Letters 1–88 always had a wider circulation than letters 89–124 and Reynolds comments that the early manuscript tradition of 89–124 "is essentially a German affair." Reynolds, ed., *Texts and Transmission*, 369–75, 373. See also Reynolds, *The Medieval Tradition of Seneca's Letters*, 104–24; and Munk Olsen, *L'étude des auteurs classiques latins*, II, 365–473.

64. Déchanet, "*Seneca noster*," 754 n. 7.

65. Macrobius's *Commentary* was known to Manegold of Lautenbach, proof that he was read in the Empire and in the area around Hohenbourg. *Liber contra Wolfelmum*, Prologue; ed. Hartmann, 39; trans. Ziomkowski, 35. For knowledge of Macrobius in the medieval period, see L. D. Reynolds, ed., *Texts and Transmission*, 222–35. See also Kelly's study of Macrobius in the Middle Ages, which includes a list of *Saturnalia* manuscripts from the late eighth to the early thirteenth century: *The Conspiracy of Allusion*, 13–35. For the medieval dissemination of the *Commentary*, see Hüttig, *Macrobius im Mittelalter*; and Caiazzo, *Lectures médiévales de Macrobe*.

66. Despite the growing emphasis on the bee as a spiritual symbol, the transformative aspect of mellification was not entirely lost. The statesman and theologian Peter of Blois (d. 1211), himself a consummate borrower of texts, stresses in

his own writings the sense of metamorphosis that had been so important to Seneca. He writes: "Why should that be accounted envy which fuses into a single study of virtue and exercise of prudence all that I have taken from my wide reading and digested with keen ardor? For as we read in the *Saturnalia* and in Seneca's epistles to Lucilius, we must imitate those bees gathering flowers whose various nectars are turned to honey and are mingled to create a single savor." Peter's use of the bee metaphor, although designed primarily to defend himself against charges of illicit borrowing, nonetheless underscored the potential originality of his work, despite its borrowed parts. Peter recognized the transformative promise of Seneca's model and claimed it as a basis for his literary authority. Peter of Blois, *Epist.* 92; PL 207, 289; trans. in Greene, 84. He repeats the idea in the prologue to his *De amicitia Christiana*; ed. Davy, 100.

67. *Vita sancti Udalrici episcopi Augustensis*, PL 142, 1187.

68. John of Salisbury, *Policraticus* VII, 10, 660a; ed. Webb, II, 133; trans. Pike, 253–54. Since John cites from several of Seneca's letters, it is likely that he knew the letters directly, and not through a florilegium. Citations from Seneca's letters in the *Policraticus* are listed in Webb, II, 499.

69. Virgil's writings concerning the bee were transmitted to the Middle Ages through Priscian, who quotes 31 lines from book 4 of the *Georgics* in his *Institutionum grammaticarum*. Rust, "The Art of Beekeeping," 365. Concerning the medieval reading of the *Georgics*, see Wilkinson, *The Georgics of Virgil*, 273–90; and for Virgil's medieval reputation, Comparetti, *Vergil in the Middle Ages*. For the influence of Virgil's bee-simile in Dante's *Paradiso*, see Rossi, "The Poetics of Resurrection."

70. Ambrose, *Hexameron*, V, 21, 67–70; PL 14, 234–35; trans. Savage, 212–15. Concerning Ambrose's writing on bees, see Misch, 34–51.

71. Paulinus, *Vita Ambrosii*, 3; ed. Pellegrino, 54; trans. Ramsey, 197.

72. The idea that the bee labored for the common good was familiar in ancient literature. See Quintilian, *Institutiones oratoriae*, V, 11, 25; ed. and trans, Cousin, III, 170. Cicero, *De Finibus*, V, 3, 19; ed. Madvig, 455. Virgil, *Georgics* IV, 153–54; ed. Mynors, lxxviii. Seneca, *Epist.* 121, 22; ed. and trans. Gummere, III, 408–9.

73. For the symbolism of the bee in the bestiary tradition, see Hassig, 52–61; and Misch, 64–69.

74. Leclercq, *Love of Learning*, 73.

75. Virgil taught that bees reproduce without coitus: *Georgics* IV, 198–99; ed. Mynors, lxxix.

76. Ambrose, *De virginibus*; ed. Gori, 99–241; trans. Ramsey, 73–116.

77. Pseudo-Augustine, *De cereo Paschali*; PL 46, 820.

78. Venantius Fortunatus, Poem 6.1; trans. George, 26. Fortunatus also linked Radegund's writing to the production of honey: "You have given me great verse on small tablets, you can create honey in the empty wax." Appendix 31; trans. George, 120.

79. See n. 82.

80. Aldhelm, *De virginitate*, 5; ed. Gwara, CCSL 124A, 63; trans. Lapidge and Herren, 62.

81. "Virgo est apicula, quae ceram fabricat, et sine coitu procreavit." Hildebert, *In Festo Purificationis Beatae Mariae sermo primus;* PL 171, 611.

82. Cited in Clayton, *The Cult of the Virgin Mary,* 258 n. 178.

83. Nulla inter aues similis est api,
     que talem gerit tipum castitatis,
     nisi que Christum portauit aluo
          inuiolata.
The Cambridge Songs, ed. and trans. Ziolkowski, 88–89.

84. See n. 77.

85. Kelly, *The Exultet in Southern Italy,* 33–34 (for the Beneventan text), 38–39 (for the Franco-Roman text). The significance of the Easter candles is treated in the *Hortus* immediately following the depiction of the crucifixion (fol. 150r) in texts drawn from Rupert of Deutz's *De divinis officiis.* HD nos. 536–38. For bees and honey in the liturgy, see Misch, 52–63 and Zenner, "From Divine Wisdom to Secret Knowledge."

86. Thomas of Cantimpré, *Bonum universale de apibus,* II, 40; trans. Platelle, 188–89. This story appears in Caesarius of Heisterbach's *Dialogus miraculorum,* IX, 8; ed. Strange, II, 172–73; trans. Scott and Bland, II, 114–15. For a discussion of Thomas's *Bonum universale de apibus,* see Misch, 70–103; Pollini, "Les Propriétés des Abeilles"; and Rubin, "The Eucharist and the Construction of Medieval Identities," 56.

87. Virgil, *Georgics,* IV, 212–18; ed. Mynnors, lxxix–lxxx. Seneca, *De Clementia,* I, 19, 2–3; ed. Basore, 408–11. Lactantius, *Divinae institutiones,* 2; ed. Heck and Wlosok, 3. Isidore, *Etymologiae,* XII, 8, 1–3; ed. Lindsay (no page numbers). However, for Semonides, the mid-seventh-century BC Greek poet, the bee represented the best type of woman—in fact, the only good woman in his view. He writes that bee wives "are the best and wisest that Zeus bestoweth upon men; these other kinds, thanks unto Him, both are and will ever be a mischief in the world." *Elegy and Iambus,* trans. Edmonds, II, 223. For a discussion of the gender of bees, see Rust, 366–67.

88. Aldhelm, *De virginitate,* 4; ed. Gwara, CCSL 124A, 53–61; trans. Lapidge and Herren, 61–62. In addition to the "peculiar chastity" of the bee, Aldhelm also praises the "harmonious fellowship," and "spontaneous inclination to voluntary servitude" by which the bee "offers an example of obedience to mortals living in this vale of tears." *De virginitate,* 6; ed. Gwara, CCSL 124A, 65–73; trans. Lapidge and Herren, 62–63.

89. An edition and translation of Hugh's letters to Heloise (nos. 16 and 17) is provided in Mews, "Hugh Metel, Heloise, and Peter Abelard," 89–91.

90. Peter the Venerable, *Epist.* 115; ed. Constable, 305; trans. Radice and Clanchy, 220.

91. Jerome wrote: "Debbora apis sive eloquentia." *Liber interpretationis hebraicorum nominum;* ed. de Lagarde, CCSL 72, 64. Rhabanus Maurus also wrote that "Debora, quae interpretatur apis, significat prophetiae suavitatem, et coelestis doctrinae dulcedinem." *De universo,* III, 1; PL 111, 56.

92. Peter Damian, *Sermo* 39; ed. Lucchesi, CCCM 57, 243. Guibert, *Moralia in Genesin* 35, 8; PL 156, 252. Rupert, *De sancta Trinitate et operibus ejus libri*

XLIII. *Commentariorum in Genesim*, VIII, 13; ed. Haacke, CCCM 21, 498. *Vita sanctae Hildegardis*, II, 6; ed. Klaes. CCCM 126, 30–31; trans. Silvas, 166–67.

93. As Mews notes: "there can be no doubting that she [Heloise] was perceived by contemporaries as a figure whose teaching and writing were widely sought after." Mews, "Heloise and Liturgical Experience at the Paraclete," 26.

94. Hugh writes "your discretion is greater than rumor has announced," suggesting that Heloise had not responded to his letter. Hugh Metel, *Epist.* 17; ed. and trans. Mews, 91.

95. Ad te concurrunt examina discipularum,
       Ut recreentur apes melle parentis apis.
Baudry of Bourgueil, *Carmina*, no. 139.15–16; ed. Hilbert, 192.

96. Trans. Derolez, *The Autograph Manuscript of the* Liber Floridus, 38.

97. *SV*, I, 953; ed. Seyfarth, CCCM 5, 38; trans. Newman, 275. For the books of the *Speculum* as "meadows," see *SV, epistula*, 58–64; ed. Seyfarth, CCCM 5, 3; trans. Newman, 270.

98. Abelard writes, "I too . . . propose to instruct your way of life through the many documents of the holy Fathers and the best customs of monasteries, gathering each blossom as it comes to mind and collecting in a single bunch what I shall see will accord with the sanctity of your calling." *Epist.* 8; ed. McLaughlin, 243; trans. Radice and Clanchy, 131.

99. Carruthers, *Book*, 192.

100. Hoc in monte (Hohenburc)   vivo fonte (sancti Spiritus)
       Potantur ovicule (domicelle),
       Esum (doctrinam) vite   sine lite
       Congestant apicule.

       Nectar clarum   scripturarum
       Potant liberaliter,
       Bibant (hic), bibant (in futuro)   vivant (nunc et semper) vivant
       Omnes eternaliter. (*HD* no. 1162)

101. *HD* no. 1162 n. a: "Neumed on a stave." As Levy notes, "musical setting was the rule rather than the exception for the verses in HD." *HD* 88.

102. Saxl, "Illustrated Medieval Encyclopedias 2," 246.

103. On this basis, Graf suggests that the women of Hohenbourg be seen as "co-authors" of the *Hortus*. Graf, 66.

Chapter 4. From Nectar to Honeycomb: Constructing the Hortus

1. Carruthers, *Book*, 35–38.
2. Green, *HD* 25.
3. Green, *HD* 17.
4. There are places in the manuscript where the order of the biblical narrative has been inverted or otherwise confused. For example, the Tower of Babel (fol. 27v) intrudes on the story of Noah and on folio 123 the parable of Dives and

Lazarus has been split between two sides, when it was probably intended as a full-page narrative depiction. *HD* Cat. Nos. 175–77.

5. Only in certain cases might an image prove to be misleading as a finding tool. Most of these are confined to the *Ecclesia* section, which, because it is largely allegorical, breaks with the biblical organization that structures the rest of the manuscript. Here, for instance, Jesus' Cleansing of the Temple (fol. 238r) is presented as a call to church reform and not as a narrative account of his life. Here too, Solomon, who had not been featured in the Old Testament section, is depicted as the builder of the true church, signified by the temple (fols. 204v–15r). The events and figures that these images portray have been removed from their biblical sequence in order to fulfill a symbolic role elsewhere in the manuscript.

6. These images are discussed in Godwin, "The Judith Illustration."

7. "Lege etiam in sententiis, rubrica in ultimis post sinum Abrahe, Petri Lombardi de ecclesiasticis ordinibus ab eo loco: Nunc ad considerationem, usque: Cum alia sacramenta." *HD* no. 792 n. 69.

8. For discussion of these transitions, see Curschmann, "Texte-Bilder-Strukturen," 383–85.

9. For a detailed discussion of these *rotae*, see Krüger and Runge, "Lifting the Veil."

10. See Chapter 1 n. 23.

11. For the practical considerations and cost of manuscript production, see Bischoff, *Latin Palaeography*, 8–19; and McKitterick, *The Carolingians*, 135–64.

12. Since baptisms were held only twice a year—at Easter and Pentecost—the combination was a natural one; see *HD* no. 363.

13. Concerning wax tablets, see Wattenbach, *Das Schriftwesen im Mittelalter*, 51–89; Bischoff, *Latin Palaeography*, 13–14; Brown, "The Role of the Wax Tablet"; Rouse and Rouse, "The Vocabulary of Wax Tablets"; Lalou, "Les tablettes de cire médiévales"; Lalou, ed., *Les Tablettes à écrire*.

14. Concerning Lambert's work on the *Liber floridus*, see Derolez, *The Autograph Manuscript*.

15. Curschmann, "Texte-Bilder-Strukturen," 384. Even so, Curschmann argues that this block of texts does not contradict Herrad's plan, since it once again follows the transitional model that Herrad had used elsewhere.

16. For the idea of medieval art as the book of the illiterate, see Diebold, *Word and Image*; Camille, "Seeing and Reading"; Chazelle, "Pictures, Books and the Illiterate"; Duggan, "Was Art Really the 'Book of the Illiterate'?"; and Curschmann, "*Pictura laicorum litteratura?*" For further discussion of this idea, see Chapter 6.

17. Hamburger, *The Visual and the Visionary*, 81. Hamburger writes, "Making a virtue of necessity, the nuns developed a visual culture of their own that was, if not entirely independent, then at least governed by its own requirements and protocols." Hamburger, *Nuns as Artists*, 10.

18. On the influences apparent in the images of the *Hortus*, see Green, *HD* 32–36. Concerning the Adam and Eve cycle, see Green, "The Adam and Eve Cycle"; for the frescoes of Regensburg, see Endres, "Romanische Deckenmalereien." Green cautions that "the Salzburg-Regensburg influence resembles tradi-

tions—predilections for certain themes and types—rather than a special genre of MS at hand in the scriptorium." *HD* 34. Certain images in the *Hortus* are similar to those in manuscripts from Regensburg, in particular the Microcosm (fol. 16v), the Mystic Winepress (fol. 241r), and the Bosom of Abraham (fol. 263v).

19. At the very least, Green suggests that the artist had two gospel books, one a contemporary Byzantine book and the other from the school of Echternach. *HD* 32–33.

20. As we have seen, not all of Herrad's sources were equally shuffled or scattered in the *Hortus*. Of the approximately 250 excerpts that Herrad took from the *Sentences*, only twenty or so appear in the main body of the *Hortus* and, with only one exception (*HD* no. 334), these are from books one and two. Excerpts from book three and especially book four—which was by far the most important book for Herrad—appear in the block of *Sentences* excerpts toward the end of the manuscript. These appear in the same order as they had in their original context. Almost fifty of these excerpts dealt with the sacrament of marriage (*HD* nos. 1039–85) and another forty with last things (*HD* nos. 1086–1124).

21. Herrad revised her selection from Honorius's sermon for the tenth Sunday after Pentecost by providing the background information to which Honorius had alluded in his reference to the day's reading: *unde legitur hodie*. She replaces this reference with more specific information: "In die Palmarum . . . " *HD* no. 379. See also *HD* nos. 386, 387, and 584.

22. *HD* no. 585. Male addresses also appear in sermons for the Paraclete. De Santis, ed., *I sermoni di Abelardo*, 125–31.

23. This idea also appears in Herrad's gloss to the Leviathan image (fol. 84r; plate 7); *HD* Cat. No. 101.

24. For other good examples of Herrad's selection technique, see *HD* nos. 246 and 519.

25. This is also the case with *HD* nos. 389 and 393.

26. See also the way in which Honorius's sermon *In adventu Domini* is divided between *HD* nos. 701, 841, 438, and 83; and his *Dominica de Passione Domini* between *HD* nos. 253 (in two separate sections), 260, 229, 231, 110, 233, 237, 382, and 449.

27. Texts from the *Elucidarium* are partially duplicated in *HD* nos. 849 and 861; *HD* nos. 849 and 866; *HD* nos. 868 and 873; and *HD* nos. 425 and 876. Duplications among texts drawn from the *Speculum ecclesiae* include: *HD* nos. 689 and 414; *HD* nos. 575 and 391; and *HD* nos. 858 and 874.

28. Bischoff, *HD* 42. Other works, such as the *Sentences, De divinis officiis*, and Ivo's *Panormia* already contained section titles. However, since Herrad often excerpted content rather than entire sections, the source titles were not always appropriate.

29. Nichols, "Introduction," 7.

30. Nichols writes: "How should the modern reader react when confronted by a manuscript into which many things, sometimes of quite diverse content, have been copied? Although the generic term used to define such a codex—*miscellany*, or volume that contains miscellaneous subject matter—lies ready to hand, the term does little to address the dynamics of individual examples of the genre. . . . It sheds

little light on the relationship of the texts to their codicological context, and it may even be misleading, suggesting, as it does, an arbitrary principle of organization for manuscripts in which there may be a perfectly clear organizing principle." Nichols and Wenzel, eds., *The Whole Book*, 3.

31. In the case of the *Liber floridus*, a manuscript to which the *Hortus* is often compared, Derolez argues that the number of interpolations is testimony to Lambert's desire to impose order on his folios. He notes: "when irregularities in the quire structure are so numerous and so intricate as is the case in the L.F., only one conclusion is possible: the author or scribe has taken great pains to place texts and pictures at definite locations in the codex and has not added them at random. In other words, the physical structure shows that he has been *organizing* his materials, instead of simply copying extracts from his sources as he encountered them." Derolez, *The Autograph Manuscript*, 17–18.

32. Green warns that "the volume was neither neat nor uniform. It had remained long years unbound; afterthoughts were included; and pages of smaller dimension were sometimes admitted." *HD* 17. For the size and placement of folios, see Evans, *HD* 1, 3. Green suggests that folios 10–16 may have formed an "intrusive" quire (*HD* 28); folios 309–15 formed a separate small booklet, described by de Bastard as "un cahier format in-4" (Evans, *HD* 1). For a revision of Green's argument regarding the so-called "intrusive" quire, see Mayo, "*Concordia Discordantium*," 47.

33. Green, *HD* 32. See also the interpolation of folio 234r–v, which de Bastard notes was inserted after the writing of the main manuscript text, but still during the same period. *HD* no. 794 n. a.

34. Curschmann, "Imagined Exegesis," 147.

35. Camille suggests that text in and on medieval images might have legitimized the image—"as if the very presence of language served to authenticate the image." Camille, "Seeing and Reading," 33.

36. On the Leviathan image, see Zellinger, "Der geköderte Leviathan"; and, concerning the deception of the devil, Constas, "The Last Temptation of Satan."

37. For other liturgical indications, see *HD* Cat. Nos. 27, 115, 126, 128, 160, and 162.

38. Herrad also included textual sections in the miniatures, some of which were quite long, and which she explicitly associated with the *Speculum ecclesiae* (*HD* Cat. Nos. 28, 101, 205, 211, 245, 307), *Gemma animae* (*HD* Cat. Nos. 45, 235, 241), *Elucidarium* (*HD* Cat. Nos. 14, 207), *Sentences* (*HD* Cat. Nos. 5, 8, 14, 16), or Rupert of Deutz (*HD* Cat. Nos. 101, 191).

39. The gloss on folio 3v (*HD* Cat. No. 4) points the reader to a selection from Peter Lombard, which is identified only by its incipit. The text itself appears on folio 103v (*HD* no. 366). The gloss on folio 8r (*HD* Cat. No. 6) directs the reader to a text beginning "aer dicitur . . . ," an excerpt from the *Summarium Heinrici* that has not survived the manuscript, if it was included in it. It is possible that it appeared as part of *HD* no. 24, which was copied only in part.

40. See, for example, *HD* Cat Nos. 14, 16, 19. *HD* Cat. No. 19 mentions "Rupertus" and there is indeed a text from Rupert that may be relevant, tucked away in a section on folio 153v (*HD* no. 543). Here Eve's formation from Adam's

rib is likened to the baptism of the church through the blood and water that flowed from Christ's side on the cross.

41. The reference appears in *HD* no. 363, where a marginal note advises: "Lege etiam de baptismo in sententiis Petri ab illo loco: Baptismum Christi, usque: sacramentum confirmationis," possibly in reference to *HD* nos. 950–55. Another note to *HD* no. 759 advises: "Lege etiam in sententiis Petri Lombardi de ordine caritatis ab eo loco: karitas est dilectio; usque: principales virtutes." However, the text to which this gloss refers cannot be located in the *Hortus*.

42. Krüger and Runge, 11.

43. Wieland explores the ways in which images can gloss texts; Wieland, "Gloss and Illustration."

44. "Quod hec vidua vicit tirannum significat quod caro Christi vicit diabolum." *HD* no. 208.

45. "Salemon et rota fortune et scala et syrene admonent nos de contemptu mundi et amore Christi." *HD* Cat. No. 299. On the Solomon cycle, see Curschmann, "Texte-Bilder-Strukturen," 394–409 and Cames, *Allégories et symboles,* 74–87.

46. The gloss to the final image of the psychomachia cycle (fol. 204r; plate 19) reads: "Hic finitur conflictus virtutum et viciorum in animabus invisibiliter pugnantium." *HD* Cat. No. 285.

47. On visual exegesis, see Esmeijer, *Divina Quaternitas* and Sicard, *Diagrammes médiévaux.* Esmeijer describes visual exegesis as "a kind of exposition of Holy Scripture in which the customary rôles of word and image have been reversed, so that the representation or programme provides the Scriptural exegesis in very compressed picture-form and the text itself is either completely omitted or else limited to explanatory inscriptions, tituli, or a very short commentary" (ix).

48. Cited in Camille, "Illuminating Thought," 352.

49. Curschmann concludes from his examination of the German glosses: "one thing seems certain from this survey of the glosses: the group which worked to produce this codex over a period of many years was small and homogeneous, and it was guided throughout by a *spiritus rector* who paid attention to the most minute detail." Curschmann, *HD* 73.

50. This is De Clercq's argument: "Hugues de Fouilloy." However, Clark comments that "there is no conclusive evidence for or against such an idea." Hugh of Fouilloy, *Aviarum;* ed. Clark, 27 n. 1. Hugh's artistry is suggested in his use of visual terms to describe his creation of the manuscript (*pingere volui*). Hugh of Fouilloy, *Aviarum* prologue 1; ed. Clark, 116. See also Clark, "The Illustrated Medieval Aviary."

51. Derolez, *The Autograph Manuscript,* 22.

52. Lewis, *The Art of Matthew Paris,* 19. On Matthew Paris as an artist, see also Alexander, *Medieval Illuminators,* 107–12.

53. Godwin, 36. Similarly, Green notes that "the various strands were introduced with great skill, the sources quarried not mechanically but with careful thought, the models freely used for best effect." *HD* 36.

54. Cames, *Byzance et la peinture romane,* 270–84; Cames, *Allégories et symboles,* 134–37. For a description of the fragments, see Zinke and Karasch, eds., *Verb-*

orgene Pracht, no. 6, 50. Greater detail is provided in Scheller, *Exemplum*, no. 8, 137–43. Scheller comments that "nowadays the relationship between the *Hortus deliciarum* and these drawings is treated with greater reserve." Scheller, 140. For more general cautions concerning the presumption of a model book, what he calls the "lost model hypothesis," see Scheller, 27. Whatever its origins, the Freiburg fragment does appear to derive from the same spiritual context as the *Hortus*, as the hymn to St. Nicholas on folio 1b recto and a Marian sequence attributed to Adam of St. Victor suggest.

55. Green writes that the artist "may not even have been conscious of the origins of much of his artistic vocabulary. A trained illuminator learned modes of expression, standard forms, a whole repertory of types, actions, and gestures, and could transform them at will to the needs of various subjects." *HD* 34.

56. Gregory of Tours, *Historia Francorum*, II, 17; trans. Thorpe, 131–32. Kitzinger makes a strong case for the influence of the patron, rather than the artist, in the shaping of a project. He writes: "One must be willing to admit, as seems indeed obvious, that a patron may not only prescribe the subject content of a work of art but may also choose the artists who are to be employed, the medium they are to use, and the models they are to follow." Kitzinger, "The Gregorian Reform and the Visual Arts," 100. For Christine de Pisan's influence in the illustration of her works, see Hindman, *Christine de Pizan's "Epistre Othéa,"* 61–99. Hindman concludes that Christine studied manuscript models, chose images, and directed the work of the illuminators of the *Epistre Othéa*. Moreover, she writes that "evidence concerning manuscript production in Paris suggests that this sort of involvement on the part of the author may have been common" (98).

57. *HD* Cat. No. 14. The image is Munich, Bayerische Staatsbibliothek, MS Clm 13002, fol. 7v. See Saxl, "Macrocosm and Microcosm"; Gillen, 66; and Cames, *Allégories et symboles*, 11–12.

58. See Chapter 5 for a detailed discussion of this image.

59. The list of novel compositions is longer still; see Green, *HD* 35–36.

60. Caviness, "Artist: 'To See, Hear, and Know All at Once'," 124.

61. Caviness, "Artist," 110. See also Caviness, "Hildegard as Designer." Concerning the invisibility of women artists, see Nochlin, "Why Have There Been No Great Women Artists?"; and the more recent discussion of Alford and Stadler, "A Discussion of Linda Nochlin's Essay."

62. Caviness, "Gender Symbolism and Text Image Relationships," 77.

63. This conclusion is not widely accepted. Newman has questioned the idea that Hildegard was the artist of the *Scivias*, arguing "if it were true both Hildegard and her biographers would surely have mentioned such a notable achievement." Newman, "Introduction," 25. Newman suggests instead that the artist was "possibly one of Hildegard's nuns." Newman, *Sister*, 18. Both Saurma-Jeltsch and Suzuki assume that Hildegard employed professional artists: Saurma-Jeltsch, *Die Miniaturen im "Liber Scivias,"* 6; Suzuki, *Bildgewordene Visionen*, 270–76. For reviews of Saurma-Jeltsch and Suzuki, see Caviness, "Hildegard of Bingen: Some Recent Books" and Niehr, "Rezension."

64. De Bastard observes "aux peintures comme à l'écriture, au moins trois mains différentes." Cited by Green, *HD* 31, who is "inclined" to see three hands

in the miniatures as well. Evans notes that "three hands" in the script may simply mean three types of script. Evans, *HD* 2.

65. This is a possibility on which de Bastard does not comment, although it was not uncommon, particularly in the early Middle Ages, for the scribe and the illuminator to be the same person. Pächt, *Book Illumination*, 176; Alexander, *Medieval Illuminators*, 6–16; and Nees, "On Carolingian Book Painters." For the overlap of scribe and artist in the twelfth century, see Alexander, "Scribes as Artists."

66. Female scribes were active at Admont, Schäftlarn, Wessobrunn, Schwartzenthann, Obermünster, Niedermünster, Wittewerun, Zwiefalten, and Lippoldsberg in the twelfth century, and at countless other female communities as well. See Beach, *Women as Scribes* for: Wittewerun (118), Wessobrunn (32–64), Admont (65–103), and Schäftlarn (104–27). For Zwiefalten, see n. 91; for Schwartzenthann, see Griffiths, "Brides and *Dominae*"; for Lamspringe, see Wolter-Von Dem Knesebeck, "Lamspringe," 469; and for Niedermünster, see Wattenbach, *Schriftwesen im Mittelalter*, 445–46. For the activity of female scribes in the early Middle Ages, see Bischoff, "Die Kölner Nonnenhandschriften"; McKitterick, "Nuns' Scriptoria"; Bishop, "The Scribes of the Corbie *a–b*"; Bodarwé, *Sanctimoniales litteratae*, 87–195; Wemple, *Women in Frankish Society*, 179–81; and Heinrich, 148–52, 190–92. The activity of female scribes demonstrates that writing was not a gendered activity, as scholars in the past have so often assumed. According to McKitterick, "writing in the early middle ages was not the exclusive concern either of monks or of male scribes and . . . the copying of books was one of the accepted occupations of at least some of the communities of women dedicated to the religious life." McKitterick, "Women and Literacy," 3.

67. For a list of books copied by Diemut, see Beach, *Women as Scribes*, 40–42.

68. *CGS*, p. 10.

69. Weis, "Le premier cahier du codex," 55, 56.

70. On the possibilities for collaboration between religious men and women within the scriptorium, see Beach, "Claustration and Collaboration," especially 71–72. Cooperation between a male and a female house for the purpose of book production was not unknown; for discussion of an earlier example, see Bodarwé, "Kontakte zweier Konvente."

71. "Adjuvantibus et consulentibus venerandis sororibus Trutwib et Gisela." *CGS*, p. 10.

72. Green, *HD* 29. In some cases, Green notes that the writing impinged on the physical space of the miniature as, for instance, on folio 60r, where Holofernes's bed was left apparently unfinished in order to allow for the texts that were to be inscribed above his head (*HD* Cat. No. 86). Green concludes: "once again the implication is that drawing or composing came first, that the scribe then wrote in the inscriptions and texts, and that the final step was the careful painting in rich, firm colour around the writing."

73. Green writes: "in my opinion the pictures most often were painted on conjugate leaves around or between which text pages were placed." *HD* 30. For an examination of the technical aspects of manuscript illumination, see Alexander,

Medieval Illuminators, 35–51; and, for cooperation between scribes and artists in the production of illuminated Bibles, see Cahn, *Romanesque Bible Illumination*, 234–42.

74. British Library Add. MS 42497. This strip seems to have served a liturgical purpose at Hohenbourg, protecting the Host from insects during the celebration of the divine office. It is comprised of two pieces of vellum, which were sewn together in order to create a single long strip, which may originally have measured some 1.4 meters in length; a section to the far right of the *recto* is now missing. The strip is divided into seventeen sections on each side, and for every two sections a single scene in the life of John the Baptist is depicted in rich illumination; additional panels may have been lost. In addition to these illuminations, a single line of text runs along the top of the strip, describing in leonine verse the subject of each image. See Millar, "Miniatures of the Life of St John the Baptist"; Millar, "The Inscription on the St John the Baptist Roll"; Walter, "Aurait-on découvert des fragments de l'*Hortus deliciarum*?"; and Green, "The Flabellum of Hohenbourg."

75. Green, *HD* 31.

76. Brown, *HD* 83. Brown's paleographical examination of the *Hortus* was limited to the legends with the Prophets since, in his opinion, copies of these "undoubtedly convey the best impression of the original script." *HD* 81.

77. For the history of one itinerant artist, see Nordenfalk, "A Travelling Milanese Artist." Concerning the activities of itinerant artists in general, see Demus, *Romanesque Mural Painting*, 152 n. 25; and for modes of artistic transmission, see Scheller, 27–28. It is possible that the Freiburg fragments formed part of a collection of models compiled by an itinerant draughtsman who gathered images as he traveled. Demus argues for the use of a model book in the composition of the *Hortus*, pointing to the depiction of Christ in Gethsemane as proof. In this image, Christ appears to address the sleeping disciples, while Peter, shown on the far side of the group, listens attentively, but faces away from him (fol. 138r). Demus argues that Christ has been misplaced in this image, which he suggests came from a model book that did not originally include the stock figure of a standing Christ. The artist copied the model and added Christ—only on the wrong side of the composition. Demus, *The Mosaics of Norman Sicily*, 447; and Demus, *Byzantine Art*, 40–43. See Green's review of the debate: *HD* Cat. No. 192.

78. Although the *Hortus* images are superior to those of the *Guta-Sintram Codex*, according to Joseph Walter, those of the Marbach *Annals* (Jena Universitätsbibliothek, MS Bose q. 6) are not so dissimilar. For discussion, see Walter, "Les miniatures," 39–40. In his view, the *Hortus*, the Marbach *Annals*, and the Evangeliary of Marbach-Schwarzenthann "form a group," although he does not go so far as to suggest that they were the product of a shared workshop. Walter, "L'Évangéliaire de Marbach-Schwarzenthann," 4–5. Elsewhere, Walter points out similarities between the *Hortus* images and the iconographic program of the Strasbourg cathedral; Walter, "Les deux roses."

79. Bayerische Hauptstaatsarchiv, Klosterliteralien Regensburg-Obermünster 1. The manuscript is discussed in Boeckler, *Die Regensburg-Prüfeninger Buch-*

malerei, 54–59; the necrology is *Necrologium monasterii superioris Ratisbonensis*, ed. Baumann, MGH Necr. 3, 334–349.

80. These two figures were discussed by Suckale, "The Canonesses of Regensburg-Obermuenster and the New Marian Piety."

81. This is a conclusion that Graf shares, based on her study of Herrad's prologue and the Hohenbourg scene at the end of the *Hortus*. Graf, 73.

82. The sorts of communication between patron and artist that Alexander notes could not have accounted for the interdependence of text and image that characterizes the *Hortus*. Alexander, *Medieval Illuminators*, 52–71. Nor is there any record of marginal instruction that may reflect Herrad's directions for the *Hortus* artists.

83. As Caviness observes in her discussion of Hildegard's artistry, "if it is to be argued that Hildegard had nothing to do with the pictures in the Rupertsberg *Scivias*, some tangible alternative has to be suggested, with a workplace, intellectual context, and other extant productions, and not some phantom atelier." "Hildegard of Bingen: Some Recent Books," 120.

84. Cited in Beach, *Women as Scribes*, 129 n. 4.

85. Seeberg, *Die Illustrationen im Admonter Nonnenbrevier*, 3–4, 18–19, 161–62.

86. He writes that the Sélestat *liber precum* (Bibliothèque Humaniste, MS 104) may have been written and illustrated by women. Hamburger, *Visual*, 190.

87. Concerning medieval women's artistic production, see Carr, "Women as Artists in the Middle Ages," and, for book art in particular, 7–13.

88. *Necrologium Zwifaltense*; ed. Baumann, MGH Necr. 1, 258, no. 22.

89. See Chapter 2, n. 109, and the discussion in Mews, "Monastic Educational Culture Revisited."

90. Württembergischen Landesbibliothek Stuttgart, Cod. Hist. 2° 415, fol. 87r. Often referred to as a choirbook, this manuscript is comprised primarily of a richly illustrated martyrology. Concerning the manuscript, see Haefeli-Sonin, *Auftraggeber und Entwurfskonzept*. The Zwiefalten Leviathan and the *Hortus* depiction both rely on sections from Honorius's *Speculum ecclesiae*. Gillen, 67.

91. *Necrologium Zwifaltense*; ed. Baumann, MGH Necr. 1, 244, no. 4 (for Matilda) and 253 no. 28 (for Albert).

92. I am grateful to Rod Thomson for notifying me of this connection.

93. Depictions of medieval women engaged in book production are discussed in Graf; and Smith, "*Scriba, Femina*: Medieval Depictions of Women Writing." Green comments that the depiction of *Rethorica* in the *Hortus* is "unprecedented." *HD* Cat. No. 33. The *Philosophia* image is discussed at length in Chapter 5.

Chapter 5. The Tree of Knowledge

1. Isidore, *Etymologies* XIV, 3, 2; ed. Lindsay (no page numbers). See, in general, Delumeau, *History of Paradise*.

2. "D. Quid est paradisus vel ubi? M. Locus amenissimus in oriente, in quo

arbores diversi generis contra varios defectos erant consite **geimpft** verbi gratia, ut, si homo congruo tempore de uno comederet, numquam amplius esuriret, congruo tempore de alio et nunquam sitiret de alio et nunquam lassaretur, ad ultimum ligno vite uteretur et amplius non senesceret, nunquam infirmaretur, nunquam moreretur." *HD* no. 76; cf. Honorius, *Elucidarium*, I, 69; ed. Lefèvre, 373.

3. Honorius writes: "Sunt ergo quatuor paradisi, scilicet paradisus voluptatis, terrestris; paradisus exsultationis, coelestis; paradisus religionis, Ecclesiarum; paradisus virtutis, animarum." *Expositio in Cantica canticorum*, II, 4; PL 172, 428. Although not all gardens were to be read as a paradise—past or future—such a reading was favored by medieval exegetes. Comito, *The Idea of the Garden in the Renaissance*, 25–50; Rhodes and Davidson, "The Garden of Paradise"; and Meyvaert, "The Medieval Monastic Garden," 47–53. On the conflation of the earthly paradise with the heavenly one in medieval thought, see Delumeau, 29.

4. Even so, the *hortus conclusus* is mentioned explicitly only twice in Herrad's text. It represents both the *domicilium virginitatis* and the Virgin Mary. *HD* nos. 314 and 769.

5. Meyvaert, "Garden"; Comito, *The Idea of the Garden*, 41–50; and Pinder, "The Cloister and the Garden." On cloisters and claustral imagery, see the essays published in *Gesta* 12 (1973) and Klein, ed., *Der mittelalterliche Kreuzgang*.

6. In sections that Herrad incorporated into the *Hortus*, Honorius repeatedly depicts the faithful as flowers; *Speculum ecclesiae*, PL 172, 1018 (*HD* no. 241); PL 172, 836 (*HD* no. 352); and *Elucidarium*, III, 81; ed. Lefèvre, 464 (*HD* no. 887).

7. On virginity (and the female monastery) as an enclosed garden, see Bugge, *Virginitas*, especially 59–67.

8. Trans. Matter, *The Voice of My Beloved*, xxv.

9. "Quis vero est ortus voluptatis nisi virgo domicilium virginitatis? De hac dicitur: Ortus conclusus, florenti cespite vernans. Ortus equidem conclusus vallo **graben** pudicitie, non timens lubricum lapsum serpentis. Ortus, inquam, conclusus, nullo assultu **elingunge** virilis luxurie violatus. Fons vero de orto procedens Christus est de virginis palacio nascens." *HD* no. 314, from "a certain doctor."

10. Rupert of Deutz, *Commentaria in Canticum canticorum*; ed. Haacke, CCCM 26. On Rupert's commentary, see van Engen, 291–98; Matter, 159–63; Astell, *The Song of Songs*, 61–71; and Fulton, 292–95.

11. "Hortus deliciarum nobis est sacratissimus tuus uterus, o Maria; quia ex eo multiplices gaudii flores colligimus." *Ad beatam virginem Deiparam. sermo panegyricus*; PL 184, 1011.

12. For negative interpretations of enclosure, see, among others, Schulenburg, "Strict Active Enclosure"; and Schulenburg, "Gender, Celibacy, and Proscriptions of Sacred Space." On enclosure in general, see Makowski, *Canon Law and Cloistered Women*; Brundage and Makowski, "Enclosure of Nuns"; Johnson, "The Cloistering of Medieval Nuns"; Johnson, "La théorie de la clôture"; Hochstetler, "The Meaning of Monastic Cloister"; Horner, *The Discourse of Enclosure*; Simmons, "The Abbey Church at Fontevraud"; and Uffmann, "Inside and Outside the Convent Walls." Ferrante argues that the cloister was depicted most often as a haven for women and a prison for men in medieval literature: Ferrante, "Im-

ages of the Cloister." For positive connotations of the wall, see Meyvaert, "The Medieval Monastic Claustrum." Book two of the *Speculum virginum*, dedicated to the explanation, defense, and encouragement of enclosure, warns its female audience that "cloistered virgins should keep the matter of sin away from their five senses." *SV, epistula*, 70–71; ed. Seyfarth, CCCM 5, 3; trans. Newman, 270. However, Pinder argues that the enclosure (and the exclusion of external distractions that it implied) emphasized by the *Speculum* author was "not merely negative" since "the virgin's enclosed space is the place in which the kiss of the Bridegroom can be received." Pinder, 167.

13. The gate and the seraph who guarded the way to the tree of life with a flaming sword are depicted on folio 19r of the *Hortus*. A section from the *Elucidarium* explains that, after the introduction of sin, paradise was encircled by a wall of fire (*igneus murus*). *HD* no. 76.

14. Comito, 34.

15. Comito writes that "the notion that the cloistered life is a 'provisional paradise' is the very basis of monastic culture." Comito, 41. See also Leclercq, "Le cloître est-il un paradis?"

16. "Porro claustrum praesefert paradisum, monasterium vero Eden securiorem locum paradisi. Fons in hoc loco voluptatis, est in monasterio fons baptismatis; lignum vitae in paradiso est corpus Domini in monasterio. Diversae arbores fructiferae sunt diversi libri sacrae Scripturae. Secretum enim claustri gerit figuram coeli. In quo justi ita a peccatoribus segregantur, sicut religiosae vitae professores a saecularibus in claustro sequestrantur. Porro monasteria praefert coelestem paradisum." Honorius Augustodunensis, *Gemma anima* I, 149; PL 172, 590; Cf. *HD* no. 789. In his *De vita claustrali*, Honorius listed ten separate symbols for the cloister, among them a port, an arbour, a couch, a prison cell, and paradise. PL 172, 1247–48.

17. Hugh of Fouilloy, *De claustro animae*, 29; PL 176, 1167. Whitehead discusses Hugh's allegory of the cloister of the soul and its influence on later medieval devotional writers in, "Making a Cloister of the Soul."

18. Writing in the sixth century, Cassiodorus cautioned against conflating the monastery with the true heavenly paradise, warning that the delights provided by the beauty of the monastery "are temporal and passing, and not to be confused with the future joys yearned for by faithful believers in Christ." Cassiodorus, *Institutiones*, I, 29; ed. Mynors, 73; trans. in Meyvaert, "Garden," 28.

19. An inscription to this image reminds the reader: "Jheronimus refert quod Adam sepultus fuerit in Calvarie loco ubi crucifixus est Dominus." *HD* Cat. No. 212.

20. The inscription reads: "Eva per crucem redempta crucem adorat." *HD* Cat No. 334.

21. Ladner characterizes the relationship between the tree of knowledge and the Cross as "half-antithetical and half-causative." Ladner, "Vegetation Symbolism," 313. Honorius writes, "Arbor crucis est lignum vitae in paradiso." *Expositio in Psalmos selectos*, PL 172, 277. For a general discussion of the cosmological tree, see Greenhill, "The Child in the Tree," 329–38 and for the sacred tree in Honorius's thought, see Dietrich, *Eruditio Sacra*, 68–83.

22. On the tree of life, see Bauerreiss, *Arbor vitae.*

23. Cf. Ezekiel 47:12, where Ezekiel associates rivers and trees with the restoration of the temple, and specifically connects the trees with healing.

24. On the symbolism of the tree in renaissance thought, see Ladner, "Vegetation Symbolism" and, on the symbolism of the tree more generally, Stauch, "Baum in der christlichen Symbolik."

25. Guerric of Igny, *Sermo ad excitandam devotionem in psalmodia*; eds. Morson and Costello, 518–19; trans. in Meyvaert, "Garden," 38.

26. The significance of the cosmological tree in Jewish legends as linking heaven and earth may have inspired the author of the fourth-century poem, *De Pascha.* Here, the tree appears as a ladder to heaven, through which souls can climb to paradise. Greenhill, 338–40. Caesarius of Arles adopted this idea, identifying Jacob's ladder with the cross. *Sermo* 87; ed. Morin, CCSL 103, 358–59.

27. For discussion of the psychomachia cycle and the Ladder of Virtues, see Chapter 7.

28. Constable highlights the centrality of the idea of a return to Eden to the reform ideology of the twelfth century. Constable, "Renewal and Reform in Religious Life," 48.

29. This poem, *Rithmus de eo quod Adam de vetito pomo comedit* (*HD* no. 69), has much in common with *De primo homine* (*HD* no. 374) which has been attributed to Herrad although she did not claim authorship for it. Many of the images in this poem are common to both, for instance the description of the devil, *vultu cum terribili* (*HD* no. 69) and *visu est horribilis* (*HD* no. 374), his generation of pain and suffering, he is *necis pater* (*HD* no. 69) and *poenae pater* (*HD* no. 374), the tears of the condemned, *nunc fletus subeunt* (*HD* no. 69) and *ibi fletus luminum* (*HD* no. 374), and the promise of God's forgiveness and of celestial rest. The juxtaposition of sin and grace, death and life, the devil and God, hell and heaven, is one that is common in Herrad's writing as well as in the presentation of her images. However, Autenrieth argues that this poem was most probably not by Herrad; she includes it among those poems that she identifies as "more artistic" (*kunstvoller*) than those that she attributes to Herrad. Autenrieth, 309 and no. 15.

30. Audi me mulier, quae dicam facito:
De fructu comede tibi prohibito,
Sic eris ut dominus, non hoc ambigito. (*HD* no. 69)

31. Cuncta nosces,
Quicquid posces
Fiet in coelestibus. (*HD* no. 69)

32. According to some interpretations, the tree of the knowledge of good and evil connoted sexual knowledge; the sin of the Fall was thus explicitly associated with human sexuality. Bugge, 5–29.

33. In fact, Herrad's description of her sources as "scriptural" did not necessarily mean that they were also biblical. As Hugh of St. Victor noted, "sacred scriptures" (here as *divina eloquia*) might include "works which holy and wise men have written at various times and which, although they are not approved by the authority of the universal church, nevertheless pass for Sacred Scriptures." *Didascalicon*, IV, 1; ed. Buttimer, 70–71; trans. Taylor, 102–3. Similarly, in Hilde-

gard's vision of "The Pillar of the Word of God" the pillar is triangular, its three sides representing the Old Testament, the New Testament, and the "exposition of the faithful doctors." *Scivias* III, 4, 5; eds. Führkötter and Carlevaris, CCCM 43A, 394; trans. Hart and Bishop, 359.

34. Hildegard did ultimately claim to have understood works of philosophy, a fact that is discussed in n. 58.

35. "Incipit Ortus deliciarum, in quo collectis floribus scripturarum assidue jocundetur turmula adolescentularum." *HD* no. 3.

36. Marenbon and McKitterick list important texts for the early medieval study of philosophy in Marenbon and McKitterick, "Philosophy and its Background," 99. None of the works that they cite appear in the *Hortus*, nor do important twelfth-century philosophers—Abelard, Gilbert of Poitiers, William of Conches, and Thierry of Chartres—figure in the manuscript. Of these four, Abelard and Gilbert of Poitiers were known at Marbach in the twelfth century. Concerning philosophy during the twelfth century, with a focus on Abelard and Gilbert, see Marenbon, "The Twelfth Century."

37. Evans, *Philosophy and Theology*, 3–16.

38. Jerome, *Epist.* 22, 29–30; ed. Hilberg, CSEL 54, 190.

39. Morrison, "Incentives for Studying the Liberal Arts," 42.

40. Augustine, *De doctrina Christiana*, II, XL, 60; ed. and trans. Green, 124–25. Herrad cites Augustine's Egyptian gold metaphor as a justification for secular literature through an excerpt from Honorius's *Speculum ecclesiae*: "non solum sacri apices ad vitam eternam nos ducunt, sed et gentilium littere nos instruunt, de quibus quedam ad edificationem proferenda sunt. Et ut nemo inde scandalizetur, sacra auctoritate exemplificetur. Filii quippe Israhel Egyptios despoliaverunt, aurum et argentum, gemmas et vestes preciosas tulerunt." *HD* no. 739.

41. Jerome, *Epist.* 70.2; ed. Hilberg, CSEL 54, 702. On the gender dynamics at work here, see Dinshaw's discussion in *Chaucer's Sexual Poetics*, 22–25.

42. Augustine, *De doctrina Christiana*, II, XLII, 63; ed. and trans. Green, 128–29.

43. Endres, "Die Dialektiker und ihre Gegner." Endres's model of an eleventh-century conflict between "dialecticians" and "anti-dialecticians" has been challenged in recent years. Resnick, "Attitudes Towards Philosophy"; and Holopainen, *Dialectic and Theology*.

44. Manegold makes a similar argument: *Liber contra Wolfelmum*, 10; ed. Hartmann, 63–65; trans. Ziomkowski, 45–46. Concerning Otloh's attitude toward secular learning, see Resnick, "*Scientia liberalis*, Dialectics, and Otloh of St. Emmeram" and "*Litterati, Spirituales*, and the Lay Christian According to Otloh of St. Emmeram"; and Evans, "*Studium discendi*: Otloh of St. Emmeram and the Seven Liberal Arts."

45. See Colossians 2:8, where Paul warns against the deceitfulness of philosophy. For criticisms of dialectic, see Resnick, "*Scientia liberalis*," 248–52 and, on dialectic in general, Stump, "Dialectic." In his condemnation of the antipapal writings of Wenrich, master of the cathedral school of Trier, Manegold focused on Wenrich's use of rhetoric, which he argued was intended to deceive his audience. For discussion, see Robinson, "The *colores rhetorici*," 222–24.

46. Robinson notes that in Manegold's hands, *philosophi* could denote equally the ancient philosophers as well as contemporary adherents to the imperial party. Robinson, "The Bible in the Investiture Contest," 76–77.

47. Like Peter Damian, Manegold and Otloh were men of learning, whose vivid condemnations of secular learning were expressed in the sort of erudite language that belies their opposition to secular studies. Evans has demonstrated Otloh's deep training in the liberal arts and his unwillingness to reject them outright, while Peter Damian's learning is evident in his every sentence. On Otloh, see Evans, "*Studium discendi*"; for Peter Damian, see Morrison, "Incentives," 34. Morrison comments, "paradoxically, his text exemplifies the very arts that Damian's teaching urged his hearers to avoid: grammar, rhetoric (including poetry), and philosophy." The same is true of Manegold; Robinson notes that "Manegold devoted considerable rhetorical skill (citing Sallust, Lucan, Horace's *Ars poetica* and Boethius's *De institutione arithmetica*, and using hyperbole and various types of paronomasia) to proving himself 'uncultivated in intellect, halting in speech, rustic in diction'." Robinson, "The *colores rhetorici*," 222.

48. Peter Damian, *Dominus vobiscum*, PL 145, 232–33; trans. in Blum, *St. Peter Damian*, 132. Similarly, Bernard of Clairvaux dismissed Plato as well as Aristotle as inappropriate to the monastic education: "What therefore did the holy apostles teach us, and indeed do they teach us? Not the art of fishing, or the making of tents, or anything of this sort: not to read Plato, not to turn Aristotle's subtleties inside out, not always to learn, and never to arrive at the knowledge of truth. They taught me to live." *In sollemnitate apostolorum Petri et Pauli*, 1, 3; *SBOp* V, 189–90.

49. Manegold, *Liber contra Wolfelmum*, 8; ed. Hartmann, 61; trans. Ziomkowski, 44. However, he was careful to note that "we do not in the least consider all the teachings of the philosophers to be damnable." *Liber contra Wolfelmum*, 1; ed. Hartmann, 44; trans. Ziomkowski, 37. Manegold warned that God did not call "the lovers of everlasting life to the study of worldly philosophy which requires one to expend almost the whole of one's attention on things that perish." *Liber contra Wolfelmum*, 20; ed. Hartmann, 89; trans. Ziomkowski, 59.

50. For a discussion of the term "philosophy," see Curtius, "Zur Geschichte des Wortes Philosophie." See the cautionary approach to philosophy of John of Salisbury; *Policraticus* VII, 1–2; ed. Webb, II, 93–99. See also Jeauneau, "Jean de Salisbury et la lecture des philosophes."

51. Ambrose, *De virginitate*, 92; ed. Gori, 72–73; trans. Callam, 46.

52. For the conflict between Bernard and Abelard, see Mews, "The Council of Sens"; Marenbon, *The Philosophy of Peter Abelard*, 26–32; and Clanchy, *Abelard*, 35–38, 215–19. For Bernard's attitudes toward the schools, see Ferruolo, 54–66 and for his attack on Gilbert, see John of Salisbury, *Historia pontificalis*, 8–13; ed. and trans. Chibnall, 15–28.

53. *Metamorphosis Goliae*, 55; ed. Huygens, 771; trans. Jaeger, 238.

54. Bernard, Epist. 106; *SBOp*, VII, 266–67. The superiority of knowledge that could be gained within the cloister to that of the schools was stressed in letters of vocation; see Leclercq, "Lettres de vocation."

55. Conrad of Hirsau, *Dialogus super auctores*, ed. Huygens, 112; trans. Min-

nis and Scott, 54. Elsewhere in the *Dialogue*, Conrad presents Paul and certain Patristic authors as learned in secular literature: ed. Huygens, 116–17; trans. Minnis and Scott, 59.

56. For the argument that the subordination of the arts to theology was characteristic of the eleventh century, see Gibson, "The *Artes* in the Eleventh Century."

57. Chenu, *Nature, Man and Society*, 304.

58. In her prologue to the *Scivias*, Hildegard writes that through her visionary experience she came to understand the Scriptures "namely the Psalter, the Gospel and the other catholic volumes of both the Old and the New Testaments." *Scivias*, Protestificatio; CCCM 43, ed. Führkötter and Carlevaris, 4; trans. Hart and Bishop, 59. Some thirty years later, she admitted that she also understood works of philosophy. *Vita sanctae Hildegardis*, II, 2; ed. Klaes, CCCM 126, 24; trans. Silvas, 160.

59. Abelard, *Epist.* 8; ed. McLaughlin, 253; trans. Radice and Clanchy, 146. Concerning Abelard's approach to philosophy, see McLaughlin, "Abelard's Conception of the Liberal Arts and Philosophy"; Luscombe, "Peter Abelard," 298–305; Luscombe, "Peter Abelard and the Poets"; and Jolivet, "Doctrines et figures."

60. Abelard, *Epist.* 17, *Fidei confessio*; PL 178, 375; trans. Radice and Clanchy, 211.

61. *De decem plagis Aegypti*; PL 172, 267. Elsewhere Honorius wrote that "the philosophers were the fathers of heretics" (*Philosophi erant patriarchae haereticorum*), following the precedent established by Tertullian of identifying philosophy as the source of heresy. *De haereticis paganorum*; PL 172, 235. However, importantly for Herrad's own approach to study, Honorius's condemnation of philosophy was not total, but was directed specifically against worldly wisdom, which he likened to the Egyptian water. According to this view, philosophers are like the fish who swam in the Egyptian water and were killed when it was changed into blood, which Honorius interprets as sin. Elsewhere, he allowed a more generous reading of philosophy, describing the exile of man as ignorance, wisdom as the *patria*, and the liberal arts as man's guide on his homeward journey. *De animae exsilio et patria*; PL 172, 1241–46. See Crouse, "Honorius Augustodunensis: The Arts as *Via ad Patriam*." Honorius writes: "De hoc exsilio ad patriam via est scientia," but nowhere in this text does he associate "scientia" with "Philosophia." PL 172, 1243.

62. For discussions of the representation of Philosophy and the liberal arts, see Bolton, "Illustrations in Manuscripts of Boethius' Works"; Courcelle, *La Consolation de philosophie*, 77–81. On the liberal arts in particular, see Katzenellenbogen, "The Representation of the Seven Liberal Arts"; Verdier, "L'iconographie des arts libéraux"; and Evans, "Allegorical Women and Practical Men." For *Philosophia* or Wisdom, see Adolf, "The Figure of Wisdom"; and Hamburger, *St. John the Divine*, 95–164. On *rotae*, see Evans, "The Geometry of the Mind," 42–43.

63. See Chapter 4 n. 93.

64. "Philosophi sapientes mundi et gentium clerici fuerunt." *HD* Cat. No. 33. The presence of Socrates and Plato in the image derives from Boethius's *Conso-

lation of Philosophy, where *Philosophia* refers to "my dear Plato" and states that she stood side by side with Socrates as he "triumphed over an unjust death." *The Consolation of Philosophy,* I, 3; ed. Bieler, CCSL 94, 5; trans. Walsh, 7.

65. The inscription beneath the *rota* describes these figures as "poete vel magi; spiritu immundo instincti." A further inscription links the inspiration of unclean spirits with the composition of magic and poetry as well as *fabulosa commenta*: "Isti immundis spiritibus inspirati scribunt artem magicam et poetriam id est fabulosa commenta." *HD* Cat. No. 33.

66. "Postquam Dominus dispersit gentes super faciem cunctarum regionum, quidam in philosophia studuerunt, qui vocati sunt philosophi, id est amatores sapientie, quidam ratione cecati et immundis spiritibus inspirati scripserunt artem magicam et insuper poetriam . . . ; et ita in cogitationibus suis evanescentes Deum creatorem reliquerunt et creaturam, scilicet solem, lunam, stellas, arbores, aquam, ignem, homines etcetera adorantes coluerunt." *HD* no. 124. This idea appears also in the titulus to *HD* no. 115: "De philosophia et de septem liberalibus artibus in quibus quidam post diluvium philosophabantur; post diluvium enim quidam in philosophia, quidam racione cecati in poetria et in arte magica studuerunt." For a survey of twelfth-century opposition to poetry, see Luscombe, "Peter Abelard and the Poets." Abelard could not relinquish the poets entirely, citing Ovid, who wrote that "it is permissible to be taught by the enemy." Cited in Luscombe, "Peter Abelard and the Poets," 168. For negative attitudes toward poetry within twelfth-century monasticism, see Conrad of Hirsau: "the poet (*poeta*) is called a maker, or one who gives shape to things, because he says what is false instead of the truth, or else sometimes intermingles truth with falsehood." *Dialogus,* ed. Huygens, 75; trans. Minnis and Scott, 43.

67. The link between philosophy and idolatry is made clear in Manegold's *Liber contra Wolfelmum,* 9; ed. Hartmann, 61–63; trans. Ziomkowski, 44–45. Manegold describes the poets and ancient philosophers, misled by the machinations of the devil, as "jesters at the wedding of idolatry."

68. For the argument that the *Philosophia* image represents a digression, see Green, *HD* 28; and Evans, *HD* 2.

69. See Newman's discussion of "Sapientia: The Goddess Incarnate," in *God and the Goddesses,* 190–244 and Newman, *Sister,* 42–89.

70. The Christological interpretation of Divine Wisdom was linked to exegesis of John 1:1 and I Corinthians 1:24. Herrad teaches the identification of Christ with Wisdom in her glosses to *HD* no. 13, where she glosses "Sapientia" as "id est Filius" and "sapientie subsistentis" as "id est Filii."

71. Concerning the personification of Philosophy in Boethius's *Consolation of Philosophy* and the problems suggested by her pagan inspiration, see Marenbon, *Boethius,* 154–59.

72. The Royal Portal at Chartres Cathedral (c. 1145–1155) is thought to have been the first façade on which the liberal arts were depicted. Later depictions include Déols (c. 1160), Laon (late twelfth century), Sens (c. 1200), and Notre Dame of Paris (thirteenth century). See Katzenellenbogen, "Representation"; and Newman, *God,* 205. For a discussion of Mary as *sedes sapientiae,* see Forsyth, *Throne of*

Wisdom. For Mary's connection to the liberal arts, see Stolz, "Maria und die Artes liberales."

73. Katzenellenbogen, "Representation," 51.

74. "Septem fontes sapientie fluunt de philosophia qui dicuntur liberales artes." *HD* Cat. No. 33.

75. "Spiritus sanctus inventor est septem liberalium artium que sunt grammatica, rethorica, dialetica, musica, arithmetica, geometria, astronomia." *HD* Cat. No. 33. The connection between the Holy Spirit and the liberal arts appears indirectly in medieval exegesis. In texts included in the *Hortus*, both Honorius Augustodunensis and Rupert of Deutz interpreted the seven pillars of Wisdom as the seven gifts of the Holy Spirit. (Honorius, *HD* nos. 602, 789; Rupert, *HD* no. 614). Rupert also presented knowledge as a gift of the Holy Spirit in his *De sancta Trinitate*, VII, 4; ed. Haacke, CCCM 24, 2042.

76. Boethius, *Consolation*, I, 1; ed. Bieler, CCSL 94, 2; trans. Walsh, 4.

77. For the association between Wisdom's seven columns and the liberal arts, see Alcuin, *Grammatica;* PL 101, 853; and Cassiodorus, *Institutiones* II, *Praef,* 2; ed. Mynors, 89. See also d'Alverny, "La Sagesse et ses sept filles."

78. This idea derives from Ecclesiasticus 1:1, "Omnis Sapientia a Deo Domino est et cum illo fuit semper et est ante aevum." The same idea appears in Hugh of St. Victor's *Didascalicon*, VI, 9; ed. Buttimer, 126; trans. Taylor, 147.

79. *HD* Cat. No. 33. Boethius attributes the idea to Plato: *Consolation*, IV, 2; ed. Bieler CCSL 94, 69; trans. Walsh, 77.

80. Cf. *HD* nos. 115 and 116 (where the order—*ethica, logica, phisica*—is inverted). Isidore presented a threefold division of *Philosophia* (*Differentiae*, II, 39, 149; PL 83, 93), Boethius a twofold division, and Hugh of St. Victor a fourfold division. Philosophy is shown with the "family tree of knowledge" emerging from her head in an eleventh-century Regensburg manuscript (Munich, Bayerische Staatsbibliothek, MS Clm 14516). For a similar depiction (in a manuscript in Leipzig), see Courcelle, 80, pl. 27.

81. "Arte regens dia que sunt ego Philosophia subjectas artes in septem divido partes." *HD* Cat. No. 33.

82. Hec exercicia   que mundi Philosophia
    Investigavit   investigata notavit
    Scripto firmavit   et alumnis insinuavit.
    Septem per studia   docet artes philosophia
    Hec elementorum   scrutatur et abdita rerum. (*HD* Cat. No. 33)
Part of this text is duplicated in *HD* no. 122.

83. The connection between the bronze bowl and the *Hortus* is discussed in Wormstall, "Eine romanische Bronzeschüssel," 247–49. My description of the bowl is taken from Weitzmann-Fiedler, *Romanische gravierte Bronzeschalen*, no. 28.

84. Although the medieval tendency was to depict the liberal arts on a ladder—as in Boethius's description of *Philosophia*, where the ladder led from the less to the more difficult subjects, and logically also from the material to the spiritual—Herrad eschewed this standard representation, as well as the Π and Θ signifying the practical and the theoretical, the two divisions of philosophy, that were typi-

cally shown on *Philosophia*'s sleeves. Her decision not to depict the arts on a ladder may have been due to her desire to differentiate between Christian and non-Christian knowledge, which the *rota* allowed her to do more easily than the ladder, which emphasized ascent within the arts, rather than distinctions between Divine and mundane wisdom.

85. *HD* Cat. No. 33.

86. Weitzmann-Fiedler, 11. For a revision of this thesis, see Cohen and Safran, "Learning from Medieval Bronze Bowls."

87. Ettlinger notes that, despite similarities between the *Hortus Philosophia* and the bronze bowl, "Herrad's diagram is clearer and its Christian content is more accentuated through reference to the Holy Ghost." Ettlinger, "Muses and Liberal Arts," 33. See also Courcelle, 80.

88. Masi, "A Newberry Diagram"; and Masi, "Boethius and the Iconography of the Liberal Arts."

89. Masi, "Boethius," 70–71.

90. Katzenellenbogen, "Representation," 49.

91. "Hec omnia scrutati sunt philosophi per mundanam sapientiam quam tamen inspiravit Spiritus sanctus." *HD* no. 36.

92. "Sic itaque philosophia cognitio est divinarum humanarumque rerum." *HD* no. 115. The idea that philosophy encompasses the knowledge of things "human and divine" appears in the writings of Clement of Alexandria, Jerome, Cassiodorus, Isidore of Seville, Alcuin, and Rhabanus Maurus, although it derives from the Stoics. Conrad of Hirsau also taught that "philosophy is the knowledge of matters human and divine in so far as this is humanly possible." *Dialogus*, ed. Huygens, 78–79; trans. Minnis and Scott, 46.

93. "Septem liberales artes, que ideo dicuntur liberales, quia liberant animum a terrenis curis et faciunt eum expeditum ad cognoscendum creatorem." *HD* no. 115. A similar idea appears in Conrad of Hirsau's *Dialogue on the Authors*. In response to the student's enquiries, the teacher explains that a " 'book' (*liber*) is so called from the verb 'to free' (*liberare*), because the man who spends his time reading often releases his mind from the anxieties and chains of the world." *Dialogus*, ed. Huygens, 74; trans. Minnis and Scott, 42.

94. Boethius, *Consolation*, I, 6; ed. Bieler, CCSL 94, 15; trans. Walsh, 17.

95. Concerning twelfth-century Platonism, see Gregory, "The Platonic Inheritance." Herrad may have been influenced by Neoplatonic thought through Honorius Augustodunensis, whose *Clavis physicae* (which she does not cite) transmitted significant portions of Eriugena's *De divisione naturae*.

96. *Confessions*, II, 6; ed. O'Donnell, 21; trans. Pine-Coffin, 50.

97. See Teske, "Augustine's Philosophy of Memory"; Teske, "Platonic Reminiscence"; and Stock, *Augustine the Reader*, 207–32.

98. *Confessions*, X, 20; ed. O'Donnell, 130; trans. Pine-Coffin, 226. Stock notes Augustine's argument that "recourse to memory is necessary if we are to know anything about God. The learner is like a student who has read, memorized, and temporarily forgotten a text. To know what he can know of God, he has to recall what he once knew." Stock, *Augustine the Reader*, 223.

99. *Confessions*, X, 24; ed. O'Donnell, 133; trans. Pine-Coffin, 230.

100. Augustine writes, "It is not strictly correct to say that there are three times, past, present, and future. It might be correct to say that there are three times, a present of past things, a present of present things, and a present of future things." *Confessions*, XI, 20; ed. O'Donnell, 157; trans. Pine-Coffin, 269.

101. Taylor notes that "Hugh presents philosophy as the instrument of a literal return to the divine Wisdom from the literal exile of the fall; as the means of restoring to man an ontological perfection which he knows, through experience, that he lacks . . ." Taylor, "Introduction," 18.

102. Hugh of St. Victor, *Didascalicon*, I, 1; ed. Buttimer, 6; trans. Taylor, 47. Hugh's conception of heaven is discussed in Feiss, "Heaven in the Theology of Hugh, Achard, and Richard of St. Victor."

103. Adelard of Bath, *De eodem et diverso*; ed. and trans. Burnett, 32–33.

104. Adelard of Bath, *De eodem et diverso*; ed. and trans. Burnett, 18–19. For a brief discussion, see also Bultot, "*Grammatica, ethica* et *contemptus mundi*," 816–18.

105. Katzenellenbogen, "Representation," 54.

106. The creation of Adam and of Eve from Adam's rib is depicted in miniatures on folio 17r; the temptation, fall, and expulsion are shown on folio 17v.

107. Bernard, *Sermo* 96; *SBOp*, VI.1, 355.

108. "Christus verus pontifex eum sua passione absolvit et eum paradiso restituit." *HD* Cat. No. 24.

109. Colish, *Mirror of Language*, 176. John of Salisbury, *Policraticus* VI, 1–2; ed. Webb, II, 93–99. Jerome, *Liber interpretationis hebraicorum nominum*; ed. de Lagarde, CCSL 72, 62. Babel was often treated as interchangeable with Babylon in medieval thought; see Alcuin, *Interrogationes*, PL 100, 533: "Et ideo civitas illa Babylon dicitur, id est, confusio, quia confusum est [ibi] labium universae terrae, et in linguas varias loquela hominum divisa." Concerning medieval interpretations of Babel, see Borst, *Der Turmbau von Babel*, II, ii.

110. See Ettlinger's discussion of the Muses in the *Hortus*.

111. Hugh of St. Victor, *Didascalicon* II, 1; ed. Buttimer, 23; trans. Taylor, 61.

112. Bernard, *Sermo* 45; *SBOp*, VI.1, 264. Other texts from Peter Lombard teach, "Quod mens proficit ad intelligendum Deum" (*HD* no. 20) and, later, "quod procreata potest cognosci creator" (*HD* no. 33).

113. Bernard, *Sermo* 102; *SBOp*, VI.1, 370. Bernard writes that it is "illam quae trahitur de occultis, per quam utique miro Dei opere agitur, ut electi quique tunsionibus et pressuris hic attriti, in aedificio veri Salomonis sine sonitu mallei postmodum construantur."

114. Isidore, *Differentiae*, II, 39, 150–54; PL 83, 94.

115. "Ethica, id est moralis, que aut repellit vicia, aut inducit virtutes." *HD* no. 116.

116. Katzenellenbogen, "Representation," 45.

117. Hugh of St. Victor; *Didascalicon*, III, 13; ed. Buttimer, 63; trans. Taylor, 96.

118. Walter of St. Victor, *Contra quatuor labyrinthos franciae*; ed. Glorieux, 201; trans. in Gibson, "The *De doctrina Christiana* in the School of St. Victor," 41.

119. Gibson, "The *De doctrina Christiana* in the School of St. Victor," 42.

120. Katzenellenbogen, "Representation," 42.

121. *SV* I, 990–98; ed. Seyfarth, CCCM 5, 39–40; trans. Newman, 276.

122. Conrad, *Dialogus*; ed. Huygens, 122–23; trans. Minnis and Scott, 64.

123. *SV epistula*, 102–4; ed. Seyfarth, CCCM 5, 4; trans. Newman, 271.

124. Latin text and translation in Bond, *The Loving Subject*, 168–69.

125. Peter the Venerable, *Epist.* 115; ed. Constable, 304; trans. Radice and Clanchy, 218.

126. Mews, "Hugh Metel," 78.

127. Munich, Bayerische Staatsbibliothek, MS Clm 9545, fol. 38r; trans. in Ziomkowski, 106.

Chapter 6. The Pleasure Garden of Learning: Reading the Hortus

1. For Herrad's potential authorship of this poem, see Chapter 3 n. 1.

2. O Rex pie,
   O Dux viae,
   Jesu Christe optime,
   Nostrum chorum
   Laudes morum
   Doce tibi promere. (*HD* no. 595)

3. "Quapropter in ipso libro oportet vos sedulo gratum querere pastum et mellitis stillicidiis animum reficere lassum, ut sponsi blandiciis semper occupate et spiritalibus deliciis saginate (id est inpinguate) transitoria secure percurratis et eterna felici jucunditate possideatis." *HD* no. 2.

4. Sit hic liber utilis,
   Tibi delectabilis
   Et non cesses volvere
   Hunc in tuo pectore. (*HD* no. 1)

5. In his *Ars poetica*, Horace suggested that the best poetry should mix the "useful" with the "delightful." *Ars poetica*, line 333; ed. Rudd, 69. Whether or not Herrad knew the source of the convention, her poem expresses the same intent.

6. Following the creation of the *Hortus*, there were fires at the monastery in 1199, 1224, 1243, 1301, 1408, and 1473. Dubled, "Recherches sur les chanoines réguliers," 9.

7. For the effect of book design on textual reception, see the discussion in Echard, "Designs for Reading."

8. The measurements are given in metric: 50–53 cm by 36–37 cm. Evans, *HD* 1.

9. The *Guta-Sintram Codex* measured 35.5 cm by 26.7 cm; Weis, "Description codicologique," 11. The Evangeliary of Marbach-Schwartzenthann measured 27 cm by 18 cm; Walter, "L'Évangéliaire de Marbach-Schwarzenthann," 5.

10. Cahn, *Romanesque Bible Illumination*; see his catalogue of manuscripts, with dimensions, 251–93.

11. Clanchy links book size to function, commenting: "The traditional large

books were intended to be placed on lecterns and displayed or read aloud in monastic communities. The new smaller formats were designed for individual private study, if they were academic books, or meditation, if they were religious." *From Memory to Written Record*, 135.

12. Pächt notes that "in general, it can be said that the more private the character of a text or book, the less the incentive to provide decoration." Pächt, 35.

13. On the various different ways in which medieval books were used, Clanchy writes, they "were studied by their owners intensively and repeatedly, over years or decades, in order to seek out their deeper levels of meaning. This involved a variety of reading strategies: hearing the text read aloud while looking at the lettering and images on the pages; repeating the text aloud with one or more companions, until it was learned by heart; construing the grammar and vocabulary of the languages of the text silently in private; translating or transposing the text, aloud or silently, into Latin, French, or English; examining the pictures and their captions, together with the illuminated letters, as a preparation for reading the imagery." *From Memory*, 194–95.

14. Peter Lombard, *Sentences*, Prologus; ed. Brady, I, 4; cited and trans. in Rouse and Rouse, "*Statim invenire*," 206. Honorius writes: "Peritissimi pictores Ambrosius et Augustinus, Hieronymus et Gregorius, et alii quamplurimi, mira caelatura et varia pictura egregie ornaverunt domum Domini; sed quia haec ob magnitudinem sui decoris hebetudinem nostri sensus excedunt, vel potius quotidiano usu obtrita jam inveteraverunt, injungitis mihi, verendi (sic) fratres, foedo pictori praeclaram picturam illustrium virorum innovare, cum vix valeam splendorem miri atque varii illorum operis considerare." *Speculum ecclesiae, Responsio Honorii*; PL 172, 814.

15. Ribémont, 59.

16. On new developments in the layout of the page in response to the exigencies of the schools, see Rouse and Rouse, "*Statim invenire*"; and Parkes, "The Influence of the Concepts of *Ordinatio* and *Compilatio*."

17. On the *lectio divina*, see Stock, "*Lectio divina* e *lectio spiritualis*"; Edsall, *Reading Like a Monk*; Leyser, "*Lectio divina, oratio pura*"; Lewis, "The English Gothic Illuminated Apocalypse"; De Vogüé, "La lecture quotidienne"; and Lefèvre, "À propos de la 'lectio divina'."

18. Hugh of St. Victor, *Didascalicon* III, 10; ed. Buttimer, 59; trans. Taylor, 93.

19. Bernard, *Sermones super Cantica canticorum*, 1.1; *SBOp* I, 3; trans. Walsh, 1.

20. As far as the placement of the gloss is concerned, only de Bastard noted the glosses in an organized way. Evans, *HD* 6. However, since he noted when a gloss was marginal, but not when it was interlinear, we can be sure that a gloss was marginal only if he notes it as such. De Bastard's default assumption seems to be that the glosses were interlinear. In the absence of information to the contrary, the reconstruction editors have simply assumed that the *Hortus* glosses were interlinear.

21. For a review of the debate, see Wieland, "Interpreting the Interpretation."

22. Lapidge, "The Study of Latin Texts."

23. Wieland, "The Glossed Manuscript," 160.

24. Wieland, "The Glossed Manuscript," 164.

25. Reynolds argues that the roles of teacher and scribe could often overlap in glossed manuscripts—a possibility that she argues presents "a very strong challenge to the notion of the 'mindless scribe,' whose function is only to copy." Reynolds, "Glossing Horace," 104.

26. For a discussion of grammatical glosses, see Wieland, *The Latin Glosses on Arator and Prudentius*, 47–97.

27. On syntactical glosses, see Wieland, *Latin Glosses*, 98–146; Robinson, "Syntactical Glosses"; and Reynolds, "*Ad auctorum expositionem.*"

28. Wieland, *Latin Glosses*, 147.

29. Bischoff, *HD* 47.

30. Flint, *Honorius Augustodunensis*, 130. See also Flint, "The Sources of the *Elucidarius.*"

31. Curschmann, *HD* 63. Curschmann provides an overview of the German glosses in *HD* 63–80.

32. Murphy writes that "one of the most obvious, yet little studied, facts about Europe in the High Middle Ages is that Latin was at all times and in all places a foreign language." Murphy, "The Teaching of Latin," 159. For studies of how Latin was learned as a second language in medieval Europe, see Porter, "The Latin Syllabus"; and *The St. Gall Tractate*, ed. and trans. Grotans and Porter.

33. Curschmann, *HD* 74. Curschmann comments that in the German glosses of the *Hortus*, "one senses a constant urge to return to the 'official' source of knowledge and to confirm once more, in writing, what one knew quite well already." *HD* 69.

34. Reynolds, *Medieval Reading*, 67.

35. A similar gloss appears in *HD* no. 799 n. 1: "Dioscorus: proprium nomen."

36. In his earlier work, Wieland argued in favor of a didactic purpose for the glosses in Cambridge University Library, MS Gg.5.35, despite their apparent randomness. Wieland, *Latin Glosses*, 191–92.

37. Wieland, *Latin Glosses*, 192–93.

38. *HD* Cat. Nos. 4, 6. See the discussion of these glosses in Chapter 4.

39. "Lege etiam in sententiis Petri Lombardi de resurrectione mortuorum ab eo loco: Causa resurrectionis, usque: Queri etiam solet an demones. Post hec legendum est ubi Dominus Jhesus justus judex vivorum et mortuorum . . ." *HD* no. 856. The first selection to which Herrad refers was most likely *Sentences* IV, d. 43, c. 2-d. 44, c. 6 (ed. Brady, II, 511–20), which possibly included the section from *HD* no. 1086 (now missing) to *HD* no. 1093. The second might refer to *Sentences*, IV, d. 43, c. 7 (ed. Brady, II, 515–16), the likely text for *HD* no. 1088 (also missing). If this was the case, then Herrad's directions do not make much sense; the first section of texts that she suggested would have included the section that she says must be read second.

40. Similarly lost to us is *HD* no. 857, which is described simply as "the sequence in which various texts on the Last Judgment should be read; possibly a continuation of 856."

41. Other repetitive glosses appear at *HD* nos. 330, 392, and 837.

42. The gloss was repetitive. The Latin lemma *ibices* is glossed *storke* and a marginal gloss essentially repeats this information: "ibis ibicis **stork** avis egyptia serpentibus inimica."

43. By contrast, Herrad's prose prologue has only two glosses for eleven lines of text in the edition. The relative poverty of the prose text versus the poem suggests that poetic pieces required more interpretative glosses than did prose compositions.

44. "Domicella" has three possible meanings: young lady, maid of honor, and canoness. All of them are relevant to the purpose of the poem.

45. Wieland, *Latin Glosses*, 7.

46. Curschmann, *HD* 69.

47. On the question of whether an illuminated manuscript can also be a classbook, see Wieland, "Gloss and Illustration." Wieland concludes that "if glossed non-illustrated manuscripts are classbooks, then glossed illustrated ones are as well" (13).

48. Pächt, *Book Illumination*, 35, 130.

49. Although, as Meier notes, many twelfth-century works combining text and image comment on the positive benefits of images without falling back on the justification for them as books for the illiterate. Meier, "Malerei des Unsichtbaren," 50.

50. For discussion of these two letters, see Chazelle, "Pictures, Books, and the Illiterate."

51. Gregory the Great, *Registrum* IX, 209; ed. Norberg, CCSL 140A, 768; trans. in Chazelle, 139.

52. Gregory the Great, *Registrum*, XI, 10; ed. Norberg, CCSL 140A, 874; trans. in Chazelle, 139.

53. However, according to Suger of St. Denis, images were permissible within the context of monastic instruction, since they could raise the soul from material to spiritual things and serve an exegetical function as part of the traditional monastic *lectio*. Rudolph, *Artistic Change at St-Denis*, 48–63; for debates concerning the role of art within the monastery, see Rudolph, *The "Things of Greater Importance."*

54. On this basis, Diebold argues that "one major form of early medieval art remained almost exclusively for the literate: illuminated manuscripts." Diebold, "Verbal, Visual, and Cultural Literacy," 89.

55. Hugh of Fouilloy, *Aviarum*, Prologue 1; ed. and trans. Clark, 116–17.

56. Hugh of Fouilloy, *Aviarum*, Prologue 2; ed. and trans. Clark, 118–19.

57. Ohly, "Probleme der mittelalterlichen Bedeutungsforschung," 55.

58. *Ancrene Wisse*; trans. Salu, 59. The physicality associated with female spirituality has been addressed by Robertson in her work on middle English devotional works for women: *Early English Devotional Prose*; "The Corporeality of Female Sanctity"; "Medieval Medical Views of Women"; and "'This Living Hand'."

Robertson observes that the female contemplative, "perceived to be rooted physically and spiritually in an inferior body and soul . . . was deemed able to perceive God only through that body." Robertson, "Medieval Medical Views of Women," 149.

59. Dinshaw, 3–27; Solterer, *The Master and Minerva*, 3–4; Schibanoff, "Taking the Gold Out of Egypt"; and Copeland, "Why Women Can't Read."

60. Guibert of Nogent, *De vita sua*, I, 14; ed. Bourgin, 51; trans. Benton, 76. Guibert describes his mother as never having "read" or "heard read" Gregory (*nec legerat, nec legi audierat*). *De vita sua*, I, 12; ed. Bourgin, 40; trans. Benton, 67. The clear implication is that she is a "nonreader," although she was obviously charged with his early education and could most likely read.

61. Guibert of Nogent, *De vita sua*, I, 19; ed. Bourgin, 79; trans. Benton, 101.

62. Mulder-Bakker, "The Metamorphosis of Woman," 114. Concerning women's roles in the transmission of knowledge, see also Mulder-Bakker, ed., *Seeing and Knowing*.

63. Mulder-Bakker, "Metamorphosis," 115.

64. For this argument, see Powell's discussion of women's classification as *auditores*, a term that, like *laici*, or *illitterati*, expressed opposition to male, clerical literacy. Powell, "The *Speculum virginum*," 114. Hamburger makes a similar observation, writing that, "Female readers stood on the boundary between lay and monastic culture and mediated between the two." *Visual*, 187.

65. "Ignorantia tua ad strophas te excitat, ut defendas, quod nescis et nescias, quod defendis. Multotiens tibi littera repetenda est, que semper in eodem neglegentie luto hesitare videris . . ." *SV*, XII, 104–6; ed. Seyfarth, CCCM 5, 352; trans. in Flanagan, "The *Speculum virginum* and Traditions of Medieval Dialogue," 93.

66. "Si forte quod legunt non intelligunt, vel proficiant ex forma subposita, quia ignorantibus litteras ipsa pictura scriptura est et exemplo excitatur ad profectum, cui littera non auget intellectum." *SV*, V, 1316–18; ed. Seyfarth, CCCM 5, 159. The image cycle of the St. Albans Psalter, designed for Christina of Markyate, explicitly invokes Gregory's justification for images, citing his letter to Serenus of Marseilles (incorrectly identified as Secundinus) in both Latin and the vernacular. *The St. Albans Psalter*, ed. Pächt et al., plate 37. Clanchy suggests that Christina "presumably 'read' the pictures by meditating on them." *From Memory*, 191.

67. *SV*, III, 1–2; ed. Seyfarth, CCCM 5, 58; trans. Newman, 281.

68. Hamburger, *Visual*, 190. He comments further "even if the body could become a vehicle of transcendence for women, medieval theology traditionally denied women access to the categories of rational and intellective—that is, nonimaginative—vision that were privileged by theory" (187). For the centrality of the body in female devotional practice, see Bynum, "The Female Body and Religious Practice" and Bynum, ". . . 'And Woman His Humanity'."

69. For limitations on women's learning and teaching, see Blamires, "Women and Preaching"; "Paradox in the Medieval Gender Doctrine"; and "The Limits of Bible Study"; as well as Blamires and Marx, "Woman Not to Preach"; and Minnis, "*De impedimento sexus*."

70. *SV epistula*, 102–4; ed. Seyfarth, CCCM 5, 4; trans. Newman, 271.

71. Newman, "Flaws in the Golden Bowl," 22.

72. See the author image in Seyfarth's edition of the *SV*; CCCM 5, plate 1; and Powell's discussion: *Mirror*, 133–73 and 192–227.

73. On the multiple uses of illuminated manuscripts, and especially the issues of literacy and images as they relate to the vernacular, see Curschmann, "Hören-Lesen-Sehen."

74. Powell writes that, "The *Speculum virginum* thus constructs its audience according to a system of binary oppositions that place—by reason of assumed natural affinity—women, listening, and pictures on one side of God's order and men, preaching or reading, and Scripture on the other." Powell, "The *Speculum virginum*," 114. Elsewhere he writes, "It is their sex, and not the literacy of the pupils which most profoundly determines the justification and function of the pictures—but not to the extent that the issue of affinity with the Latin text becomes irrelevant." Powell, *Mirror*, 120–21.

75. For the use of spontaneous translation from Latin to the vernacular and back again, see Clanchy, *From Memory*, 206–11.

76. For this reason, it is more correct to speak of Herrad's "audience" than of her "readers." For models of "hearing" and "listening" rather than private reading, see Clanchy, *From Memory*, 253–93. Reynolds writes of "communal reading, communicated orally." She notes that, "the glosses are merely the written traces of a much fuller reading practice, and what is more, they are part of a shift in the history of reading itself, away from the solitary rumination of monastic *lectio* to the more public forum of the classroom." *Medieval Reading*, 29.

77. Until the thirteenth century, women were allowed to teach within female monastic communities. However, beginning in the early thirteenth century, limitations appear on the reception of girls into female communities for the purposes of education. Bériou, "The Right of Women to Give Religious Instruction," 143 n. 17.

78. For the Regensburg influence on the *Speculum virginum*, see Goggin, *The Illuminations of the Clairvaux* Speculum virginum, 110–37. On the place of diagrams in twelfth-century thought, see Meier, "Die Quadratur des Kreises"; Meier, "Malerei des Unsichtbaren"; Sicard, *Diagrammes médiévaux*; and Evans, "Fictive painting."

79. For the salvific implications of ladders and trees, see the discussion in Chapter 5. Concerning the *Speculum*, see Goggin, 26–27.

80. "Hec persona virtutis significat omnes sanctos et electos qui angelica custodia perducuntur ad celestia premia." *HD* Cat. No. 296.

81. On the psychomachia as a tool for contemplation, see Carruthers, *Craft*, 143–50. Newhauser observes that treatises on the vices and virtues could be used as part of the private reflection that formed an essential part of the individual's preparation for confession. *The Treatise on Vices and Virtues*, 85.

82. "Milicia est vita hominis super terram." *HD* Cat. No. 258.

83. For didactic images, see Kühnel, *The End of Time in the Order of Things*; Gorman, "The Diagrams in the Oldest Manuscripts of Cassiodorus' *Institutiones*"; Gorman, "The Diagrams in the Oldest Manuscripts of Isidore's *De natura*

rerum"; Eastwood, "The Diagram of the Four Elements"; Bober, "An Illustrated Medieval School-book"; Masi, "A Newberry Diagram"; and Bolton. Concerning the use of images in the school of St. Victor, see Sicard, *Diagrammes médiévaux*, 141–54.

84. Cited in Darlington, "Gerbert, the Teacher," 472.

85. Germanisches Nationalmuseum MS 27773, fols. 73v–74v. This manuscript contains two parts, the first of which (fols. 1–99) dates from the second half of the twelfth century and was most likely copied at Marbach; the second part (fols. 100–129) dates from around 1260 and comes from Paris. The first part provides a clear foundation in the arts of the trivium—grammar, rhetoric, and dialectic— through excerpts from Priscian's *De nomine pronomine et verbo* and *Institutiones grammaticae* (fols. 10r–20r), Cicero's letter to Lucius Veturius (fols. 25r–36r), the pseudo-Ciceronian *Rhetorica ad Herennium* (fols. 92r–97r), and various other teaching texts including an *Ars metrica* (fols. 1r–10r), the *Regulae de primis syllabis* of John of Beauvais (fols. 36r–40v), and a dialectical text entitled the *Excerpta Norimbergensia* (fols. 41r–54v). Schemas are provided for metaphysics—substance, genus, species, etcetera (fols. 84v–86r). Brief sections are included from a commentary on Donatus's *Ars minor* (fol. 81v), Porphyry's *Isagoge*, Aristotle's *Categoriae*, and the *Periermenias* with commentary by Boethius. A text on adverbs of location gives the following examples, locating the manuscript in the environs of Marbach: "Marbaci didici" (fol. 21r) and "Swarcendan fugio" (fol. 21v). See Wattenbach, "Eine alte Grammatik"; and Knepper, *Das Schul- und Unterrichtswesen in Elsass*, 157–66.

86. Germanisches Nationalmuseum MS 27773, fol. 84v.

87. Alan of Lille, *On the Six Wings of the Seraph*; trans. Balint.

88. See Chapter 7 for a discussion of the psychomachia cycle.

89. Evans offers a classification of the "main types of visual aid: the typographic, the stemmatic, the geometric and the emblematic." Evans, "The Geometry of the Mind," 35. For the concept of "divine order" within geometric schemata, see Caviness, "Images of Divine Order and the Third Mode of Seeing." On didactic miniatures, see also Pächt, 155–60.

90. For the discussion of images within the schoolroom, see Wirth, "Von mittelalterlichen Bildern und Lehrfiguren im Dienste der Schule und des Unterrichts," 367. Reading in general could also require discussion; Noakes writes that reading was "a community experience in which the interpretation of the text any single listener or reader developed was the product, not of his understanding of the text alone, but of a combination of questions and insights supplied by others." Cited in Camille, "Seeing and Reading," 33.

91. Morrison uses the *Hortus* to illustrate his concept of the "nuclear perspective." *History as a Visual Art*, 113–20.

92. On images as memory tools, see Friedman, "Les images mnémotechniques." On the role of memory in medieval education, see Riché, "Le rôle de la mémoire dans l'enseignement médiéval."

93. Evans, "Fictive Painting"; Sicard, *Diagrammes médiévaux*; Zinn, "*De gradibus Ascensionum*"; and Zinn, "Hugh of St. Victor, Isaiah's Vision, and *De arca Noe*."

94. Hugh of St. Victor, "De tribus maximis circumstantiis gestorum"; ed. Green, 490; trans. Carruthers, 264. For discussion of Hugh's approach to memory, see Zinn, "Hugh of Saint Victor and the Art of Memory."

95. A text from Peter Comestor also notes that the veil of Moses's tabernacle was beautifully decorated with pictures of flowers and animals. *HD* no. 157.

96. Carruthers, *Craft*, 142. Carruthers argues that the distinction between verbal and visual memory was not relevant to medieval authors: "the letters used for writing were considered to be as visual as what we call 'images' today; . . . as a result the page as a whole, the complete parchment with its lettering and all its decoration, was considered a cognitively valuable 'picture'." *Craft*, 122.

97. Carruthers, *Craft*, 101. Elsewhere, she argues that fear is the first step in the memory work of prayer. *Craft*, 175. Fulton comments on the role of images with memory: "as we have seen, Honorius and his contemporaries (including his teacher Anselm) believed that to excite the memory, to leave a sharp impression, images must arouse some intense emotion, if not fear, then anxiety, disgust, wonder, anger, or grief." Fulton, 262.

98. Carruthers, *Book*, 38.

99. Hugh, "De tribus maximis"; ed. Green, 490; trans. Carruthers, 264. For further discussion of the book and page layout as mnemonic tools, see Carruthers, *Book*, 194, 215–18.

100. Sit hic liber utilis,
    Tibi delectabilis
    Et non cesses volvere (pertractare)
    Hunc (librum) in tuo pectore (memoria). (*HD* no. 1)

101. The Bible provides several examples of "digesting" knowledge: John the Evangelist eats a scroll (Revelation 10:9), as does Ezekiel, for whom eating as the internalization of knowledge was also the first step in the digestion metaphor for imitative composition (Ezekiel 3:1–3).

102. *Utilitas* was one of the six headings of the "Type C" prologue identified by Hunt and discussed by Minnis. Hunt, "The Introductions to the 'Artes'"; Minnis, *Medieval Theory of Authorship*, 23.

103. *De doctrina Christiana*, II, VI, 7; ed. and trans. Green, 60–63.

104. Hugh of St. Victor, *Didascalicon*, V, 2; ed. Buttimer, 96; trans. Taylor, 121.

105. Hugh of St. Victor, *Didascalicon*, V, 7; ed. Buttimer, 107; trans. Taylor, 129.

106. Hugh of St. Victor, *Didascalicon*, IV, 1; ed. Buttimer, 70; trans. Taylor, 102.

Chapter 7. Reforming Women in the Garden of Delights

1. Green writes that, "the striking effect of this page is owed to its severely limited colour scheme, its unusual framing device, and its rare dark background even more than to the horrors it depicts." *HD* Cat. No. 338. See Gillen's discussion of this image: Gillen, 27–31.

2. Cames suggests that this figure represents Herod, whom Herrad notes had committed suicide following the Massacre of the Innocents (fol. 98r; *HD* Cat. No. 117). Cames, *Allégories et symboles*, 43.

3. "Vermis impiorum non morietur et ignis illorum in sempiternum non extinguetur." *HD* Cat. No. 338.

4. The scene is reminiscent of a verse in *De primo homine*, a poem that may have been written by Herrad (*HD* no. 374):

The god of hell sits on the throne
Which smokes with pitch-black fire;
His face is horrifying.
There is pain to those who are burning
For different vices
He hands down his punishment to each.

Orcus sedens solio
Ignis pice fumido,
Visus ejus horridus
Dolor est aestuantibus;
Pro diversis viciis
Poenas tradit singulis.

5. For other depictions of avarice in art of the eleventh and twelfth centuries, see Baumann, "The Deadliest Sin."

6. *Praeceptum*, 3; in Lawless, *Augustine of Hippo*, 80–81.

7. "Nichil quis appellet suum singulariter, sed ad omnia dicat *nostrum*, nisi de culpis et patre et matre." *Consuetudines*, 34; ed. Siegwart, 141.

8. For the damnation of priests and other religious in descriptions of hell, see *Visions of Heaven and Hell Before Dante*, ed. Gardiner.

9. Few of the booklet's texts were copied before 1870; however, many of its titles were preserved, providing a rough sense of its original contents. The booklet was composed of half or quarter leaves. For discussion of the role of the booklet in medieval manuscripts, see Robinson, "The 'Booklet'." The *Hortus* may have contained a second booklet, which included a series of poems from Petrus Pictor wrongly attributed to Anselm. *HD* nos. 460–86; fols. 134r–37v. Following *HD* no. 486, an *explicit* concludes the section: "Explicit libellus Anshelmi cantuariensis episcopi de sacramentis."

10. "*Incipiunt auctoritates* that none should have the governance of the church and the care of souls, except those who live regularly (*nisi regulariter viventes*)." *HD* no. 1131. Although *regularis* was used to denote those who lived according the Benedictine Rule, it was also a common descriptor for reformed canons.

11. On Gregory's reform of the canons, see Bardy, "Saint Gregoire VII."

12. *HD* no. 1134: "namque apostolorum sequaces sunt canonici." *HD* no. 1142: "quod omnes sacerdotes regularem agere vitam deberent." *HD* no. 1143: "Quod nullus debeat habere curas animarum vel regimen parrochiarum nisi qui de communi vita secundum consuetudinem primitive Ecclesie assumatur."

13. "Illi enim qui modo ecclesiis preficiuntur, dum res earum fidelium oblatione Deo dicatas variis et exquisitis cibi et potus et vestimentorum aliarumque rerum deliciis eis abutentes consumunt . . . " *HD* no. 1136. The criticism of ornate clothing also appears in the collection published by Leclercq. "Un témoignage sur l'influence de Grégoire VII," 194, no. 118: "Ut clerici non affectent ornatum vestium."

14. "Quia coerceri nec volunt nec possunt vel virga pastorali vel lege regulari vel certe disciplina timoris Domini." *HD* no. 1155. Although this passage did not form part of the booklet, it extends many of the booklet's concerns. The charge that canons bring scandal to the church echoes Gerhoch of Reichersberg's claim that priests' wives watched as churches were transformed from houses of prayer into theaters. *De investigatione Antichristi*, I, 5; ed. Sackur, MGH Libelli 3, 315–16.

15. Essential studies of the *Hortus* psychomachia are Cames, *Allégories et symboles*, 54–73; Norman, *Metamorphoses of an Allegory*, 88–97 (whose study is largely dependent on Cames); and McGuire, "Psychomachia."

16. The gendering of the Virtues and Vices is not simply a function of Latin grammar, as Nugent argues: "*Virtus* or Virago?"

17. Hildegard's *Scivias* also included descriptions of the Virtues personified as women, elaborately dressed; however, she omits the Vices, which do not appear—as they do in Herrad's presentation—as female personifications. *Scivias* III, 6, 27–35; ed. Führkötter and Carlevaris, CCCM 43A, 450–61; trans. Hart and Bishop, 400–408.

18. Prudentius, *Psychomachia*. For an introduction to the *Psychomachia*, see Nugent, *Allegory and Poetics*.

19. For illustrated manuscripts of Prudentius's *Psychomachia*, see Stettiner, *Die illustrierten Prudentiushandschriften*; and Woodruff, "The Illustrated Manuscripts of Prudentius." The foundational study of the influence of Prudentius in art is still that of Katzenellenbogen, *Allegories of the Virtues and Vices*. See also O'Reilly, *Studies in the Iconography of the Virtues and Vices*; and Nugent, *Allegory and Poetics*.

20. Pride's downfall foreshadows the downfall of the Whore of Babylon, who is depicted first riding sidesaddle (fol. 258r) and then toppled from her manyheaded mount into a pit of flames (fol. 258v). See Wright, "The Great Whore."

21. See the discussion of Avarice in Prudentius's *Psychomachia* in Newhauser, *Early History of Greed*, 79–85.

22. *De fructibus carnis et spiritus* (PL 176, 997–1006); concerning Conrad's possible authorship of this piece, see Bultot, "L'auteur et la fonction littéraire du 'De fructibus carnis et spiritus'."

23. Newhauser comments that, "Conrad of Hirsau designed his *Liber de fructu carnis et spiritus* with the need foremost in his mind of making the symmetry of differences between good and evil as visibly comprehensible as possible." Newhauser, *Vices and Virtues*, 119. On the emergence of a standard grouping of the vices, see Bloomfield, *Seven Deadly Sins*, 43–67.

24. "Duas itaque arbusculas fructu et ascensu dissimiles, et rudi, et novello cuilibet converso, adjunctis vitiorum sive virtutum paucis diffinitiunculis proponimus, ex quarum radice fructuum proventus pateat, et quae arbor ex duabus eli-

genda sit allectus fructu discernat. Et quidem superbia fructus carnis radix est, fructus spiritus humilitas." *De fructibus carnis et spiritus*, Prologus; PL 176, 997.

25. Morrison argues that these folios may have been intended to introduce the psychomachia cycle, but that the illuminator placed them at its end by mistake. Morrison, *History as a Visual Art*, 117.

26. Avarice and Pride had jockeyed for the dubious honor of chief vice throughout the Middle Ages. For changing categorizations of the vices, see Newhauser, *Vices and Virtues*, 180–202.

27. Little, "Pride Goes Before Avarice." On avarice, see also Murray, *Reason and Society*, 59–80. Newhauser challenges the view that anxiety concerning avarice was a function of the later medieval period, when an increasingly commercial economy raised fears about the unfettered pursuit of money, arguing that "pride's hegemony was by no means universal" in the early Middle Ages. He writes: "in the period before the advent of a money economy avarice was already available to serve as the chief sin whenever the overriding concern of the author was to convert his addressees from a material ideology, such as moral theologians identified in pagan religion, or to teach a lesson in *contemptus mundi*." Newhauser, *Vices and Virtues*, 199–200. This idea is explored more fully in Newhauser, *Greed*. Newhauser argues that the tendency to concentrate on avarice as desire for money has obscured its early history as a vice that included any worldly desire.

28. The use of the wheel to denote the battle of the Virtues and Vices is discussed briefly in Newhauser, *Vices and Virtues*, 163. Will has pointed out similarities between the depiction of Mercy in the *Hortus* and a bas-relief representing the works of Mercy at the abbey of Petershausen. Will, "*Currus misericordiae*."

29. Eli and his sons were invoked as a model of evil in a letter from Peter Damian to Nicholas II. *Epist*. 61, 8–10; trans. Blum, III, 7–9.

30. Cassian, *De institutis coenobiorum*, 12.7; ed. and trans. Guy, 458–59. The texts of the *Hortus* are not always consistent in presenting avarice as the chief vice. Since most of these texts had been drawn from traditional Benedictine authors, they tended to maintain a monastic emphasis on Pride. In a text copied from Honorius Augustodunensis, Pride appears as the chief vice (*principale vicium*), accompanied by six others. *HD* no. 265. Elsewhere, Pride is the "queen of all sins" (*omnis regina peccati*) (*HD* no. 751), the "root of all evil" (*radix omnium malorum*) (*HD* no. 911), the means through which the devil tempted Adam and Eve (*HD* no. 78), the cause of the devil's fall from heaven (*HD* no. 94), and the reason for man's separation from God (*HD* nos. 786, 752). The devil is the "prince of pride," in a gloss to the psychomachia cycle. *HD* Cat. No. 258. The images of the *Hortus* allowed Herrad to break from her texts in order to express her own point of view—one that was potentially more critical of the church than that presented in many of her sources.

31. "Que est hec insania, acquirere aurum et perdere celum?" *HD* Cat. No. 282.

32. Cited in Cowdrey, *Pope Gregory VII*, 46.

33. The connection between avarice, the desire for belongings, simony, the wrongful desire for office, and the abuse of the church, is discussed in the texts of the *Hortus* booklet, which warn that "only those who scorn property should be

chosen for the governance of the church" (*HD* no. 1137). Simony was mentioned explicitly only once in the titles of the booklet: "Quod tres species symonie diligenter observant in acquirendis Ecclesiis, ne si quid minus fecerint, cicius perdant." *HD* no. 1153. The three types of simony to which the text refers were identified by Gregory the Great: *Homiliae* I, 4; PL 76, 1091–92. Simony was also treated in several excerpts from Peter Lombard's *Sentences*. *HD* nos. 1036–37.

34. Matthew 21:12–13; Mark 11:15; Luke 19:45–46; John 2:14–16. Of these, only John describes the whip of cords, which the *Hortus* artist includes in her rendition.

35. "In bove. Sermonem vendunt." *HD* Cat. No. 304. Gregory the Great wrote that "Boves sunt praedicatores Ecclesiae, qui dum praedicant, arant." *In librum primum Regum*, V, 4; PL 79, 370.

36. "Judas mercator pessimus significat usurarios quos omnes expellit Dominus, quia spem suam ponunt in diviciis et volunt ut nummus vincat, nummus regnet, nummus imperet." *HD* Cat. No. 304.

37. "Ypocrita vendit ovem id est religionem causa questus vel propter humanum favorem. Ipse enim arroganter loquitur dicens: Non sum sicut ceteri hominum." *HD* Cat. No. 304.

38. Surviving details include an isolated whip of cords, which would have been held by Christ but now hangs suspended in the air; a merchant holding a set of scales; a brigand with the bloody head of his victim; a young lover (*fornicator*) with his girlfriend; and an unfinished sketch of a magician, improbably balancing a miniature castle (*turris*) on his nose. The symbolism of the tower is discussed by Cames, who suggests that the figure represents the female companion of Simon Magus. Cames, *Allégories et symboles*, 101. For Cames, avarice is the key to understanding Herrad's Cleansing image. In his view, the temple in the image represented the heavenly kingdom, from which wrongdoers will be expelled. Cames, *Allégories et symboles*, 97. Cames discusses the entire image in *Allégories et symboles*, 96–103.

39. On leprosy as a manifestation of spiritual illness, see Brody, *Disease of the Soul*.

40. The link between avarice and simony is discussed in Little, 21. Little writes that, "by the later eleventh century attacks on simony came to include—and eventually to concentrate upon—attacks against money and avarice." Leclercq explores the characterization of simony as heresy in "*Simoniaca heresis*." Newhauser provides an appendix of imagery used in connection with discussions of avarice in the early Middle Ages. *Greed*, 132–42. He writes that Simon Magus was associated with avarice by Gregory the Great, Peter Damian, and Otloh of St. Emmeram (140); Gehazi was associated with avarice by Origen, Palladius, Chrysostom, Evagrius Ponticus, Jerome, Cassian, Ambrose, Rhabanus Maurus, Pseudo-Rhabanus, and Peter Damian (136).

41. The association of avarice with the temptation of the eyes began with the fourth-century Egyptian monk Evagrius Ponticus and was adopted by John Cassian, although only in relation to the version of the temptation provided in Matthew. Newhauser, *Greed*, 47–57, 61–69. The three temptations of I John 2:16 were generally associated in later medieval exegesis with the temptations of Adam in the

garden and of Christ in the wilderness. On medieval interpretations of the three temptations, see Howard, *The Three Temptations*, 43–75.

42. "Illa est symonia que fit verbo pactionis, gezia que spe remunerationis unde Gezi lepra percussus et sui flagizii luit supplicium, et nobis delectabile reliquit exemplum." (Simony is that which is made by the word of an agreement, Gezia that which is made by the hope of remuneration, whence Gehazi was struck with leprosy, and paid the punishment of his disgrace, and left a useful example for us.) *HD* Cat. No. 123.

43. "Hoc solum vicium Christus tali mercimonio **choufe** domum Dei pollui non patiens, flagello facto de funiculis cum proprii corporis opprobria sustinuisset punivit, kathedras vendentium columbas evertit. Non itaque glorientur, qui in kathedris resident nisi justitiam exercuerint, cum et ipsi cadant." *HD* Cat. No. 123.

44. Robinson, "'Political Allegory'," 71. Cowdrey discusses John of Mantua's use of political allegory in the commentary on the Song of Songs that he composed for Matilda of Tuscany: Cowdrey, *Pope Gregory VII*, 303.

45. Rough notes that the cleansing was "virtually a Reformist possession." Rough, *Reformist Illuminations*, 19.

46. Bruno of Segni, *In Lucam*, 46; PL 165, 440. Concerning Bruno's career, see North, "Polemic, Apathy and Authorial Initiative."

47. Green comments on the originality of the *Hortus* Cleansing, observing that while some of the details of the image can be seen in earlier depictions, "the allegorizing of the event is unknown to me earlier." *HD* Cat. No. 304.

48. Morgan Library, New York, M. 492. See Rough, 5 n. 14, for a description of the manuscript.

49. Rough, 51. Cohen calls the Cleansing image "a visual corollary to the forceful written commentaries" of the reformers. Cohen, "The Art of Reform," 994.

50. For further discussion of this poem, see Constable, *Three Studies in Medieval Religious and Social Thought*, 51–52.

51. Katzenellenbogen, *Allegories of the Virtues and Vices*, 22–26; Newhauser, *Vices and Virtues*, 157–58; and Evans, who discusses the *scala virtutis* as a reflection of medieval thought-processes in "The Geometry of the Mind," 39–40.

52. "Salemon et rota fortune et scala et syrene admonent nos de contemptu mundi et amore Christi." *HD* Cat. No. 299. For studies of *contemptus mundi*, see Bultot, *La doctrine du mépris du monde* and de Certeau, *Le mépris du monde*.

53. "Pietas per contemptum mundi excludit avariciam." *HD* no. 750.

54. "Que humana voce cantat est avaricia, que suis auditoribus hujus mundi modulatur carmina." *HD* no. 756.

55. Spernere mundum, spernere nullum, spernere sese.
Spernere sperni se, quatuor haec bona sunt. (*HD* no. 735)

56. Pulvere terreno   contempto currite celo,
Que nunc absconsum   valeatis cernere sponsum. (*HD* Cat. No. 346)

57. "Iste clericus omnes falsos clericos designans crapule, luxurie, symonie, aliisque viciis deditur retrorsum cadit et minime ad acquirendam vite coronam in altum vadit." *HD* Cat. No. 296.

58. "Iste monachus falsorum monachorum typum gerit qui proprietatibus et

pecunie inhians cor suum a divinis officiis abstrahit et ubi est thesaurus suus immobiliter figit." *HD* Cat. No. 296. Cf. Luke 12:34.

59. "Hec persona virtutis significat omnes sanctos et electos qui angelica custodia perducuntur ad celestia premia." *HD* Cat. No. 296. The image of the *persona virtutis* reaching the apex of the ladder is matched in the miniature of the Just in Heaven (fol. 244v) by a female figure, who again signifies all the holy and the elect (*omnes sanctos et electos*) and who is embraced by God who wipes away her tears. *HD* Cat. No. 318.

60. "Pseudo pape cum episcopis et clericis qui non in Christi nomine sed pro transitoria mercede predicaverunt et vitam suam viciis maculaverunt." *HD* Cat. No. 335.

61. "Qui proprietatibus crapula ceterisque viciis ordinem suum violaverunt." *HD* Cat. No. 335.

62. For the interplay of text and image in the Solomon cycle, see Curschmann, "Texte-Bilder-Strukturen," 394–409. The Solomon cycle of the *Hortus* was examined by Ganz, "On the Unity."

63. Ganz, 49.

64. "Saperatis [superatis] viciorum pugnis et venenata invidia draconis, sequitur requies pacifica veri Salemonis." *HD* Cat. No. 286. Curschmann suggests "superatis" instead of "saperatis" as it appears in the *Hortus* edition. Curschmann, "Texte-Bilder-Strukturen," 394. On the facing page, a text from Rupert's commentary on the Song of Songs identifies Solomon's bed with the virginal uterus of Mary. *HD* no. 711.

65. Hildegard's *Scivias* also included a cycle of *Ecclesia* images (associated with *Scivias* II, 3–6; ed. Führkötter and Carlevaris, CCCM 43, 133–306; trans. Hart and Bishop, 341–408) and a vision of *Ecclesia* (*Scivias* III, 9; ed. Führkötter and Carlevaris, CCCM 43, 515–44; trans. Hart and Bishop, 451–69). See also Newman, *Sister*, 196–249.

66. "Avaricia dicit: Lingo fraude quasi vulpis dolo vel vi sectans lucra rodo ut leo crudelis." *HD* Cat. No. 282.

67. "Sacerdotes vero sunt fenestre, per quos lumen divine noticie debuit subjectis splendescere. Sed heu! terra super fenestras crevit, et lumen intrare non sinit, quia cupiditas terrenarum rerum visum mentis sacerdotum excecat, et ideo lumen divine scientie per eos minime in Ecclesia radiat." *HD* no. 251.

68. "Si autem nec bene vivunt nec docent, sunt fumus qui ignem obfuscat et aciem oculorum reverberat **widerslehet**; de his dicitur: Stelle non luxerunt, ideo de celo ceciderunt." *HD* no. 805.

69. See Introduction n. 26.

70. Moore, "Family, Community and Cult," 56.

Conclusion: A Book for Women?

1. Bynum, "The Spirituality of Regular Canons," 57.

2. Hathaway, 34. As Kelly observes, "rewriting, therefore, is the sphere within which medieval writers in the scholastic tradition sought and achieved origi-

nality." Kelly, *The Conspiracy of Allusion*, xiii. Summit makes a similar point concerning women's involvement in compilation; she writes that, "while the process of writing by compiling pays homage to a system of *auctoritas* based on citation and *traditio*, it would be wrong to assume that compilation was necessarily a noncreative act." Summit, "Women and Authorship," 100.

3. For Caviness, several themes, nonetheless, "mark it as a women's book." Caviness, "Anchoress, Abbess, and Queen," 117. She points to the Tree of Jesse image (fol. 80v), a subject that she notes is often associated with women, as well as the depiction of the daughters of Jerusalem (fol. 209v), an image unique to the *Hortus*. HD Cat. No. 293. These are only two of the many images in the manuscript that either highlight women or include visual cues that would have been directly relevant to its female audience.

4. For discussion of this point, see Reudenbach, "Individuum ohne Bildnis?"

5. O nivei flores   dantes virtutis odores,
   Semper divina   pausantes in theoria,
   Pulvere terreno   contempto currite celo,
   celo
   Que nunc absconsum   valeatis cernere sponsum.

HD fol. 323r; HD Cat. No. 346. Relinde also addresses a poem to the women; see the discussion in Chapter 4.

6. Cf. HD no. 792: "Nigredo hujus indumenti est contemptus mundi."

7. Cf. HD no. 789, where virgins appear below martyrs in a text from Honorius.

8. "Facies habebant mulierum, quia nil ita mentem hominis a Deo alienat quam amor mulierum." HD no. 756.

9. "Visus (glossed 'mulierum') Sampsonem pessumdedit et Salemonem." HD no. 754 n. 63.

10. "Molentes non duo sed due scribuntur, quia conjungati non ut viri ad spiritalia eriguntur sed ut femine ad carnalia inflectuntur." HD Cat. No. 148.

11. Morrison, *History as a Visual Art*, 161.

12. Morrison sees the marginal placement of the canoness in this image as an example of Herrad's ambivalence toward women. *History as a Visual Art*, 162.

Bibliography

PRIMARY SOURCES

Abelard. *Epist. 7.* Ed. J. T. Muckle, "The Letter of Heloise on Religious Life and Abelard's First Reply." *Mediaeval Studies* 17 (1955): 253–81. Trans. Vera Morton, "The History of Women's Roles in Christianity." In *Guidance for Women in Twelfth-Century Convents.* Cambridge: D.S. Brewer, 2003. 52–95.
———. *Epist. 8.* Ed. T. P. McLaughlin, "Abelard's Rule for Religious Women." *Mediaeval Studies* 18 (1956): 241–92. Trans. Betty Radice and M. T. Clanchy in *The Letters of Abelard and Heloise.* New York: Penguin, 2003. 130–210.
———. *Epist. 17.* "Fidei confessio." PL 178: 375–78.
———. *Sermon 30. De eleemosyna pro sanctimonialibus de Paraclito.* Ed. Aldo Granata, "La dottrina dell'Elemosina nel sermone 'Pro sanctimonialibus de Paraclito' di Abelardo." *Aevum* 47 (1973): 32–59, 54–59.
Ad Beatam Virginem Deiparam sermo Panegyricus. PL 184: 1009–14.
Adelard of Bath. *De eodem et diverso.* Ed. and trans. Charles Burnett, *Conversations with His Nephew: On the Same and the Different, Questions on Natural Science, and On Birds.* Cambridge: Cambridge University Press, 1998.
Alan of Lille. *On the Six Wings of the Seraph.* Trans. Bridget Balint in Mary Carruthers and Jan M. Ziolkowski, eds., *The Medieval Craft of Memory: An Anthology of Texts and Pictures.* Philadelphia: University of Pennsylvania Press, 2002. 83–102.
Alcuin. *Interrogationes.* PL 100: 515–70.
———. *Grammatica.* PL 101: 849–902.
Aldhelm. *De virginitate.* Ed. Scott Gwara and Rudolf Ehwald, *Prosa de virginitate: cum glosa latina atque anglosaxonica.* CCSL 124–124A. Turnhout: Brepols, 2001. Trans. Michael Lapidge and Michael Herren in *Aldhelm, the Prose Works.* Cambridge: Cambridge University Press, 1979. 59–132.
Ambrose of Milan. *De virginibus.* Ed. and trans. Franco Gori in *Verginità, e, Vedovanza.* Sancti Ambrosii episcopi Mediolanensis Opera 14.1, Opere morali II.I. Milan: Bibliotheca Ambrosiana, 1989. 99–241. Trans. Boniface Ramsey in *Ambrose.* Early Church Fathers 3. London: Routledge, 1997. 73–116.
———. *De virginitate.* Ed. and trans. Franco Gori in *Verginità, e, Vedovanza.* Sancti Ambrosii episcopi Mediolanensis Opera 14.1, Opere morali II.II. Milan: Bibliotheca Ambrosiana, 1989. 11–107. Trans. Daniel Callam, *On Virginity.* Toronto: Peregrina, 1989.
———. *Hexameron.* PL 14: 123–274. Trans. John J. Savage in *Hexameron, Paradise, and Cain and Abel.* New York: Fathers of the Church, 1961.

Ancrene Wisse. Trans. M. B. Salu, *The Ancrene riwle: (the Corpus Ms.,* Ancrene wisse*)*. Exeter: Exeter University Press, 1990. (Originally published: London: Burns & Oates, 1955).

Annales Admontenses. Ed. Wilhelm Wattenbach, MGH SS 9. Hannover: Hahn, 1851. 569–93.

Annales Marbacenses qui dicuntur (Cronica Hohenburgensis cum continuatione et additamentis neoburgensibus). Ed. Hermann Bloch. MGH SSRG 9. Hannover: Hahn, 1907.

Aristotle. *History of Animals, Books VII-X.* Ed. and trans. D. M. Balme. Cambridge, Mass.: Harvard University Press, 1991.

Augustine of Hippo. *City of God.* Ed. Bernhard Dombart and Alfons Kalb, *De civitate Dei.* CCSL 47–48. Turnhout: Brepols, 1955. Trans. Henry Bettenson, *Concerning the City of God Against the Pagans.* New York: Penguin Books, 2003.

———. *Confessions.* Ed. James J. O'Donnell, *Confessions,* vol. 1, *Introduction and Text.* Oxford: Clarendon Press, 1992. Trans. R. S. Pine-Coffin, *Confessions.* London: Penguin Books, 1961.

———. *De doctrina Christiana.* Ed. and trans. R. P. H. Green. Oxford: Clarendon Press, 1995.

———. *De Trinitate.* Ed. W. J. Mountain. CCSL 50–50A. Turnhout: Brepols, 1968.

Baudry of Bourgueil. *Carmina.* Ed. Karlheinz Hilbert. Editiones Heidelbergenses 19. Heidelberg: Winter, 1979.

Bernard of Clairvaux. *Sancti Bernardi Opera.* Ed. J. Leclercq, C. H. Talbot, and H. M. Rochais. 8 vols. Rome: Editiones Cistercienses, 1957–1998.

———. *On the Song of Songs I.* Trans. Kilian Walsh. Cistercian Fathers series 4. Spencer, Mass.: Cistercian Publications, 1971.

Bernold of Constance. *Chronicon.* Ed. Ian Stuart Robinson, trans. Ian Stuart Robinson and Helga Robinson-Hammerstein in *Bertholds und Bernolds Chroniken.* Ausgewählte Quellen zur deutschen Geschichte des Mittelalters 14. Darmstadt: Wissenschaftliche Buchgesellschaft, 2002. 279–433.

Boethius. *The Consolation of Philosophy.* Ed. Ludwig Bieler, *Anicii Manlii Severini Boethii Philosophiae consolatio.* CCSL 94. Turnhout: Brepols, 1957. Trans. P. G. Walsh. Oxford: Oxford University Press, 1999.

Boso. *Boso's Life of Alexander III.* Ed. and trans. G. M. Ellis. Oxford: Blackwell, 1973.

Bruno of Segni. *Commentaria in Lucam.* PL 165: 333–452.

Caesarius of Arles. *Sermones.* Ed. Germain Morin. 2 vols. CCSL 103–4. Turnhout: Brepols, 1953.

Caesarius of Heisterbach. *Dialogus miraculorum.* Ed. Josephus Strange. 2 vols. Cologne: J.M. Heberle, 1851. Trans. H. von E. Scott and C. C. Swinton Bland, *The Dialogue on Miracles.* 2 vols. London: G. Routledge, 1929.

The Cambridge Songs (Carmina Cantabrigiensia). Ed. and trans. Jan M. Ziolkowski. Tempe, Ariz.: Medieval and Renaissance Texts and Studies, 1998.

Cassian, John. *De institutis coenobiorum.* Ed. and trans. Jean-Claude Guy, *Institutions cénobitiques.* Sources chrétiennes 109. Paris: Éditions du Cerf, 1965.

Cassiodorus. *Institutiones.* Ed. R. A. B. Mynors. Oxford: Clarendon Press, 1937.

Chronicon Ebersheimense. Ed. Ludwig Weiland. MGH SS 23. Hannover: Hahn, 1874. 427–53.

Chronicon Lippoldesbergense. Ed. Wilhelm Arndt. MGH SS 20. Hannover: Hahn, 1868. 546–58.

Cicero. *De divinatione.* Ed. Arthur Stanley Pease. Urbana: University of Illinois, 1920.

———. *De finibus bonorum et malorum.* Ed. J. N. Madvig. Hildesheim: Georg Olms, 1963.

Le Codex Guta-Sintram: manuscrit 37 de la Bibliothèque du Grand séminaire de Strasbourg. Ed. Béatrice Weis. 2 vols. Lucerne: Editions Fac-similés, 1983.

Conrad of Hirsau. *Dialogus super auctores.* In R. B. C. Huygens, ed., *Accessus ad auctores, Bernard d'Utrecht, Conrad d'Hirsau: Dialogus super auctores.* Leiden: E. J. Brill, 1970. 71–131. Extracts trans. in Alastair J. Minnis and A. B. Scott, eds., *Medieval Literary Theory and Criticism, c. 1100-c. 1375: The Commentary-Tradition.* Oxford: Clarendon Press, 1988. 39–64.

Die Consuetudines des Augustiner-Chorherrenstiftes Marbach im Elsass (12. Jahrhundert). Ed. Josef Siegwart. Fribourg: Universitätsverlag, 1965.

Decrees of the Ecumenical Councils. Ed. and trans. Norman P. Tanner. 2 vols. Washington, D.C.: Georgetown University Press, 1990.

Defensor. *Liber scintillarum.* Ed. H. M. Rochais. CCSL 117. Turnhout: Brepols, 1957.

De fructibus carnis et spiritus. PL 176: 997–1006.

Dietler, Seraphin. *Chronik des klosters Schönensteinbach.* Ed. Joh. v. Schlumberger. Gebweiler: J. Boltze, 1897.

Elisabeth of Schönau. *Die Visionen der hl. Elisabeth und die Schriften der Aebte Ekbert und Emecho von Schönau.* Ed. F. W. E. Roth. Brünn: Verlag der Studien aus dem Benedictiner- und Cistercienser-Orden, 1884. Trans. Anne L. Clark, *Elisabeth of Schönau: The Complete Works.* New York: Paulist Press, 2000.

Gerhoch of Reichersberg. *De investigatione Antichristi Liber I.* Ed. Ernest Sackur. MGH Libelli 3. Hannover: Hahn, 1897. 304–95.

Gilbert of Poitiers. *The Commentaries on Boethius.* Ed. Nikolaus M. Häring. Toronto: Pontifical Institute of Mediaeval Studies, 1966.

Gregory the Great. *Homiliae in Evangelia.* PL 76: 1071–312.

———. *In librum primum Regum.* PL 79: 17–468.

———. *Registrum epistularum.* Ed. Dag Norberg. CCSL 140–40A. Turnhout: Brepols, 1982.

Gregory of Tours. *Historia Francorum.* Trans. Lewis Thorpe, *The History of the Franks.* Harmondsworth: Penguin, 1974.

Guerric of Igny. *Sermons II.* Ed. John Morson and Hilary Costello. Sources chrétiennes 202. Paris: Éditions du Cerf, 1973.

Guibert of Nogent. *De vita sua.* Ed. Georges Bourgin, *Guibert de Nogent: histoire de sa vie, 1053–1124.* Paris: A. Picard et fils, 1907. Trans. John F. Benton, *Self and Society in Medieval France: The Memoirs of Abbot Guibert of Nogent.*

Toronto: University of Toronto Press in association with the Medieval Academy of America, 1984.

———. *Moralia in Genesin.* PL 156: 19–337.

Heinrich von Nördlingen. *Letters.* Trans. Lucia Corsini, *Heinrich von Nördlingen e Margaretha Ebner: le lettere 1332–1350,* Medioevo tedesco 9. Pisa: ETS, 2001.

Heloise. *Epist. 6.* "The Letter of Heloise on Religious Life and Abelard's First Reply." Ed. J. T. Muckle. *Mediaeval Studies* 17 (1955): 241–53. Trans. Betty Radice and M. T. Clanchy in *The Letters of Abelard and Heloise.* New York: Penguin, 2003. 93–111.

Herrad of Hohenbourg. *Hortus deliciarum.* Ed. Rosalie Green, Michael Evans, Christine Bischoff, and Michael Curschmann. 2 vols. London: Warburg Institute, 1979.

Hildebert of Lavardin. *Carmina minora.* Ed. A. Brian Scott. Leipzig: Teubner, 1969.

———. *In festo purificationis Beatae Mariae Sermo Primus.* PL 171: 611–15.

Hildegard of Bingen. *Letters.* Ed. L. Van Acker, *Hildegardis Bingensis Epistolarium.* CCCM 91, 91A, 91B (co-ed. M. Klaes-Hachmöller). Turnhout: Brepols, 1991. Trans. Joseph L. Baird and Radd K. Ehrman, *The Letters of Hildegard of Bingen,* 3 vols. New York: Oxford University Press, 1994–2004.

———. *Scivias.* Ed. Aldegundis Führkötter, with Angela Carlevaris. CCCM 43, 43A. Turnholt: Brepols, 1978. Trans. Mother Columba Hart and Jane Bishop, *Scivias.* New York: Paulist Press, 1990.

Honorius Augustodunensis. *De luminaribus ecclesiae.* PL 172: 197–234.

———. *Elucidarium.* Ed. Yves Lefèvre, *L'Elucidarium et les lucidaires.* Bibliothèque des Ecoles françaises d'Athènes et de Rome 180. Paris: E. de Boccard, 1954.

———. *Opera.* PL 172: 9–1270.

———. *Quod monachis liceat predicare.* In *Honorius Augustodunensis. Beitrag zur Geschichte des geistigen Lebens im 12. Jahrhundert.* Ed. Joseph A. Endres. Kempten Munich: J. Kösel, 1906. 147–50.

Horace. *Ars poetica.* Ed. Niall Rudd, *Epistles, Book II and Epistle to the Pisones (Ars poetica).* Cambridge: Cambridge University Press, 1989.

———. *The Odes.* Ed. Kenneth Quinn. London: Bristol Classical Press, 1997. Trans. W. G. Shepherd, *The Complete Odes and Epodes with the Centennial Hymn.* New York: Penguin, 1983.

Hugh of Fouilloy. *Aviarum.* Ed. and trans. Willene B. Clark, *The Medieval Book of Birds: Hugh of Fouilloy's Aviarum.* Binghamton, N.Y.: Medieval and Renaissance Texts and Studies, 1992.

———. *De claustro animae.* PL 176: 1017–182.

Hugh Metel. *Epist. 16–17.* "Hugh Metel, Heloise, and Peter Abelard: The Letters of an Augustinian Canon and the Challenge of Innovation in Twelfth-Century Lorraine." Trans. Constant J. Mews. *Viator* 32 (2001): 89–91.

Hugh of St. Victor. "De tribus maximis circumstantiis gestorum." Ed. William M. Green. *Speculum* 18 (1943): 484–93. Trans. in Mary J. Carruthers, *The Book of Memory: A Study of Memory in Medieval Culture.* Cambridge: Cambridge University Press, 1990. 261–66.

———. *Didascalicon de studio legendi: A Critical Text.* Ed. Charles Henry Buttimer. Washington, D.C.: Catholic University Press, 1939. Trans. Jerome Taylor, *Didascalicon: A Medieval Guide to the Arts.* New York: Columbia University Press, 1961.

Idung of Prüfening. *Dialogus duorum monachorum.* Trans. Jeremiah F. O'Sullivan, Joseph Leahey, and Grace Perrigo, *Cistercians and Cluniacs: The Case for Cîteaux.* Kalamazoo, Mich.: Cistercian Publications, 1977. 21–141.

Institutio sanctimonialium. Ed. Albert Werminghoff. MGH Legum Sectio 3, Conc. II, 1. Hannover: Hahn, 1906. 421–56.

Isidore. *Differentiae.* PL 83: 1–98.

———. *Etymologies.* Ed. W. M. Lindsay, *Etymologiae.* 2 vols. Oxford: Clarendon Press, 1911; reprinted 1962.

Jerome. *Hebraicae quaestiones in libro Geneseos.* Ed. Paulus de Lagarde. In *S. Hieronymi presbyteri opera. Pars I: Opera exegetica.* CCSL 72. Turnhout: Brepols, 1959. 59–161.

———. *Liber interpretationis hebraicorum nominum.* Ed. Paulus de Lagarde. In *S. Hieronymi presbyteri opera. Pars I: Opera exegetica.* CCSL 72. Turnhout: Brepols, 1959. 1–56.

———. *Sancti Evsebii Hieronymi Epistulae.* Ed. Isidore Hilberg. CSEL 54–56. Vienna: F. Tempsky, 1910–1918.

John of Salisbury. *Historia pontificalis.* Ed. and trans. Marjorie Chibnall, *Memoirs of the Papal Court.* London: Nelson, 1956.

———. *Policraticus.* Ed. C. C. J. Webb, *Ioannis Saresberiensis episcopi Carnotensis Policratici.* 2 vols. Oxford: Clarendon Press, 1909. Trans. (in part) Joseph B. Pike, *Frivolities of Courtiers and Footprints of Philosophers.* Minneapolis: University of Minnesota Press, 1938.

Lactantius, *Divinae institutiones.* Ed. Eberhard Heck and Antonie Wlosok, *Epitome divinarum institutionum.* Stuttgart: Teubner, 1994.

Libellus de diversis ordinibus et professionibus qui sunt in aecclesia. Ed. and trans. G. Constable and B. Smith. Oxford: Clarendon Press, 1972.

Liber florum. Prologue. In Richard William Hunt, "*Liber florum*: A Twelfth-Century Theological Florilegium," in Roland Hissette, Guibert Michiels, and Dirk van den Auweele, eds., *Sapientiae doctrina: mélanges de théologie et de littérature médiévales offerts à Dom Hildebrand Bascour O.S.B.* Leuven: Abbaye du mont César, 1980. 138–39.

Macrobius. *Saturnalia.* Ed. James Willis. 2nd ed. Stuttgart: Teubner, 1994. Trans. Percival Vaughan Davies, *The Saturnalia.* New York: Columbia University Press, 1969.

Manegold of Lautenbach. *Liber ad Gebehardum.* Ed. Kuno Francke. MGH Libelli 1. Hannover: Hahn, 1891. 300–430.

———. *Liber contra Wolfelmum.* Ed. Wilfried Hartmann. MGH Quellen zur Geistesgeschichte des Mittelalters 8. Weimar: Böhlau, 1972. Trans. Robert Ziomkowski, *Liber contra Wolfelmum.* Dallas Medieval Texts and Translations 1. Dudley, Mass.: Peeters, 2002.

The Medieval Craft of Memory: An Anthology of Texts and Pictures. Ed. Mary Carruthers and Jan M. Ziolkowski. Philadelphia: University of Pennsylvania Press, 2002.

Metamorphosis Goliae. Ed. R. B. C. Huygens, "Mitteilungen aus Handschriften." *Studi Medievali* ser. 3, 3 (1962): 764–72. Trans. C. Stephen Jaeger in *Ennobling Love: In Search of a Lost Sensibility*. Philadelphia: University of Pennsylvania Press, 1999. 229–39.

Necrologium conventus Marpach prope Eguisheim, in Alsatia superior. In "L'abbaye de Marbach." Ed. C. Hoffman. *Bulletin de la Société pour la conservation des monuments historiques d'Alsace* 2 ser. 20 (1902): 67–230, 173–222.

Necrologium monasterii S. Arbogasti. In *Nouvelles œuvres inédites*. Ed. Philippe André Grandidier. Colmar: H. Hüffel, 1897–1900. 5: 169–72.

Necrologium monasterii superioris Ratisbonensis. In *Dioceses Brixinensis, Frisingensis, Ratisbonensis*. Ed. F. L. Baumann. MGH Necr. Germ. 3. Berlin: Weidmann, 1905. 334–49.

Necrologium Zwifaltense. In *Dioeceses Augustensis, Constantiensis, Curiensis*. Ed. F. L. Baumann. MGH Necr. Germ. 1. Berlin: Weidmann, 1888. 240–68.

Otto of St. Blasien. *Chronici ab Ottone Frisingensi Conscripti Continuatio*. Ed. Roger Wilmans. MGH SS 20. Hannover: Hahn, 1868. 302–37.

Otto of Freising. *Ottonis et Rahewini Gesta Friderici I imperatoris*. Ed. G. Waitz. 3rd ed. MGH SSRG 46. Hannover: Hahn, 1978. Trans. Charles Christopher Mierow, *The Deeds of Frederick Barbarossa*. New York: Columbia University Press, 1953.

Paulinus of Milan. *Vita Ambrosii*. Ed. Michele Pellegrino, *Vita di S. Ambrogio*. Rome: Editrice Studium, 1961. Trans. Boniface Ramsey, "The Life of Saint Ambrose." In *Ambrose*. Early Church Fathers 3. London: Routledge, 1997. 196–218.

Peltre, P. *La vie de Ste Odile Vièrge Première Abbesse d'Hohenbourg Diocèse de Strasbourg*. Strasbourg, 1699.

Peter Comestor. *Historia scholastica*. PL 198: 1049–722.

———. *Historia scholastica*, Prologue. Ed. A. Sylwan, "Petrus Comestor, *Historia Scholastica*: une nouvelle édition," *Sacris Erudiri* 39 (2000): 345–82, 379.

Peter Damian. *Dominus Vobiscum*. PL 145: 231–52.

———. *Sermones*. Ed. Giovanni Lucchesi. CCCM 57. Turnhout: Brepols, 1983.

———. *The Letters of Peter Damian*. Trans. Owen J. Blum. 5 vols. Washington, D.C.: Catholic University of American Press, 1989-.

Peter Lombard. *Sentences*. Ed. Ignatius C. Brady, *Sententiae in IV libris distinctae*. 3rd ed. 2 vols. Spicilegium Bonaventurianum 4–5. Grottaferrata: Editiones Collegii S. Bonaventurae ad Claras Aquas, 1971–1981.

Peter of Blois. *De amicitia Christiana*. Ed. M.-M. Davy, *Un traité de l'amour du XIIe siècle*. Paris: E. de Boccard, 1932.

———. *Epist. 92*. PL 207: 289–91.

Peter the Venerable. *Epist. 115*. Ed. Giles Constable, *The Letters of Peter the Venerable*. Cambridge, Mass.: Harvard University Press, 1967. I: 303–8. Trans. Betty Radice and M. T. Clanchy in *The Letters of Abelard and Heloise*. New York: Penguin, 2003. 217–23.

Prudentius. *Psychomachia*. Ed. and trans. H. J. Thomson in *Prudentius*. Cambridge, Mass.: Harvard University Press, 1962. I: 274–343.

Pseudo-Augustine. *Sermo 1, De cereo Paschali*. PL 46: 818–21.

Quintilian. *Institutiones oratoriae*. Ed. and trans. Jean Cousin, *Institution Oratoire*. 3 vols. Paris: Société d'édition "Les Belles Lettres," 1975–1980.

Die Reinhardsbrunner Briefsammlung. Ed. Friedel Peeck. MGH Epistolae selectae 5. Munich: Monumenta Germaniae Historica, 1978.

Rhabanus Maurus. *De universo*. PL 111: 9–614.

Richard of Poitiers. *Chronicon. Ex Ricardi Pictaviensis Chronica*. Ed. G. Waitz. MGH SS 26. Hannover: Hahn, 1882. 74–82.

Rupert of Deutz. *Altercatio monachi et clerici, quod liceat monacho praedicare*. PL 170: 537–42.

———. *Commentaria in Canticum canticorum*. Ed. Rhaban Haacke. CCCM 26. Turnhout: Brepols, 1974.

———. *De sancta Trinitate et operibus eius*. Ed. Rhaban Haacke. CCCM 21–24. Turnhout: Brepols, 1971–1973.

———. *Liber de divinis officiis*. Ed. Rhaban Haacke. CCCM 7. Turnhout: Brepols, 1967.

The St. Albans Psalter (Albani Psalter). Ed. Otto Pächt, C. R. Dodwell, and Francis Wormald. Studies of the Warburg Institute 25. London: Warburg Institute, University of London, 1960.

The St. Gall Tractate: A Medieval Guide to Rhetorical Syntax. Ed. and trans. A. Grotans and D. Porter. Columbia, S.C.: Camden House, 1995.

Semonides. Poem 7. In *Greek Elegy and Iambus*. Ed. and trans. J. M. Edmonds. Cambridge, Mass.: Harvard University Press, 1993. II: 217–25.

Seneca. *Ad Lucilium Epistulae morales*. Trans. Richard M. Gummere. Loeb Classical Library 75–77. New York: G.P. Putnam's Sons, 1920.

———. *De Clementia*. Trans. John W. Basore, "On Mercy." In *Moral Essays*. 3 vols. Cambridge, Mass., 1958. I: 356–447.

Speculum virginum. Ed. Jutta Seyfarth. CCCM 5. Turnhout: Brepols, 1990. Extracts trans. Barbara Newman, "*Speculum virginum*: Selected Excerpts." In Constant J. Mews, ed., *Listen, Daughter: The* Speculum virginum *and the Formation of Religious Women in the Middle Ages*. New York: Palgrave, 2001. 269–96.

Thomas of Cantimpré. *Bonum universale de apibus*. Trans. Henri Platelle, *Les exemples du "Livre des abeilles": Une vision médiévale*. Turnhout: Brepols, 1997.

Die Urkunden Friedrichs I. Ed. Heinrich Appelt, with Rainer Maria Herkenrath, Walter Koch, et al. MGH DDRG 10.1–5. Hannover: Hahn, 1975–1990.

Venantius Fortunatus. *Poems*. Trans. Judith George, *Venantius Fortunatus: Personal and Political Poems*. Liverpool: Liverpool University Press, 1995.

Vincent of Beauvais. *Libellus totius operis apologeticus*. Ed. Serge Lusignan, *Préface au Speculum maius de Vincent de Beauvais: réfraction et diffraction*. Montréal: Bellarmin, 1979.

Virgil. *Georgics*. Ed. R. A. B. Mynors. New York: Oxford University Press, 1990.

Visions of Heaven and Hell Before Dante. Ed. Eileen Gardiner. New York: Italica Press, 1988.

Vita Eigilis abbatis Fuldensis auctore Candido. Ed. W. Wattenbach. MGH SS 15.1. Hannover: Hahn, 1887. 221–33.

Vita Leonis noni. Ed. Michel Parisse and trans. Monique Goullet, *La vie du Pape Léon IX: Brunon, évêque de Toul.* Paris: Belles Lettres, 1997.

Vita Odiliae Abbatissae Hohenburgensis. Ed. Wilhelm Levison. MGH SSRM 6. Hannover: Hahn, 1913 (reprinted 1979). 24–50.

Vita sanctae Hildegardis. Ed. Monica Klaes. CCCM 126. Turnhout: Brepols, 1993. Trans. Anna Silvas in *Jutta and Hildegard: The Biographical Sources.* Medieval Women: Texts and Contexts 1. Turnhout: Brepols, 1998. 118–210.

Vita sancti Udalrici episcopi Augustensis. PL 142: 1183–204.

Walter of Châtillon. *Carmina II.* Ed. H. Boehmer. MGH Libelli 3. Hannover: Hahn, 1897. 558–60.

Walter of St. Victor. *Contra quatuor labyrinthos franciae.* Ed. P. Glorieux, "Le *Contra quatuor labyrinthos franciæ* de Guathier de Saint-Victor," *Archives d'histoire doctrinale et littéraire du moyen âge* 19 (1952): 187–335.

Women and Monasticism in Medieval Europe: Sisters and Patrons of the Cistercian Reform. Trans. Constance Berman. TEAMS Document of Practice Series. Kalamazoo, Mich.: Medieval Institute Publications, 2002.

RESOURCE WORKS AND MANUSCRIPT CATALOGUES

Alsatia aevi Merovingici, Carolingici, Saxonici, Salici, Suevici diplomatica. Ed. Johann Daniel Schoepflin. 2 vols. Mannheim: Ex Typographia Academica, 1772–1775.

Catalogue général des manuscrits des bibliothèques publiques de France. Paris: Librarie Plon, 1886- .

Gallia Christiana in provincias ecclesiasticas distributa. Ed. Denis de Sainte-Marthe, rev. Paul Piolin. Paris: Victor Palmé, 1744- .

Die Handschriften des klosters Zwiefalten. Ed. Karl Löffler. Archiv für bibliographie, buch- und bibliothekswesen. Supplement 6. Linz: F. Winkler, 1931.

Handschriftenerbe des deutschen Mittelalters. Ed. Sigrid Krämer. 3 vols. Mittelalterliche Bibliothekskataloge Deutschlands und der Schweiz, Supplement 1. Munich: Beck, 1989–1990.

Katalog der illuminierten Handschriften der Württembergischen Landesbibliothek Stuttgart. 3 vols. Denkmäler der Buchkunst, vols. 7–8, 12. Stuttgart: A. Hiersemann, 1987- .

Die lateinischen mittelalterlichen Handschriften. Ed. Hardo Hilg. Die Handschriften der Germanischen Nationalmuseums Nürnberg, 2. Wiesbaden: Harrassowitz, 1983- .

Die lateinischen mittelalterlichen Handschriften der Universitätsbibliothek Freiburg im Breisgau: (ab Hs. 231). Ed. Winfried Hagenmaier. Kataloge der Universitätsbibliothek Freiburg im Breisgau, 1, 3. Wiesbaden: Harrassowitz, 1980.

Ouy, Gilbert, ed. *Les manuscrits de l'abbaye de Saint-Victor: catalogue établi sur la base du répertoire de Claude de Grandrue (1514).* 2 vols. Bibliotheca Victorina 10. Turnhout: Brepols, 1999.

Nova subsidia diplomatica . . . Ed. Stefan Alexander Würdtwein. 14 vols. Heidelberg: T. Goebhardt, 1781–1792.

SECONDARY SOURCES

Adolf, Helen. "The Figure of Wisdom in the Middle Ages." In *Arts libéraux et philosophie au moyen âge: Actes du quatrième Congrès international de philosophie médiévale.* Montréal: Institut d'études médiévales, 1969. 429–43.

Alexander, Jonathan J. G. *Medieval Illuminators and Their Methods of Work.* New Haven, Conn.: Yale University Press, 1992.

———. "Scribes as Artists: The Arabesque Initial in Twelfth-Century English Manuscripts." In M. B. Parkes and Andrew G. Watson, eds., *Medieval Scribes, Manuscripts and Libraries: Essays Presented to N. R. Ker.* London: Scolar Press, 1978. 87–116.

Alford, Elizabeth and Ingrid Stadler. "A Discussion of Linda Nochlin's Essay, 'Why Have There Been No Great Women Artists?' " In Ingrid Stadler, ed., *Contemporary Art and Its Philosophical Problems.* Buffalo, N.Y.: Prometheus Books, 1987. 45–59.

Arduini, Maria. *Rupert von Deutz und der "status christianitatis" seiner Zeit: symbolisch-prophetische Deutung der Geschichte.* Cologne: Böhlau, 1987.

Arts libéraux et philosophie au moyen âge: Actes du quatrième Congrès international de philosophie médiévale. Montréal: Institut d'études médiévales, 1969.

Astell, Ann. *The Song of Songs in the Middle Ages.* Ithaca, N.Y.: Cornell University Press, 1990.

Autenrieth, Johanne. "Einige Bemerkungen zu den Gedichten im *Hortus deliciarum* Herrads von Landsberg." In Johanne Autenrieth and Franz Brunhölzl, eds., *Festschrift Bernhard Bischoff zu seinem 65. Geburtstag dargebracht von Freunden, Kollegen und Schülern.* Stuttgart: A. Hiersemann, 1971. 307–21.

Baldwin, Marshall W. *Alexander III and the Twelfth Century.* Glen Rock, N.J.: Newman Press, 1968.

Bardy, Gustave. "Saint Gregoire VII et la reforme canoniale au XIe siècle." *Studi Gregoriani* 1 (1947): 47–64.

Barth, Médard. *Die Heilige Odilia, Schutzherrin des Elsass: Ihr Kult im Volk und Kirche.* Strasbourg: Gesellschaft für Elsässische Kirchengeschichte, 1938.

Barthes, Roland. "The Death of the Author." In Roland Barthes, *Image, Music, Text.* Trans. Stephen Heath. London: Fontana, 1977. 142–48.

Bauerreiss, Romuald. *Arbor vitae: Der "Lebensbaum" und seine Verwendung in Liturgie, Kunst und Brauchtum des Abendlandes.* Abhandlungen der Bayerischen Benediktiner-Akademie 3. Munich: Neuer Filser-Verlag, 1938.

———. "Honorius von Canterbury und Kuno I. der Raitenbucher, Bischof von Regensburg 1126–1132." *Studien und Mitteilungen zur Geschichte des Benediktinerordens und seiner Zweige* 67 (1956): 306–13.

Baumann, Priscilla. "The Deadliest Sin: Warnings Against Avarice and Usury on Romanesque Capitals in Auvergne." *Church History* 59 (1990): 7–18.

Baumont, Georges. "Notice historique sur la bibliothèque publique de Saint-Dié." *Le Pays Lorrain et le pays Messin* 12 (1920): 241–50.

Beach, Alison I. "Claustration and Collaboration Between the Sexes in the Twelfth-Century Scriptorium." In Sharon Farmer and Barbara H. Rosenwein, eds., *Monks and Nuns, Saints and Outcasts: Religion in Medieval Society*. Ithaca, N.Y.: Cornell University Press, 2000. 57–75.

———. *Women as Scribes: Book Production and Monastic Reform in Twelfth-Century Bavaria*. Cambridge: Cambridge University Press, 2004.

Becq, Annie, ed. *L'Encyclopédisme: Actes du colloque de Caen, 12–16 janvier 1987*. Paris: Aux Amateurs de Livres, 1991.

Becquet, Jean. *Vie canoniale en France aux Xe–XIIe siècles*. London: Variorum Reprints, 1985.

Bell, David N. *What Nuns Read: Books and Libraries in Medieval English Nunneries*. Kalamazoo, Mich.: Cistercian Publications, 1995.

Benoit, A. "L'abbaye d'Étival: sa bibliothèque, ses manuscrits, ses archives." *Bulletin de la Société Philomatique Vosgienne* (1884–1885): 79–92.

Benson, Robert L. and Giles Constable, eds., with Carol D. Lanham. *Renaissance and Renewal in the Twelfth Century*. Toronto: University of Toronto Press and Medieval Academy of America, 1991.

Bergmann, Bettina. "The Roman House as Memory Theater: The House of the Tragic Poet in Pompeii." *Art Bulletin* 76 (1994): 225–56.

Bériou, Nicole. "The Right of Women to Give Religious Instruction in the Thirteenth Century." In Beverly Kienzle and Pamela Walker, eds., *Women Preachers and Prophets Through Two Millennia of Christianity*. Berkeley: University of California Press, 1998. 134–45.

Berman, Constance H. "Were There Twelfth-Century Cistercian Nuns?" *Church History* 68 (1999): 824–64.

Bernards, Matthäus. *Speculum virginum: Geistigkeit und Seelenleben der Frau im Hochmittelalter*. Cologne: Böhlau, 1955.

Bischoff, Bernhard. "Die Kölner Nonnenhandschriften und das Skriptorium von Chelles." *Mittelalterliche Studien* 1 (1966): 16–34.

———. *Latin Palaeography: Antiquity and the Middle Ages*. Trans. Dáibhí ó Cróinín and David Ganz. Cambridge: Cambridge University Press, 1990.

Bishop, T. A. M. "The Scribes of the Corbie *a-b*." In Peter Godman and Roger Collins, eds., *Charlemagne's Heir: New Perspectives on the Reign of Louis the Pious (814–840)*. Oxford: Clarendon Press, 1990. 523–36.

Blamires, Alcuin. "*Caput a femina, membra a viris*: Gender Polemic in Abelard's Letter 'On the Authority and Dignity of the Nun's Profession.'" In David Townsend and Andrew Taylor, eds., *The Tongue of the Fathers: Gender and Ideology in Twelfth-Century Latin*. Philadelphia: University of Pennsylvania Press, 1998. 55–79.

———. "The Limits of Bible Study for Medieval Women." In Lesley Smith and Jane Taylor, eds., *Women, the Book and the Godly: Select Proceedings of the St. Hilda's Conference, 1993*. 2 vols. Woodbridge, Suffolk: D.S. Brewer, 1995. 1: 1–12.

———. "Paradox in the Medieval Gender Doctrine of Head and Body." In Peter

Biller and A. J. Minnis, eds., *Medieval Theology and the Natural Body*. York Studies in Medieval Theology 1. Rochester, N.Y.: York Medieval Press, 1997. 13–29.

———. "Women and Preaching in Medieval Orthodoxy, Heresy, and Saints' Lives." *Viator* 26 (1995): 135–52.

Blamires, Alcuin and C. W. Marx. "Woman Not to Preach: A Disputation in British Library MS Harley 31." *Journal of Medieval Latin* 3 (1993): 34–49.

Bloomfield, Morton W. *The Seven Deadly Sins: An Introduction to the History of a Religious Concept*. East Lansing: Michigan State College Press, 1952.

Blum, Owen J. *St. Peter Damian: His Teaching on the Spiritual Life*. Washington, D.C.: Catholic University of America Press, 1947.

Blumenthal, Uta-Renate. *The Investiture Controversy: Church and Monarchy from the Ninth to the Twelfth Century*. Philadelphia: University of Pennsylvania Press, 1988.

Bober, Harry. "An Illustrated Medieval School-book of Bede's 'De natura rerum'." *Journal of the Walters Art Gallery* 19–20 (1956–1957): 65–97.

Bodarwé, Katrinette. "Kontakte zweier Konvente. Essen und Werden im Spiegel ihrer Handschriften." In Heinz Finger, ed., *Bücherschätze der rheinischen Kulturgeschichte: Aus der Arbeit mit den historischen Sondersammlungen der Universitäts- und Landesbibliothek Düsseldorf 1979 bis 1999*. Studia humaniora 34. Düsseldorf: Droste-Verlag, 2001. 49–68.

———. *Sanctimoniales litteratae: Schriftlichkeit und Bildung in den ottonischen Frauenkommunitäten Gandersheim, Essen und Quedlinburg*. Münster: Aschendorff, 2004.

Boeckler, Albert. *Die Regensburg-Prüfeninger Buchmalerei des XII. und XIII. Jahrhunderts*. Miniaturen aus Handschriften der Bayerischen Staatsbibliothek in München 8. Munich: A. Reusch, 1924.

Bolton, Diane. "Illustrations in Manuscripts of Boethius' Works." In Margaret Gibson, ed., *Boethius: His Life, Thought and Influence*. Oxford: Blackwell, 1981. 428–37.

Bond, Gerald A. *The Loving Subject: Desire, Eloquence, and Power in Romanesque France*. Philadelphia: University of Pennsylvania Press, 1995.

Borst, Arno. *Der Turmbau von Babel: Geschichte der Meinungen über Ursprung und Vielfalt der Sprachen und Völker*. 4 vols. Stuttgart: A. Hiersemann, 1957–1963.

Bourgain, Pascale. "Les verbes en rapport avec le concept d'auteur." In Michel Zimmerman, ed., *Auctor et auctoritas: invention et conformisme dans l'écriture médiévale: actes du colloque tenu à l'Université de Versailles-Saint-Quentin-en-Yvelines, 14–16 juin 1999*. Paris: École des chartes, 2001. 361–74.

Brasington, Bruce C. "*Recte docens vel credens*: Glosses to the Prologue to Ivo of Chartres' *Panormia* and Monastic Study of Canon Law." In Gert Melville, ed., *De ordine vitae: Zu Normvorstellungen, Organisationsformen und Schriftgebrauch im mittelalterlichen Ordenswesen*. Vita Regularis 1. Münster: Lit, 1996. 101–23.

———. "Religious Reform and Legal Study: Manuscripts of Canonistic Works by Ivo of Chartres at Cloister Schäftlarn." *Manuscripta* 39 (1995): 186–93.

Brody, Saul Nathaniel. *The Disease of the Soul: Leprosy in Medieval Literature.* Ithaca, N.Y.: Cornell University Press, 1974.

Brooke, Christopher. *The Monastic World, 1000–1300.* London: Elek, 1974.

Brown, Michelle P. "The Role of the Wax Tablet in Medieval Literacy: A Reconsideration in Light of a Recent Find from York." *British Library Journal* 20 (1994): 1–16.

Brundage, James A. and Elizabeth M. Makowski. "Enclosure of Nuns: The Decretal *Periculoso* and Its Commentators." *Journal of Medieval History* 20 (1994): 143–55.

Bugge, John. *Virginitas: An Essay in the History of a Medieval Ideal.* The Hague: Martinus Nijhoff, 1975.

Bultot, Robert. "L'auteur et la fonction littéraire du 'De fructibus carnis et spiritus'." *Recherches de théologie ancienne et médiévale* 30 (1963): 148–54.

———.*La doctrine du mépris du monde, en Occident, de S. Ambroise à Innocent III.* 6 vols. Louvain: Éditions Nauwelaerts, 1963–1964.

———."*Grammatica, ethica* et *contemptus mundi* au XIIe et XIIIe siècles." In *Arts libéraux et philosophie au moyen âge: Actes du quatrième Congrès international de philosophie médiévale.* Montréal: Institut d'études médiévales, 1969. 815–27.

Burg, André Marcel. "Quelle règle sainte Odile introduisit-elle à Hohenbourg?" *Archives de l'Église d'Alsace* n.s. 7 (1956): 123–24.

Büttner, Heinrich. "Die Beziehungen der heiligen Hildegard von Bingen zur Kurie, Erzbischof und Kaiser." In Ludwig Lenhart, ed., *Universitas, Dienst an Wahrheit und Leben: Festschift für Bischof Dr. Albert Stohr im Auftrag der Katholisch-Theologischen Fakultät der Johannes Gutenberg-Universität Mainz.* 2 vols. Mainz: M. Gruenwald, 1960. II: 60–68.

———. "Kaiserin Richgard und die Abtei Andlau." *Archives de l'Église d'Alsace* n.s. 7 (1956): 83–91.

———."Studien zur Geschichte des Stiftes Hohenburg im Elsaß während des Hochmittelalters." *Zeitschrift für die Geschichte des Oberrheins* 52 (1939): 103–38.

Bynum, Caroline Walker. ". . . 'And Woman His Humanity': Female Imagery in the Religious Writing of the Later Middle Ages." In Caroline Walker Bynum, Stevan Harrell, and Paula Richman, eds., *Gender and Religion: On the Complexity of Symbols.* Boston: Beacon Press, 1986. 257–88.

———. *Docere verbo et exemplo: An Aspect of Twelfth-Century Spirituality.* Harvard Theological Studies 31. Missoula, Mont.: Scholars Press, 1979.

———. "The Female Body and Religious Practice in the Later Middle Ages." In Caroline Walker Bynum, *Fragmentation and Redemption: Essays on Gender And The Human Body in Medieval Religion.* New York: Zone Books, 1991. 181–238.

———. "The Spirituality of Regular Canons in the Twelfth Century." In *Jesus as Mother: Studies in the Spirituality of the High Middle Ages.* Berkeley: University of California Press, 1982. 22–58.

———. "Women Mystics in the Thirteenth Century: The Case of the Nuns of

Helfta." In *Jesus as Mother: Studies in the Spirituality of the High Middle Ages.* Berkeley: University of California Press, 1982. 170–262.

Cahn, Walter. *Romanesque Bible Illumination.* Ithaca, N.Y.: Cornell University Press, 1982.

Caiazzo, Irene. *Lectures médiévales de Macrobe: les Glosae Colonienses super Macrobium.* Paris: Vrin, 2002.

Cames, Gérard. *Allégories et symboles dans l'Hortus deliciarum.* Leiden: Brill, 1971.

———. *Byzance et la peinture romane de Germanie.* Paris: A. et J. Picard, 1966.

———. "Un nouveau fleuron de l'enluminure Romane en Alsace: l'Évangélistaire de Saint-Pierre, Perg. 7 à Karlsruhe." *Cahiers alsaciens d'archéologie d'art et d'histoire* 7 (1963): 43–72.

Camille, Michael. "Illuminating Thought: The Trivial Arts in British Library, Burney Ms. 275." In Paul Binski and William Noel, eds., *New Offerings, Ancient Treasure: Studies in Medieval Art for George Henderson.* Thrupp, Stroud, Gloucestershire: Sutton, 2001. 343–66.

———. "Seeing and Reading: Some Visual Implications of Medieval Literacy and Illiteracy." *Art History* 8 (1985): 26–49.

Carr, Annemarie Weyl. "Women as Artists in the Middle Ages: 'The Dark Is Light Enough'." In Delia Gaze, ed., *Dictionary of Women Artists.* 2 vols. Chicago: Fitzroy Dearborn Publishers, 1997. I: 3–21.

Carruthers, Mary J. *The Book of Memory: A Study of Memory in Medieval Culture.* Cambridge: Cambridge University Press, 1990.

———. *The Craft of Thought: Meditation, Rhetoric and the Making of Images, 400–1200.* Cambridge: Cambridge University Press, 1998.

Carruthers, Mary and Jan M. Ziolkowski, eds. *The Medieval Craft of Memory: An Anthology of Texts and Pictures.* Philadelphia: University of Pennsylvania Press, 2002.

Caviness, Madeline H. "Anchoress, Abbess, and Queen: Donors and Patrons or Intercessors and Matrons?" In June Hall McCash, ed., *The Cultural Patronage of Medieval Women.* Athens: University of Georgia Press, 1996. 105–54.

———. "Artist: 'To See, Hear, and Know All at Once'." In Barbara Newman, ed., *Voice of the Living Light: Hildegard of Bingen and Her World.* Berkeley: University of California Press, 1998. 110–24.

———. "Gender Symbolism and Text Image Relationships: Hildegard of Bingen's *Scivias.*" In *Art in the Medieval West and Its Audience.* Aldershot: Ashgate, 2001. VII.

———. "Hildegard as Designer of the Illustrations to her Works." In *Art in the Medieval West and Its Audience.* Aldershot: Ashgate, 2001. VIII.

———. "Hildegard of Bingen: Some Recent Books." *Speculum* 77 (2002): 113–20.

———. "Images of Divine Order and the Third Mode of Seeing." *Gesta* 22 (1983): 99–120.

Châtillon, François. "Recherches critiques sur les différents personnages nommés Manegold." *Revue du moyen âge latin* 9 (1953): 153–70.

Châtillon, Jean. "La culture de l'école de Saint-Victor au 12e siècle." In Maurice de Gandillac and Éduard Jeauneau, eds., *Entretiens sur la Renaissance du 12e siècle.* Paris: La Haye, 1968. 147–60.

————. "Un commentaire anonyme de la Règle de saint Augustin." In Béatrice Weis, ed., *Le Codex Guta-Sintram: Manuscrit 37 de la Bibliothèque du Grand séminaire de Strasbourg*. 2 vols. Lucerne: Editions Facsimilés, 1983. II: 180–91.

————. *Le mouvement canonial au moyen âge: Réforme de l'église, spiritualité et culture*. Ed. Patrice Sicard. Bibliotheca Victorina 3. Paris: Brepols, 1992.

Chazelle, Celia M. "Pictures, Books, and the Illiterate: Pope Gregory I's Letters to Serenus of Marseilles." *Word and Image* 6 (1990): 138–53.

Chenu, Marie-Dominique. "*Auctor, actor, autor.*" *Bulletin du Cange* 3 (1927): 81–86.

————. *Nature, Man, and Society in the Twelfth Century: Essays on New Theological Perspectives in the Latin West*. Ed. and trans. Jerome Taylor and Lester K. Little. Toronto: University of Toronto Press with Medieval Academy of America, 1997.

Chèvre, André. *Lucelle: histoire d'une ancienne abbaye cistercienne*. Delémont: Bibliothèque jurassienne, 1973.

Clanchy, M. T. *Abelard: A Medieval Life*. Oxford: Blackwell, 1997.

————. *From Memory to Written Record: England 1066–1307*. 2nd ed. Oxford: Blackwell, 1993.

Clark, Willene B. "The Illustrated Medieval Aviary and the Lay-Brotherhood." *Gesta* 21 (1982): 63–74.

Clark, Anne L. *Elisabeth of Schönau: A Twelfth-Century Visionary*. Philadelphia: University of Pennsylvania Press, 1992.

————. "Repression or Collaboration? The Case of Elisabeth and Ekbert of Schönau." In Scott L. Waugh and Peter D. Diehl, eds., *Christendom and Its Discontents: Exclusion, Persecution and Rebellion, 1000–1500*. Cambridge: Cambridge University Press, 1996. 151–67.

Clayton, Mary. *The Cult of the Virgin Mary in Anglo-Saxon England*. Cambridge: Cambridge University Press, 1990.

Clementi, Dione. "The Circumstances of Count Tancred's Accession to the Kingdom of Sicily, Duchy of Apulia and the Principality of Capua." In *Mélanges Antonio Marongiu*. Brussels: Éditions de la Librarie encyclopédique, 1968. 57–80.

Coakley, John. "Friars, Sanctity, and Gender: Mendicant Encounters with Saints, 1250–1325." In Clare A. Lees, ed., *Medieval Masculinities: Regarding Men in the Middle Ages*. Medieval Cultures 7. Minneapolis: University of Minnesota Press, 1994. 91–110.

————. "Gender and the Authority of Friars: The Significance of Holy Women for Thirteenth-Century Franciscans and Dominicans." *Church History* 60 (1991): 445–60.

Cohen, Adam S. "The Art of Reform in a Bavarian Nunnery Around the Year 1000." *Speculum* 74 (1999): 992–1020.

————. *The* Uta Codex: *Art, Philosophy, and Reform in Eleventh-Century Germany*. University Park: Pennnsylvania State University Press, 2000.

Cohen, Adam S. and Linda Safran. "Learning from Medieval Bronze Bowls," *Word and Image* 22 (2006): 211–18.

Cohen-Mushlin, Aliza. "The Twelfth-Century Scriptorium at Frankenthal." In

Linda L. Brownrigg, ed., *Medieval Book Production: Assessing the Evidence: Proceedings of the Second Conference of the Seminar in the History of the Book to 1500. Oxford, July 1988*. Los Altos Hills, Calif.: Anderson-Lovelace, 1990. 85–101.

Colish, Marcia L. *The Mirror of Language: A Study in the Medieval Theory of Knowledge*. Rev. ed. Lincoln: University of Nebraska Press, 1983.

———. *Peter Lombard*. 2 vols. Leiden: Brill, 1994.

Comito, Terry. *The Idea of the Garden in the Renaissance*. New Brunswick, N.J.: Rutgers University Press, 1978.

Comparetti, Domenico. *Vergil in the Middle Ages*. Trans. E. F. M. Benecke. Princeton, N.J.: Princeton University Press, 1997.

Constable, Giles. *The Reformation of the Twelfth Century*. Cambridge: Cambridge University Press, 1996.

———. "Renewal and Reform in Religious Life: Concepts and Realities." In Robert L. Benson and Giles Constable, eds., with Carol D. Lanham, *Renaissance and Renewal in the Twelfth Century*. Toronto: University of Toronto Press and the Medieval Academy of America, 1991. 37–67.

———. *Three Studies in Medieval Religious and Social Thought*. Cambridge: Cambridge University Press, 1995.

Constas, Nicholas P. "The Last Temptation of Satan: Divine Deception in Greek Patristic Interpretations of the Passion Narrative." *Harvard Theological Review* 97 (2004): 139–63.

Cook, Arthur Bernard. "The Bee in Greek Mythology." *Journal of Hellenic Studies* 15 (1895): 1–24.

Copeland, Rita. "Why Women Can't Read: Medieval Hermeneutics, Statutory Law, and the Lollard Heresy Trials." In Susan Sage Heinzelman and Zipporah Batshaw Wiseman, eds., *Representing Women: Law, Literature, and Feminism*. Durham, N.C.: Duke University Press, 1994. 253–86.

Courcelle, Pierre. *La Consolation de philosophie dans la tradition littéraire. Antécédents et postérité de Boèce*. Paris: Études Augustiniennes, 1967.

Cowdrey, H. E. J. *Pope Gregory VII, 1073–1085*. Oxford: Clarendon Press, 1998.

Crouse, Robert Darwin. "Honorius Augustodunensis: The Arts as *Via ad Patriam*." In *Arts libéraux et philosophie au moyen âge: Actes du quatrième Congrès international de philosophie médiévale*. Montréal: Institut d'études médiévales, 1969. 531–39.

Crusius, Irene, ed. *Studien zum Kanonissenstift*. Göttingen: Vandenhoeck und Ruprecht, 2001.

Curschmann, Michael. "Hören-Lesen-Sehen: Buch und Schriftlichkeit im Selbverständnis der volkssprachlichen literarischen Kultur Deutschlands um 1200." *Beiträge zur Geschichte der deutschen Sprache und Literatur* 106 (1984): 218–57.

———. "Imagined Exegesis: Text and Picture in the Exegetical Works of Rupert of Deutz, Honorius Augustodunensis, and Gerhoch of Reichersberg." *Traditio* 44 (1988): 145–69.

———. *"Pictura laicorum litteratura?* Überlegungen zum Verhältnis von Bild und volkssprachlicher Schriftlichkeit im Hoch- und Spätmittelalter bis zum

Codex Manesse." In Hagen Keller, Klaus Grubmüller and Nikolaus Stau-
    bach, eds., *Pragmatische Schriftlichkeit im Mittelalter: Erscheinungsformen
    und Entwicklungsstufen.* Munich: Fink, 1992. 211–29.
————. "Texte-Bilder-Strukturen. Der *Hortus deliciarum* und die frühmittelhoch-
    deutsche Geistlichendichtung." *Deutsche Vierteljahrsschrift für Literaturwis-
    senschaft und Geistesgeschichte* 55 (1981): 379–418.
Curtius, Ernest Robert. "Zur Geschichte des Wortes Philosophie im Mittelalter."
    Romanische Forschungen 57 (1943): 290–309.
d'Alverny, Marie-Thérèse. "La Sagesse et ses sept filles: Recherches sur les allégo-
    ries de la Philosophie et des Arts Libéraux du IX au XII siècle." In Marie-
    Thérèse d'Alverny, *Études sur le symbolisme de la Sagesse et l'iconographie méd-
    iévale.* Ed. Charles Burnett. Aldershot: Variorum, 1993. I.
Daly, Saralyn R. "Peter Comestor: Master of Histories." *Speculum* 32 (1957):
    62–73.
Darlington, Oscar G. "Gerbert, the Teacher." *American Historical Review* 52
    (1947): 456–76.
de Certeau, M. et al. *Le mépris du monde: la notion de mépris du monde dans la
    tradition spirituelle occidentale.* Paris: Éditions du Cerf, 1965.
de Clercq, Charles. "Hugues de Fouilloy, imagier de ses propres oeuvres?" *Revue
    du Nord* 45 (1963): 31–42.
de Gandillac, Maurice, Jacques Fontaine, Jean Châtillon, and Michel Lemoine,
    eds. *La Pensée encyclopédique au Moyen âge.* Paris: Editions de la Baconnière,
    1966.
de Ghellinck, J. *Le mouvement théologique du XII siècle.* 2nd ed. Bruges: Éditions
    "De Tempel," 1948.
de Lubac, Henri. *Medieval Exegesis.* 2 vols. Grand Rapids, Mich.: W. B. Eerdmans,
    2000. Vol. 2. Trans. E. M. Macierowski.
de Santis, Paola, ed. *I sermoni di Abelardo per le monache del Paracleto.* Mediae-
    valia Lovaniensia Ser. 1 Studia 31. Leuven: Leuven University Press, 2002.
de Vogüé, Adalbert. "La lecture quotidienne dans les monastères (300–700)."
    Collectanea Cisterciensia 51 (1989): 241–51.
Déchanet, J.-M. "*Seneca noster:* Des lettres à Lucilius à la lettre aux Frères du
    Mont-Dieu." In *Mélanges Joseph de Ghellinck.* 2 vols. Gembloux: J. Duculot,
    1951. 2: 753–66.
Delumeau, Jean. *History of Paradise: The Garden of Eden in Myth and Tradition.*
    Trans. Matthew O'Connell. New York: Continuum, 1995.
Demus, Otto. *Byzantine Art and the West.* New York: New York University Press,
    1970.
————. *The Mosaics of Norman Sicily.* London: Routledge and Paul, 1949.
————. *Romanesque Mural Painting.* Trans. Mary Whittall. London: Thames and
    Hudson, 1970.
Dereine, Charles. "Chanoines: des origines au XIIIe siècle." *Dictionnaire d'his-
    toire et de géographie ecclésiastiques* 12 (1953): col. 353–405.
————. "L'élaboration du statut canonique des chanoines réguliers, spécialement
    sous Urbain II." *Revue d'Histoire Ecclésiastique* 46 (1951): 534–65.

———. "Saint-Ruf et ses coutumes aux XIe et XIIe siècles." *Revue Bénédictine* 15 (1949): 161–82.

———. "Vie commune, règle de Saint Augustin et chanoines réguliers au XIe siècles." *Revue d'histoire ecclésiastique* 61 (1946): 365–406.

Derolez, Albert. *The Autograph Manuscript of the* Liber Floridus: *A Key to the Encyclopedia of Lambert of Saint-Omer.* Corpus Christianorum: Autographa Medii Aevi, 4. Turnhout: Brepols, 1998.

Dickinson, J. C. *The Origins of the Austin Canons and Their Introduction into England.* London: S.P.C.K., 1950.

Diebold, William J. "Verbal, Visual, and Cultural Literacy in Medieval Art: Word and Image in the Psalter of Charles the Bald." *Word and Image* 8 (1992): 89–99.

———. *Word and Image: An Introduction to Early Medieval Art.* Boulder, Colo.: Westview Press, 2000.

Dietrich, Paul Alan. "Eruditio Sacra: Symbol and Pedagogy in the Thought of Honorius Augustodunensis." Ph.D. dissertation, University of Chicago, 1981.

Dinshaw, Carolyn. *Chaucer's Sexual Poetics.* Madison: University of Wisconsin Press, 1989.

Dolbeau, François. "Quelques aspects des relations entre bibliothèques d'établissements religieux (XIIe–XVe siècles)." In *Naissance et fonctionnement des réseaux monastiques et canoniaux: Actes du Premier Colloque International du C.E.R.C.O.M., Saint-Etienne, 16–18 Septembre 1985.* Saint-Etienne: Publications Université Jean-Monnet, 1991. 495–509.

Dronke, Peter. *Women Writers of the Middle Ages: A Critical Study of Texts from Perpetua (d. 203) to Marguerite Porete (d. 1310).* Cambridge: Cambridge University Press, 1984.

Dubled, Henri. "L'Avouerie des monastères en Alsace au Moyen Age (VIIIe–XIIe siècle)." *Archives de l'Église d'Alsace* n.s. 10 (1959): 1–88.

———. "Recherches sur les chanoines réguliers de Saint-Augustin au diocèse de Strasbourg." *Archives de l'Église d'Alsace* n.s. 16 (1967–1968): 5–52.

Duggan, Lawrence G. "Was Art Really the 'Book of the Illiterate'?" *Word and Image* 5 (1989): 227–51.

Eastwood, Bruce S. "The Diagram of the Four Elements in the Oldest Manuscripts of Isidore's *De natura rerum.*" *Studi medievali* ser. 3, 42 (2001): 547–64.

Echard, Siân. "Designs for Reading: Some Manuscripts of Gower's *Confessio Amantis.*" In William Marx, ed., *Sources, Exemplars, and Copy-Texts: Influence and Transmission.* Essays from the Lampeter Conference of the Early Book Society, 1997. *Trivium* 31 (1999): 59–72.

Edsall, Mary Agnes. "Reading Like a Monk: Lectio Divina, Religious Literature, and Lay Devotion." Ph.D. dissertation, Columbia University, 2000.

Ehlers, Joachim. "Das Augustinerchorherrenstift St. Viktor in der Pariser Schul- und Studienlandschaft des 12. Jahrhunderts." In Georg Wieland, ed., *Aufbruch, Wandel, Erneuerung: Beiträge zur "Renaissance" des 12. Jahrhunderts.* Stuttgart: Frommann-Holzboog, 1995. 100–122.

El Kholi, Susann. *Lektüre in Frauenkonventen des ostfränkisch-deutschen Reiches vom 8. Jahrhundert bis zur Mitte des 13. Jahrhunderts.* Würzburger Wissenschaftliche Schriften 203. Würzburg: Königshausen and Neumann, 1997.

Elkins, Sharon K. *Holy Women of Twelfth-Century England.* Chapel Hill: University of North Carolina Press, 1988.

Elliott, Dyan. *Fallen Bodies: Pollution, Sexuality, and Demonology in the Middle Ages.* Philadelphia: University of Pennsylvania Press, 1999.

Endres, Joseph Anton. "Die Dialektiker und ihre Gegner im 11. Jahrhundert." *Philosophisches Jahrbuch* 19 (1906): 20–33.

———. *Honorius Augustodunensis: Beitrag zur Geschichte des geistigen Lebens im 12. Jahrhundert.* Munich: J. Kösel, 1906.

———. "Romanische Deckenmalereien und ihre Tituli zu St. Emmeram in Regensburg." *Zeitschrift für christliche Kunst* 15 (1902): 235–40.

Engels, L. J. "*Adtendite a falsis prophetis* (Ms. Colmar 128, ff. 152v/153v). Un texte de Pierre Abélard contre les Cisterciens retrouvé?" In *Corona Gratiarum: Miscellanea patristica, historica et liturgica Eligio Dekkers O. S. B. XII lustra complenti oblata.* 2 vols. Bruges: Sint Pietersabdij, 1975. 2: 195–228.

Esmeijer, Anna C. *Divina Quaternitas: A Preliminary Study in the Method and Application of Visual Exegesis.* Assen: Gorcum, 1978.

Étaix, Raymond. "Les homélies capitulaires." In Béatrice Weis, ed., *Le Codex Guta-Sintram: manuscrit 37 de la Bibliothèque du Grand séminaire de Strasbourg.* 2 vols. Lucerne: Editions Fac-similés, 1983. 2: 167–73.

Ettlinger, L. D. "Muses and Liberal Arts: Two miniatures from Herrad of Landsberg's *Hortus Deliciarum.*" In Douglas Fraser, Howard Hibbard, and Milton J. Lewine, eds., *Essays in the History of Art Presented to Rudolf Wittkower.* London: Phaidon, 1969. 29–35.

Evans, Gillian R. "*Studium discendi*: Otloh of St. Emmeram and the Seven Liberal Arts." *Recherches de théologie ancienne et médiévale* 44 (1977): 29–54.

———. *Philosophy and Theology in the Middle Ages.* London: Routledge, 1993.

Evans, Michael. "Allegorical Women and Practical Men: the Iconography of the *Artes* Reconsidered." In Derek Baker, ed., *Medieval Women: Dedicated and Presented to Professor Rosalind M.T. Hill . . .* Studies in Church History Subsidia 1. Oxford: Blackwell, 1978. 305–29.

———. "Fictive Painting in Twelfth-Century Paris." In John Onians, ed., *Sight and Insight: Essays on Art and Culture in Honour of E. H. Gombrich at 85.* London: Phaidon Press, 1994. 73–87.

———. "The Geometry of the Mind." *Architectural Association Quarterly* 12 (1980): 32–55.

Fassler, Margot. *Gothic Song: Victorine Sequences and Augustinian Reform in Twelfth-Century Paris.* Cambridge: Cambridge University Press, 1993.

———. "Who Was Adam of St. Victor? The Evidence of the Sequence Manuscripts." *Journal of the American Musicological Society* 37 (1984): 233–69.

Feiss, Hugh, "Heaven in the Theology of Hugh, Achard, and Richard of St Victor." In Jan Swango Emerson and Hugh Feiss, eds., *Imagining Heaven in the Middle Ages: A Book of Essays.* New York: Garland, 2000. 145–63.

Ferrante, Joan M. "The Education of Women in the Middle Ages in Theory, Fact, and Fantasy." In Patricia H. Labalme, ed., *Beyond Their Sex: Learned Women of the European Past*. New York: New York University Press, 1980. 9–42.

———. "Images of the Cloister—Haven or Prison." *Mediaevalia* 12 (1989): 57–66.

Ferruolo, Stephen C. *The Origins of the University: The Schools of Paris and Their Critics 1100–1215*. Stanford, Calif.: Stanford University Press, 1985.

Flanagan, Sabina. "The *Speculum virginum* and Traditions of Medieval Dialogue." In Constant J. Mews, ed., *Listen, Daughter: The* Speculum virginum *and the Formation of Religious Women in the Middle Ages*. New York: Palgrave, 2001. 181–200.

Flint, Valerie I. J. "Honorius Augustodunensis of Regensburg." In P. J. Geary, ed., *Authors of the Middle Ages*. II, 6. Aldershot: Variorum, 1995. 95–128

———. *Ideas in the Medieval West: Texts and Their Contexts*. London: Variorum Reprints, 1988.

———. "The Place and Purpose of the Works of Honorius Augustodunensis." In *Ideas in the Medieval West: Texts and Their Contexts*. London: Variorum Reprints, 1988. XII.

———. "The Sources of the *Elucidarius* of Honorius Augustodunensis." In *Ideas in the Medieval West: Texts and Their Contexts*. London: Variorum Reprints, 1988. X.

Forsyth, Ilene H. *Throne of Wisdom: Wood Sculptures of the Madonna in Romanesque France*. Princeton, N.J.: Princeton University Press, 1972.

Foucault, Michel. "What Is an Author?" In Donald F. Bouchard, ed., *Language, Counter-Memory, Practice: Selected Essays and Interviews*. Trans. Donald F. Bouchard and Sherry Simon. Ithaca, N.Y.: Cornell University Press, 1977. 113–38.

Fournier, Paul and Gabriel Le Bras, eds. *Histoire des collections canoniques en Occident: depuis les fausses décrétales jusqu'au Décret de Gratien*. Paris: Recueil Sirey, 1931–1932.

Fowler, Robert L. "Encyclopaedias: Definitions and Theoretical Problems." In Peter Binkley, ed., *Pre-modern Encyclopaedic Texts: Proceedings of the Second COMERS Congress, Groningen, 1–4 July 1996*. Leiden: Brill, 1997. 3–29.

Fransen, Gérard. "La tradition manuscrite de la *Panormie* d'Yves de Chartres." In Stanley Chodorow, ed., *Proceedings of the Eighth International Congress of Medieval Canon Law, San Diego, University of California at La Jolla, 21–27 August 1988*. Monumenta Iuris Canonici, Series C: Subsidia, 9. Vatican City: Biblioteca Apostolica Vaticana, 1992. 23–25.

Frassetto, Michael, ed. *Medieval Purity and Piety: Essays on Medieval Clerical Celibacy and Religious Reform*. New York: Garland, 1998.

Friedman, John B. "Les images mnémotechniques dans les manuscrits de l'époque gothique." In Bruno Roy and Paul Zumthor, eds., *Jeux de mémoire: aspects de la mnémotechnie médiévale*. Montréal: Presses de l'Université de Montréal, 1985. 169–84.

Fröhlich, Walter. "The Marriage of Henry VI and Constance of Sicily: Prelude and Consequences." *Anglo-Norman Studies* 15 (1992): 99–115.

Fullenwider, H. F. "Das *Mellificium*: die 'Honigmanufaktur' als Anthologie-

Gattung der Neulateinischen Literatur." *Humanistica lovaniensia* 33 (1984): 135–44.

Fulton, Rachel. *From Judgment to Passion: Devotion to Christ and the Virgin Mary, 800–1200.* New York: Columbia University Press, 2002.

Gambier-Parry, T. R. "Lending Books in a Medieval Nunnery." *Bodleian Quarterly Record* 5 (1927): 188–90.

Ganz, P. F. "On the Unity of the Middle High German *Lob Salomons.*" In *Mediaeval German Studies: Presented to Frederick Norman.* London: Institute of Germanic Studies, 1965. 46–59.

Gasse-Grandjean, Marie-José. *Les livres dans les abbayes vosgiennes du moyen âge.* Nancy: Presses Universitaires de Nancy, 1992.

Georgel, Marc Antoine. *L'abbaye d'Étival, Ordre de Prémontré: du XIIe au XVIIe siècle.* Bibliotheca analectorum praemonstratensium 3. Louvain: Averbode, 1962.

Georgianna, Linda. "In Any Corner of Heaven: Heloise's Critique of the Monastic Life." In Bonnie Wheeler, ed., *Listening to Heloise: The Voice of a Twelfth-Century Woman.* New York: St. Martin's Press, 2000. 187–216.

Gibson, Margaret T. "The *Artes* in the Eleventh Century." In *Arts libéraux et philosophie au moyen âge: Actes du quatrième Congrès international de philosophie médiévale.* Montréal: Institut d'études médiévales, 1969. 121–26.

———. "The *De doctrina Christiana* in the School of St. Victor." In Edward D. English, ed., *Reading and Wisdom: The* De doctrina Christiana *of Augustine in the Middle Ages.* Notre Dame, Ind.: University of Notre Dame Press, 1995. 41–47.

Gilchrist, John. "The Gregorian Reform Tradition and Pope Alexander III." In *Canon Law in the Age of Reform, 11th–12th Centuries.* Aldershot: Variorum, 1993.

Gillen, Otto. *Ikonographische Studien zum* Hortus deliciarum *der Herrad von Landsberg.* Berlin: Deutscher Kunstverlag, 1931.

Gilomen-Schenkel, Elsanne. "Engelberg, Interlaken und andere autonome Doppelklöster im Südwesten des Reiches (11.–13. Jh.). Zur Quellenproblematik und zur historiographischen Tradition." In Kaspar Elm and Michel Parisse, eds., *Doppelklöster und andere Formen der Symbiose männlicher und weiblicher Religiosen im Mittelalter.* Berlin: Duncker and Humblot, 1992. 115–33.

———. " 'Officium paterne providentie' ou 'Supercilium noxie dominationis': Remarques sur les couvents de bénédictines au Sud-Ouest du Saint-Empire." In *Les Religieuses dans le cloître et dans le monde des origines à nos jours: Actes du deuxième colloque international du C.E.R.C.O.R., Poitiers, 29 septembre–2 octobre 1988.* Saint-Étienne: Publications de l'Université de Saint-Étienne, 1994. 367–71.

Godwin, Frances G. "The Judith Illustration of the *Hortus deliciarum.*" *Extrait de la Gazette des beaux arts* ser. 5, 36 (1949): 25–46.

Goggin, Cheryl Gohdes. "The Illuminations of the Clairvaux Speculum virginum (Troyes, Bibliothèque municipale, MS. 252)." Ph.D. dissertation, Indiana University, 1982.

Gold, Penny Schine. *The Lady and the Virgin: Image, Attitude, and Experience in Twelfth-Century France*. Chicago: University of Chicago Press, 1985.

———."Male/Female Cooperation: The Example of Fontevrault." In Lillian Thomas Shank and John A. Nichols, eds., *Medieval Religious Women*. Vol. 1, *Distant Echoes*. Cistercian Studies Series 71. Kalamazoo, Mich.: Cistercian Publications, 1984. 151–68.

Golding, Brian. *Gilbert of Sempringham and the Gilbertine Order, c.1130–c.1300*. Oxford: Clarendon Press, 1995.

———. "Hermits, Monks and Women in Twelfth Century France and England: The Experience of Obazine and Sempringham." In Judith Loades, ed., *Monastic Studies: The Continuity of Tradition*. Bangor, Maine: Headstart History, 1990. 127–45.

Gorman, Michael M. "The Diagrams in the Oldest Manuscripts of Cassiodorus' *Institutiones*." *Revue bénédictine* 110 (2000): 27–41.

———. "The Diagrams in the Oldest Manuscripts of Isidore's *De natura rerum*, With a Note on the Manuscript Tradition of Isidore's Works." *Studi medievali* ser. 3, 42 (2001): 529–45.

———. "Hugh of St. Victor." In Jorge J. E. Gracia and Timothy B. Noone, eds., *A Companion to Philosophy in the Middle Ages*. Blackwell Companions to Philosophy 24. Oxford: Blackwell, 2003. 320–25.

———. "A List of Books Lent by the Cathedral Library in Verona in the Eleventh Century." *Scriptorium* 56 (2002): 320–23.

Gottschall, Dagmar. *Das "Elucidarium" des Honorius Augustodunensis: Untersuchungen zu seiner Überlieferungs- und Rezeptionsgeschichte im deutschsprachigen Raum mit Ausgabe der niederdeutschen Übersetzung*. Tübingen: M. Niemeyer, 1992.

Graf, Katrin. *Bildnisse schreibender Frauen im Mittelalter 9. bis Anfang 13. Jahrhundert*. Basel: Schwabe, 2002.

Grandidier, Philippe André. *Oeuvres historiques inédites de Ph. And. Grandidier*. L. Sprach, ed., 6 vols. Colmar: Au bureau de la Revue d'Alsace, 1865–1867.

Green, Rosalie B. "The Adam and Eve Cycle in the *Hortus deliciarum*." In Kurt Weitzmann, ed., *Late Classical and Mediaeval Studies in Honor of Albert Mathias Friend, Jr.* Princeton, N.J.: Princeton University Press, 1955. 340–47.

———. "The Flabellum of Hohenbourg." *Art Bulletin* 33 (1951): 153–55.

Greene, Thomas M. *The Light in Troy: Imitation and Discovery in Renaissance Poetry*. New Haven, Conn.: Yale University Press, 1982.

Greenhill, Eleanor Simmons. "The Child in the Tree: A Study of the Cosmological Tree in Christian Tradition." *Traditio* 10 (1954): 323–71.

Gregory, Tullio. "The Platonic Inheritance." In Peter Dronke, ed., *A History of Twelfth-Century Western Philosophy*. Cambridge: Cambridge University Press, 1988. 54–80.

Griffiths, Fiona J. "Brides and *Dominae*: Abelard's *Cura monialium* at the Augustinian Monastery of Marbach." *Viator* 34 (2003): 57–88.

———. "'Men's Duty to Provide for Women's Needs': Abelard, Heloise, and Their Negotiation of the *Cura monialium*." *Journal of Medieval History* 30 (2004): 1–24.

Grundmann, Herbert. *Religious Movements in the Middle Ages: The Historical Links Between Heresy, the Mendicant Orders and the Women's Religious Movement in the Twelfth and Thirteenth Centuries.* Trans. Steven Rowan. Notre Dame, Ind.: University of Notre Dame Press, 1995.

Guldentops, Guy. "The Sagacity of the Bees: An Aristotelian Topos in Thirteenth-Century Philosophy." In Carlos Steel, Guy Guldentops, Pieter Beullens, eds., *Aristotle's Animals in the Middle Ages and Renaissance.* Leuven: Leuven University Press, 1999. 275–96.

Gurevich, Aron. "The *Elucidarium*: Popular Theology and Folk Religiosity in the Middle Ages." In *Medieval Popular Culture: Problems of Belief and Perception.* Trans. János M. Bak and Paul A. Hollingsworth. Cambridge: Cambridge University Press, 1988. 153–75.

Haaby, Charles. *Stift Lautenbach.* Alsatia monastica 2. Kevelaer: Butzon and Bercker, 1958.

Haacke, Rhaban. "Nachlese zur Überlieferung der Schriften Ruperts von Deutz." *Deutsches Archiv* 26 (1970): 528–40.

———. "Überlieferung der Schriften Ruperts von Deutz." *Deutsches Archiv* 16 (1960): 397–436.

Haefeli-Sonin, Zuzana. *Auftraggeber und Entwurfskonzept im Zweifaltener Martyrolog des 12. Jahrhunderts: Stuttgart, Württembergische Landesbibliothek cod. hist. 2415.* New York: P. Lang, 1992.

Hamburger, Jeffrey F. "Brother, Bride and *alter Christus*: The Virginal Body of John the Evangelist in Medieval Art, Theology and Literature." In Ursula Peters, ed., *Text und Kultur: Mittelalterliche Literatur 1150–1450.* Stuttgart: Metzler, 2001. 296–327.

———. *Nuns as Artists: The Visual Culture of a Medieval Convent.* Berkeley: University of California Press, 1997.

———. *St. John the Divine: The Deified Evangelist in Medieval Art and Theology.* Berkeley: University of California Press, 2002.

———. *The Visual and the Visionary: Art and Female Spirituality in Late Medieval Germany.* New York: Zone Books, 1998.

———. "Women and the Written Word in Medieval Switzerland." In Susanne Bieri and Walther Fuchs, eds., *Building for Books: Traditions and Visions.* Berlin: Birkhäuser, 2001. 122–63.

Hamesse, Jacqueline. "Les florilèges philosophiques du XIIIe siècle." In *Les genres littéraires dans les sources théologiques et philosophiques médiévales: Définition, critique et exploitation: Actes du Colloque international de Louvain-la-Neuve, 25–27 mai 1981.* Louvain-la-Neuve: Institut d'Études Médiévales de l'Université Catholique de Louvain, 1982. 181–91.

———, ed. *Les prologues médiévaux.* Textes et études du moyen âge 15. Turnhout: Brepols, 2000.

———. "Le vocabulaire des florilèges médiévaux." In Olga Weijers, ed., *Méthodes et instruments du travail intellectuel au moyen âge: Études sur le vocabulaire.* Turnhout: Brepols, 1990. 209–30.

Häring, Nikolaus M. "Auctoritas in der sozialen und intellektuellen Struktur des zwölften Jahrhunderts." In Albert Zimmermann, ed., *Soziale Ordnungen im*

Selbstverständnis des Mittelalters. 2 vols. Berlin: de Gruyter, 1979–1980. 2: 517–33.

———. "Handschriftliches zu den Werken Gilberts Bischof von Poitiers (1142–1154)." *Revue d'histoire des textes* 8 (1978): 133–94.

———. "Introduction." In Gilbert of Poitiers, *The Commentaries on Boethius.* Ed. Nikolaus M. Häring. Toronto: Pontifical Institute of Mediaeval Studies, 1966. 3–47.

Haskins, Charles Homer. *The Renaissance of the Twelfth Century.* Cambridge, Mass.: Harvard University Press, 1927.

Hassig, Debra. *Medieval Bestiaries: Text, Image, Ideology.* Cambridge: Cambridge University Press, 1995.

Hathaway, Neil. "*Compilatio*: From Plagiarism to Compiling." *Viator* 20 (1989): 19–44.

Haupt, Josef. *Das hohe Lied, übersetz von Williram, erklärt von Rilindis und Herrat, aus der einzigen Handschrift der Hoffbibliothek zu Wien.* Vienna: Braumüller, 1864.

Haverkamp, Alfred. "Tenxwind von Andernach und Hildegard von Bingen: Zwei 'Weltanschauungen' in der Mitte des 12. Jahrhunderts." In Lutz Fenske, Werner Rösener and Thomas Zotz, eds., *Institutionen, Kultur und Gesellschaft im Mittelalter: Festschrift für Josef Fleckenstein zu seinem 65. Geburtstag.* Sigmaringen: J. Thorbecke, 1984. 515–48.

Head, Thomas. "'Monastic' and 'Scholastic' Theology: A Change of Paradigm?" In Nancy van Deusen and Alvin E. Ford, eds., *Paradigms in Medieval Thought Applications in Medieval Disciplines: A Symposium.* Lewiston, N.Y.: Edwin Mellen Press, 1990. 127–41.

Heinrich, Mary Pia. *The Canonesses and Education in the Early Middle Ages.* Washington, D.C.: Catholic University of America, 1924.

Heinzer, Felix. "Buchkultur und Bibliotheksgeschichte Hirsaus." In Klaus Schreiner, ed., *Hirsau, St. Peter und Paul, 1091–1991.* Vol. II. *Geschichte, Lebens- und Verfassungsformen eines Reformklosters.* Forschungen und Berichte der Archäologie des Mittelalters in Baden-Württemberg 10. Stuttgart: K. Theiss, 1991. 259–96.

Herlihy, David. "Did Women Have a Renaissance? A Reconsideration." *Medievalia et Humanistica* 13 (1985): 1–22.

Hilpisch, Stephen. "Erzbischof Hillin von Trier, 1152–1169." *Archiv für mittelrheinische Kirchengeschichte* 7 (1955): 9–21.

Hindman, Sandra L. *Christine de Pizan's "Epistre Othéa": Painting and Politics at the Court of Charles VI.* Toronto: Pontifical Institute of Mediaeval Studies, 1986.

Hirsch, Hans. "Die Urkundenfälschungen des Klosters Ebersheim und die Entstehung des Chronicon Ebersheimense." In *Festschrift Hans Nabholz.* Zürich: A.-G. Gebr. Leemann and Co., 1934. 23–53.

Hochstetler, Donald. "The Meaning of Monastic Cloister For Women According to Caesarius of Arles." In Thomas F. X. Noble and John J. Contreni, eds., *Religion, Culture, and Society in the Early Middle Ages: Studies in Honor of*

Richard E. Sullivan. Kalamazoo, Mich.: Medieval Institute Publications, 1987. 27–40.

Hollingsworth, Cristopher. *Poetics of the Hive: The Insect Metaphor in Literature.* Iowa City: University of Iowa Press, 2001.

Hollywood, Amy. *The Soul as Virgin Wife: Mechthild of Magdeburg, Marguerite Porete, and Meister Eckhart.* Notre Dame, Ind.: University of Notre Dame, 1995.

Holopainen, Toivo J. *Dialectic and Theology in the Eleventh Century.* Leiden: Brill, 1996.

Horner, Shari. *The Discourse of Enclosure: Representing Women in Old English Literature.* Albany: SUNY Press, 2001.

Hotchin, Julie. "Abbot as Guardian and Cultivator of Virtues: Two Perspectives on the *Cura monialium* in Practice." In Linda Rasmussen, Valerie Spear, and Diane Tillotson, eds., *Our Medieval Heritage: Essays in Honour of John Tillotson for his 60th Birthday.* Cardiff: Merton Priory Press, 2002. 50–64.

———. "Female Religious Life and the *Cura monialium* in Hirsau Monasticism, 1080 to 1150." In Constant J. Mews, ed., *Listen, Daughter: The Speculum virginum and the Formation of Religious Women in the Middle Ages.* New York: Palgrave, 2001. 59–83.

———. "Women's Reading and Monastic Reform in Twelfth Century Germany: The Library of the Nuns of Lippoldsberg." In Alison I. Beach, ed., *Manuscripts and Monastic Culture: The Twelfth-Century Renaissance in Germany.* Turnhout: Brepols, forthcoming.

Howard, Donald R. *The Three Temptations: Medieval Man in Search of the World.* Princeton, N.J.: Princeton University Press, 1966.

Hunt, Richard William. "The Introductions to the 'Artes' in the Twelfth Century." In *Studia mediaevalia in honorem admodum Reverendi Patris Raymundi Josephi Martin.* Bruges: De Tempel, 1948. 85–12.

Hutchison, Ann M. "What the Nuns Read: Literary Evidence from the English Bridgettine House, Syon Abbey." *Mediaeval Studies* 57 (1995): 205–22.

Hüttig, Albrecht. *Macrobius im Mittelalter: Ein Beitrag zur Rezeptionsgeschichte der* Commentarii in Somnium Scipionis. Frankfurt: P. Lang, 1990.

Idoux, M. C. "Relations d'Étival avec les monastères Alsacians d'Andlau et de Hohenbourg." *Annales de la Societé d'Emulation du Département des Vosges* 89 (1913): 3–108.

Jacqueline, B. "À propos des *Dictatus papae*: Les *Auctoritates apostolice sedis* d'Avranches." *Revue historique de droit français et étranger* sér. 4, 34 (1956): 569–74.

Jaeger, C. Stephen. *The Envy of Angels: Cathedral Schools and Social Ideals in Medieval Europe, 950–1200.* Philadelphia: University of Pennsylvania Press, 1994.

———. "Pessimism in the Twelfth-Century 'Renaissance'." *Speculum* 78 (2003): 1151–83.

Jeauneau, Édouard. "Jean de Salisbury et la lecture des philosophes." In Michael Wilks, ed., *The World of John of Salisbury.* Studies in Church History Subsidia 3. Oxford: Blackwell, 1984. 77–108.

Johnson, Penelope D. "The Cloistering of Medieval Nuns: Release or Repression, Reality or Fantasy?" In Dorothy O. Helly and Susan M. Reverby, eds., *Gendered Domains: Rethinking Public and Private in Women's History*. Ithaca, N.Y.: Cornell University Press, 1992. 27–39.

———. *Equal in Monastic Profession: Religious Women in Medieval France*. Chicago: University of Chicago Press, 1991.

———. "La théorie de la clôture et l'activité réelle des moniales françaises du XIe au XIIIe siècle." In *Les Religieuses dans le cloître et dans le monde des origines à nos jours: Actes du Deuxième Colloque International du C.E.R.C.O.R., Poitiers, 29 septembre–2 octobre 1988*. Poitiers: Publications de l'Université de Saint-Étienne, 1994. 491–505.

Jolivet, Jean. "Doctrines et figures de philosophes chez Abélard." In Rudolf Thomas, ed., *Petrus Abaelardus (1079–1142): Person, Werk und Wirkung*. Trierer theologische Studien 38. Trier: Paulinus-Verlag, 1980. 103–20.

Karp, Sandra Rae. "Peter Comestor's Historia scholastica: A Study in the Development of Literal Scriptural Exegesis." Ph.D. dissertation, Tulane University, 1978.

Karpp, Gerhard. "Bemerkungen zu den mittelalterlichen Handschriften des adeligen Damenstifts in Essen (9.–19. Jahrhundert)." *Scriptorium* 45 (1991): 163–204.

Katzenellenbogen, Adolf. *Allegories of the Virtues and Vices in Mediaeval Art from Early Christian Times to the Thirteenth Century*. Trans. Alan J. P. Crick. Toronto: University of Toronto Press and Medieval Academy of America, 1989.

———. "The Representation of the Seven Liberal Arts." In Marshall Clagett, Gaines Post and Robert Reynolds, eds., *Twelfth-Century Europe and the Foundations of Modern Society*. Madison: University of Wisconsin Press, 1966. 39–55.

Kelly, Douglas. *The Conspiracy of Allusion: Description, Rewriting, and Authorship from Macrobius to Medieval Romance*. Leiden: Brill, 1999.

Kelly, Thomas Forrest. *The Exultet in Southern Italy*. New York: Oxford University Press, 1996.

Kempf, Friedrich. "Ein zweiter '*Dictatus papae*'? Ein Beitrag zum Depositionsanspruch Gregors VII." *Archivum Historiae Pontificiae* 13 (1975): 119–39.

Kerby-Fulton, Kathryn. "Prophet and Reformer: 'Smoke in the Vineyard'." In Barbara Newman, ed., *Voice of the Living Light: Hildegard of Bingen and Her World*. Berkeley: University of California Press, 1998. 70–90.

———. "A Return to 'The First Dawn of Justice': Hildegard's Visions of Clerical Reform and the Eremitical Life." *American Benedictine Review* 40 (1989): 383–407.

Kerr, Berenice M. *Religious Life for Women, c.1100–c.1350: Fontevraud in England*. New York: Oxford University Press, 1999.

Kienzle, Beverly Mayne. "Defending the Lord's Vineyard: Hildegard of Bingen's Preaching Against the Cathars." In Carolyn Muessig, ed., *Medieval Monastic Preaching*. New York: Brill, 1998. 163–81.

———. "*Operatrix in vinea Domini*: Hildegard's Public Preaching and Polemics Against the Cathars." *Heresis* 26–27 (1996): 43–56.

Kitzinger, Ernst. "The Gregorian Reform and the Visual Arts: A Problem of Method." *Transactions of the Royal Historical Society* ser. 5, 22 (1972): 87–102.

Klein, Peter K., ed. *Der mittelalterliche Kreuzgang: Architektur, Funktion und Programm.* Regensburg: Schnell and Steiner, 2004.

Knepper, Joseph. *Das Schul- und Unterrichtswesen im Elsass von den Anfängen bis Gegen das Jahr 1530.* Strasbourg: Heitz and Mündel, 1905.

Kottje, Raymund. "*Claustra sine armario?* Zum Unterschied von Kloster und Stift im Mittelalter." In Joachim F. Angerer and Josef Lenzenweger, eds., *Consuetudines monasticae: Eine Festgabe für Kassius Hallinger aus Anlass seines 70. Geburtstages.* Studia Anselmiana 85. Rome: Pontificio Atheneo S. Anselmo, 1982. 125–44.

———. "Klosterbibliotheken und monastische Kultur in der zweiten Hälfte des 11. Jahrhunderts." *Zeitschrift für Kirchengeschichte* 80 (1969): 145–62.

Krüger, Annette and Gabriele Runge. "Lifting the Veil: Two Typological Diagrams in the *Hortus deliciarum.*" *Journal of the Warburg and Courtauld Institutes* 60 (1997): 1–22.

Kühnel, Bianca. *The End of Time in the Order of Things: Science and Eschatology in Early Medieval Art.* Regensburg: Schnell & Steiner, 2003.

Küsters, Urban. "Formen und Modelle religiöser Frauengemeinschaften im Umkreis der Hirsauer Reform des 11. und 12. Jahrhunderts." In Klaus Schreiner, ed., *Hirsau, St. Peter und Paul, 1091–1991.* Vol. 2. *Geschichte, Lebens- und Verfassungsformen eines Reformklosters.* Forschungen und Berichte der Archäologie des Mittelalters in Baden-Württemberg 10. Stuttgart: K. Theiss, 1991. 195–220.

Ladner, Gerhart B. "St Gregory of Nyssa and St Augustine on the Symbolism of the Cross." In Kurt Weitzmann, ed., *Late Classical and Medieval Studies in Honor of A. M. Friend, Jr.* Princeton, N.J.: Princeton University Press, 1955. 88–95.

———. "Terms and Ideas of Renewal." In Robert L. Benson and Giles Constable, eds., with Carol D. Lanham, *Renaissance and Renewal in the Twelfth Century.* Toronto: University of Toronto Press and Medieval Academy of America, 1991. 1–33.

———. "Vegetation Symbolism and the Concept of Renaissance." In Millard Meiss, ed., *De artibus opuscula XL: Essays in Honor of Erwin Panofsky.* New York: New York University Press, 1961. 303–22.

Lalou, Élisabeth. "Les tablettes de cire médiévales." *Bibliothèque de l'École des Chartes* 147 (1989): 123–40.

———, ed. *Les Tablettes à écrire de l'antiquité à l'époque moderne.* Turnhout: Brepols, 1992.

Lapidge, Michael. "The Study of Latin Texts in Late Anglo-Saxon England: The Evidence of Latin Glosses." In Nicholas Brooks, ed., *Latin and the Vernacular Languages in Early Medieval Britain.* Leicester: Leicester University Press, 1982. 99–140.

Laudage, Johannes. *Alexander III. und Friedrich Barbarossa.* Cologne: Böhlau, 1997.

Lawless, George. *Augustine of Hippo and His Monastic Rule*. Oxford: Clarendon Press, 1987.

Leclercq, Jean. "Le cloître est-il un paradis?" In *Le message des moines à notre temps*. Paris: A. Fayard, 1958. 141–59.

———. "Lettres de vocation à la vie monastique," *Analecta monastica* 3 sér 37 (1955): 169–97.

———. *The Love of Learning and the Desire for God*. Trans. Catherine Misrahi. 3rd ed. New York: Fordham University Press, 1982.

———. "Naming the Theologies of the Early Twelfth Century." *Mediaeval Studies* 53 (1991): 327–36.

———. "The Renewal of Theology." In Robert L. Benson and Giles Constable, eds., with Carol D. Lanham, *Renaissance and Renewal in the Twelfth Century*. Toronto: University of Toronto Press and the Medieval Academy of America, 1991. 68–87.

———. "*Simoniaca heresis*." *Studi Gregoriani* 1 (1947): 523–30.

———. "Un témoignage sur l'influence de Grégoire VII dans la réforme canoniale." *Studi Gregoriani* 6 (1959–61): 173–227.

Lefèvre, Placide. "À propos de la 'lectio divina' dans la vie monastique et canoniale." *Revue d'histoire ecclésiastique* 67 (1972): 800–809.

Lewis, Gertrud Jaron. *By Women, For Women, About Women: The Sister-Books of Fourteenth-Century Germany*. Toronto: Pontifical Institute of Mediaeval Studies, 1996.

Lewis, Suzanne. *The Art of Matthew Paris in the* Chronica Majora. Berkeley: University of California Press, 1987.

———. "The English Gothic Illuminated Apocalypse, *Lectio Divina*, and the Art of Memory." *Word and Image* 7 (1991): 1–32.

Leyser, Conrad. "Custom, Truth, and Gender in Eleventh-Century Reform." In R. N. Swanson, ed., *Gender and Christian Religion*. Studies in Church History 34. Woodbridge, Suffolk: Boydell Press, 1998. 75–91.

———. "*Lectio divina, oratio pura*: Rhetoric and the Techniques of Asceticism in the Conferences of John Cassian." In G. Barone, Marina Caffier, and Francesco Scorza Barcellona, eds., *Modelli di santità e modelli di comportamento*. Turin: Rosenberg and Sellier, 1994. 79–105.

Leyser, Henrietta. *Hermits and the New Monasticism: A Study of Religious Communities in Western Europe, 1000–1150*. New York: St. Martin's Press, 1984.

Leyser, Karl J. *Rule and Conflict in an Early Medieval Society: Ottonian Saxony*. London: Edward Arnold, 1979.

Little, Lester K. "Pride Goes Before Avarice: Social Change and the Vices in Latin Christendom." *American Historical Review* 76 (1971): 16–49.

Longère, Jean, ed. *L'abbaye parisienne de Saint-Victor au Moyen Age*. Paris: Brepols, 1991.

Luff, Robert. *Wissensvermittlung im europäischen Mittelalter: "Imago-mundi"-Werke und ihre Prologe*. Tübingen: M. Niemeyer, 1999.

Luscombe, David E. "Masters and Their Books in the Schools of the Twelfth Century." *Proceedings of the PMR Conference* 8 (1984): 17–33.

———. "Peter Abelard." In Peter Dronke, ed., *A History of Twelfth-Century Western Philosophy*. Cambridge: Cambridge University Press, 1988. 279–307.

———. "Peter Abelard and the Poets." In John Marenbon, ed., *Poetry and Philosophy in the Middle Ages: A Festschrift for Peter Dronke*. Boston: Brill, 2001. 155–71.

———. "Peter Comestor." In Katherine Walsh and Diana Wood, eds., *The Bible in the Medieval World: Essays in Memory of Beryl Smalley*. Studies in Church History Subsidia 4. Oxford: Blackwell, 1985. 109–29.

———. *The School of Peter Abelard: The Influence of Abelard's Thought in the Early Scholastic Period*. London: Cambridge University Press, 1969.

MacLean, Simon. "Queenship, Nunneries and Royal Widowhood in Carolingian Europe." *Past and Present* 178 (2003): 3–38.

Madertoner, Willibald. *Die zwiespältige Papstwahl des Jahres 1159*. Vienna: VWGÖ, 1978.

Makowski, Elizabeth. *Canon Law and Cloistered Women: Periculoso and Its Commentators, 1298–1545*. Washington, D.C.: Catholic University of America Press, 1997.

Mâle, Emile. *The Gothic Image: Religious Art in France of the Thirteenth Century*. Trans. Dora Nussey. New York: Harper and Row, 1972.

Mantz, Francis. *Le mur païen: Histoire et mystères archéologiques autour du Mont Sainte-Odile*. Strasbourg: Nuée bleue, 1991.

Marenbon, John. *Boethius*. Oxford: Oxford University Press, 2003.

———. "Gilbert of Poitiers." In Peter Dronke, ed., *A History of Twelfth-Century Western Philosophy*. Cambridge: Cambridge University Press, 1988. 328–52.

———. *The Philosophy of Peter Abelard*. Cambridge: Cambridge University Press, 1997.

———. "The Twelfth Century." In John Marenbon, ed., *Medieval Philosophy*. Routledge History of Philosophy 3. New York: Routledge, 1998. 150–87.

Marenbon, John and Rosamond McKitterick. "Philosophy and Its Background in the Early Medieval West." In John Marenbon, ed., *Medieval Philosophy*. Routledge History of Philosophy 3. New York: Routledge, 1998. 96–119.

Marignan, Albert. *Étude sur le manuscrit de l'Hortus deliciarum*. Strasbourg: J. H. E. Heitz, 1910.

Mariotte, Jean-Yves. "Les staufen en Alsace au XIIe siècle d'après leurs diplomes." *Revue d'Alsace* 119 (1993): 43–74.

Masi, Michael. "Boethius and the Iconography of the Liberal Arts." *Latomus* 33 (1974): 57–75.

———. "A Newberry Diagram of the Liberal Arts." *Gesta* 11 (1972): 52–56.

Mathis, Marcel. "Les prieures monastiques et canoniaux d'Alsace." *Archives de l'Église d'Alsace* 49 (1990/1991): 133–87.

Matter, E. Ann. *The Voice of My Beloved: The Song of Songs in Western Medieval Christianity*. Philadelphia: University of Pennsylvania Press, 1990.

Matthew, Donald. *The Norman Kingdom of Sicily*. Cambridge Medieval Textbooks. Cambridge: Cambridge University Press, 1992.

Mayo, Penelope C. "*Concordia Discordantium*: A Twelfth-Century Illustration of Time and Eternity." In Susan A. Stein and George D. McKee, eds., *Album*

Amicorum Kenneth C. Lindsay: Essays on Art and Literature. Binghamton, N.Y.: Dept. of Art and Art History, SUNY Binghamton, 1990. 29–56.

McGuire, Therese B. "Psychomachia: A Battle of the Virtues and Vices in Herrad of Landsberg's Miniatures." *Fifteenth Century Studies* 16 (1990): 189–97.

McKitterick, Rosamond. *The Carolingians and the Written Word.* Cambridge: Cambridge University Press, 1989.

———. "Nuns' Scriptoria in England and Francia in the Eighth Century." In *Books, Scribes and Learning in the Frankish Kingdoms, 6th–9th Centuries.* Aldershot: Variorum, 1994. VII.

———. "Women and Literacy in the Early Middle Ages." In *Books, Scribes and Learning in the Frankish Kingdoms, 6th–9th Centuries.* Aldershot: Variorum, 1994, XIII.

McLaughlin, Mary Martin. "Abelard's Conception of the Liberal Arts and Philosophy." In *Arts libéraux et philosophie au moyen âge: Actes du quatrième Congrès international de philosophie médiévale.* Montréal: Institut d'études médiévales, 1969. 523–30.

McNamara, Jo Ann. "The 'Herrenfrage': The Restructuring of the Gender System, 1050–1150." In Clare A. Lees, ed., *Medieval Masculinities: Regarding Men in the Middle Ages.* Medieval Cultures 7. Minneapolis: University of Minnesota Press, 1994. 3–29.

———. *Sisters in Arms: Catholic Nuns Through Two Millennia.* Cambridge, Mass.: Harvard University Press, 1996.

———. "Women and Power Through the Family Revisited." In Mary C. Erler and Maryanne Kowaleski, eds., *Gendering the Master Narrative: Women and Power in the Middle Ages.* Ithaca, N.Y.: Cornell University Press, 2003. 17–30.

Meier, Christel. "*Ecce auctor*: Beiträge zur Ikonographie literarischer Urheberschaft im Mittelalter." *Frühmittelalterstudien* 34 (2000): 338–92.

———. "Grundzüge der mittelalterlichen Enzyklopädik. Zu Inhalten, Formen und Funktionen einer problematischen Gattung." In Ludger Grenzmann and Karl Stackmann, eds., *Literatur und Laienbildung im Spätmittelalter und in der Reformationszeit: Symposion Wolfenbüttel 1981.* Stuttgart: J.B. Metzler, 1984. 467–500.

———. "Malerei des Unsichtbaren. Über den Zusammenhang von Erkenntnistheorie und Bildstruktur im Mittelalter." In Wolfgang Harms, ed., *Text und Bild, Bild und Text: DFG-Symposion 1988.* Stuttgart : J.B. Metzler, 1990. 35–65.

———. "Organisation of Knowledge and Encyclopaedic *Ordo*: Functions and Purposes of a Universal Literary Genre." In Peter Binkley, ed., *Pre-modern Encyclopaedic Texts: Proceedings of the Second COMERS Congress, Groningen, 1–4 July 1996.* Leiden: Brill, 1997. 103–26.

———. "Die Quadratur des Kreises: Die Diagrammatik des 12. Jahrhunderts als symbolische Denk- und Darstellungsform." In Alexander Patschovsky, ed., *Die Bildwelt der Diagramme Joachims von Fiore: zur Medialität religiös-politischer Programme im Mittelalter.* Ostfildern: J. Thorbecke, 2003. 23–53.

Meister, Aloys. *Die Hohenstaufen im Elsass: Mit besonderer berücksichtigung des reichsbesitzes und des familiengutes derselben im Elsass 1079–1255.* Inaugural-dissertation, Strassburg: Mainz, 1890.

Mews, Constant J. "From *Scivias* to the *Liber Divinorum Operum*: Hildegard's Apocalyptic Imagination and the Call to Reform." *Journal of Religious History* 24 (2000): 44–56.

———. "Monastic Educational Culture Revisited: The Witness of Zwiefalten and the Hirsau Reform." In George Ferzoco and Carolyn Muessig, eds., *Medieval Monastic Education*. London: Leicester University Press, 2000. 182–97.

———. "Hildegard, Visions and Religious Reform." In Rainer Berndt, ed., *"Im Angesicht Gottes suche der Mensch sich selbst": Hildegard von Bingen (1098–1998)*. Erudiri Sapientia 2. Berlin: Akademie Verlag, 2001. 325–42.

———. "Hugh Metel, Heloise, and Peter Abelard: The Letters of an Augustinian Canon and the Challenge of Innovation in Twelfth-Century Lorraine." *Viator* 32 (2001): 59–91.

———, ed. *Listen, Daughter: The* Speculum virginum *and the Formation of Religious Women in the Middle Ages*. New York: Palgrave, 2001.

———. "Heloise and Liturgical Experience at the Paraclete." *Plainsong and Medieval Music* 11 (2002): 25–35.

———. "The Council of Sens (1141): Abelard, Bernard, and the Fear of Social Upheaval." *Speculum* 77 (2002): 342–82.

———. "Virginity, Theology, and Pedagogy in the *Speculum virginum*." In Constant J. Mews, ed., *Listen, Daughter: The* Speculum virginum *and the Formation of Religious Women in the Middle Ages*. New York: Palgrave, 2001. 15–40.

Meyvaert, Paul. "The Medieval Monastic Claustrum." *Gesta* 12 (1973): 53–59.

———. "The Medieval Monastic Garden." In Elisabeth Blair MacDougall, ed., *Medieval Gardens*. Washington, D.C.: Dumbarton Oaks Research Library and Collection, 1986. 25–53.

Milis, Ludo. *L'Ordre des chanoines réguliers d'Arrouaise: son histoire et son organisation, de la fondation de l'abbaye-mère (vers 1090) à la fin des chapitres annuels (1471)*. Brugge: De Tempel, 1969.

Millar, Eric George. "The Inscription on the St John the Baptist Roll." *British Museum Quarterly* 6 (1931–1932): 108–9.

———. "Miniatures of the Life of St John the Baptist." *British Museum Quarterly* 6 (1931–1932): 1–3

Miller, Jacqueline T., *Poetic License: Authority and Authorship in Medieval and Renaissance Contexts*. New York: Oxford University Press, 1986.

Minnis, Alastair J. "*De impedimento sexus*: Women's Bodies and Medieval Impediments to Female Ordination." In Peter Biller and A. J. Minnis, eds., *Medieval Theology and the Natural Body*. York Studies in Medieval Theology 1. Rochester, N.Y.: York Medieval Press, 1997. 109–39.

———. "Late-Medieval Discussions of *Compilatio* and the Rôle of the *Compilator*." *Beiträge zur Geschichte der deutschen Sprache und Literatur* 101 (1979): 385–421.

———. *Medieval Theory of Authorship: Scholastic Literary Attitudes in the Later Middle Ages*. London: Scolar Press, 1984.

Misch, Manfred. *Apis est animal, apis est ecclesia: Ein Beitrag zum Verhältnis von Naturkunde und Theologie in spätantiker und mittelalterlicher Literatur*. Frankfurt: Peter Lang, 1974.

Mois, Jakob. *Das Stift Rottenbuch in der Kirchenreform des XI.–XII. Jahrhunderts: Ein Beitrag zur Ordens-Geschichte der Augustiner-Chorherren.* Munich: Verlag des Erzbischöflichen Ordinariats, 1953.

Mooney, Catherine M., ed. *Gendered Voices: Medieval Saints and Their Interpreters.* Philadelphia: University of Pennsylvania Press, 1999.

Moore, R. I. "Family, Community and Cult on the Eve of the Gregorian Reform." *Transactions of the Royal Historical Society* 5th ser. 30 (1980): 49–69.

———. *The Origins of European Dissent.* Toronto: University of Toronto Press and Medieval Academy of America, 1994.

Mordek, Hubert. "*Proprie auctoritates apostolice sedis.* Ein zweiter *Dictatus papae* Gregors VII.?" *Deutsches Archiv für Erforschung des Mittelalters* 28 (1972): 105–32.

Morey, James H. "Peter Comestor, Biblical Paraphrase and the Medieval Popular Bible." *Speculum* 68 (1993): 6–35.

Morgan, Teresa. *Literate Education in the Hellenistic and Roman Worlds.* Cambridge: Cambridge University Press, 1998.

Morrison, Karl F. *History as a Visual Art in the Twelfth-Century Renaissance.* Princeton, N.J.: Princeton University Press, 1990.

———. "Incentives for Studying the Liberal Arts." In David L. Wagner, ed., *The Seven Liberal Arts in the Middle Ages.* Bloomington: Indiana University Press, 1983. 32–57.

Moss, Ann. *Printed Commonplace-Books and The Structuring of Renaissance Thought.* New York: Clarendon Press, 1996.

Mulder-Bakker, Anneke B. "The Metamorphosis of Woman: Transmission of Knowledge and the Problems of Gender." In Pauline Stafford and Anneke B. Mulder-Bakker, eds., *Gendering the Middle Ages, Gender and History* Special Issue (2001): 112–34.

———, ed. *Seeing and Knowing: Women and Learning in Medieval Europe 1200–1550.* Medieval Women: Texts and Contexts 11. Turnhout: Brepols, 2004.

Munk Olsen, B. *L'étude des auteurs classiques latins aux XIe et XIIe siècles.* 3 vols. Paris: Editions du Centre national de la recherche scientifique, 1982–1989.

Murphy, James J. "The Teaching of Latin as a Second Language in the 12th Century." *Historiographia Linguistica* 7 (1980): 159–75.

Murray, Alexander. *Reason and Society in the Middle Ages.* Oxford: Clarendon Press, 1978.

Nees, Lawrence. "On Carolingian Book Painters: The Ottoboni Gospels and Its Transfiguration Master." *Art Bulletin* 83 (2001): 209–39.

Newhauser, Richard. *The Early History of Greed: The Sin of Avarice in Early Medieval Thought and Literature.* Cambridge: Cambridge University Press, 2000.

———. *The Treatise on Vices and Virtues in Latin and the Vernacular.* Typologie des sources du Moyen Âge occidental 68. Turnhout: Brepols, 1993.

Newman, Barbara. "Flaws in the Golden Bowl: Gender and Spiritual Formation in the Twelfth Century." In *From Virile Woman to WomanChrist: Studies in Medieval Religion and Literature.* Philadelphia: University of Pennsylvania Press, 1995. 19–45.

———. *God and the Goddesses: Vision, Poetry, and Belief in the Middle Ages*. Philadelphia: University of Pennsylvania Press, 2003.

———. "Hildegard of Bingen: Visions and Validation." *Church History* 54 (1985): 163–75.

———. "Introduction." In Hildegard of Bingen, *Scivias*. Trans. Mother Columba Hart and Jane Bishop. New York: Paulist Press, 1990. 9–53.

———. "'Sibyl of the Rhine': Hildegard's Life and Times." In Barbara Newman, ed., *Voice of the Living Light: Hildegard of Bingen and Her World*. Berkeley: University of California Press, 1998. 1–29.

———. *Sister of Wisdom: St. Hildegard's Theology of the Feminine*. Berkeley: University of California Press, 1987.

Nichols, Stephen G. "Introduction: Philology in a Manuscript Culture." *Speculum* 65 (1990): 1–10.

Nichols, Stephen G. and Siegfried Wenzel, eds. *The Whole Book: Cultural Perspectives on the Medieval Miscellany*. Ann Arbor: University of Michigan Press, 1996.

Niehr, Klaus. "Rezension." *Zeitschrift für deutsches Altertum und deutsche Literatur* 129 (2000): 215–22.

Nochlin, Linda. "Why Have There Been No Great Women Artists?" *Art News* 69 (1971): 22–39, 67–71.

Nordenfalk, Carl. "A Travelling Milanese Artist in France at the Beginning of the XI. Century." In Edoardo Arslan, ed., *Arte del primo millennio: Atti dell IIo convegno per lo studio dell'arte dell'alto medio evo tenuto presso l'Università di Pavia nel settembre 1950*. Turin: Viglongo, 1953. 374–80.

Norman, Joanne S. *Metamorphoses of an Allegory: The Iconography of the Psychomachia in Medieval Art*. New York: Peter Lang, 1988.

North, William L. "Polemic, Apathy, and Authorial Initiative in Gregorian Rome: The Curious Case of Bruno of Segni." *Haskins Society Journal* 13 (2001): 113–25.

Nugent, S. Georgia. *Allegory and Poetics: The Structure and Imagery of Prudentius' "Psychomachia."* Frankfurt: P. Lang, 1985.

———. "*Virtus* or Virago? The Female Personifications of Prudentius's *Psychomachia*." In Colum Hourihane, ed., *Virtue and Vice: The Personifications in the Index of Christian Art*. Princeton, N.J.: Index of Christian Art, 2000. 13–28.

Obermeier, Anita. *The History and Anatomy of Auctorial Self-Criticism in the European Middle Ages*. Amsterdam: Rodopi, 1999.

Ohly, Friedrich. "Probleme der mittelalterlichen Bedeutungsforschung und das Taubenbild des Hugo de Folieto." *Schriften zur mittelalterlichen Bedeutungsforschung*. Darmstadt: Wissenschaftliche Buchgesellschaft, 1977. 32–92.

Opll, Ferdinand. *Das Itinerar Kaiser Friedrich Barbarossas (1152–1190)*. Cologne: Böhlau, 1978.

O'Reilly, Jennifer. *Studies in the Iconography of the Virtues and Vices in the Middle Ages*. New York: Garland, 1988.

Pacaut, Marcel. *Alexandre III: Étude sur la conception du pouvoir pontifical dans sa pensée et dans son oeuvre*. L'église et l'état au moyen âge 2. Paris: J. Vrin, 1956.

———. *Frédéric Barberousse*. Paris: Fayard, 1991.

Pächt, Otto. *Book Illumination in the Middle Ages*. Trans. Kay Davenport. London: H. Miller, 1986.

Parisse, Michel. "Les chanoines réguliers en Lorraine. Fondations, expansion (XIe–XIIe siècles)." *Annales de l'Est* 20 (1968): 347–88.

———. "Les chanoinesses dans l'Empire Germanique (IXe-XIe s.)." *Francia* 6 (1978): 107–26.

———. "Être moine ou chanoine à la fin du IXe siècle." In Patrick Henriet and Anne-Marie Legras, eds., *Au cloître et dans le monde: Femmes, hommes et sociétés (IXe–XVe siècle): Mélanges en l'honneur de Paulette L'Hermite-Leclercq*. Paris: Presses de l'Université de Paris-Sorbonne, 2000. 91–101.

———. "Les femmes au monastère dans le Nord d'Allemagne du IXe au XIe siècle: Conditions sociale et religieuses." In Werner Affeldt, ed., *Frauen in Spätantike und Frühmittelalter: Lebensbedingungen—Lebensnormen—Lebensformen*. Sigmaringen: J. Thorbecke, 1990. 311–24.

———. *Les nonnes au Moyen Age*. Le Puy: C. Bonneton, 1983.

Parkes, M. "The Influence of the Concepts of *Ordinatio* and *Compilatio* on the Development of the Book." In J. J. G. Alexander and M. T. Gibson, eds., *Medieval Learning and Literature: Essays Presented to Richard William Hunt*. Oxford: Clarendon Press, 1976. 115–41.

Pétry, François and Robert Will. *Le Mont Sainte-Odile, Bas-Rhin*. Paris: Ministère de la culture, de la communication, des grands travaux et du Bicentenaire, Direction du patrimoine, Sous-direction de l'archéologie: Impr. nationale, 1988.

Pfister, Christian. *Le duché mérovingien d'Alsace et la Légende de Sainte Odile*. Paris: Berger-Levrault, 1892.

———. "La légende de sainte Odile." In *Pages alsaciennes*. Paris: Les Belles lettres, 1927. 87–119.

Pigman III, G. W. "Versions of Imitation in the Renaissance." *Renaissance Quarterly* 33 (1980): 1–32.

Pinder, Janice M. "The Cloister and the Garden: Gendered Images of Religious Life from the Twelfth and Thirteenth Centuries." In Constant J. Mews, ed., *Listen, Daughter: The* Speculum virginum *and the Formation of Religious Women in the Middle Ages*. New York: Palgrave, 2001. 159–79.

Pollini, Nadia. "Les Propriétés des Abeilles dans le *Bonum Universale de Apibus* de Thomas de Cantimpré (1200–1270)." *Micrologus: natura, scienze e società medievali: Nature, Sciences, and Medieval Societies* 8 (2000): 261–96.

Poor, Sara S. *Mechthild of Magdeburg and Her Book: Gender and the Making of Textual Authority*. Philadelphia: University of Pennsylvania Press, 2004.

Porter, David W. "The Latin Syllabus in Anglo-Saxon Monastic Schools." *Neophilologus* 78 (1994): 463–82.

Powell, Morgan. "The Mirror and the Woman: Instruction for Religious Women and the Emergence of Vernacular Poetics, 1120–1250." Ph.D. dissertation, Princeton University, 1997.

————. "The *Speculum virginum* and the Audio-Visual Poetics of Women's Religious Instruction." In Constant J. Mews, ed., *Listen, Daughter: The* Speculum virginum *and the Formation of Religious Women in the Middle Ages.* New York: Palgrave, 2001. 111–35.

Radspieler, Hans. "Regilind aus Admont, Äbtissin von Bergen und Hohenburg. Reformerin—Lehrerin—Dichterin." *Neuburger Kollectaneenblatt* 115 (1962): 33–48.

Reinhardt, Hans. "Eine Handschrift des 12. Jahrhunderts in der Basler Universitätsbibliothek, die Buchmalerei des elsässischen Klosters Marbach und eine Scheibe aus dem Straßburger Münster." *Basler Zeitschrift für Geschichte und Altertumskunde* 77 (1977): 5–21.

Resnick, Irven M. "Attitudes Toward Philosophy and Dialectic During the Gregorian Reform." *Journal of Religious History* 16 (1990): 115–25.

————. "*Litterati, Spirituales,* and Lay Christians According to Otloh of Saint Emmeram." *Church History* 55 (1986): 165–78.

————. "Scientia liberalis, Dialectics, and Otloh of St. Emmeram." *Revue Bénédictine* 97 (1987): 241–52.

Reudenbach, Bruno. "Individuum ohne Bildnis? Zum Problem künstlerischer Ausdrucksformen von Individualität im Mittelalter." In Jan A. Aertsen and Andreas Speer, eds., *Individuum und Individualität im Mittelalter.* Berlin: Walter de Gruyter, 1996. 807–18.

Reynolds, L. D., ed. *Texts and Transmission: A Survey of the Latin Classics.* Oxford: Clarendon Press, 1983.

————. *The Medieval Tradition of Seneca's Letters.* Oxford: Oxford University Press, 1965.

Reynolds, Suzanne. "*Ad auctorum expositionem*: Syntactic Theory and Interpretative Practice in the Twelfth Century." *Histoire, Epistémologie, Langage* 12 (1990): 31–51.

————. "Glossing Horace: Using the Classics in the Medieval Classroom." In Claudine A. Chavannes-Mazel and Margaret M. Smith, eds., *Medieval Manuscripts of the Latin Classics: Production and Use; Proceedings of the Seminar in the History of the Book to 1500, Leiden 1993.* Los Altos Hills, Calif.: Anderson-Lovelace, 1996. 103–17.

————. *Medieval Reading: Grammar, Rhetoric and the Classical Text.* Cambridge: Cambridge University Press, 1996.

Rhodes, J. T. and Clifford Davidson. "The Garden of Paradise." In Clifford Davidson ed., *The Iconography of Heaven.* Kalamazoo, Mich.: Medieval Institute Publications, 1994. 69–109.

Ribémont, Bernard. "On the Definition of an Encyclopaedic Genre in the Middle Ages." In Peter Binkley, ed., *Pre-modern Encyclopaedic Texts: Proceedings of the Second COMERS Congress, Groningen, 1–4 July 1996.* Leiden: Brill, 1997. 47–61.

Riché, Pierre. "Le rôle de la mémoire dans l'enseignement médiéval." In Pierre Riché, *Education et culture dans l'Occident medieval.* London: Variorum, 1993.

Rigg, A. G. "Anthologies and Florilegia." In F. A. C. Mantello and A. G. Rigg, eds., *Medieval Latin: An Introduction and Bibliographical Guide*. Washington, D.C.: Catholic University of America Press, 1996. 708–12.

Robertson, Elizabeth. "The Corporeality of Female Sanctity in *The Life of Saint Margaret*." In Renate Blumenfeld-Kosinski and Timea Szell, eds., *Images of Sainthood in Medieval Europe*. Ithaca, N.Y.: Cornell University Press, 1991. 268–87.

———. *Early English Devotional Prose and the Female Audience*. Knoxville: University of Tennessee Press, 1990.

———. "Medieval Medical Views of Women and Female Spirituality in the *Ancrene Wisse* and Julian of Norwich's *Showings*." In Linda Lomperis and Sarah Stanbury, eds., *Feminist Approaches to the Body in Medieval Literature*. Philadelphia: University of Pennsylvania Press, 1993. 142–67.

———. " 'This Living Hand': Thirteenth-Century Female Literacy, Materialist Immanence, and the Reader of the *Ancrene Wisse*." *Speculum* 78 (2003): 1–36.

Robinson, Fred C. "Syntactical Glosses in Latin Manuscripts of Anglo-Saxon Provenance." *Speculum* 48 (1973): 443–75.

Robinson, I. S. *Authority and Resistance in the Investiture Contest: The Polemical Literature of the Late Eleventh Century*. Manchester: Manchester University Press, 1978.

———. "The Bible in the Investiture Contest: The South German Gregorian Circle." In Katherine Walsh and Diana Wood, eds., *The Bible in the Medieval World: Essays in Memory of Beryl Smalley*. Studies in Church History Subsidia 4. Oxford: B. Blackwell, 1985. 61–84.

———. "The *colores rhetorici* in the Investiture Contest." *Traditio* 32 (1976): 209–38.

———. "The Friendship Circle of Bernold of Constance and the Dissemination of Gregorian Ideas in Late Eleventh-Century Germany." In Julian Haseldine, ed., *Friendship in Medieval Europe*. Stroud: Sutton, 1999. 185–98.

———. *The Papacy 1073–1198: Continuity and Innovation*. Cambridge: Cambridge University Press, 1990.

———. " 'Political Allegory' in the Biblical Exegesis of Bruno of Segni." *Recherches de théologie ancienne et médiévale* 50 (1983): 69–98.

———. "Pope Gregory VII (1073–1085)." *Journal of Ecclesiastical History* 36 (1985): 439–83.

Robinson, P. R. "The 'Booklet': A Self-Contained Unit in Composite Manuscripts." *Codicologica* 3 (1980): 46–69.

Rossi, Albert L. "The Poetics of Resurrection: Virgil's Bees (*Paradiso* XXXI, 1–12)." *Romantic Review* 80 (1989): 305–24.

Rough, Robert H. *The Reformist Illuminations in the Gospels of Matilda, Countess of Tuscany*. The Hague: Nijhoff, 1973.

Rouse, Mary A. and Richard H. Rouse. "Florilegia of Patristic Texts." In *Les genres littéraires dans les sources théologiques et philosophiques médiévales: définition, critique et exploitation: Actes du Colloque international de Louvain-la-Neuve, 25–27 mai 1981*. Louvain-la-Neuve: Institut d'Études Médiévales de l'Université Catholique de Louvain, 1982. 165–80.

————. "*Statim invenire*: Schools, Preachers, and New Attitudes to the Page." In Robert L. Benson and Giles Constable, eds., with Carol D. Lanham, *Renaissance and Renewal in the Twelfth Century*. Toronto: University of Toronto Press and Medieval Academy of America, 1991. 201–25.

————. "The Vocabulary of Wax Tablets." *Harvard Library Bulletin* n.s. 1.3 (1990): 12–19.

Rubin, Miri. "The Eucharist and the Construction of Medieval Identities." In David Aers, ed., *Culture and History, 1350–1600: Essays on English Communities, Identities, and Writing*. Detroit: Wayne State University Press, 1992. 43–63.

Rudolph, Conrad. *Artistic Change at St-Denis: Abbot Suger's Program and the Early Twelfth-Century Controversy over Art*. Princeton, N.J.: Princeton University Press, 1990.

————. *The "Things of Greater Importance": Bernard of Clairvaux's* Apologia *and the Medieval Attitude Toward Art*. Philadelphia: University of Pennsylvania Press, 1990.

Rust, Martha Dana. "The Art of Beekeeping Meets the Art of Grammar: A Gloss of 'Columcille's Circle.'" *Philological Quarterly* 78 (1999): 359–86.

Sanford, Eva Matthews. "Honorius, *Presbyter* and *Scholasticus*." *Speculum* 23 (1948): 397–425.

Saurma-Jeltsch, Lieselotte E. *Die Miniaturen im "Liber Scivias" der Hildegard von Bingen: die Wucht der Vision und die Ordnung der Bilder*. Wiesbaden: Reichert, 1998.

Saxl, Fritz. "Illustrated Medieval Encyclopedias 2: The Christian Transformation." *Lectures*. 2 vols. London: Warburg Institute, University of London, 1957. 1: 242–54.

————. "Macrocosm and Microcosm in Mediaeval Pictures." *Lectures*. 2 vols. London: Warburg Institute, University of London, 1957. 1: 58–72.

Schäfer, Karl Heinrich. *Die Kanonissenstifter im deutschen Mittelalter: Ihre Entwicklung und innere Einrichtung im Zusammenhang mit dem altchristlichen Sanktimonialentum*. Stuttgart: F. Enke, 1907.

Scheller, Robert W. *Exemplum: Model-Book Drawings and the Practice of Artistic Transmission in the Middle Ages (ca. 900–ca. 1470)*. Trans. Michael Hoyle. Amsterdam: Amsterdam University Press, 1995.

Schibanoff, Susan. "Taking the Gold Out of Egypt: The Art of Reading as a Woman." In Elizabeth A. Flynn and Patrocinio P. Schweickart, eds., *Gender and Reading: Essays on Readers, Texts, and Contexts*. Baltimore: Johns Hopkins University Press, 1986. 83–106.

Schilp, Thomas. *Norm und Wirklichkeit religiöser Frauengemeinschaften im Frühmittelalter: Die "Institutio sanctimonialium Aquisgranensis" des Jahres 816 und die Problematik der Verfassung von Frauenkommunitäten*. Göttingen: Vandenhoeck & Ruprecht, 1998.

Schmale, Franz-Josef, with Irene Schmale-Ott and Dieter Berg. *Deutschlands Geschichtsquellen im Mittelalter*. Vol. 1, *Vom Tode Kaiser Heinrichs V. bis zum Ende des Interregnum*. Darmstadt: Wissenschaftliche Buchgesellschaft, 1976.

Schmidt, Charles. *Herrade de Landsberg*. 2nd ed. Strasbourg: J.H.E. Heitz, 1897.

Schulenburg, Jane Tibbetts. "Gender, Celibacy, and Proscriptions of Sacred Space: Symbol and Practice." In Michael Frassetto, ed., *Medieval Purity and Piety: Essays on Medieval Clerical Celibacy and Religious Reform*. New York: Garland, 1998. 353–76.

———. "Strict Active Enclosure and Its Effects on the Female Monastic Experience (ca. 500–1100)." In Lillian Thomas Shank and John A. Nichols, eds., *Medieval Religious Women*. Vol. 1, *Distant Echoes*. Cistercian Studies Series 71. Kalamazoo, Mich.: Cistercian Publications, 1984. 51–86.

Scott, Joan W. "Gender: A Useful Category of Historical Anaylsis." *American Historical Review* 91 (1986): 1053–75.

Seeberg, Stefanie. *Die Illustrationen im Admonter Nonnenbrevier von 1180. Marienkrönung und Nonnenfrömmigkeit—Die Rolle der Brevierillustration in der Entwicklung von Bildthemen im 12. Jahrhundert*. Imagines Medii Aevi 8. Wiesbaden: Reichert, 2002.

Semmler, Josef, "Klosterreform und Gregorianische Reform: Die Chorherrenstifter Marbach und Hördt im Investiturstreit." *Studi Gregoriani* 6 (1959–1961): 165–72.

Sicard, Patrice. *Diagrammes médiévaux et exégèse visuelle: Le Libellus de formatione arche de Hugues de Saint-Victor*. Paris: Brepols, 1993.

———. *Hugues de Saint-Victor et son école: Introduction, choix de texte, traduction et commentaires*. Turnhout: Brepols, 1991.

Siegwart, Josef. *Die Chorherren- und Chorfrauengemeinschaften in der deutschsprachigen Schweiz vom 6. Jahrhundert bis 1160*. Freiburg: Universitätsverlag, 1962.

———. *Die Consuetudines des Augustiner-Chorherrenstiftes Marbach im Elsass (12. Jahrhundert)*. Fribourg: Universitätsverlag, 1965.

Silvestre, Hubert. "Les manuscrits des Oeuvres de Rupert." *Revue Bénédictine* 88 (1978): 286–89.

Simmons, Loraine N. "The Abbey Church at Fontevraud in the Later Twelfth Century: Anxiety, Authority and Architecture in Female Spiritual Life." *Gesta* 31 (1992): 99–107.

Simonsfeld, Henry. *Jahrbücher des deutschen Reiches unter Friedrich I*. Leipzig: Duncker and Humblot, 1908.

Smalley, Beryl. *The Study of the Bible in the Middle Ages*. 2nd ed. Oxford: Blackwell, 1952.

Smith, Lesley. "Lending Books: The Growth of a Medieval Question from Langton to Bonaventure." In Lesley Smith and Benedicta Ward, eds., *Intellectual Life in the Middle Ages: Essays Presented to Margaret Gibson*. London: Hambledon Press, 1992. 265–79.

———. "*Scriba, Femina*: Medieval Depictions of Women Writing." In Lesley Smith and Jane H. M. Taylor, eds., *Women and the Book: Assessing the Visual Evidence*. Toronto: University of Toronto Press, 1996. 21–44.

Solterer, Helen. *The Master and Minerva: Disputing Women in French Medieval Culture*. Berkeley: University of California Press, 1995.

Sorrentino, Janet. "In Houses of Nuns, in Houses of Canons: A Liturgical Dimension to Double Monasteries." *Journal of Medieval History* 28 (2002): 361–72.

Southern, R. W. *Scholastic Humanism and the Unification of Europe*. Vol. II. *The Heroic Age*. Oxford: Blackwell, 2001.

Stammberger, Ralf M. W. "*De longe veritas videtur diversa iudicia parit*: Hugh of Saint Victor and Peter Abelard." *Revista Portuguesa de Filosofia* 58 (2002): 65–92.

Stauch, Liselotte. "Baum in der christlichen Symbolik." In Otto Schmitt, ed., *Reallexikon zur deutschen Kunstgeschichte*. Stuttgart: J.B. Metzler, 1933–. 2: 63–72.

Stettiner, Richard, *Die illustrierten Prudentiushandschriften*. Berlin: J.S. Preuss, 1895.

Stock, Brian. *Augustine the Reader: Meditation, Self-knowledge, and the Ethics of Interpretation*. Cambridge, Mass.: Belknap Press, 1996.

———. "*Lectio divina* e *lectio spiritualis*: la scrittura come pratica contemplativa nel Medioevo." *Lettere italiane* 52 (2000): 169–83.

Stolz, Michael. "Maria und die Artes liberales: Aspekte einer mittelalterlichen Zuordnung." In Claudia Opitz et al., eds., *Maria in der Welt: Marienverehrung im Kontext der Sozialgeschichte 10–18 Jahrhundert*. Zurich: Chronos, 1993. 95–120.

Stump, Eleanore. "Dialectic." In David L. Wagner, ed., *The Seven Liberal Arts in the Middle Ages*. Bloomington: Indiana University Press, 1983. 125–46.

Suckale, Robert. "The Canonesses of Regensburg-Obermuenster and the New Marian Piety." Paper presented at the conference Crown and Veil: The Art of Female Monasticism in the Middle Ages, 750–1530, Harvard University, May 13, 2004.

Summit, Jennifer. *Lost Property: The Woman Writer and English Literary History, 1380–1589*. Chicago: University of Chicago Press, 2000.

———. "Women and Authorship." In Carolyn Dinshaw and David Wallace, eds., *The Cambridge Companion to Medieval Women's Writing*. Cambridge: Cambridge University Press, 2003. 91–108.

Suzuki, Keiko. *Bildgewordene Visionen oder Visionserzählungen: Vergleichende Studie über die Visionsdarstellungen in der Rupertsberger "Scivias"-Handschrift und im Luccheser "Liber divinorum operum"-Codex der Hildegard von Bingen*. Bern: Peter Lang, 1998.

Sylwan, A. "Petrus Comestor, *Historia Scholastica*: une nouvelle édition." *Sacris Erudiri* 39 (2000): 345–82.

Taylor, Jerome, "Introduction." In Hugh of St. Victor. *Didascalicon: A Medieval Guide to the Arts*. Trans. Jerome Taylor. New York: Columbia University Press, 1961. 3–39.

Tellenbach, Gerd. *The Church in Western Europe from the Tenth to the Early Twelfth Century*. Trans. Timothy Reuter. Cambridge: Cambridge University Press, 1993.

Teske, Roland. "Augustine's Philosophy of Memory." In Eleonore Stump and Norman Kretzmann, eds., *The Cambridge Companion to Augustine*. Cambridge: Cambridge University Press, 2001. 148–58.

———. "Platonic Reminiscence and Memory of the Present in St. Augustine." *New Scholasticism* 58 (1984): 220–35.

Thompson Sally. "The Problem of the Cistercian Nuns in the Twelfth and Early Thirteenth Centuries." In Derek Baker, ed., *Medieval Women: Dedicated and Presented to Professor Rosalind M. T. Hill.* Studies in Church History Subsidia 1. Oxford: Blackwell, 1978. 227–52.

Twomey, Michael W. "Medieval Encyclopedias." In R. E. Kaske, Arthur Groos, and Michael W. Twomey, eds., *Medieval Christian Literary Imagery: A Guide to Interpretation.* Toronto: University of Toronto Press, 1988. 182–215.

Uffmann, Heike. "Inside and Outside the Convent Walls: The Norm and Practice of Enclosure in the Reformed Nunneries of Late Medieval Germany." *Medieval History Journal* 4 (2001): 83–108.

Van Engen, John H. *Rupert of Deutz.* Publications of the UCLA Centre for Medieval and Renaissance Studies 18. Berkeley: University of California Press, 1983.

Van Winter, Johanna Maria. "The Education of the Daughters of the Nobility in the Ottonian Empire." In Adelbert Davids, ed., *The Empress Theophano: Byzantium and the West at the Turn of the First Millennium.* Cambridge: Cambridge University Press, 1995. 86–98.

Venarde, Bruce L. *Women's Monasticism and Medieval Society: Nunneries in France and England, 890–1215.* Ithaca, N.Y.: Cornell University Press, 1997.

Verdier, Philippe. "L'iconographie des arts libéraux dans l'art du moyen âge jusqu'à la fin du quinzième siècle." *Arts libéraux et philosophie au moyen âge: Actes du quatrième Congrès international de philosophie médiévale.* Montréal: Institut d'études médiévales, 1969. 305–55.

Verheijen, Luc. *La Règle de saint Augustin.* 2 vols. Paris: Études augustiniennes, 1967.

von Moos, Peter. *Hildebert von Lavardin, 1056–1133: Humanitas an der Schwelle des höfischen Zeitalters.* Pariser historische Studien 3. Stuttgart: A. Hiersemann, 1965.

von Stackelberg, Jürgen. "Das Bienengleichnis: ein Beitrag zur Geschichte der literarischen *Imitatio.*" *Romanische Forschungen* 68 (1956): 271–93.

Wagner, Georg. *Untersuchungen über die Standesverhältnisse Elsässischer Klöster.* Strasbourg: Heitz and Mündel, 1911.

Walter, Joseph. "Aurait-on découvert des fragments de l'*Hortus deliciarum*?" *Archives alsaciennes d'histoire de l'art* 10 (1931): 1–8.

———. "L'Évangéliaire de Marbach-Schwarzenthann de la fin du XIIe siècle (Cod. Laudun. 550)." *Archives alsaciennes d'histoire de l'art* 9 (1930): 1–20.

———. "Les deux roses du transept sud de la cathédrale de Strasbourg." *Archives alsaciennes d'histoire de l'art* 7 (1928): 13–33.

———. "Les miniatures du Codex Guta-Sintram de Marbach-Schwartzenthann (1154)." *Archives alsaciennes d'histoire de l'art* 4 (1925): 1–40.

Wattenbach, Wilhelm. "Eine alte Grammatik." *Anzeiger für Kunde der deutschen Vorzeit* (1872): 119–22.

———. *Das Schriftwesen im Mittelalter.* 4th ed. Graz: Akademische Druck- u. Verlagsanstalt, 1958.

Weinfurter, Stefan. "Neuere Forschung zu den Regularkanonikern im Deutschen Reich des 11. und 12. Jahrhunderts." *Historische Zeitschrift* 224 (1977): 379–97.

————. "Reformkanoniker und Reichsepiskopat im Hochmittelalter." *Historisches Jahrbuch* 87/98 (1977–1978): 158–93.

Weis, Béatrice, ed. *Le Codex Guta-Sintram: manuscrit 37 de la Bibliothèque du Grand séminaire de Strasbourg*. 2 vols. Lucerne: Editions Fac-similés, 1983.

————. "Description codicologique." In Béatrice Weis, ed., *Le Codex Guta-Sintram: manuscrit 37 de la Bibliothèque du Grand séminaire de Strasbourg*. 2 vols. Lucerne: Editions Fac-similés, 1983. 2: 11.

————. "Die Nekrologien von Schwartzenthann und Marbach im Elsaß." *Zeitschrift für die Geschichte des Oberrheins* 128 (1980): 51–68.

————. "Le premier cahier du codex." In Béatrice Weis, ed., *Le Codex Guta-Sintram: manuscrit 37 de la Bibliothèque du Grand séminaire de Strasbourg*. 2 vols. Lucerne: Editions Fac-similés, 1983. 2: 49–64.

Weitzmann-Fiedler, Josepha. *Romanische gravierte Bronzeschalen*. Berlin: Deutscher Verlag für Kunstwissenschaft, 1981.

Wemple, Suzanne. "Female Monasticism in Italy and Its Comparison with France and Germany from the Ninth Through the Eleventh Century." In Werner Affeldt, ed., *Frauen in Spätantike und Frühmittelalter: Lebensbedingungen—Lebensnormen—Lebensformen*. Sigmaringen: Jan Thorbecke, 1990. 291–310.

————. *Women in Frankish Society: Marriage and the Cloister, 500 to 900*. Philadelphia: University of Pennsylvania Press, 1981.

Wendehorst, Alfred and Stefan Benz. "Verzeichnis der Stifte der Augustiner-Chorherren und -Chorfrauen." *Jahrbuch für fränkische Landesforschung* 56 (1996): 1–110.

Whitehead, Christiania. "Making a Cloister of the Soul in Medieval Religious Treatises." *Medium Ævum* 67 (1998): 1–29.

Wieland, Gernot Rudolf. "Gloss and Illustration: Two Means to the Same End?" In Phillip Pulsiano and Elaine M. Treharne, eds., *Anglo-Saxon Manuscripts and Their Heritage*. Aldershot: Ashgate, 1998. 1–20.

————. "The Glossed Manuscript: Classbook or Library Book?" *Anglo-Saxon England* 14 (1985): 153–73.

————. "Interpreting the Interpretation: The Polysemy of the Latin Gloss." *Journal of Medieval Latin* 8 (1998): 59–71.

————. *The Latin Glosses on Arator and Prudentius in Cambridge University Library, MS Gg.5.35*. Toronto: Pontifical Institute of Mediaeval Studies, 1983.

Wilkinson, L. P. *The Georgics of Virgil: A Critical Survey*. Cambridge: Cambridge University Press, 1969.

Will, Robert. "*Currus misericordiae*: contribution à l'iconographie des vertus." *Revue du moyen âge latin* 6 (1950): 299–312.

————. "Les origines de l'abbesse Relinde de Hohenbourg." *Archives de l'église d'Alsace* n.s. 21 (1974): 1–12.

Wilsdorf, Christian. "Les très anciennes forteresses du Mont Sainte-Odile et de Frankenbourg dans les textes du Moyen Age." In *Mélanges offerts à Jean Jacques Hatt. Cahiers alsaciens d'archéologie d'art et d'histoire* 36 (1993): 207–10.

Wimmer, Elisabeth. *Biene und Honig in der Bildersprache der lateinischen Kirchenschriftsteller*. Vienna: Österreichischer Kunst- und Kulturverlag, 1998.

Winnlen, Jean Charles. *Schönensteinbach: Une communauté religieuse féminine 1138–1792*. Altkirch: Société d'histoire sundgauvienne, 1993.

Wirth, Karl-August. "Von mittelalterlichen Bildern und Lehrfiguren im Dienste der Schule und des Unterrichts." In Bernd Moeller et al., eds., *Studien zum städtischen Bildungswesen des späten Mittlelalters und der frühen Neuzeit*. Göttingen: Vandenhoeck and Ruprecht, 1983. 256–370.

Wittwer, Peter. "Quellen zur Liturgie der Chorherren von Marbach. Zugleich ein Beitrag zur Erforschung der Bildung von Ordensliturgien." *Archiv für Liturgiewissenschaft* 32 (1990): 307–61.

Wogan-Browne, Jocelyn and Glyn S. Burgess, trans. *Virgin Lives and Holy Deaths: Two Exemplary Biographies for Anglo-Norman Women*. London: J.M. Dent, 1996.

Wojtowytsch, Myron. "*Proprie auctoritates apostolice sedis*. Bemerkungen zu einer bisher unbeachteten Überlieferung." *Deutsches Archiv* 40 (1984): 612–21.

Wolbrink, Shelley Amiste. "Women in the Premonstratensian Order of Northwestern Germany, 1120–1250." *Catholic Historical Review* 89 (2003): 387–408.

Wolter-Von Dem Knesebeck, Harald. "Lamspringe, ein unbekanntes Scriptorium des Hamersleben-Halberstädter Reformkreises zur Zeit Heinrichs des Löwen." In Jochen Luckhardt and Franz Niehoff, eds., *Heinrich der Löwe und seine Zeit: Herrschaft und Repräsentation der Welfen 1125–1235*. Katalog der Ausstellung Braunschweig 1995, 2 vols. Munich: Hirmer, 1995. II: 468–77.

Woodruff, Helen. "The Illustrated Manuscripts of Prudentius." *Art Studies* 7 (1929): 33–79.

Wormstall, Albert. "Eine romanische Bronzeschüssel aus Westfalen." *Zeitschrift für christliche Kunst* 8 (1897): 239–50.

Wright, Rosemary Muir. "The Great Whore in the Illustrated Apocalypse Cycles." *Journal of Medieval History* 23 (1997): 191–210.

Zellinger, Johannes. "Der geköderte Leviathan im *Hortus deliciarum* der Herrad von Landsperg." *Historisches Jahrbuch* 45 (1925): 161–77.

Zenner, Marie-Thérèse. "From Divine Wisdom to Secret Knowledge: The Cosmology of the Honeybee in the Church Calendar." *Micrologus: Natura, scienze e società medievali: Nature, Sciences, and Medieval Societies* 8 (2000): 103–24.

Ziegelbauer, Magnoald. *Historia rei literariae O.S.B.* 4 vols. Würzbourg: M. Veith, 1754.

Zimmerman, Michel, ed. *Auctor et auctoritas: invention et conformisme dans l'écriture médiévale: actes du colloque tenu à l'Université de Versailles-Saint-Quentin-en-Yvelines, 14–16 juin 1999*. Paris: École des chartes, 2001.

Zinn, Grover A. "*De gradibus Ascensionum*: The Stages of Contemplative Ascent in Two Treatises on Noah's Ark by Hugh of St. Victor." *Studies in Medieval Culture* 5 (1975): 61–79.

———."*Historia fundamentum est*: The Role of History in the Contemplative Life According to Hugh of St. Victor." In George H. Shriver, ed., *Contemporary Reflections on the Medieval Christian Tradition: Essays in Honor of Ray C. Petry*. Durham, N.C.: Duke University Press, 1974. 135–58.

————. "Hugh of Saint Victor and the Art of Memory." *Viator* 5 (1974): 211–34.

————. "Hugh of St. Victor, Isaiah's Vision, and *De arca Noe*." In Diana Wood, ed., *The Church and the Arts*. Oxford: Blackwell, 1992. 99–116.

Zinke, Detlef and Angela Karasch. *Verborgene Pracht: mittelalterliche Buchkunst aus acht Jahrhunderten in Freiburger Sammlungen*. Lindenberg: J. Fink, 2002.

Ziolkowski, Jan. "A Bouquet of Wisdom and Invective: Houghton MS. Lat 300." *Harvard Library Bulletin* n.s. 1, 3 (1990): 20–45.

Ziomkowski, Robert. "Introduction," and "Appendix: Biographical Dossier." In Manegold of Lautenbach. *Liber contra Wolfelmum*. Trans. Robert Ziomkowski. Dallas Medieval Texts and Translations 1. Dudley, Mass.: Peeters, 2002. 1–31, 105–40.

Index

216; and Marbach, 39–41, 51; and reform
at Hohenbourg, 29–32, 44, 49–50; role in
Hortus project, 7, 54–55, 75–76, 113, 126;
and Zwiefalten, 131
Renaissance: and women, 12–13, 160–61,
222–23; and the *Hortus*, 22–23, 72–75, 160–
62, 213–14, 222–23
Resnick, Irven, 146
Rethorica, 132, 148
Revelation, 136, 138, 140, 141, 142, 318 n. 101
Reynolds, L. D., 98–99
Reynolds, Suzanne, 174–75
Rhabanus Maurus, 98, 291 n. 91, 309 n. 92
Rheinhardsbrunn, 71, 76
Rhetorica ad Herennium, 77, 122, 317 n. 85
Rottenbuch, 33, 267 n. 80
Rough, Robert, 204
Runge, Gabriele, 121
Rupert of Deutz, 64, 67–68; and bees, 104;
Commentaria in Canticum canticorum,
68, 137, 324 n. 64; and Hildegard, 14, 71;
and *Hortus* glosses, 178; and knowledge of
Seneca, 98–99; manuscript dissemination
of, 69; manuscripts owned by female communities, 279 n. 78; and Marbach, 77; and
monastic preaching, 68, 69; and reform
concerns in the *Hortus*, 52, 56; and salvation history, 109; as a source for the *Hortus*, 3, 17–18, 56, 67–68, 71–72, 80
——, *De divinis officiis*, 67–68; dedicated
to Cuno of Raitenbuch, 69; Herrad's use
of, 113, 116, 117; in the *Hortus*, 68, 87, 120,
172, 220, 294 n. 28; as glosses to *Hortus*
images, 120; known at Lippoldsberg, 71;
known at Schäftlarn, 70; manuscript dissemination of, 278 74
Rupertsberg: and Frederick Barbarossa, 59;
Hildegard as *magistra*, 48, 222; and pastoral care, 40–41, 59

Sapientia, 150, 152, 157, 175
Schäftlarn, 70, 279 n. 78, 298 n. 66
Schism (1159–1177), 53–54, 56–57, 58–60
Schönau, 59
Schwartzenthann, 35, 36–37, 38, 47; and
books, 76; and book production, 40; and
female scribes, 13, 127, 298 n. 66. See also
Guta-Sintram Codex; Guta of Schwart-
zenthann
Scott, A. B., 192

Scribes, female, 298 n. 66; at Admont, 70;
Guda, 130; at Hohenbourg, 2, 19, 126,
127–28, 130–32; at Lippoldsberg, 71; at Ob-
ermünster, 129–30; at Schäftlarn, 70; at
Schwartzenthann, 13, 36, 126–27; at Wes-
sobrunn, 126; at Zwiefalten, 75, 131–32. *See
also* Guta of Schwartzenthann
Semonides, 291 n. 87
Seneca: apian metaphor, 92–97, 105–6; bee
and martial imagery, 103; and Herrad, 99–
100, 102, 105, 115, 134–35; medieval knowl-
edge of, 98–99
Serenus, bishop of Marseilles, 179
Seuse, Heinrich, 14
Sibylle, queen of Sicily, 26–27, 114, 273 n. 14
Simon Magus, 202, 322 n. 38
Simony, 20, 195, 207, 208, 210, 211; and the
Cleansing of the Temple, 201–4; and Ru-
pert of Deutz, 67
Sindold of Rheinhardsbrunn, 71
Sintram of Marbach, 13, 36–37, 126–27, 129,
130
Socrates, in the *Hortus*, 144–45, 148–50, 152,
159, 170; at Marbach, 187; shown on
bronze bowl, 151–52; and women, 162
Solomon, 121, 125, 189, 205, 208–9, 278 n. 62;
and organization of the *Hortus*, 293 n. 5;
and women, 220
Song of Songs: and enclosure, 137–38; and
Hohenbourg, 56; and Honorius Augustodunensis, 277 n. 62; in the *Hortus*, 209,
261 n. 15; and political allegory, 323 n. 44;
and Rupert of Deutz, 68, 137; and the
Speculum virginum, 5, 183; and women,
136, 137
Sophia, 150
Sophocles, 97–98
Speculum virginum, 4–5; and enclosure, 301
n. 12; and floral metaphor, 105; and images, 20, 182–85, 187, 205; and women and
learning, 9, 105–6, 161, 182–84, 216; and
women's religious life, 4, 6, 12, 21, 216
St. Arbogast, 44; necrology, 27, 28
St. Victor, and manuscript dissemination, 75;
and Marbach, 79; and scholarship, 32, 73–
74, 159–60, 214
St. Gorgon, Herrad's foundation at, 42–47,
51; and the *Hortus*, 53, 126, 132, 210, 215
Steinbach, 38, 40, 274 n. 24
Suger of St. Denis, 314 n. 53

Acknowledgments

THIS BOOK IS ABOUT TEACHING AND LEARNING within the context of a community—in this case the community of women at Hohenbourg in the twelfth century. In writing it, I have benefited enormously from the generosity of several communities and the wisdom of many individuals; it gives me enormous pleasure to be able to thank them here. My thanks are due first to the intellectual community in which I first encountered the *Hortus deliciarum*, when I was a graduate student at Cambridge University. Anna Sapir Abulafia and Liesbeth van Houts guided me in the early stages of my research and have maintained their enthusiasm for the project in the intervening years; I am so grateful to them for their continuing encouragement and unstinting generosity of time and energy. My thanks are due also to the Cambridge Commonwealth Trust and to Trinity Hall, which provided a home at Cambridge, and, especially, to Christopher Padfield, whose confidence in me, and generosity toward me, I will always remember with gratitude. The Institute of Historical Research awarded me a research fellowship during the final year of my doctorate and provided an academic base in London; I am so grateful to Jinty Nelson for her encouragement during that year and her friendship ever since.

I was fortunate to have been able to write this book in the calm and quiet of the Radcliffe Institute for Advanced Study, where I was a fellow in 2003–2004. Not only did the Radcliffe allow me the precious gift of time to think and to write, but the intellectual curiosity, collegiality, and optimism that pervaded the institute made it easy to do both. I am grateful to Jenny Knust, a fellow "fellow," for her friendship and shared enthusiasm for all things related to gender and religion and, above all, for her careful reading and insightful comments on several early drafts of this work. Katy Park, Arielle Saiber, and Irene Winter, also fellows, supported my project as it developed, sharing their work and engaging generously with mine. The vibrant community at Eliot House, where I lived while at the Radcliffe, provided a welcome and ever-cheerful break from the seclusion of writing. I am grateful to Lino Pertile and Anna Bensted for welcoming me into the Eliot community and for making it such a rich and friendly place.

During the course of my work on the *Hortus*, I have been fortunate in the friends and mentors I have found. My first thanks are due to Constant Mews, whose intellectual generosity and friendship over the years have never once faltered. His work on the links between women and twelfth-century monastic reform provided the starting point for my understanding of the context and significance of the *Hortus*. My thanks are due also to Connie Berman for her generous support for the project and conversations concerning women and twelfth-century reform; to Stacy Klein for her friendship over many years and her gracious and thoughtful engagement with my work; to Bruce Venarde for his comments on several draft chapters and suggestions concerning my translations; to Miri Rubin, Jan Ziolkowski, and Beverly Kienzle for their early and continued encouragement of my work on Herrad; to Morgan Powell, David Tabak, and Helen Jacupke for their valuable comments on drafts of several chapters; to Alison Beach, Adam Cohen, and Julie Hotchin for their friendship and many helpful exchanges over the years; and to my research assistants, Jonathan Gnoza, Emily Graham, Susan Valentine, and Sarah Zeiser for their unfailing good cheer and excellent work. At the University of Pennsylvania Press, Jerry Singerman provided expert and patient guidance through the publication process; he deserves my heartfelt thanks. The Medieval Academy of America supported the publication of this book, providing generous funds for the inclusion of images from the *Hortus*; I am grateful to the Academy and to its director, Rick Emmerson. Finally, I am greatly indebted to Barbara Newman and Jeffrey Hamburger, who have supported my work on the *Hortus* with generosity, kindness, and wisdom. Both read the manuscript in its entirety, helped to refine its argument, and saved me from many errors. Their work has served as an inspiration for my own in countless ways; it is a privilege to thank them each here. Of course, it goes without saying that any errors that remain are my own.

There are few words sufficient to thank my family, who have supported me in every project, not just this one. To my grandparents, Gerald and Kitty Anna Griffiths, I owe the practical and material encouragement that made it possible for me to study Herrad to begin with. Their perseverance and hard work have been models for my own. To my parents, Ian and Christine Griffiths, whose selfless dedication to their children's education allowed me countless opportunities, I owe every encouragement during the long and sometimes frustrating years of research that led to this book.

To Rupert, who arrived just in time, I owe a happiness beyond words. And last, but never least, how to thank Ronald, without whom I know that nothing is possible? Perhaps just by saying that I dedicate this book to you.

*   *   *

Some of the translations in the appendix were previously published in Fiona J. Griffiths, "Herrad of Hohenbourg and the Poetry of the *Hortus celiciarum*: *Cantat tibi cantica*," in *Women Writing Latin*, ed. Laurie Churchill (London: Routledge, 2002), 2: 231–63. Reprinted by permission of Routledge/Taylor & Francis Group.

Texts from the Warburg Institute reconstruction (volume 2) of the *Hortus*, text nos. 1, 2, 1162, 1163, 374, 595, and texts (volume 1) from the penultimate folios of the manuscript HD fol. 322v–323r, Cat. Nos. 345, 346, are reprinted by permission of the Warburg Institute.